TARNISHED WARRIOR
MAJOR–GENERAL JAMES WILKINSON

THE MACMILLAN COMPANY
NEW YORK · BOSTON · CHICAGO · DALLAS
ATLANTA · SAN FRANCISCO

MACMILLAN AND CO., Limited
LONDON · BOMBAY · CALCUTTA · MADRAS
MELBOURNE

THE MACMILLAN COMPANY
OF CANADA, Limited
TORONTO

Major-General James Wilkinson from a portrait by Gilbert Stuart.

Courtesy of Mr. and Mrs. Henry G. Allen, New Orleans, La.

TARNISHED WARRIOR

Major-General JAMES WILKINSON

BY

JAMES RIPLEY JACOBS
MAJOR, U.S. ARMY, RETIRED

NEW YORK
THE MACMILLAN COMPANY
1938

To My Wife

BERYL MARTIN JACOBS

"Some men are sordid, some vain, some ambitious. To detect the predominant passion, to lay hold of it, is the profound part of political science."—Wilkinson to Gardoqui, Jan. 1, 1789, in Fortier, *A History of Louisiana*, II, 141–142.

PREFACE

MOST of those who were friends of the first four Presidents were not far travelers within the limits of their country; they seldom ventured out of the State that had given them birth. Few cared to suffer the hardships of crossing the Appalachians or to incur danger from Indians beyond the Mississippi unless they were dominated by a great personal desire or acting under government orders that they could not readily evade. For the general population, New Orleans, Detroit, and Albany were merely geographical expressions—outposts on the periphery of a wilderness that only pioneers were wont to explore. The more conservative who succeeded in meeting competition along the eastern seaboard did not harken to the call of cheap lands across the mountains or in the fecund river valleys of the Southwest unless the spirit of adventure conquered the discerning judgment that had created their opulence. In time, these who remained at home became more set in English patterns; even their passing was marked by tombstones cut like those in quiet country churchyards across the sea. The frontier, with its years of hardships, was for hardy young men who yearned for a greater and more exciting future than that which their drab and conventional birthplaces indifferently offered them. They were the more daring few who cleared and plowed under new lands and created a virile democracy. For their less aggressive countrymen they won an imperial domain. In payment they demanded the elimination of certain outworn political theories and social practices. As frontiersmen they were concerned with essentials; they had slight esteem for conventions; they created a type distinctly American. To critical foreigners these representatives of new ideals of living often appeared gross, frequently dishonest, commonly illiterate, and generally egotistical beyond limit; in their myopia they overlooked those worthier qualities of bravery, open friendliness, tenacity of purpose, and a heartening confidence in all the vicissitudes of life. Of the many able men in the early days of the United States not a few displayed several of these estimable qualities while they lagged little behind their critics in culture and Old World vices.

James Wilkinson was such a one. Possessing a formal education somewhat better than that of the successful planters of his day, he supplemented it by extensive travel and a wide range of friends throughout a long and active career. From 1777 to 1825 there were few persons of importance within the United States whom he did not claim sooner or later as friend or enemy. He made both easily. Simultaneously, no significant event in the United States escaped his comment, and often he was personally concerned in it. Moving constantly from place to place, he was hailed as the bearer of the latest news from where he had last raised his marquee or found shelter in the home of friends; and if he did not tell profusely what he knew in person, he wrote it verbosely by letter. He seldom judged men or things without bias, and often judged them so hastily that his opinion is of little value; he was, in fact, a strong partisan and a sturdy advocate, and if it redounded to his personal advantage he could do much for those whom he liked. Whatever he did was usually embroidered with ballyhoo: he was a great showman, never disturbed by a sense of modesty. Habitually vigorous in manner and speech, he seldom failed to make an impression and often gained stanch adherents for his cause. Open-handed with what he had, he was chronically in need of money to support his entertaining and display, but he was consistently casual concerning the sources from which his funds came. If the Spaniards, for example, were willing to pay for information and advice, he did not hesitate to give both, although he commanded the Army of the United States; if his own government could be induced to pay a questionable item, he did not hesitate to include it in his vouchers. Loyalty to his friends and his government endured only so long as his personal interests were served. This cardinal weakness has raised against him a great mountain of odium that some persons have obviously tried to heighten. His faults were so numerous and striking that one need never consult the chronicles of the prejudiced in order to add interest to the story of his colorful career. Were he nothing more than the peerless archvillain that John Randolph and others have painted, even the dull-witted must wonder why Washington, John Adams, and Jefferson allowed him to be commander of the Army for nearly twenty precarious years of the Republic.

In time of war Wilkinson proved unfit for high military command. His ability was not pronounced in the conduct of active operations;

it lay in a sort of practical diplomacy, often dubious in its ethics though usually acceptable in his time. His conclusions were not arrived at by the careful process of synthetic reasoning; they were based more frequently on a superficial examination of information that was easily available but not always true. He did not weigh right or wrong in an apothecary's scales. Had he insisted upon a finely measured and unbending justice he would not have been acceptable to those along the Mississippi and the Ohio; for their rules of conduct were sometimes as rude as their clothes and as rough as the houses that they built and the food that they ate. They were concerned with the fundamentals of living, and whether or not a few more Spaniards or Indians were robbed or killed or cheated mattered little to them so long as they were permitted to follow unhampered their own ways of life on the rim of the wilderness. Wilkinson's knowledge of these adventurers and the country that they would possess was exceeded by few, if any, of the Presidential advisers. Since some of the most pressing problems of the first three administrations concerned the frontier, Wilkinson proved of distinct help in solving them. Oftentimes, though very ruefully accepting the task that the President, his commander-in-chief, assigned him, he did not dare to rebel openly like those who were controlled only by ties of a common political faith. If failure attended his efforts, no particular odium fell upon the party in power: it was regarded as just another Army blunder. If he met with success, the administration might claim it as another reason for continuing things as they were. Wilkinson was an energetic helper in this species of partisan propaganda. As a clever politician he skillfully catered first to the Federalists, then to the Democratic-Republicans, convincing both of his friendship and ability to serve them. Unfortunately he can never be properly appraised until the history of the early Army is completely told and the valley of the Mississippi surrenders a few of its long-held secrets of intrigue.

Whatever success this biography attains in solving the riddles of Wilkinson's character is largely due to the cheerful and intelligent assistance of many scholars. Nevertheless, to none of them are to be imputed errors of fact or opinion that this book may contain. Particular thanks are due to Mr. T. R. Hay, Great Neck, New York, who has often given me the results of his own study of Wilkinson's part in American history. My sister, Miss Elizabeth C. Jacobs, Marfa, Texas, has unselfishly collaborated with me on the last chapter and greatly improved others by careful revision. To Major Charles W. Elliott, U.S.A. (Retired), I am under great obligation: he has frequently furnished me with necessary data, he has constantly helped me with his broad scholarship and stimulating criticism. Professors Ralph V. Harlow and Gaston Moffatt, both of Syracuse University, have given me much appreciated encouragement and advice. Professor I. J. Cox, Northwestern University, has lent me valuable manuscript material and suggested to me where more of it might be found. Messrs. T. E. Roberts and H. C. Durston, of The Manlius School, have read my manuscript and made valuable suggestions. In the same way my wife, Beryl Martin Jacobs, has made a distinct contribution. She has also relieved me frequently of the tedium incident to writing and given me a more human understanding of the story that I have endeavored to tell. Commander Theodore Wilkinson, United States Navy; Mrs. Nancy Hamilton Allen, New Orleans; and Mrs. Thomas B. Mackall, Mackall's Landing, Maryland, have kindly supplied information about General Wilkinson's family. I am also under obligation to a number of others for helpful notes or manuscripts: Mr. C. W. Andrews, Syracuse, N.Y.; Mrs. C. G. Brandon, Natchez, Miss.; Mrs. Elvert M. Davis, Philadelphia, Pa.; Miss Laurie Gray, Gray Court, S.C.; Mr. George Middleton, Washington, D.C., Mrs. W. H. Palmer, Jr., St. Davids, Pa.; Mr. E. A. Parsons, New Orleans, La.; Mr. Thomas W. Streeter, Morristown, N.J.

The following institutions and persons associated with them have been uncommonly kind in assisting my research:

Library of Alabama Polytechnic Institute
Auburn, Alabama
Miss Mary E. Martin

American Antiquarian Society
Worcester, Mass.
Mr. Robert W. G. Vail

Library of the Army War College
Washington, D.C.
Colonel Hjalmar Erickson, U.S. Army (Retired)
Miss Nannie Cramer Barndollar

The Public Library of the City of Boston
Mr. Zoltán Haraszti

Buffalo Historical Society, Buffalo, N.Y.
Mr. Robert W. Bingham

Public Archives of Canada, Ottawa, Canada
Mr. Francis J. Audet

Chicago Historical Society
Mr. L. H. Shattuck
Miss Alice Daly

Public Library of Cincinnati, Cincinnati, Ohio
Miss Mary R. Cochran

Library of Congress, Washington, D.C.
Dr. J. Franklin Jameson
Dr. Thomas P. Martin

Connecticut State Library, Hartford, Conn.
Mr. George S. Goddard
Miss M. E. Case

The Filson Club, Louisville, Ky.
Miss Ludie J. Kinkead

Henry E. Huntington Library and Art Gallery
San Marino, Calif.
Mr. Reginald Berti Haselden

Kentucky State Historical Society
Frankfort, Ky.
Mrs. Jouett Taylor Cannon

Hall of Records, Annapolis, Md.
Miss Elizabeth W. Meade

Massachusetts Historical Society
Boston, Mass.
Mr. Julius H. Tuttle

The Library, United States Military Academy
West Point, N.Y.
Lieutenant-Colonel Elbert E. Farman, U.S. Army (Retired)

Missouri Historical Society, St. Louis, Mo.
Miss Anne Kinnaird

The New York State Historical Association
Ticonderoga, N.Y.
Mr. E. P. Alexander

The New York Historical Society, New York City
Mr. Alexander J. Wall

The New York Public Library, New York City
Mr. Victor H. Paltsits
Miss M. C. Weaks

New York State Library, Albany, N.Y.
Mr. James I. Wyer
Miss Edna L. Jacobsen

The Newberry Library, Chicago, Ill.
Mr. George B. Utley

Northwestern University Library, Evanston, Ill.
Mr. Theodore W. Koch

Historical and Philosophical Society of Ohio
Cincinnati, Ohio
Miss Eleanor S. Wilby

The Oneida Historical Society, Utica, N.Y.
Mrs. Thomas D. Watkins

The Historical Society of Pennsylvania
Philadelphia, Pa.
Dr. Julian P. Boyd
Miss Mary M. Townsend
Miss Catherine H. Miller

State Library of Commonwealth of Pennsylvania
Harrisburg, Pa.
Mr. Curtis W. Garrison

Library of the American Philosophical Society
Philadelphia, Pa.
Miss Laura E. Hanson

Library of the University of Pittsburgh
Pittsburgh, Pa.
Mr. Howard Dice

Library of Syracuse University, Syracuse, N.Y.
Mr. Wharton Miller
Mrs. Ida O. Benderson
Mrs. Emilie Du Bois Benedict

State Library and Historical Commission
Austin, Texas
Miss Harriet Smither

Library of the University of Texas
Austin, Texas
Mr. J. Haggard-Villasana

Ticonderoga Museum, Ticonderoga, N.Y.
Mr. S. H. P. Pell

Old Records Section, Adjutant-General's Office,
War Department, Washington, D.C.
Mr. Charles E. Gause

The State Historical Society of Wisconsin
Madison, Wis.
Miss Annie A. Nunns

Several publishing companies have allowed me to make use of copyright material: The Burrows Bros. Co., Cincinnati, Ohio; Dodd, Mead, New York; Houghton Mifflin, Boston. This courtesy has saved me much inconvenience and is greatly appreciated.

JAMES RIPLEY JACOBS

THE MANLIUS SCHOOL
Manlius, N.Y.

CONTENTS

ILLUSTRATIONS

CHAPTER I

DOCTOR BY PROFESSION, SOLDIER BY CHOICE

FORTY miles southeast of Washington a few fishermen live sparingly on the bounty of tourists and the sale of oysters gathered from the waters of the Patuxent. They are friendly, these folk, and talk in quiet neighborly voices about their own doings. They are not the kind who travel far in the journeyings of the mind, nor do they think deeply except on very personal things. Like their thoughts, their wants are not extensive. If life is hard, they still are happy in their brightening Maryland sunshine; usually whimsical over misfortunes, they take their turns of adversity with an easy faith in a rewarding future. When food and shelter are sufficient, they see no reason to exert themselves as do the more prosperous farmers who live across the river and in the rolling country of the hinterland.

The eighteenth century forebears of these farmers were men who often held great areas of land touched by arms of the Atlantic. From their own wharves, boats were loaded in summer and fall with the harvest of their crops destined for Baltimore Town or ports across the sea. They were wealthy enough in this world's goods until tobacco lost its primacy and their fields wore out with constant planting. Generous to a fault, hospitable to friends and strangers alike, gallant toward women, sensitive in matters of honor, and often unskillful in barter and business, they made a pleasant people with whom to dwell.

In the days of the early Baltimores their creed was Catholicism, although members of other sects were tolerated and came to Maryland in great numbers. But with the accession of William and Mary to the throne in 1689, important changes occurred in the province: a royal government was instituted; the Church of England was established, and an irksome tax levied for its support. For years living was dangerous for those who continued to make confession to the priests

1

still lingering among them. Sometimes they had to wear swords for
their personal protection, and for a time they were permitted to wor-
ship only in special rooms of their own homes. However, after the
Calverts had turned Protestant and were again governors, the
Catholics, scattered here and there, were no longer considered a
menace. Persecution then abated, and at the beginning of the American Revolution the Angelus was sometimes heard as Protestants
returned to their homes upon the rounded hills.

As religious bigotry diminished, the planters were better able to
concentrate upon matters of more worldly concern—land, hogsheads
of well cured tobacco, and numbers of dutiful slaves. These were their
principal interests, even if their epitaphs beneath a spreading oak
would indicate far otherwise. Their kin, like most others, judged
kindly in the presence of eternity.

In this Maryland of early days, James Wilkinson was born in
1757, three miles northeast of the present village of Benedict, on the
south side of Hunting Creek. The arrival of another boy was welcome
news to family and friends—particularly to young Joseph, who was
then about three and needed a playmate. In the course of time these
two boys were to have a couple of sisters. These four rounded out the
family circle.[1]

The father, Joseph Wilkinson, was an esteemed merchant-planter.
He died when James was not quite seven, leaving to his dependents a
considerable estate. The growing boy remembered little about his
father except that he was oversensitive about his honor and enjoined
his son to be likewise. The mother, Betty Heighe, lived until 1802,
and on her devolved the task of raising the family. Having, in addition to strength of body and mind, many Christian virtues, she won
from her children not only affection but a great deal of admiration.[2]

She and her husband both came from good English families, were
followers of the Protestant faith, and often bent their heads in prayer
beneath the barreled ceiling of All Saints Church. Whether merchant,
planter, or doctor, their ancestors had acquired property and, with
meticulous care, saw that it was bequeathed as they desired. The
families seldom had many members, and each heir's portion of slaves,
land, tobacco, and cattle was proportionately large. Other things of
lesser value were also handed down—joiners' tools, pewter dishes and

[1] Wilkinson, *Memoirs,* I, 7–9.
[2] *Ibid.,* 7–9, and gravestone records about four miles northwest of Prince Frederick.

silver plate; a suit of child's bed linen; a "feather bed for Althea on her sixteenth birthday or earlier" should she marry; Bibles, concordances, commentaries and expositions of the oracles of God; "ten pounds current money of England for Elizabeth and Mary" in token of paternal affection; "a handsome suit of mourning and a mourning ring of 20s sterling price." [3]

Land, slaves, and valuables of this kind could come only from people of consequence. Even if their last thought was of decent burial and remission of sins, they were yet very careful to see that their possessions were reserved only for kinsmen of their choice.

With this background of piety and property James Wilkinson passed into his teens, acquiring a tolerant idea of most sects and an easy disregard for money except for the pleasure it might bring. He doubtless knew many of the fox-hunting gentry, particularly those who ranged through his mother's plantation, and from them took some of his patterns of conduct. He learned to admire comely women who gracefully rode clean-limbed horses of pedigree. He acquired a desire for long reaches of fruitful acres and for negroes stripping tobacco and singing in the sun. He often pricked up his ears to the blowing of a cow's horn along the winding reaches of Hunting Creek, for the sound meant the visiting of relatives and friends, either at his home or somewhere along the Patuxent. His days would soon be filled with bustling interest. He delighted to see the house overflowing and guests becoming convivial around the board. He early learned to move easily among them, because they came so often and stayed so long. He sometimes wormed in below the salt and aped the manners of a man, for he matured early, this fatherless boy of keen mind and attractive ways.

When he was twelve years old, he had to leave a genial home like this and go to Baltimore for inoculation against smallpox. Here he remained a month or more while he was being successfully treated. He was thrilled; the town was different from that world of his between the Chesapeake and the Patuxent. [4]

The study of "inferior" mathematics and the Latin classics had no corresponding call of interest, even if David Hunter, a graduate of the University of Glasgow, was his tutor. He did not make marked progress in either; when about fourteen, he was placed under Dr.

[3] *Ibid.*, Appendix I–IV.
[4] *Ibid.*, 10–13.

John Bond, a relative, to begin the study of medicine. The doctor had served in the French and Indian War, and delighted in telling stories of his regiment. To these Wilkinson was deeply attentive, for he was a virile lad, and all his friends were then discussing imperial efforts to tax and resistance to the British Crown. For him the lore of surgeons and apothecaries could not compete with that of soldiers and arms and shining deeds.[5]

Nevertheless, in the hope that he might still become a doctor, it was thought best to send him where he might enjoy the best training along the Atlantic seaboard. From Plum Point, the home of his grandmother Heighe, the lad made his way up the Chesapeake, then across the isthmus and up the Delaware to Philadelphia, the largest and most interesting city of the Colonies. He arrived here in his seventeenth year, perhaps on an autumn evening in 1773.[6] Probably there were relations or friends who met the lad and took him to their home.

In Philadelphia his eyes were opened to unaccustomed sights. Along its straight and well paved streets fine ladies and gentlemen were constantly riding in coaches or on horseback. In spite of Quaker restraint, they wore heavily powdered wigs, flaring coats of radiant color, taboured shirts, silver buckles, fine breeches, bodices, stomachers, and gaily patterned silks and satins. People of quality had not yet yielded to the pressure of patriotism and the fashion for provincial things. Humbler folk were very differently clad; their clothes were suited for rugged tasks. German and Irish workmen, redemptioners, and apprentices went about their business in stout leather breeches and woolens. Sailors clattered by in coarse jackets and ill-fitting shoes; they were hardy and brown with the weathering of the ocean, ill-smelling with grog and the fish of the sea. These people were all very new to the growing James, whose vision had been limited to his mother's plantation, Baltimore, and the sweep of the Patuxent and the Chesapeake. He would learn much from them before his course of study was ended.

Within the cosmopolitan city of Philadelphia he would also find unusual opportunities for the study of "physic and surgery." Nowhere in the New World existed such a coterie of distinguished physicians. Dr. William Shippen, Jr., father of medical science in Philadelphia, was just beginning his great aid to women through the teaching

[5] *Ibid.*, 12.
[6] *Ibid.*, 12–13.

of obstetrics. Dr. Benjamin Rush, brilliant and learned in the lore of the Old World, was in the early morning of his dynamic career. These two and Doctors John Morgan, William Smith, Thomas Bond, and others induced the College of Pennsylvania in 1767 to have a regular course of medicine, which was to be followed by a year's service as interne in the Pennsylvania Hospital. At about the same time Dr. Thomas Bond originated the idea of clinical lectures. Sometimes the doctor took several students to the bedside of the sick and there made a few remarks; on other occasions the clinic was held in a large room so that a greater number might be present. Patients were in the immediate care of student-apprentices living in the same building and directly supervised by a regular physician. What these neophytes gained from experience was considered full payment for their services.[7]

Wilkinson's training often required his presence at the Pennsylvania Hospital. It was built of red brick during the early days of the French and Indian War through the generosity of the British Parliament and many individual contributors. With its gray marble pilasters, Palladian windows, Ionic columns, and winding stairways, it was a fitting monument to skillful craftsmen and liberal donors.[8] This style of architecture, as well as other types equally attractive, was part and parcel of Philadelphia, making the city an inviting, substantial place in which to dwell. The Quakers were not only peaceful and godly; they were diligent and thorough in whatever work their hands took up. Their two-and-one-half-story homes, so disarmingly simple in general design, were carefully built, brick on brick or stone on stone, by men who would not prostitute their craftsmanship for personal gain.

The more prosperous Quakers and "World's People" Wilkinson frequently visited. He moved in and out among the Shippens, Biddles, Bonds, and others of equal prominence, rather avoiding the company of swaggering young blades who sometimes "lost their rudder" or "filled their heads with bees." He was careful of appearances, and, with his rare capacity for making friends easily, he tried to cultivate the esteem of worth-while people. He often raised a heavy bronze knocker beneath the fanlight of a pedimented doorway and was en-

[7] Scharf and Wescott, *History of Philadelphia, 1609–1884,* II, 1588, 1607, 1670–1671.
[8] For a description of the hospital, see Cousins and Riley, *The Colonial Architecture of Philadelphia,* 212–214.

thusiastically welcomed to a comfortable seat beside an open fire of glowing hickory logs.

Philadelphia, no longer a part of the frontier, had evolved a serene but somewhat complicated civilization. Wilkinson enjoyed the best of it, and the houses that he built and the gardens that he planted in after years near the edge of the wilderness seem to have their originals in his memory of earlier days. Perhaps he also echoed the wishes of Ann Biddle, that charming woman whom he later married. Maybe he hoped that by such efforts her nostalgia would be less keen for friends and home and garden along the Delaware; perhaps she would not yearn so much for the peace and comfort of the city where her early years had been so happily spent.

Oddly enough, while she was being carefully reared as a Quaker, Wilkinson was turning more and more to soldiers and splendid deeds. The very day after he arrived in Philadelphia for the first time he went out to Northern Liberties, where the 18th Royal Irish Infantry was stationed, along with a detachment of Royal Artillery. Dr. John Bond, his Maryland tutor, had kindled an interest in the British service, and recent events increased it. When he saw the Irish in their colorful uniforms on guard and parade he was greatly thrilled. Before long the officers were his friends, and he frequently spent hours with them until their departure in 1774 for Boston [9]—a hotbed of revolution.

There in December, 1773, the belligerent Samuel Adams and some of his followers had staged a $90,000 "tea-party" at the expense of the East India Company. Great Britain had tried to bring Boston to account through the "Intolerable Acts"; but she had succeeded only in angering the merchants whose port was closed and the demagogues whose mouths were shut by the prohibition of town meetings. Resentful of punishment, they began glorifying themselves and others as martyrs to the cause of liberty. In their propaganda they were successful; for the citizens received plenty of food and sympathy, and steps were taken for the meeting of the First Continental Congress.

It met in Philadelphia, September 5, 1774. The delegates assembled in Carpenter's Hall, not far from the Pennsylvania Hospital, where Wilkinson probably was. They gave greater impetus to a movement Boston had partly initiated, setting the minds of the Colonists to seething over their petition to the King, addresses to the people, and plans for suspension of trade with Great Britain. Wilkinson, always

[9] *Memoirs,* I, 13.

alert and in the thick of things, doubtless neglected his medicine in trying to keep up with his study of the bigwigs who passed in and out of Carpenter's Hall. If "arms was his profession and politics his hobby," when he grew older, the incidents of these Philadelphia days were enough to incite a zeal for both. He might have espoused them immediately if he had been allowed to do as he pleased.

Instead, he had to leave the City of Brotherly Love and political turmoil in the spring of 1775 and begin the practice of medicine near Monocacy, Maryland, thirty miles up the Potomac from Georgetown.[10] He was now away from stirring things and able people, just an eighteen-year-old rustic mending bones and joints and prescribing pills and herbs. And this was at a time when his country was in rebellion, when the battles of Lexington and Concord were being fought.

He let his profession take care of itself and rode off each week to drill with an independent company. His patriotic ardor still unsatisfied, he became a volunteer in a rifle corps under Colonel William Thompson, of Pennsylvania. Before long he was with the Colonial forces investing Boston, near which the bloody battle of Bunker Hill had been fought on June 17, 1775.[11] Since then General William Howe had been sitting sluggishly by, seeing the Americans increase in numbers and seize points that enfiladed his position. He was a Whig by sentiment and loved his wine, women, and cards. He was in no mood to repeat a tactical blunder like that of Bunker Hill; he determined to evacuate Boston, and on St. Patrick's Day, 1776, the fleet weighed anchor for the chill Nova Scotia shore. With his troops went 1,000 loyalists without possessions or prospects, tearfully and forlornly huddled beneath the bellying sails.[12]

Wilkinson was quick to hear the news of the British departure, and before an hour had passed he and Colonels James Reed and John Stark were going over the ground where the two field officers had fought, several months before. They answered readily the questions of this interesting, affable boy; they liked to have him along, while he was delighted with the information and the attention that they gave him. He was the type of young officer that would bend or blend, tactfully courting the friendship of those who might promote his advancement.

[10] *Ibid.,* 14 ff.
[11] *Ibid.,* 15–16. Wilkinson was made captain, Mar., 1776, to rank from Sept. 6, 1775. Heitman, *Historical Register and Dictionary of the U.S. Army,* II, 1037.
[12] Wrong, *Canada and the American Revolution,* 307.

Wilkinson remained in or around Boston until the beginning of April. As an aide of General Nathanael Greene, the best of Washington's generals, he was serving an apprenticeship under admirable auspices. He continued in this capacity until Greene's command was transferred to New York, when he was assigned to a company of Colonel James Reed's New Hampshire regiment. Toward the end of the month he was among reinforcements that were marching to the army in Canada.[13]

If the "fourteenth colony" was to be won, new life must be injected into the crippled forces that were already there. They had been worn down by hardships seldom experienced by heroic men. General Montgomery had been killed and Benedict Arnold had fallen while making valiant efforts to take Quebec in the midst of a blinding snowstorm on the last day of the year 1775. They had been defeated when the winter was worst and no shelter was available. Their rations were uniformly poor; clothing was scant, and their money was worthless. They had been scourged by smallpox and were soon to be demoralized further by "Apostles of Confusion"—a committee of Congress. And General David Wooster, the successor of Arnold, was an illiterate bigot without capacity. Although victory was never possible with the men and means that the Colonies could provide, more troops were being sent to Canada.[14]

Some time during the first part of May, Wilkinson and his company reached Albany, only to linger in the neighborhood for a few days and then start north for the St. Lawrence country. They traveled by water as much as they could, for they were encumbered with provisions and equipment, roads were poor, and wheeled transportation was scarce. Near the south end of Lake George they scrambled into bateaux, and did not disembark until near Fort Ticonderoga. At this place, after changing to other boats and stowing away more rations, they bent their oars for Crown Point. On the open stretches of Champlain's chill blue water, a storm descended upon them; they were lashed by a violent wind and pelted with hail and heavy rain. Finding a haven on the lee side of Valcour Island, they rested there until a favoring breeze began to fill their blanket sails. By the 22nd of May they were in St. Johns, a frowzy village filled with men who had dropped away from organizations en route to or from the St.

[13] *Memoirs*, I, 34, 38.
[14] Smith, *Our Struggle for the Fourteenth Colony*, II, *passim*.

Lawrence. Wilkinson attached about fourteen of these dirty, hungry deserters to his company and pushed on to Lachine, where General Benedict Arnold, according to reports, had a handful of men trying to protect Montreal. Wilkinson determined to hasten to his camp rather than to Sorel, the headquarters of the army in Canada. The distance to Arnold was shorter; his sector was threatened with immediate invasion, and few Americans had won greater praise for leadership and valor. Under him a stalwart young officer might have rare opportunities for distinction. On May 23, 1776, Wilkinson reported to him.[15]

Arnold could readily perceive that a youth of unusual force and ability had joined him. Not yet twenty years old, Wilkinson had brought nearly one hundred men safely up the Hudson, through Lakes George and Champlain, across a tangled stretch of wilderness, and over the St. Lawrence at one of its treacherous points. The task had required initiative, physical hardihood, and the frequent exercise of good judgment. If he had not possessed the character of a soldier he would never have courted an opportunity to suffer privations and danger merely for the purpose of bringing help to a defeated army in which many had ingloriously died. The qualities that he had shown, along with his supreme confidence and insatiable ambition, were destined to insure his rapid advancement.

Luck, too, favored Wilkinson's cause. On the very day that he reported, Arnold was badly needing reinforcements to break the hostile net that was hemming him in. No help was possible from Montreal, down the St. Lawrence, where the garrison was half clothed, nearly starved, and dying from smallpox. Farther on in the same direction, at the mouth of the Sorel, General John Thomas, sick and turning blind, had begun to withdraw his heavy guns and baggage; for General John Sullivan had not yet come from the south, bringing fresh men and new hope. Up the St. Lawrence, conditions were even more foreboding. Outlying detachments had been driven in, and now Arnold and his troops were the only ones left to bar the way to Montreal. In fear of a rumored attack he had details of men furiously digging intrenchments at Lachine when Wilkinson arrived.[16]

Soon outguards could hear the beat of hostile drums, and a prisoner declared the enemy were preparing to advance. It was only

[15] *Memoirs*, I, 39–41.
[16] Smith, *op. cit.*, II, 371–395; Wilkinson, *Memoirs*, I, 41.

two days after Wilkinson's arrival, and never before had he been so close to actual fighting. He was frightened; in reality, he was no more than a nineteen-year-old boy. About midnight he sat down and wrote to General Nathanael Green, his patron of a few months before, telling him of the "sweet situation" they were in, intimating Montreal would be abandoned and they might be taken. The letter was informing even if it did end with some stilted eloquence about duty and personal sacrifice.

Appreciating its value, Greene sent it on to General Washington, who in turn forwarded it to Congress.[17] It went quickly along a channel best designed to serve military purposes and focus attention on the writer. As a clever piece of personal publicity, no better scheme could have been devised for announcing that Wilkinson had arrived in Canada and was assiduous in his country's service.

Fortunately his prognosis was not entirely correct; Arnold's "handful of brave fellows" was not sacrificed. Colonel De Haas arrived on May 25 with five hundred Pennsylvanians, and with these reinforcements Arnold began an offensive, pursuing the British as far as Fort Anne. Here he summoned a council of war that even captains attended. Wilkinson, of course, was present, and acted as recorder of the proceedings. He and his facile pen were frequently in demand. Arnold wanted to ascend the Grand River by night and fall on the rear of the enemy at daybreak, hoping in this way to free some American prisoners recently taken. The idea was too daring for several of the senior officers, who argued that the Indians would discern the movement and begin a massacre. Only the young bloods like Captains Harmar, Butler, and Wilkinson were eager to make the attempt. The project was voted down, and Arnold, though much irritated, ceased to urge it.[18]

Two or three days later Arnold set out for Montreal, leaving Colonel De Haas in command at Fort Anne. On May 30, the Colonel received a peremptory order to attack a near-by Iroquois village. Another council of war followed. In spite of this order and the opposition of a few determined spirits, De Haas did nothing except retreat to Lachine. Wilkinson was sent to the General to make the best of this act of insubordination and cowardice. Arnold booked them all as cowards. Wilkinson remonstrated, declaring De Haas was to blame.

[17] *Memoirs*, I, 43–44.
[18] *Ibid.*, 44–46.

Arnold meditated, and then asked him to remain for supper. Refusing the invitation, he went hungry to the lousy tavern, and, sulking, slept in his rain-drenched clothes. He was just a boy, but already his shadows were like those he would cast as an older man.[19]

In the morning he was ordered to join the Lachine troops, soon transferred to Montreal. When they arrived there, he was requested to join Arnold as an aide-de-camp. He accepted gladly; he was flattered by "the preference of an officer, who at that period acquired great celebrity." He might have added that in this new position his peculiar abilities would find their best expression, and his chances of promotion would be considerably improved.

If he had known what was in store for him as a staff officer he might have declined. A few days after his appointment he was given a few men and some invoices and told to collect supplies from the inhabitants. The requisitions were designed to meet the needs of the army, although they included many things of value not essential for soldiers. The owners, of course, would not willingly deliver the goods and thereby forfeit any indemnity that they might expect from the British Crown. Nor did they want Continental money in payment; it had little value then and would have less after the departure of American troops. Wilkinson withered under the abuse that was heaped upon him, particularly when he tried to make away with a quarter-cask of Madeira. His thirst and strength of purpose were not so well developed as in later years. In disgust, he returned and asked Arnold to relieve him from the detail. The General did so, remarking that Wilkinson was "more nice than wise." [20]

Arnold knew that his sick, starved, and naked army had to be fed and clothed, and that requisitions upon the conquered people were his only resource, but he was not careful about the character of the articles collected or the uses to which they were subsequently put. Out of such a situation grew peculation, thefts, investigations, courts-martial, and black hatreds—a sordid story of those who would first be rich, and then perhaps be honest. Brave and resourceful, Arnold had led eight hundred men suffering incredible hardships through the lengths of the forests of Maine, and then, in the midst of a blinding snowstorm, had thrown them, ragged, hungry, and diseased, against the strongest citadel on the American continent. The tale is epic.

[19] *Ibid.*, 47–48.
[20] *Ibid.*, 48–49.

How easy would have been his translation to a worthy place in Valhalla had his wound proved fatal in the shadow of the rock of Quebec!

Wilkinson had much to learn from this masterful man. In the critical hour of battle and the long drab intervals between, the rank and file turned to Arnold. The power of his will and the fear of his own hot anger won from his followers their last ounce of strength, whether in the open shock of arms or in the "fatigue of long hard marches; the dreariness of prolonged, uncomfortable encampments; the disappointment of defeat; the discouragements and hardships of retreat." [21] Such great qualities of leadership, Wilkinson seemed unable to acquire. Though no coward, he could not convince subordinates that he was entirely brave, that he would suffer and ignominiously die with them. His value to the service consisted in his adaptability, eagerness to please, diplomatic smoothness, and unusual strength of mind and body. He was best fitted for staff duty. Others appreciated this fact and chose him as one of their aides.

Before long Arnold sent him with important messages to General Sullivan, who, as commonly supposed, was at Sorel. When Wilkinson had traveled on his way as far as Varennes he found the place filled with redcoats—a good-sized force and only fourteen miles from Montreal. Though the British were pushing a daring offensive, nobody seemed the wiser. Once they had seized Longueuil, Chambly, and St. Johns, the whole American army might be trapped and an immediate invasion of New York made possible.[22]

Wilkinson quickly estimated the situation. Realizing that Arnold was ignorant of the British advance and must be immediately informed, he rode like the wind to tell him. By six o'clock that evening he was back at headquarters, and the General knew that the British were on the way to cut off his retreat. Meanwhile news had come of Sullivan's withdrawal from Sorel; consequently Arnold was free to evacuate Montreal. The movement immediately began. In two hours boats were shoving off and troops were starting on their way to St. Johns via Laprairie.[23]

Wilkinson was again dispatched to General Sullivan with a request for troops to cover Arnold's retreat. Not reaching Longueuil until dusk, he still had a dozen miles to go through storm and driving rain.

[21] Steele, *American Campaigns*, I, 39.
[22] Smith, *op. cit.*, II, 428–429.
[23] *Ibid.*, 438–439, and Wilkinson, *Memoirs*, I, 49–51.

About nine o'clock he arrived at Chambly, where he found the advance guard of the army, overcome with fatigue and demoralized by its own fears. Men were scattered here and there, buried in sleep, and without a single sentinel on watch for their safety. Not once was he challenged en route to army headquarters, where he reported the advance of the British and the dilemma of Arnold. Sullivan decided to send reinforcements of five hundred men from the rear guard commanded by Baron de Woedtke, of the sore seat and quenchless thirst; and Wilkinson was told to find him and deliver the order. Again he started out in that night of utter darkness; once he nearly fell in the river; for a time he lost his way. Woedtke could not be found—comfortably drunk somewhere, the rumor ran. Within a month or two strong liquor and scarlet women would complete the baron's dissolution. At length Wilkinson took shelter in a filthy cabin and waited until dawn would make easier his search; but he met with no better results.[24]

Acting on another's suggestion, he then sought aid from Colonel Anthony Wayne—the "Mad Anthony" of valorous deeds at Three Rivers, Brandywine, Germantown, and many another place. He responded with characteristic decision; stationing himself at a bridge, he halted and formed into organizations all those who came to pass over. With this nondescript detachment he started to reinforce Arnold. After two hours' marching he learned that the British had let slip their great opportunity. They were no longer sailing up the St. Lawrence, for the winds had proved contrary and the current was strong.[25]

Wayne, therefore, reversed his march and started back to rejoin Sullivan, cluttering the rear of his route with felled trees and demolished bridges. Still haunted by fears of British pursuit, his men plodded on. By June 16, they had reached a fort that Montgomery had taken the year before, and close by they found a village of canvas sheltering their own comrades in arms. For two days they remained at St. Johns, waiting for other troops and stores. Then the army of retreat, burning what it could not carry, pushed southward once more, wearily driving the cumbersome boats against the current of the Sorel toward Nut Island.

Only two lingered behind—Arnold and Wilkinson. Both rode

[24] Smith, *op. cit.*, II, 439–440; Wilkinson, *Memoirs*, I, 51–53; Graydon, *Memoirs*, 139.

[25] Smith, *op. cit.*, II, 440–441; Wilkinson, *Memoirs*, I, 53–55; Moore, *Diary of the American Revolution*, I, 459.

quickly down the road to Chambly to look upon the vanguard of the army of John Burgoyne, "Lieutenant-General of his Majesty's Armies in America, Colonel of the Queen's regiment of light dragoons, Governor of Fort William, in North Britain, one of the Representatives of the Commons of Great Britain in Parliament." In spite of such a relay of titles he had few practical ideas about leading troops in the wilderness that lay before him, while the two officers in homespun, now observing his men, were well versed in the lore of forest and stream. Within a year or more the three were to meet along the waters of the Hudson, where Burgoyne would give full proof of incapacity. Once satisfying themselves that the British were not in hot pursuit, Arnold and Wilkinson galloped away, returning to the river that they had just left. After killing and stripping their horses, they loaded their dunnage into a boat, which the melodramatic Arnold shoved off with his own hand that he might be the last to leave the enemy's country. The same night they reached Nut Island, twelve miles distant, where the rest of the troops were drearily encamped.[26]

In this dark hour of the defeated army, the half-starved troops were so weak and exhausted that they fell asleep at the oars. Once on the low and swampy land of Nut Island, they perished miserably from malaria and virulent smallpox. Without supplies or medicines, the doctors could do nothing. The burial pits grew larger, but they were daily filled with the dead wrapped in filthy blankets. In spite of increased suffering and disaster, Sullivan refused to retreat farther until he received orders from Major-General Philip Schuyler, then commanding the Northern Department. Before long they came; and on the first day of July "the wreck of the army gathered itself painfully and pitifully at Crown Point, humiliated, woebegone, and utterly demoralized." [27]

Arnold was not in the number. He and Wilkinson had already left on June 19 for Albany in order to carry dispatches to Schuyler, who was then commanding the area into which Sullivan and his army had come. For over a year Arnold had carried on as few men could; a leave would afford a pleasant change and might give opportunity for clearing himself of evil tales about those confiscated Canadian goods that had just arrived in Albany. He was also a widower of a few years, and, like his bachelor companion, had a turn for gayety and women.

[26] Wilkinson, *Memoirs*, I, 54–55.
[27] Smith, *op. cit.*, II, 444–445.

A hard journey would be well repaid if it ended on that fine estate of General Schuyler. He was an engaging host possessed of charming daughters and a lovely garden—more than enough to make laggards of good soldiers.[28]

Wilkinson did not remain long in the neighborhood to enjoy the pleasures that it offered. Changes in the Northern Department helped to send him soon on his way back to Lake Champlain. Major-General Horatio Gates arrived on June 27, rather puffed up over his recent promotion and assignment to the army that had just returned from Canada. He had been up to his old game of intrigue while others were suffering the worst hardships of war. When Sullivan heard that he had been superseded he asked to retire from Schuyler's department and seek the acceptance of his resignation from Congress.[29] With this shifting of generals in an already demoralized command, Gates, Schuyler, and Arnold decided to go to Crown Point and look over the situation. Thinking Wilkinson might be useful, one of them ordered him to set out quickly and arrange for their coming. After the generals had arrived and conferred, they decided to remove their bedridden forces to Ticonderoga. Of the 5,200 men 2,800 needed hospital care. A few field officers remonstrated against the evacuation, for they believed that Crown Point should be held at all costs. Nevertheless, the movement went forward, and Arnold, Wilkinson, and others were left behind to clear the place completely of men and supplies.[30]

After this work was finished Arnold went to Ticonderoga and for a time used most of his energy in trying to prosecute Colonel Hazen for alleged negligence in caring for the goods that had been confiscated in Canada. When the court refused to accept the testimony of one Major Scott, principal witness for the prosecution, because of his apparent interest in the case, Arnold declared its action unjust and without precedent. Thereupon the court asked for a retraction of his statement. Arnold declared he would not comply but expressed a willingness to give the satisfaction that the "nice honor" of any member required. The wrangle grew in strength and scope. Each had hardy partisans. At the time Wilkinson thought Arnold "the intrepid, gen-

---

[28] Wilkinson, *Memoirs*, I, 60. To Varick, July 4, 1776, Miscel. MSS, N.Y. Public Library.

[29] Gates to Hancock, July 16, 1776, Wilkinson, *Memoirs*, I, 62; Sullivan to Schuyler, July 6, 1776, in Hammond, *Letters and Papers of General John Sullivan*, I, 280–281.

[30] Wilkinson, *Memoirs*, I, 62–64, 67; "Autobiography of John Trumbull," in *Bulletin of Fort Ticonderoga Museum*, Jan., 1933, pp. 5–6.

erous, friendly, upright Honest Man," and indignantly asked, ". . . is it for Men, who can't boast more than an easy enjoyment of the Continental Provision, to blast the Reputation of Him, who having encountered the greatest perils, surmounted extremest hardships, fought and bled in a Cause which they have only encumbered?"[31] Gates held a somewhat similar opinion, and showed it by dissolving the court and appointing Arnold to the important command of the squadron proposed for the defense of Lake Champlain.[32]

Without delay Arnold vigorously applied himself to the task of turning forests into boats and soldiers into sailors. Before long he was flying the broad pennant of commodore from the masthead of the *Royal Savage*, the best of his flotilla of fifteen ships. With an ill assorted lot of schooners, gondolas, and galleys, he moved north along the waters of Champlain to meet the enemy under Sir Guy Carleton, who was descending from Canada with a fleet and an army of 12,000 men. Twice they joined battle, October 11 and 13. In the first engagement the Americans held their own; in the second all their vessels were sunk. The British, however, had no reason to gloat; they had been delayed so long that they could not move southward and secure the valley of the Hudson before the winter. Again, Arnold had done well by his country.[33]

Wilkinson did not share in the glory of his exploits; during the summer he had retired from the General's official family. His own sickness and the friendliness of high ranking officers may have induced him to seek another connection. Once having made it, he was destined soon to see new fields of adventure opening before him.

[31] Wilkinson to Varick, Aug. 5, 1776. Varick Papers, Tomlinson Collection, N.Y. Public Library.
[32] Wilkinson, *Memoirs*, I, 70–74; Gates to Pres. of Congress, July 29 and Sept. 2, 1776, in Force, *American Archives*, 5th Series, I, 649, 1267–1268.
[33] *Bulletin of Fort Ticonderoga Museum*, Jan., 1929, pp. 16, 17. "Benedict Arnold," in *Dictionary of American Biography*, I, 362–367.

CHAPTER II

BOY–GENERAL

DURING the summer of 1776 a new spirit animated the Americans who were taking part in the Revolution. It sprang from no elation of victory, rather from a grim determination to win the war in spite of every obstacle. Incensed by the acts of George III and inspired by the Declaration of Independence, they fought no longer merely for their rights as Englishmen. They were engaged in a war of secession from the British Empire. If victorious, they would have full opportunity to carry out their theories of "liberty and equality"; if defeated, they might reasonably expect the imposition of more galling conditions than any that they had suffered before the days of Lexington and Concord. Little in the first year and a half of the Revolution augured well for their ultimate success. Boston, of course, had been taken, but its value was slight compared with that of New York City, from which Washington was driven during September, 1776. While he was in full retreat across New Jersey, the Colonists learned the harrowing details incident to the ignominious failure of their expedition into Canada. With the northern frontier unprotected, the British assumed the offensive, an offensive that Arnold halted by his gallant action with an improvised fleet on Lake Champlain during October. Once the enemy were in retreat in this area, Gates dismissed the militia, established a garrison under Wayne at Ticonderoga, and began a concentration of the rest of his troops at Albany.

Wilkinson had no part in these autumn operations of the Champlain valley. By the good offices of Gates, he was promoted to brigade-major on July 20 and assigned to the 3rd Brigade at Mount Independence. On September 4 he was transferred with the same rank and duties to the command of Brigadier-General Arthur St. Clair, one of Washington's faithful officers who subsequently became gov-

ernor of the Northwest Territory.[1] While elated over his rise in rank,
Wilkinson was stricken with typhoid fever and incapacitated for two
or three months. More than a thousand troops died of the disease,
and few expected him to survive. With others critically ill he was sent
to the south end of Lake George, where Dr. Jonathan Potts became
his personal physician. In spite of attentive care, he grew worse, and
boards were sawed for his coffin. Taking a turn for the better, he
improved so much by October that he could make the trip to Albany
in a wagon. There he was helped, at least, by being far away from
burial squads and the slow beat of funeral drums. The Van Rensse-
laers took him in and tended him kindly.[2] Among friends and in a
comfortable home, Wilkinson began to mend, and toward the last of
November he was able to resume his duties.

He could no longer act as brigade-major for his old organization,
the 4th Brigade, for it had been recently discharged. Gates was on
his way to General Washington in New Jersey with reinforcements
from the Northern Department; he had progressed as far as Esopus
(Kingston) when Wilkinson, now convalescent, reported and began
to do errands for him. On arriving at Van Kempt's, a settlement in the
rough country near the Delaware, the straggling troops suffered intensely from cold; they lacked clothing, shoes, transportation, and
provisions, and, in this desolate region, covered deep with snow, Gates
did not know the whereabouts of either Washington or the enemy.
On December 12 Wilkinson was dispatched to find the commander-
in-chief and ascertain what route to pursue.[3] Making his way over
the hills to Sussex Court House, he learned that Washington had
crossed the Delaware to escape the British in close pursuit. He immediately wrote this news to Gates, expressing at the same time his
intention of pushing on quickly to the headquarters of the commander-
in-chief.[4] On hearing how hard it was to get a boat for reaching the
opposite shore of the Delaware, he changed his plans and determined
to find General Charles Lee, now second in command of the Army, who
was supposed to be at Morristown, a place much closer at hand.[5] He

[1] *Memoirs,* I, 83; "Deputy Adjutant-General's Orderly Book," in *The Bulletin of
Fort Ticonderoga Museum,* Jan., 1933, p. 35, and July, 1933, p. 87.
[2] *Memoirs,* I, 86, 99; Wilkinson to Gates, Oct. 25, 1776, in Force, *American Archives,*
5th Series, II, 1243.
[3] *Memoirs,* I, 100; Gates to Washington, Dec. 12, 1776, in Force, *Amer. Archives,*
5th Series, III, 1190.
[4] To Gates, Dec. 12, 1776, in Force, *Amer. Archives,* 5th Series, III, 1190–1191.
[5] *Memoirs,* I, 101.

must have known that Gates would choose to serve under Lee, an old friend, rather than under Washington, of whom he was inordinately jealous. It was possible that Lee might order Gates's four regiments to join him instead of making the longer and more difficult march to Washington; lately he had done this very thing in the case of three other organizations.[6]

While riding along at night, Wilkinson stumbled on a tavern, and went in to inquire where Lee might be found. Nobody apparently could inform him except the old woman of the place, who suggested that two strange officers upstairs in bed might know. A chambermaid, sent to awaken them, was soon screaming at the top of her voice though not because they were asleep or deaf. Wilkinson, Don Quixote in person, grabbed his pistols and started to the rescue of the nearly ravished Dulcinea. He found her trembling in a corner and two officers somewhat the worse for toddy. Naked and unarmed, they rose up in bed only to look into a pair of huge pistols and a gaudy apparition clothed in French capot, scarlet undercoat, and gold-laced hat. It was time for Lee's private secretary and Colonel Gibson to quake. Only a realization of Wilkinson's identity brought them relief —then the maid went back to her chores, the officers to their clothes, and Wilkinson again upon his way.[7]

By four o'clock the same morning he had reached White's Tavern, where Lee was quartered. The General received him in bed, read the message, and bade him "take repose." Wilkinson, finding a place to rest among the officers of the staff, rose early to wait upon him again at eight. But the General had to take time out to confer with his adjutant-general and to pour out his wrath upon the peruked Connecticut Light Horse who, sick of the war, wanted to go home. Damned by him, they went. Not until ten o'clock was he able to write a reply to Gates and begin his breakfast with Wilkinson.[8]

When both had nearly finished eating Wilkinson turned and peered out of the window. Just one look was enough. A troop of British dragoons were charging down the road toward the tavern. Lee had only thirteen men as a bodyguard, and his division was four miles distant. The General raged because members of the "damned guard" did not fire. They were without arms, two hundred yards away, on

[6] Gates to Washington, Dec. 12, 1776, in Wilkinson, *Memoirs*, I, 100–101.
[7] *Ibid.*, I, 101–102.
[8] *Ibid.*, I, 102–108.

the south side of a house, pleasantly warming themselves in the winter sun. When Wilkinson poked his head out, the dragoons greeted him with curt, dirty words—a broad enough hint to get his pistols and prepare for resistance. Lee, still unseen, could not get a satisfactory place to hide: the breastwork over the fireplace was too small, and his dignity would not permit the use of a feather bed that the landlady offered. After surrounding the tavern, the raiders swore that they would burn it to the ground unless the General came forth and surrendered. Wilkinson was ignored: their net was cast for bigger fish. Lee quickly appeared bareheaded, in bedroom slippers, blanket coat, and dirty shirt. Mounting him on Wilkinson's horse and tormenting him with stableyard wit, they joyfully bore away one whom some erroneously believed to be "the American Palladium," [9] but who was, in fact, nothing more than a spindle-shanked, long-nosed, dog-loving eccentric of dubious loyalty and questionable military capacity.

Before Lee was captured he had written an answer to Gates, and Wilkinson now hastened to deliver it. In this letter he termed Washington "damnably deficient"; he declared the army was without supplies, Tories were everywhere, the country's counsels were weak, and unless the Whigs burnt Philadelphia, the cause of liberty was lost. Under the circumstances, Gates was bidden to seek safety by marching his forces to join the main army, if he thought he could do so quickly enough to help.[10]

Lee had disobeyed orders in lagging along the way, and was consequently liable to be court-martialed or relieved from command. To justify his action and show up Washington by contrast, Lee, according to Wilkinson, was contemplating an attack on the British at Princeton. A brilliant stroke with his own small forces might have resulted in foisting him upon the Army as commander-in-chief. The possibility of any such disaster was fortunately prevented by his capture.[11]

When Gates heard that Lee was in British hands he was greatly disturbed. In compliance with orders he started his troops for the Delaware, and on December 20 arrived at Washington's headquarters near Coryell's ferry.[12]

[9] *Ibid*, I, 102–107; Irving, *Life of George Washington*, II, 459–460; Winsor, *Narrative and Critical History of America*, II, 369.
[10] Lee to Gates, Dec. 13, 1776, in Wilkinson, *Memoirs*, I, 108.
[11] *Ibid.*, 108–110.
[12] *Ibid.*, I, 114.

Never had the morale of the army been so low. The loss of New York and Fort Washington, the ensuing retreat, accumulating hardships, and offers of easy British pardon had caused many to desert and others to lose their fighting edge. Washington realized that if the army was to be saved from disintegration, he must rekindle its hopes with a brilliant stroke.[13] On December 23, he informed Colonel Joseph Reed of a contemplated raid on Trenton.[14]

With a battle imminent, Gates complained of sickness and declined the command at Bristol that Washington had offered him; he prepared to leave for Philadelphia, where Mrs. Gates had recently come for a visit. He also wanted to see several merchants of the city who seemed eager to obtain a contract for supplying his half-naked men with clothes.[15] Now a surplus major-general, he could be spared for such an errand. Perhaps by a warm fire in a comfortable house, he might improve his health and figure out a scheme for regaining his former importance. Not far off was Baltimore, Maryland, where Congress was sitting. A journey thither might disclose how he and Washington stood with some of its influential members.

Wilkinson traveled with him, although then a staff officer of St. Clair, who had recently been given another brigade. His old commander wondered that he would go at a time when a fight was in the wind. Wilkinson, in later years, tried to excuse himself on a plea of ignorance, in spite of the fact that orders had been issued on the 23rd for troops to draw rations for three days and even Tories knew that Washington was planning an offensive. More likely he was flattered by Gates's friendliness and felt the lure of Philadelphia and a burning desire to see the charming Ann Biddle. Hence the two set out and, after a wearisome ride, reached the City Tavern, where they lodged for Christmas Eve. Gates was dyspeptic and croaked mournfully of Washington and his plans; he felt that the one which he was going to propose to Congress would save the Republic.[16]

Wilkinson wisely determined to return to his brigade, which he reached about dusk on Christmas Day after delivering a letter from Gates to Washington at McKonky's Ferry. Stopping for a moment from observing the passage of troops to the New Jersey side, the com-

[13] Upton, *The Military Policy of the United States*, 23–24.
[14] Washington to Reed, Dec. 23, 1776, in Wilkinson, *Memoirs*, I, 125–126.
[15] Stryker, *The Battles of Trenton and Princeton*, 60, 131, and Irwin to Gates, Nov. 3, 1776, in Force, *Amer. Archives*, 5th Series, III, 492.
[16] Stryker, *op. cit.*, 131; Wilkinson, *Memoirs*, I, 126–127.

mander-in-chief asked Gates's whereabouts and made a mental note that he was on the way to Baltimore.[17] Gates's absence was not deeply regretted; he could have done little to help upon that wintry night.

It was bitterly cold, and a cutting wind swept down the Delaware, now filled with floes of ice and eddying currents. At the ferry stood the massive and vigorous Henry Knox, bellowing orders. From the most ponderous of Boston booksellers, he had developed into one of Washington's favorite generals. Toward eleven o'clock snow began to fall, increasing confusion and discomfort. Colonel John Glover's regiment of seafaring Marblehead men was in charge of the crossing. These hardy fellows in blue jackets and leather-buttoned trousers knew rough weather and how to handle the black Durham boats across the thousand feet or more of treacherous water. With only about thirty shivering figures in a boat, the transfer was slow; after nine hours of going and coming, Glover had landed twenty-four hundred men safely on the Jersey side.[18]

At four o'clock the eight-mile march to Trenton began. The army operated in two divisions; the right under John Sullivan, that doughty general who had led the Americans back from Canada, took the route closer to the river, while the left, commanded by Washington in person, covering about the same distance, followed the Pennington road. Coöperating troops were to cross from points opposite Trenton and Bordentown, but these failed to get over. Hence on Sullivan's and Washington's troops alone the burden of battle fell.

Moving to the southeast, they first encountered a hostile picket about eight o'clock. It was posted near the Pennington road on the outskirts of Trenton. When firing began Hessian reinforcements came running up; they pulled their triggers once and fled helter-skelter down the road across the Assunpink to Bordentown and safety. Lieutenant Jacob Piel, brigade adjutant, hearing the rattle of musketry, knocked loudly on the quarters of Colonel Rall, then commanding at Trenton. The colonel, late at wine and cards, still slept. Once awakened, he answered from an upstairs window, and was soon in the street already swept by artillery from the road junction near the north end of the village. For a few moments he wavered in confusion and then gave orders for the Rall and the Lossberg regiments to drive the invaders from the town. Both organizations completely failed, and the retreat

[17] Wilkinson, *Memoirs*, I, 127–128.
[18] Stryker, *op. cit.*, 113, 133–138.

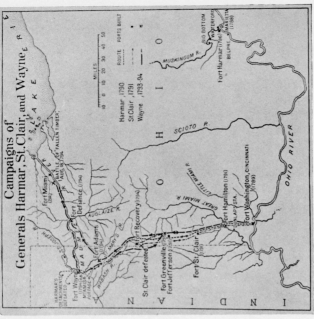

Fort Recovery.

Reproduced from "The Pageant of America" II, 87. Copyright Yale University Press.

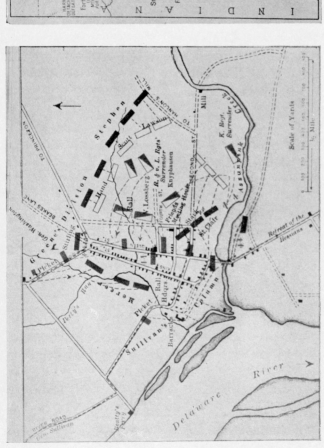

Map of the Battle of Trenton.

Courtesy of The Burrows Bros. Co. From E. M. Avery, "A History of the United States and Its People," II, 47.

began. Rall suffered two fearful wounds, and was carried into the Methodist Church, a dour-looking building where some of his artillerists were quartered. No one immediately exercised control, and the two regiments milled about in the orchards east of town. Firing continued. Often a figure in scarlet or blue or black stumbled and lay quietly beneath the trees, and the snow fell gently on his upturned face or heavy mass of braided hair.[19]

The Knyphausen regiment fared no better than the other two. When attacked by Sullivan's men on the south end of Trenton it resisted stoutly. But General Arthur St. Clair, pushing the Hessians hard with his brigade, drove them eastward from the houses of the town. Seventeen years before he had shown the same indomitable spirit on the Plains of Abraham when Quebec yielded to Wolfe. Once the enemy were in the open, Wilkinson, his aide, yelled out to them to surrender. A Lieutenant Wiederhold soon approached, and through him Captain von Biesenrodt, actually commanding, was informed of the terms. The captain objected to them, and the parley was resumed. This time St. Clair took an active part, and he swore to blow the Knyphausen regiment to hell unless it immediately surrendered. The threat proved effective.[20]

Wilkinson was then dispatched to inform Sullivan of the news. With the same message he went on to Washington, who received it just when Rall, mortally wounded, was being carried to one of the houses of the town. Elated with victory, the commander-in-chief pressed Wilkinson's hand and exclaimed, "This is a glorious day for our country." [21]

It was. The whole cause of liberty had been reborn in the hearts of all those who fought and labored for the army's success. A thousand of the enemy had been killed or captured at the expense of five American casualties—two killed and three wounded.[22] The prisoners were sent to Philadelphia, where "Old Put" (Israel Putnam) gave orders to his officers to clear their own men "out of the Barrok to make room for the hashon Prisoners." [23]

Perhaps others might have been taken if Washington had been able to push on and gain the most from victory. Unfortunately his men

[19] *Ibid.*, 145–177.
[20] *Ibid.*, 183–184.
[21] *Ibid.*, 185, and Wilkinson, *Memoirs*, I, 129–131.
[22] Carrington, *Battles of the Revolution*, 274–275.
[23] Stryker, *op. cit.*, 214.

were exhausted, and he could do nothing in the next few days except remain at Trenton and retard the advance of the British. In spite of his efforts they drove him from the village on January 2, and soon their artillery began to pound his new position along the high ground south of Assunpink Creek. His left rested on the Delaware, and once his right was turned his whole force might be driven into the river.

In this dilemma he called a council of his ranking officers at St. Clair's headquarters, where they decided to evacuate their position secretly and attack the British at Princeton. Wilkinson claims St. Clair suggested the idea. He may have done so, although there were others whose estimate of the situation could have been more impressive. General Dickinson was far better acquainted with the neighborhood roads over which the march was to be made, and Colonel Joseph Reed, the adjutant-general, had, besides this knowledge, the latest and most accurate information of the dispersed condition of the enemy's forces.[24]

Once the decision was made, orders were promptly issued for the movement. A few men were detailed to stay behind and maintain the fiction of a camp. They kept the fires burning brightly with fragrant cedar rails and dug into the soil as if for a line of intrenchments. The British, only a hundred and fifty yards away, could easily hear the challenge of sentinels and the sound of tools upon the frozen earth. They were completely deceived; they expected with some short, bloody work in the morning to wipe out the stain of the Hessian defeat by the capture of Washington's forces.

Meanwhile, the Americans were wrapping the wheels of the gun carriages with cast-off clothing to deaden the rumble of artillery over the frost-bitten ground. Rags had served a useful purpose before; they had bound the bleeding feet of shoeless men on the night march to Trenton. At about one o'clock on the morning of January 3 the march began. The road was rough and winding, the night dark and cold. Men grew weary and stumbled sleepily over the stumps along the uncleared way. Bruised, hungry, and shivering they moved slowly and profanely on.[25]

At dawn they reached the outskirts of Princeton, where the 40th Regiment alone remained of the British brigade quartered there. The 17th and 55th regiments had already left and were just then passing over the Stony Creek bridge on the way to reinforce Cornwallis at

[24] Wilkinson, *Memoirs,* I, 140; Stryker, *op. cit.,* 271–273.
[25] Stryker, *op. cit.,* 274–278.

Trenton. Lieutenant-Colonel Mawhood was in command and rode near the head of the column on a small brown pony. A couple of his favorite spaniels ran close beside. Suddenly catching sight of the American advance party under General Mercer, he immediately faced his troops about and raced back across the bridge to higher ground and natural cover. The Americans made for the same point. The lines drew close, not more than one hundred and twenty feet apart; volley followed volley, and a cloud of smoke drifted lazily through the bare limbs of orchard trees. Men fought savagely, and warm blood ebbed away upon the frozen ground. Mercer went down with seven wounds. The British left him for dead, and pursued his routed men. Wilkinson, seeing the sorry state of things, ran to tell St. Clair, who, in turn, calmed his fears and told him to keep the bad news to himself. Meanwhile Washington rode forward and put new spirit into his beaten men. Mifflin, in rose-colored blanket coat, came hurrying up with reinforcements; St. Clair also brought help. The balance of battle turned. The 17th ran pell-mell across the fields to Maidenhead, and the 55th were "fox-chased" back to Princeton, where they joined with some of the 40th and made a stand upon the college grounds. Though Nassau Hall proved a strong point of resistance, it was soon surrounded and covered by artillery fire. From its stone walls a ricocheting ball nearly killed the horse on which Wilkinson rode. Up in front as usual, he could have seen one hundred and ninety-four of the British file out of the building and surrender. About two hundred others escaped by running off to Brunswick at top speed. All told, the British lost four hundred in killed, wounded, and prisoners. The Americans suffered only forty casualties.[26]

Meanwhile Cornwallis had learned what Washington was doing. He was "in a most infernal sweat—running puffing and blowing and swearing at being so outwitted." [27] To prevent further disaster he started on a forced march to Princeton, where he arrived about noon, just in time to see the American rear-guard pass out of sight with the plunder of a second victory. Washington, of course, wanted to push on and capture Brunswick with all its British supplies and military chest of £70,000, but his men were too fatigued for another march and fight. Once beyond the danger of pursuit they rested for a while, and then ultimately went into camp at Morristown, a place well suited for

[26] Wilkinson, *Memoirs*, I, 140–148. Stryker, *op. cit.*, 278–302.
[27] Stryker, *op. cit.*, 288.

launching or repelling an attack and for obtaining adequate forage and provisions.[28]

Wilkinson was not among the troops that were stationed there. He perhaps had no desire to remain in a cheerless camp during midwinter. He had already experienced much of the wretchedness of war; he had often looked upon stark, naked suffering and putrid death in squalid places. He had seen bright waters and clean, green forests fouled by his afflicted countrymen in their dismal retreat from unconquerable Canada. He knew the exhaustion from long hard marching and the suffering from continued cold. The battles of Trenton and Princeton had opened his eyes to the hideous wounds that may be made by soft lead bullets and cannon balls. Partly because of his youthful vigor and practical mind, he had come through a year of fighting unscathed. In a short time he had established an enviable reputation, gained a modicum of glory, and won the friendship and support of his high-ranking superiors. Schuyler, Gates, St. Clair, and others were ready to exert a helpful influence in case he wanted a detail for which he was apparently fitted.

Thus it happened that Wilkinson was one of the officers assigned to the new battalions authorized on December 27, 1776; he was promoted to the grade of lieutenant-colonel and finally assigned to the regiment of Colonel Thomas Hartley, an officer with whom he had served in Canada. Partly because of his pleasing and convincing manner, he was selected to secure men for these last increments of the Army. He was sent to Maryland and Pennsylvania to enlist recruits, carrying with him blank commissions for the officers of his organization.[29] The detail offered no chances for distinction, but it did have compensations. For a while, at least, he would not have to perform a round of monotonous duties in an uncomfortable camp. The winter was not harsh along the shores of Maryland, and here and in Philadelphia he might find many friends who would take him in and listen eagerly to his doings since 1773. Though his stories might grow old, they seldom lacked interest to others or credit to himself. His mother listened and carried her head a trifle higher; his elder brother Joseph and his younger sisters were quickened with family pride. The youthful James had traveled far and was now at home in the full glory of success.

[28] Washington's report to Congress, Jan. 5, 1777, in *Ibid.*, 460–462.
[29] *Memoirs*, I, 157–158.

By the beginning of March, 1777, his recruiting parties were operating, and he had taken station in Philadelphia, the rendezvous of his regiment and the home of his future bride. One of his friends there was Gates, who had been oscillating since Christmas between Philadelphia and Baltimore under pretense of restoring his health but actually to promote his advancement through political intrigue. On March 25 Congress gave Gates what he wanted—the command of the Northern Department. Thereupon, Wilkinson was asked to become a member of his staff, a position that he accepted only after Washington had given reluctant consent.[30]

Some may have wondered why any officer would be willing to give up a lieutenant-colonelcy in the line for a lower grade on the staff of Gates, who was then just another major-general. Wilkinson offers in explanation that important operations were impending in the Northern Department, he knew its terrain in detail, and he valued distinction more than rank.[31] He might have added that Gates was companionable, overlooked his foibles with paternal indulgence, and perhaps gave him promises of rapid promotion. As an officer of field rank he could not expect the same treatment at the hands of Washington. Few men had the courage and ability to pass through his hard school for regimental commanders at Morristown, Valley Forge, Yorktown, and all the trying places in between. Youth and brilliance did not alone suffice; Wilkinson may have realized that he did not have the other necessary qualities in an adequate degree.

Although Gates had set out for the Northern Department about the first of April, Wilkinson delayed and did not reach the dreary posts near the upper Hudson until the month had almost ended.[32] At Albany he wrote to Wayne telling him of Gates's superseding Schuyler, of his own appointment, and of St. Clair's expected coming. At this time he greatly admired Wayne—that same "Mad Anthony" who had helped him get reinforcements to protect Arnold at a critical juncture during the Canadian campaign. He was just the man that Fort Ticonderoga then needed. In a letter to Gates, Wilkinson declared that to transfer him elsewhere would be "ill-natured, ill-judged and impolitic." This newly made staff officer was not wanting in opinions or words to express them.[33]

[30] *Ibid.*, 159–160.
[31] *Ibid.*, 160.
[32] *Ibid.*, 162.
[33] To Gates, May 11, 1777, in Gates Papers, N.Y. Historical Society.

On May 13 Wilkinson reached Ticonderoga and three days later made a scathing report on conditions there: the general in command was incapable of strengthening the defenses or perfecting the line of communications with Albany; provisions were scarce, returns in confusion, muskets and artillery in need of repair; clothing was not fit to be worn; the fleet was disorganized and without stores; men were sick and had no fight left in them. Nor were these the only things wrong. In the eyes of this boy-inspector: the adjutants were blockheads, the brigade-majors ignorant of their duties, and the general commanding had little or no ability, education, or experience.[34] Little wonder that Wilkinson begged Gates or St. Clair to come and bring order out of chaos.

On June 12, 1777, St. Clair arrived at Ticonderoga as a result of another shuffling of general officers. He set vigorously to work, although he could foresee that twenty-five hundred men with inadequate provisions and dilapidated defenses could not long sustain a well-planned attack.[35] Neither Congress nor the people would materially help to remedy these conditions, but they were still insistent that the place be held. Whoever abandoned it and saved his men might expect abuse from designing politicians who pandered to the whims of ignorant constituents.

Perhaps Gates visualized these contingencies more clearly than St. Clair; at any rate, he was too wily to accept command of the fort when it was offered to him by his successor, Schuyler, whom Congress had restored to the command of the Northern Department on May 22.[36] Wilkinson hated to see his patron displaced and without any assignment. On June 7 he wrote to Gates bitterly arraigning the members of Congress for what they had done:

"They have injured themselves, they have insulted you, and by so doing have been guilty of the foulest ingratitude. How base, how pitiful, or how little deserving the name is the Public Power which individual consequence can intimidate or bribe to its purposes." [37]

Lately Wilkinson had special reason to feel kindly toward Gates, who, just before actual relief, had appointed him "deputy adjutant-

[34] To Gates, May 16, 22, 26, 1777, in Wilkinson, *Memoirs*, I, 162–167; to Gates, May 26, 31, 1777, in Gates Papers, N.Y. Historical Society.
[35] *Memoirs*, I, 174–176.
[36] Nickerson, *The Turning Point of the Revolution*, 136; Wilkinson, *Memoirs*, I, 168.
[37] To Gates, June 7, 1777, in Lossing, *Life and Times of Philip Schuyler*, II, 183; to Gates, June 10, 1777, in Wilkinson, *Memoirs*, I, 172–173.

general to the army of the Northern Department of America" on the 24th of May.[38] The honor was highly flattering and might be retained under Schuyler. He had read the auspices correctly when he had resigned his lieutenant-colonelcy in March. Now he was a grade higher, at a time and place where his peculiar abilities would show to the best advantage in a series of events that were close at hand. Already the stage was being set.

In June, 1777, about eight thousand British, Germans, Tories, and Indians left Canada and began moving southward through the valley of Lake Champlain. They were commanded by one Lieutenant-General Burgoyne, literary dilettante, favorite of the King, and reputed bastard. Strangely out of his element but never wavering in a belief in his omniscience, this young general of sloping forehead and heavy nose indited brochures to scalping Indians in his best "Ciceronian manner," marched his troops through the woods as on parade, drank champagne and flirted with pretty women wherever found, and spoke contemptuously of the Colonists in their slatternly clothes, believing their conquest easy for the well drilled soldiers of the Crown.

Such was the unconventional leader of this extraordinary army that trudged along through the dripping aisles of forest trees. Pioneers were constantly panting from clearing the way and building bridges for those three thousand German hirelings of his to pass over with their heavy boots and clanking broadswords. Excepting the chasseurs, they were immobile and bovine and were no more fitted for frontier fighting than savages were for warfare in Flanders. The Englishmen, knowing something of colonial warfare, did not fall an easy prey to the Indians, even if their scarlet coats made them conspicuous targets against an emerald background bright with summer rain. They were well trained and inspired with traditions of success, but were burdened with lumbering carts and useless guns and knew nothing of the country in which they marched. For scouting they trusted to Indians, cruel, filthy, and hideous with war paint, useful only so long as they were swollen with food and allowed the privilege of plunder. Women of quality beheld them, and trembling, looked carefully to their little ones who traveled with them in the rear-guard of this vainglorious column.[39]

[38] G.O., Hqrs., May 24, 1777, in Wilkinson, *Memoirs*, I, 170.
[39] Nickerson, *op. cit., passim;* Channing, *A History of the United States,* III, 255–261; Winsor, *Narrative and Critical History of America,* VI, 293–296.

Never before had such a heterogeneous and well equipped expedition descended from Canada. The Americans sensed the might of empire and grew fearful as the days drew near for the issue of battle. By the 1st of July the British had reached the south end of Lake Champlain. They had brushed aside all resistance—only Ticonderoga, frowning before them, barred their farther advance.[40]

Fortunately for the invaders, confusion and divided counsels weakened the twenty-five hundred effective defenders. Tactics and politics were at odds. Wilkinson's idea, as he says, was to have fifteen hundred men hold Ticonderoga with plenty of supplies and a few light guns, ready to oppose a feint or scamper quickly away in case of serious attack. Schuyler could not agree to any such plan; instead he called a council of war made up of St. Clair, De Fermoy, Poor, and Patterson. Its decision was to maintain Ticonderoga and Mount Independence "as long as possible, consistent with the safety of troops and stores." [41] The task fell upon the shoulders of the forty-three-year-old St. Clair, whose patriotism and character were of a much higher order than his military ability. For no good reason Mount Defiance, on the side of Lake George and commanding both of the above places, remained unfortified.[42] Muddy thinking and ambiguous orders continued to handicap the defenders.

In great anxiety Wilkinson wrote to Gates: "O! that you were here! the fertility of your soul might save this important pass." [43] Probably he would have handled the situation better than the general in immediate command, Arthur St. Clair. The letter was soothing ointment for Gates's recently wounded pride. He was still in shadows; his machinations had not yet succeeded. He knew that the army need suffer only a few apparent disasters and Schuyler would be replaced by another who promised success. Events were already shaping themselves for just this outcome.

On July 2 the vanguard of the British took possession of Mount Hope. Three days after, they occupied Mount Defiance, and from this point their guns commanded the most important positions of the American defenses. At three o'clock on the afternoon of the same day a late but wise decision was made; a council of war decided to

---

[40] Nickerson, *op. cit.*, 140.
[41] Wilkinson, *Memoirs*, I, 175.
[42] Memoirs of John Armstrong, Sparks MSS; extract from the Autobiography of John Trumbull, in *Bulletin of Fort Ticonderoga Museum*, January, 1933, pp. 7–8.
[43] To Gates, June 25, 1777, in *Memoirs*, I, 177–178.

evacuate Ticonderoga and Mount Independence that very night. The army would have suffered less had the same conclusion been reached earlier; on the other hand, St. Clair states he would then have got a hanging instead of a court-martial.[44]

The evacuation on short notice was a task for able and experienced men, and there were few of them on hand. Already the British, less than a mile away, were holding points from which they could readily observe what the Americans were doing. Once they noticed any unusual activity, they might begin an offensive. Therefore special pickets were placed and nothing else was done until evening. The Americans hoped that the darkness of that short summer night might hide their hurried preparations for immediate departure. A strong wind blew from the northeast, and ruffled the waters of Champlain, and only a few bateaux would be brought close enough to the Ticonderoga landing for loading artillery and ammunition. Fifteen tons of powder were stored away, and the worst cases of the sick were carried on board— the former soon to be blown up, and the latter captured when the British overtook the slow-moving flotilla at Skenesboro under the ineffective Colonel Long.

Over at Mount Independence on the opposite side of Champlain, De Fermoy, brigadier-general, ex-roommate of St. Clair, and more especially habitual drunkard, sat blear-eyed amidst his dunnage and looked drowsily upon the confusion that his incompetence had created. To this critical point Wilkinson, who had been scurrying around delivering orders and placing pickets, was sent to help accelerate the preparations for departure. The efficient young quartermaster, Lieutenant-Colonel Udrey Hay, was dispatched on the same errand. Major Isaac B. Dunn, an aide, moved backward and forward along the bridge to tell St. Clair how matters were going. Groups of disorderly men cluttered his way. Some were carrying baggage and supplies across for loading; others bore articles of personal plunder, which in a few weary hours of marching they were destined to drop along the stony trail or fling resentfully into the forest.

About two o'clock most of the work had been done at Ticonderoga, and St. Clair went over and joined the troops at Mount Independence. Here the men had grown weary of work and belligerently refused to do more, even so little as loading some of the General's papers. As

---

[44] Nickerson, *op. cit.*, 140–143. "The Trial of Major-General St. Clair," in *Collections of the N.Y. Historical Society for the Year 1880*, III, 157.

a final token of incapacity De Fermoy set his quarters on fire, thereby warning the British of the movement on foot. After all had evacuated Fort Ticonderoga, a detachment was ordered to blow up the bridge. The enemy found it intact but a keg of Madeira empty.

Near daybreak the bateaux began sliding slowly through the water. A long, demoralized column took up its march to Hubbardton, twenty-two miles distant. Those in the advance-guard seemed to hasten their steps when they entered the dark forest that shut their route closely in. They could not escape by either flank, and in the rear came the British against whom they dared not turn. Here and there officers urged on the laggards: some were sick with measles and plodded heavily along; others wabbled drunkenly by, fearful neither of punishment nor of an oncoming enemy. Nine hundred lately arrived militia cared for nothing except their own willful and ignorant ways, entering and leaving their places in column when and wherever they chose. Whatever the result, they halted if they wanted to appease their hunger or thirst; but, when stricken with terror, they surpassed all others in speed.[45] Rear-guard detachments reached Hubbardton on the evening of July 6. Here they halted, unwilling to march two hours more and thus join the main body at Castleton as ordered. Next morning they paid for their disobedience and folly by being overtaken and routed.[46]

The American detachments retreating by water were luckier, although their movement was so slow that Burgoyne, commanding in person, overtook them at Skenesboro. Here his dispositions were faulty, and the country exceedingly rough. In consequence, they escaped to Fort Anne, eleven miles distant, only losing their stores and a few men. Several days later they reached Fort Edward.[47]

At this place St. Clair and Wilkinson, last heard of at Castleton, arrived on July 12. Learning of the American disasters at Hubbardton and Skenesboro, St. Clair had pushed eastward by a circuitous route, and, after seven days of painfully hard marching through a mountain wilderness flooded with rain, he had finally reached Fort Edward. His reinforcements and six hundred militia from Peekskill now raised Schuyler's forces to forty-four hundred men. Besides, Washington

---

[45] The data for this retreat are taken largely from "The Trial of Major-General St. Clair" in *Collections of the N.Y. Historical Society for the Year 1880,* III, 1–171, and Nickerson, *op. cit.,* 142–147.

[46] Nickerson, *op. cit.,* 146–153.

[47] *Ibid.,* 154–157.

had sent him Lincoln and Arnold in order to make easier the handling of New England contingents. Keeping his army at Fort Edward, Schuyler awaited the coming of Burgoyne, who moved slowly forward over indifferent roads, now well obstructed by the work of a thousand or more American axmen.[48]

With the capture of Ticonderoga, Burgoyne had become elated, the Americans proportionately dismayed. Many of the weak and most of the prejudiced had turned upon St. Clair and Schuyler as the direct cause of such apparent disaster. Gates stirred the pot of small politics, for thereby he hoped to command once more the Northern Department. St. Clair, soldier that he was, took all the blame himself in an effort to exculpate Schuyler. Still the stories grew—British firing silver balls into the camp of the traitors for those two generals who had abandoned their country's stronghold for filthy lucre.[49] Tales like these were told and other fanciful lies, but many believed.

Wilkinson had been through the worst of the retreat with St. Clair and appreciated his worth. Hence he became the General's indignant defender against the ignorant and malicious. Writing to the editor of a Boston paper, he asked him not to prejudge St. Clair or "disgrace your paper with the malicious innuendoes of every envious talkative puppy . . . Believe me, Sir, if virtue or justice has existence, the man who stands condemned for retreating from Ticonderoga, will ere long be thanked for the salvation of three thousand men, who instead of being in captivity are now opposing our enemy." [50]

Wilkinson spoke the truth, and had the manhood to proclaim it among those who were not inclined to listen.

As Schuyler continued to retreat, he increased the ultimate chance of victory at the expense of his own immediate reputation. By the time Burgoyne had reached Fort Edward, Schuyler was four miles to the south, occupying a position that had been selected by Colonel Tadeusz Kosciuszko, Wilkinson's tentmate and chief of engineers. Not daring to remain here, he pushed on toward Albany, passing through Saratoga and Stillwater and finally reaching Van Schaick's Island, near the juncture of the Mohawk with the Hudson, on the 18th of August. On the next day Gates arrived and superseded him in command.[51]

[48] *Ibid.*, 175.
[49] *Ibid.*, 161; Wilkinson, *Memoirs*, I, 198.
[50] *Memoirs*, I, 199.
[51] *Ibid.*, I, 207.

The opposition of New England to Schuyler, Indian outrages, the fall of Ticonderoga, and Gates's machinations, all had operated to cause this third change within a year of commanding generals of the Northern Department. Congress had made additional effort to mortify Schuyler by directing that he and St. Clair be held for trial because of the evacuation of Ticonderoga. Gates, showing no inclination to ameliorate this trying situation for Schuyler, displayed toward him the frowzy manners of an ill born boor.[52]

Wilkinson, although a partisan of Gates, felt that Schuyler had been greatly wronged, and that, too, when victory was close at hand.[53] A detachment of approximately a thousand men whom Burgoyne had sent out to collect supplies, had been routed at Bennington, Vermont, on August 16; Lieutenant-Colonel Barry St. Leger, bringing reinforcements from the west, had advanced to Oriskany, New York, only to suffer defeat on the 6th and retreat thereafter to Canada. Burgoyne's own advance was increasingly slow. His engineers had to build bridge after bridge across marsh land for troops and artillery to pass over. One was two miles long.[54] On firmer ground they found no relief from toil, for they had to clear the roadway of huge trees that Americans had felled across it. When they would rest from such labor, they could not, because of swarms of pestilent mosquitoes.[55] With hardships mounting, and diminished prospect of booty, many deserted, particularly Indian and Canadian allies.

Gates's army, on the contrary, was growing in spirit and numbers. The militia were eager to "join up" when victory and plunder seemed to be in easy reach. Colonel Daniel Morgan's corps had come from Washington's forces, and through its scouting a better knowledge of enemy movements was more quickly obtained. The tide had begun to turn. Gates, moving north over the route along which Schuyler had lately retreated, halted at Bemis Heights.

Wilkinson claims credit for suggesting to Gates the occupation of this position.[56] As chief of staff it behooved him to do so if he thought the place well designed for defeating the enemy. Four times, at least, during the last two years he had gone to and from Ticonderoga, and perhaps then and on other occasions he had ridden along the main-

[52] Nickerson, *op. cit.*, 280–282.
[53] Wilkinson, *Memoirs*, I, 222–223.
[54] Andrews, *History of the War with America, etc.*, II, 390.
[55] Stedman, *The History of the . . . American War*, I, 305.
[56] *Memoirs*, I, 232.

traveled route and looked upward from Bemis Tavern to the swelling hills that rose quickly from the ill cleared fields along the Hudson. His experience around Boston, the Canadian campaign, the battles of Trenton and Princeton, and his recent retreat with St. Clair, all would have trained his "eye for ground." If he himself did not sense the tactical advantages of the position, there were plenty of people in the neighborhood, like John Neilson, who were ready to suggest its occupation to him in the hope they would be protected by their countrymen, not ravished and plundered by the enemy. If he did not come by the idea from his own observation or in talking with settlers near by, he may have got it from his own blanket companion and Gates's chief engineer, Kosciuszko. More likely Wilkinson was only one of several who recommended Bemis Heights to Gates; and the General, after ruminating upon the matter for a while, dispatched Arnold, his ablest subordinate in troop leading, and Kosciuszko, who was to plan the defense works, to examine the position.[57] Influenced by the report of these two, he chose Bemis Heights, and after it had proved so desirable in the test of battle he did not bestir himself to share with others the glory of its selection. That was Gates's way—and Wilkinson's also.

With Bemis Heights actually occupied on September 12, troops immediately began to make intrenchments and breastworks. Gates sensed that Burgoyne was continuing southward, though ignorant of what progress he had made and what were his immediate intentions. Making use of Wilkinson's offer, the General sent him on reconnaissance with twenty picked riflemen and one hundred and fifty infantrymen. The detachment left on the evening of the 12th, and by the next morning had reached the high ground near the west bank of the Hudson and approximately three miles from Saratoga. Not satisfied with what he had learned so far, Wilkinson took four men and advanced a mile or two more. From a position near Fish Creek, he could see companies of the British prepared to march and others making ready to join them from across the Hudson. He concluded that Burgoyne's army was on its way to Stillwater, and so informed Gates when he returned. His deductions proved correct. Within a few days the enemy were only two miles from the American position.[58]

Soon real fighting began. Yellowing leaves and chill evening winds

[57] Winsor, *Narrative and Critical History of America,* VI, 304.
[58] Wilkinson, *Memoirs,* I, 233–235; Nickerson, *op. cit.,* 291.

had warned Burgoyne that he must hasten south to better winter quarters. Troops had been deserting; supplies had been running low, and no encouraging news had come from Clinton. If he were to save himself from the reputation of Carleton and Howe, he must perform a brilliant stroke. On the morning of September 19 he personally led his troops to battle, hoping first to turn the American left and then perhaps to advance with his whole army and secure the road to Albany.[59] When Gates learned of the movement he ordered Colonel Morgan to take his corps and counterattack Burgoyne. Gates seemed to sense the enemy's general plan, but, for a time at least, he did not realize where the attack was being most vigorously pressed.[60] He held most of his men closely in camp and waited developments; the numbers of reinforcements actually sent were insufficient, and their efforts poorly coördinated.

By half-past twelve, troops were heavily engaged in small-arms firing. Riding toward the sound of it, Wilkinson reached Freeman's Farm and fell in with Major Henry Dearborn, a subordinate of Morgan, trying to reorganize his men after a stiff fight with the enemy. The troops of Lieutenant-Colonel Butler had been routed also and were fleeing in every direction. Morgan, confessing that his own were "scattered God knows where," was trying to assemble them with his "turkey call." Wilkinson brought news of a few and probably told him that reinforcements would come to his aid.[61]

They did come, seven regiments strong, though not when and where they were most needed. From about three o'clock until dark, hard fighting continued, success favoring first one side, then the other, along the open spaces of Freeman's narrow farm. Here and in the near-by woods and rain-washed gullies they clashed in grisly combat. The Americans advanced slowly, picking off man after man with their unexcelled marksmanship, only to give way when the British met them in clashing charges with the cold steel of sword and bayonet. The colonial frontiersmen from New York, Pennsylvania, and elsewhere knew how to handle their individual weapons and how to make the best use of the terrain and trees, but they were unable to combine their efforts toward the winning of a common objective. Though on the field as a representative of the commanding general, Wilkinson

[59] Nickerson, *op. cit.*, 303–304.
[60] Wilkinson, *Memoirs*, I, 240; Dearborn to Wilkinson, Dec. 20, 1816, in *Bulletin of Fort Ticonderoga Museum*, June, 1929, p. 10.
[61] *Memoirs*, I, 236–238.

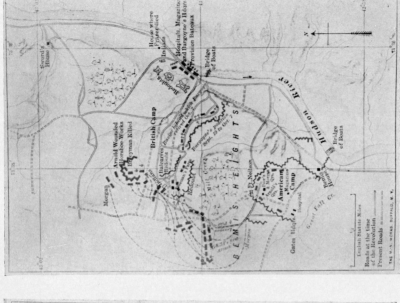

Map of the Battle of Bemis Heights.

Courtesy of The Burrows Bros. Co. From E. M. Avery, "A History of the United States and Its People," VI, 122.

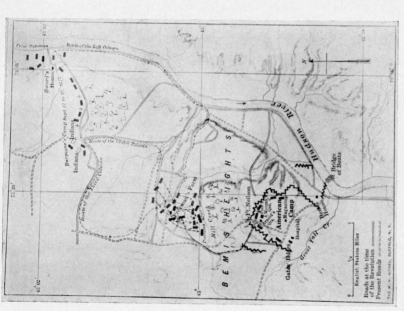

Map of the Battle of Freeman's Farm.

Courtesy of The Burrows Bros. Co. From E. M. Avery, "A History of the United States and Its People," VI, 113.

could not direct them; he was too young and inexperienced to cope with such a situation. No officer of sufficient rank was near enough to coördinate the fighting of the colonels and detachment commanders until toward evening General Learned was ordered out with five more regiments. By then it was too late; the battle had already ended in a stalemate. Approximately six hundred British had been "killed, wounded, or taken," while the Americans had suffered only three hundred and twenty casualties.[62] Both sides had furnished examples of great valor. Even the British were now ready to admit that there were Americans who knew how to die as bravely as the rank and file of England's most distinguished regiments.

If Arnold had taken personal control early on the 19th, the battle of Freeman's Farm might have been a decisive victory for the Americans. Doubtless he wanted to do so, but was restrained in camp by Gates, who wished to keep several of his ablest subordinates with him until he knew against what part of his line the main attack was being made.[63] Apparently several hours passed before Gates was aware that his left was being enveloped. About this time Colonel Morgan Lewis came riding up and told him that the battle was in a deadlock. Then Arnold, with a "By God, I will soon put an end to it," was off— but not far. Wilkinson, at Gates's order, rode after him, directing his return.[64] The hour was too late except for a night operation, a hazardous undertaking for even the bravest and best. Possibly to prevent any attempt of this sort, Gates wanted Arnold held in check; he therefore ordered the rather inconsequential Learned to march out with troops for the sole purpose of holding the ground that their companions had taken. Always ravenous for glory, Gates, in spite of his dislike for Arnold, would have allowed him to go if the occasion had demanded. Gates felt that he could ill afford to risk disaster; his conservative thinking ruled the day.

On the other hand, Arnold's reputation does not suffer even if Wilkinson's story be true that he did not take part in the actual fighting on that autumn day.[65] At the time Arnold was a major-general, and his particular duty was to dispose of his forces in accordance with orders so that they would promote the chances of victory, not to lead

[62] Nickerson, *op. cit.*, 319.
[63] Dearborn to Wilkinson, Dec. 20, 1815, in *Bulletin of Fort Ticonderoga Museum*, Jan., 1929, p. 10.
[64] *Memoirs*, I, 245–246.
[65] *Ibid.*, I, 245.

them personally in the restricted area of Freeman's Farm where he
might distinguish himself for bravery only to lose the direction and
control of the units of his command. Nevertheless, he was doubtless
irritated that his former aide should have been the person to prevent
him from giving a new exhibition of leadership and valor.

Between September 19 and October 7 the rift between the two
increased. In the course of his staff duties Wilkinson declared that
Morgan's riflemen and light infantry, known as the élite corps, should
be directly under the orders of headquarters and not under those of
Arnold. Gates sustained him and made the suggested change in spite
of previous arrangements to the contrary. Arnold, in high dudgeon,
went to headquarters and had hard words with Gates, who merely
ridiculed him and his contention. Angrier than ever, he persisted in
his claim; he also accused Wilkinson of annexing the New York militia
to Glover's Brigade after he had directed them to join Poor's in compliance with Gates's order; furthermore, he said that his division had
not received due credit for its fighting on the 19th, and that when he
was about headquarters he was coldly received. Wearying of his subordinate's belligerence, Gates relieved him from command. Arnold
then asked leave to go to Philadelphia, and, although it was granted,
he fulminated more and did not go.[66]

At times Arnold was disloyal, undisciplined, dishonest, and untruthful. No matter how able a leader he was in battle, these glaring
faults totally unfitted him for continuing long as a desirable subordinate. On the other hand, Gates was narrow and jealous, just the
type to goad him into a display of some of these most objectionable
qualities. When once he had fallen into such an error, Gates relieved
him from command, as he had a perfect right to do.[67] He may have
also felt that Arnold's services were not essential for victory. The
reconnaissance of Wilkinson, Hardin, and others had revealed how
the British army was disintegrating and its supplies were dwindling.[68]
For the Americans, on the contrary, reinforcements were arriving
daily, and both their rations and their ammunition had sensibly increased. Gates now knew that he had only to wait until Burgoyne
retreated or attacked in desperation.[69]

---

[66] For the letters passing between Arnold and Gates at this time, see *Ibid.,* I,
254–261.
[67] Hancock to Gates, Aug. 14, 1777, in *Ibid.,* I, 225–226.
[68] Nickerson, *op. cit.,* 354–357; Wilkinson, *Memoirs,* I, 264–265.
[69] Gates to Washington, Oct. 5, 1777, in Wilkinson, *Memoirs,* I, 266.

His estimate of the situation proved correct. On the morning of October 7, drums began to beat the alarm. Wilkinson went to investigate and found a large detachment of the British in a near-by wheatfield.[70] When Gates was informed of the fact he ordered out Morgan, who in turn decided to strike this hostile force on the right; Poor and his brigade planned to envelop it on the left, Learned and his brigade to attack the center. These three commanders soon encountered about fifteen hundred troops whom Burgoyne had sent out on a vague, indefinite mission.[71]

The British were entirely too few for any decisive action, and in less than one hour after the battle had joined they were in full retreat. Some of Burgoyne's best men had fallen. Nearly half a company of grenadiers lay dead or wounded in a single area no larger than a garden patch. Elsewhere, too, casualties had been severe. A few of the wounded were given treatment by American surgeons, at least one of whom gloated that his hands were red from such a task; others were the spoil of ruffians who were out to loot both the living and the dead. From one of these raffish stragglers Wilkinson rescued Major Ackland, commander of the grenadiers.[72]

Much needed matériel also fell into the hands of exulting Americans. When New Hampshire men had captured a twelve-pounder, Colonel Cilley stopped long enough to straddle it and from this warming seat to deliver himself of a laconic speech of dedication.[73]

Do what they might, British officers could not stem the rush of fugitives until they reached their intrenched camp. In it the Germans were on the right, next Tories and spineless Canadians, farther on troops under Lord Balcarres. Partly protected by intrenchments, the defense stiffened; the second stage of battle began. Arnold, without command, had taken one, and now pushed the assault against Balcarres with fiery zeal. Meeting with no success, he then rode on a shining bay through a line of fire to the opposite flank of the enemy. Here Germans were holding out sturdily behind an improvised rampart of rails until he charged them. They could not withstand such a dynamic spirit of battle; they broke and fled, but with a retreating volley they felled both horse and rider. Thus John Armstrong (then an aide of Gates and thirty-five years later Secretary of War) was able

[70] Wilkinson, *Memoirs*, I, 267–268.
[71] Nickerson, *op. cit.*, 357–360.
[72] *Memoirs*, I, 270–271.
[73] Nickerson, *op. cit.*, 361; Wilkinson, *Memoirs*, I, 270.

to overtake him and deliver Gates's order to withdraw. By this time Arnold had done decisive work: the hostile defenses were crumbling there and elsewhere, Burgoyne's whole position was threatened. Only the coming of darkness saved the British from greater defeat.[74] Even so, they had suffered approximately seven hundred and fifty casualties.[75]

During the night of the 7th the British withdrew north of the Great Ravine. Next day Burgoyne, the play boy of the King's court, decided to retreat still farther after Major-General Fraser, one of his ablest subordinates, had been buried on a neighboring hilltop and the supply boats had made a little distance against the current of the Hudson. By daylight of the 9th troops had marched only four miles— hungry, exhausted, and cold, their tattered uniforms wet through with chilling rain. A continual downpour made their footsteps heavier and filled the creeks to overflowing. The men trudged miserably on, abandoning wagon after wagon sunk deep in mud. Deserters slunk away from the column, and snipers, hiding behind rocks and trees, fired at those who remained in ranks and marched slowly past. It was too hardy a war for Burgoyne, that dramaturgic technician. Toward evening, he took shelter in the Schuyler mansion, where he found physical comfort for his drooping spirits. Near by his rain-soaked troops made camp in the mud, failing to push on and increase their chances of escape. Not even did he allow Lieutenant-Colonel Sutherland to attack the Berkshire men under General John Fellows, who were then blocking the only remaining avenue of retreat; he satisfied himself with merely strengthening his position north of Fish Creek.[76]

While Burgoyne was retreating slowly Gates did little to improve his advantage. Time was taken to draw and cook rations and obtain more ammunition before taking up the pursuit. Fellows was merely warned of his isolated position across the Hudson and left to use his own measures in preserving his safety. On the night of the 10th Gates planned to attack next morning. Wilkinson was hesitant because he thought that the British were in a strong position and could shatter any offensive. Gates bade him rise early and verify his theory by reconnaissance. Apparently he did so.[77]

At dawn of the 11th the Americans began to advance under cover

[74] Nickerson, *op. cit.*, 365–367.
[75] Brandow, *The Story of Old Saratoga*, 17.
[76] Nickerson, *op. cit.*, 370–378.
[77] Wilkinson, *Memoirs*, I, 282–286; Nickerson, *op. cit.*, 372–373.

of a heavy fog. Morgan, on the left as usual, crossed the upper reaches of Fish Creek and headed directly for a hill overlooking it and the Hudson. Although he did not know that a British strong point had been established near the crest, he sensed danger ahead, and, when met by Wilkinson, readily agreed to incline more to the west. Soon afterwards Wilkinson moved eastward and, finding Learned, guided him and his two brigades across the creek and unwittingly headed them against the British intrenchments, then completely hidden by the fog. Other American units farther down the creek and nearer the Hudson grew suspicious and halted. Seeing what a plight they themselves were in when the fog lifted, they ran quickly to the rear, suffering little from hostile fire. Unfortunately, Learned kept moving up the slope just where Burgoyne wanted him to go. Wilkinson, perceiving what a sacrifice was in prospect, hastened back and ordered him to retreat. After considerable demurring, Learned complied. Wilkinson's initiative and persistence had prevented disaster.[78]

Gates now wisely made no further effort to advance. The Americans could wait; the British could not. Realizing that the net around him was tightening, Burgoyne called a council of war on the 12th, and it decided to hasten the retreat, abandoning baggage and artillery. Nothing was done, however. Next day another council of war was held, and this time all were for surrender on honorable conditions. Lieutenant-Colonel Kingston was sent to arrange the details with Gates, who, in anticipation of the turn of events, had already carefully written out his own terms. As a whole, Burgoyne found them acceptable; he wanted only one important and several insignificant changes made. Gates agreed to them all, even to the one stipulating that those surrendering would be returned to England if they promised not to serve again in North America during the war; he merely requested that all negotiations be ended by two P.M. of the 15th. Believing that Gates's desire for haste sprang from a fear of British coming up the Hudson, Burgoyne asked for more time. Gates acquiesced.[79]

The arrangement of the terms of surrender was left in the hands of Captain James H. Craig and Lieutenant-Colonel Nicholas Sutherland, who negotiated with Wilkinson and General William Whipple. By eight in the evening the four had composed their differences and

[78] *Memoirs*, I, 286–289; Nickerson, *op. cit.*, 382–383.
[79] Nickerson, *op. cit.*, 384–389; Wilkinson, *Memoirs*, I, 298–309.

articles were signed. About three hours later Wilkinson received a
note saying that Burgoyne agreed to everything except the word
"capitulation" for which he wished "convention" substituted. For
the third time Gates found no objection, and, after sending word to
that effect, lay down to sleep.[80]

On the next morning, the 16th, Burgoyne wanted more delay; he
had just heard the erroneous report that Sir Henry Clinton had
advanced to Albany. He thereupon demanded that two of his officers
count the American forces so that he would be sure of their superiority.
Of course, Gates did not countenance such an impudent and lunatic
request, and Wilkinson was sent to inform Burgoyne accordingly and
to demand an "immediate and decisive reply." [81] Burgoyne refused,
the truce was to end in an hour, and Wilkinson started back—a failure
on a definite mission. He had gone only a few hundred yards when
Kingston came running after him, and pleaded that it be extended
another hour. Burgoyne, meanwhile having consulted his officers,
remained obdurate and sent Sutherland to inform Wilkinson of the
final decision. Wilkinson, then reading part of Craig's letter in which
Burgoyne had stated all was satisfactory except the word "capitulation," declared that he expected to keep it as a reminder of British
good faith. Sutherland asked for the loan of the letter as an aid to
win over his general; and, when given it, ran quickly back to his camp.
Gates sent word to break off negotiations, but Wilkinson held on,
replying that he was doing the best that he could and would see him
in half an hour. Soon after Sutherland reappeared with Burgoyne's
signature to the papers. Greatly relieved, Wilkinson returned with
them to Gates.[82]

Seldom has a youth of twenty been so important in arranging details for so significant a surrender. Certainly none in American history pretends to an equal claim. Matthew Lyon believed that Wilkinson was then the "likeliest young man I ever saw." [83] He was the same
one who, in later years, charged John Adams, the President, with "un-
bounded thirst for ridiculous pomp and for foolish adulation," and
had to suffer four months' imprisonment and a thousand-dollar fine
as a consequence. Gates seemed to hold an equally flattering opinion

[80] Wilkinson, *Memoirs*, I, 309–311.
[81] Nickerson, *op. cit.*, 395–396.
[82] *Memoirs*, II, 312–317.
[83] Lyon to Jefferson, Aug. 12, 1801, Jefferson Papers (Library of Congress), Vol.
115.

of his aide. Perhaps he saw in him a repetition of his own early struggles in the British service. He could recall how others had smoothed the way for him in his upward climb, and he overlooked few opportunities to do the same for his favorite subordinate.

When the surrender of the British army actually occurred at Saratoga, Wilkinson was given an important part. Early in the morning of the 17th, he started to the camp of Burgoyne, who, accompanied by staff and general officers, soon returned with him to the headquarters of Gates. At the head of the American camp the two met— Burgoyne in rich uniform of scarlet and gold, Gates, wigless, wearing his spectacles, and in a plain blue frock. When about sword's distance from each other, both halted, and Wilkinson introduced them. Then Burgoyne, always the actor, took his cue, raised his hat, and declared:

"The fortune of war, General Gates, has made me your prisoner."

Gates, not to be outdone, replied:

"I shall always be ready to bear testimony that it has not been through any fault of your excellency." [84]

After the others had been introduced, Wilkinson went to supervise other details incident to the surrender of the defeated army.[85]

Probably as a result of his hard and trying work, Wilkinson fell ill with "convulsive colic" from which he suffered extremely. Not until the 20th of October was he able to leave Albany for York, Pennsylvania, where Congress was then sitting. He had been chosen as Gates's messenger for making an official report of the surrender at Saratoga. Washington was to be meanly ignored. With other papers he bore a very flattering letter in which Congress was asked to reward him with the brevet of brigadier-general.[86] In spite of this recommendation from Gates for promotion and the eagerness of Congress for news, Wilkinson did not hasten his journey.

The approximate distance from Albany to York via Kingston, Easton, and Reading is 285 miles, and Wilkinson took eleven days to travel it. He was not well, the weather was bad, and he found plenty of friends along the way. At Hurley he spent a little while with George Clinton and Gouverneur Morris. At Easton the attraction was greater and his stay longer. Here as director general of hos-

[84] Nickerson, *op. cit.*, 399–400; Wilkinson, *Memoirs*, I, 321–322.
[85] Wilkinson, *Memoirs*, I, 322.
[86] *Ibid.*, I, 323–324.

pitals was Dr. William Shippen, whom Wilkinson when a medical student had known in Philadelphia. From him and others, he heard much of Thomas Conway, a French soldier of Irish antecedents who had been made a brigadier-general in the American forces and was allied with others in secret efforts to undermine the prestige of Washington. And best of all, that charming Ann Biddle, his fiancée, was visiting in the town. She was always a ready listener to the brave stories of her returning knight. Two days was only too short a time to spend with friends and betrothed, even if Congress was waiting for what he might tell.[87]

On the 27th he left for Reading, fifty miles distant, arriving there in the evening, and falling in the hands of old soldiers and veteran politicians. General Mifflin was there in a smug fit of blues. At tea, he and two Congressmen, as invited guests, quizzed Wilkinson about Gates's victory, while they croaked on Washington's misfortunes, damning him by contrast and with the help of Conway's thirteen reasons for the American defeat at Brandywine on September 11.[88]

Next day it rained in torrents, and Wilkinson lay over; his health was not good and hospitality was alluring. Lord Stirling, an American major-general, invited him to dinner. His two aides, one McWilliams and James Monroe, were also guests. The General delighted in telling his own experiences; he liked to have brilliant youngsters with him for a pot-luck dinner while he was mending from a spill from his horse. Even if he preferred his own trumpet solos, he gave others a chance once in a while, listening attentively to their part in the symphony of news and comment. The hours slipped quickly by for those congenial comrades in arms—an open fire, a big-bellied flagon under a friendly roof pelted with cold autumn rain. It was easy for mutual confidences under the influence of Monongahela brew, and when Wilkinson's turn came, he was off his guard, and told McWilliams things that were only for the ears of Gates and himself. His host learned of them, and before long Washington knew that Conway and Gates were plotting to supplant him.[89]

Not until about midnight did the party break up. Next day and part of the following Wilkinson remained in Reading. The Schuylkill,

[87] *Ibid.*, I, 330–331, 338.
[88] *Ibid.*, I, 331.
[89] *Ibid.*, I, 331–332; Hatch, *The Administration of the American Revolutionary Army*, 29.

as he said, had overflowed its banks, and swept away all ferryboats.[90] This was not much of an excuse for the delay of an officer who bore messages for Congress, and had at one time crossed the Delaware in a blizzard and the St. Lawrence under hostile fire. Maybe he was enjoying more of his friends, such as the able lawyer Edward Biddle, a relative of his fiancée, or Alexander Graydon, a youthful friend for whom he had a great regard.

When he finally reached York, about fifty miles distant, on Friday the 31st, he found that John Hancock had resigned and Charles Thompson was acting as President of Congress. After he had delivered the public dispatches and answered various questions by members of Congress, he noticed a tendency of many to criticize Gates. With the idea of putting his own papers in better order and drawing up a brief for the General's defense, he asked to withdraw and reappear before the body later. After consulting with Samuel Adams and others he wrote out a message to Congress in Gates's name. On November 3 he again came before its members and defended the lenient terms of surrender. The task was now much easier, for Henry Laurens was friendly and had been elected President.[91]

Next day Wilkinson wrote Gates a letter in which the General was advised against allowing copies to be made of official papers. By granting the privilege, the details of Saratoga had already reached Congress, and some of its members had been outspoken in criticizing the liberal terms given Burgoyne. Of course he had shown that they were warranted by the conditions. He also added that the public noticed that Washington had received no official notice of the surrender, and that he himself was still without mark of Congress' approbation. Even so, he was not mortified; in his own words, " . . . my hearty contempt of the follies of the world will shield me from such pitiful sensations." [92]

Nevertheless, this "promising military genius" was distinctly disappointed when others were receiving official recognition. On November 3, Gates besides being voted the thanks of Congress, like Arnold and Lincoln, had been given a gold medal in appreciation of his services. Next day it awarded "elegant swords" to three more officers.[93] In spite of Gates's request some were loath to honor Wilkinson, who

[90] *Memoirs*, I, 332.
[91] *Ibid.*, I, 332–333.
[92] To Gates, Nov. 4, 1777, in *Ibid.*, I., 336–338.
[93] Ford and Hunt, *Journals of the Continental Congress*, IX, 861–862.

was already high-ranking for his years and had taken about twice the necessary time to bring them dispatches of the highest importance. Perhaps the gift of a horsewhip and a pair of spurs would be better and more suggestive gifts. Such at least was the idea of one or two.[94] However, in the great joy of victory sober thinking took a holiday; much to the resentment of older and more experienced officers, Wilkinson was given the brevet of brigadier-general on November 6, 1777.[95]

Shortly after delivering the papers concerned with Burgoyne's surrender, Wilkinson left York, going to Reading and spending several days with friends, then traveling to White Marsh, where he expected to find Washington and make another official report of Saratoga. Gates did not dare to ignore completely the commander-in-chief, although he could show studied discourtesy in long delay. Undisturbed, Washington treated his messenger with kindness and attention, asking various questions about Gates's recent operations and present dispositions.[96]

He also showed similar forbearance toward the disreputable General Thomas Conway, who was then in camp and had written a bitter and disloyal letter concerning him to Gates. Fearful of disclosure, Conway now approached Wilkinson and asked if he recalled having read certain expressions in it. Wilkinson replied that he did not remember them. When wine was flowing and spirits high he might tell all to Lord Stirling, but never when sober and thoughtful to this plotting and ill-balanced Conway.[97] He was still unaware of what a Pandora's box had been opened by talking indiscreetly at Reading. For several days he continued with the Grand Army, strutting a little, renewing his friendships, and learning much about the battle of Germantown. And then he set out for Easton, where that "sprightly" Ann Biddle awaited his coming. Of course he lingered several days with her. It was not until the 9th of December that this fledgling brigadier was back at Albany, working once more as adjutant-general of the Northern Department.[98]

[94] McKean to John Adams, Nov. 20, 1815, and Adams to McKean, Nov. 26, 1915, in McKean Papers (Hist. Soc. of Pa. Library), Vol. IV.

[95] Ford and Hunt, *Journals of the Continental Congress*, IX, 870.

[96] Wilkinson, *Memoirs*, I, 339–340.

[97] *Ibid*, I, 341; Declaration of Conway, Jan. 3, 1778, in Hammond, *Letters and Papers of Sullivan*, II, 1–2.

[98] *Memoirs*, I, 369.

CHAPTER III

AN ARDENT DUELIST ACQUIRES
A THANKLESS JOB

DURING the early days of the Revolution many officers who had fought in European wars took passage across the Atlantic and entered the service of the Colonies. They came from France, Ireland, Poland, and Prussia, egged on by a hope of glory and a desire to recoup their dwindling fortunes. A few of them, like Lafayette and Steuben, rendered distinguished service; the great majority did not measure up to the high rank that they usually demanded and Congress supinely granted. Of these professional soldiers Thomas Conway was exceptionally objectionable. He became an American brigadier-general in May, 1777, shortly after his arrival from France, where he had served eighteen years in the French Army. He was a reputed expert in the handling of infantry—a quality that he soon failed to demonstrate at the battles of Brandywine and Germantown during September and October. Even so, and in spite of Washington's resolute opposition, Congress promoted him to the grade of major-general on December 14. Heartened by the support that politicians had apparently given, he tried to get Washington relieved and Gates placed in supreme command. This attempt, known as the "Conway Cabal," proved abortive; it resulted in the confusion of the conspirators and the enhanced reputation of Washington. The affair might have ended differently if Wilkinson had failed to disclose it to Colonel McWilliams when both of them were at Reading in the quarters of Lord Stirling, during October, 1777. In this way the earl learned that Conway had written to Gates: "Heaven has determined to save your country, or a weak General [Washington] and bad counsellors would have ruined it."[1] Ere long Washington was acquainted with these very words by a letter from Stirling.

[1] Gates to Wilkinson, Feb. 23, 1778, in Wilkinson, *Memoirs*, I, 386–387.

Apparently Gates was not aware until the 3rd of December that some of his private correspondence was becoming common knowledge. At this time he received a note at Albany from Thomas Mifflin informing him: "An extract from General Conway's letter to you has been procured, and sent to headquarters. . . . General Washington enclosed it to General Conway without remark . . . take care of your generosity and frank disposition; they cannot injure yourself, but may injure some of your best friends." [2]

Possessed of this disturbing information, Gates immediately sat down and wrote a letter to Conway, both as a reply to one received and as a direct attempt to find out more about what Mifflin had written. After expressing the hope that Conway's resignation, if offered, would not be accepted and warning him that "military discipline" among a free people is not easily obtained, Gates closed the letter with a significant "P.S." stating that "extracts from your letters" have been conveyed to Washington, occasioning "an eclaircissement in which you acted with all the dignity of a virtuous soldier. I entreat you, dear General, to let me know which of the letters was copied off. It is of the greatest importance, that I should detect the person who has been guilty of that act of infidelity." [3]

With the identity of the culprit unknown, investigation continued. On the very day that Wilkinson arrived in Albany, December 8, 1777, Gates talked with him about the person suspected as author of the "eclaircissement"; namely, Colonel Alexander Hamilton, who had visited him early in November to get reinforcements for Washington's army. While the staff was out, as Gates said, Colonel Hamilton was "left alone an hour in this room, during which time, he took Conway's letter out of that closet, and copied it, and the copy has been furnished to Washington." Wilkinson tried to dissuade his general from this belief, suggesting instead that Colonel Troup, one of the aides-de-camp, might inadvertently have given Hamilton the substance of the letter. Gates persisted, declaring that both the thief and the receiver would be disgraced.

Thus Wilkinson tells this part of the story, calling on the "Searcher of all Hearts" to witness its truth. He adds that he felt no personal solicitude about the matter, because Gates had "read the letter publicly in his presence" and he himself "had never spoken of it with evil

[2] Mifflin to Gates, Nov. 28, 1777, in *Ibid.*, 374.
[3] Gates to Conway, Dec. 3, 1777, in *Ibid.*, 374–376.

intentions, or at all, except when mentioned to him." [4] Feeling so about the letter, Wilkinson strangely refrained from telling his share in its disclosure. The fault appears greater in view of the fact that he described Gates later as one who easily pardoned. More unbecoming was his effort to throw upon another the responsibility for revealing a staff secret that he himself, when talkative from liquor, had told at Reading. He was soon to learn that the truth would ultimately leak out, and when it did his suggestion of Troup's guilt would prove another reason for increasing the anger of Gates.

For a few weeks no new development occurred in the thickening plot; Wilkinson was beyond the range of news and intrigue. In compliance with orders he went on an inspection tour, visiting Fort Schuyler and other places, traveling as far as Oneida Castle. By the first of February he had completed his work and was back in Albany.[5] Gates was not there. He had received notification of appointment as President of the Board of War and had left for York to begin his new duties. Wilkinson planned to hasten to the very same place; he had just received a letter announcing his election as the Board's secretary. On February 3, he wrote to the President of Congress accepting the position, but intimating that he preferred to serve his country in a different capacity.[6] Apparently Gates and Wilkinson would soon be working together as harmoniously as ever before.

The outcome was to be far otherwise. On the 5th of February, Wilkinson received a most disturbing letter from Lord Stirling. He wanted to know if Conway had written to Gates, "Heaven surely is determined to save the American cause, or a weak General and bad councils had long since lost it, or words to that effect." [7] According to Stirling this was what Wilkinson had once stated to be in the letter; but, according to Conway, Wilkinson had subsequently denied it in the presence of several officers at White Marsh.[8] Stirling now wanted the truth about the alleged denial and a copy of the bedeviling letter. It took a fine piece of effrontery to ask Wilkinson to convict himself by his own evidence and to aggravate his original offense by sending

---

[4] *Ibid.*, I, 372–373.
[5] *Ibid.*, 381–382.
[6] To Pres. of Congress, Feb. 3, 1778, Papers of the Continental Congress (Library of Congress).
[7] Stirling to Wilkinson, Jan. 6, 1778, in *Memoirs*, I, 382–383, and Papers of the Continental Congress.
[8] Statement of Conway, Jan. 3, 1778, in Hammond, *Letters and Papers of Major-General Sullivan*, II, 1–2.

a copy of the private correspondence of his general to one who designed to use it for embarrassing purposes.

In answer Wilkinson declared that he could not recall all that he had said while Stirling's guest; in respect to Conway's questions, he had replied to them dubiously. There was no need of straining one's veracity; Conway himself had declared that the charges he made had been justified. Stirling could not extract much satisfaction out of this part of the letter; he must have derived less out of the remainder:

"I can scarce credit my senses, when I read the paragraph in which you request an extract from a private letter, which had fallen under my observation. I may have been indiscreet, my Lord, but be assured I am not dishonourable." [9]

Soon after making this spirited reply, Wilkinson left Albany for York. Traveling by way of Reading, he reached Lancaster on the 21st of February. Next day, hoping to benefit his cause, he sent Congress copies of the letters that had passed between himself and Stirling.[10] By means of them the earl was revealed as being loyal to Washington but opprobriously stupid in dealing with a brilliant young aide who had let out a secret that he now wanted to hide—one had unwittingly delivered up his general, the other had premeditatedly betrayed his guest.

In the meanwhile Gates had learned that Wilkinson was responsible for the original disclosure of Conway's letter. He did not hesitate to abuse his former aide in the "grossest language." Thirty-eight years afterward Wilkinson describes his immediate reaction:

". . . although my feelings and affections were outraged, my resolution was not appalled, I remembered the injunction of a dying father, I worshipped honor as the jewel of my soul, and did not pause for the course to be pursued; but I owed it to disparity of years and rank, to former connexion, and the affection of my breast, to drain the cup of conciliation, and seek an explanation, which I believed the exposition of my correspondence with Lord Stirling would produce, as it ought to have done; because it acquitted me of sinister intention, and stamped the report of his Lordship to Washington, with palpable falsehood." [11]

Wilkinson belonged to Don Quixote's school of thought. There

[9] To Stirling, Feb. 4, 1778, in *Memoirs*, I, 383–384, and Papers of the Continental Congress.
[10] To Pres. of Congress, Feb. 22, 1778, Papers of the Continental Congress.
[11] *Memoirs*, I, 385.

were many of his type in the Army, but only a few of them were equally lurid in expressing themselves or so ready to expose their persons to prove their questioned honor. He was young, wholly without humor, and supremely confident. Thus far he had been brilliantly triumphant; hence he saw no need to abandon those rules of conduct that he erroneously believed to be the keystone of his dazzling career.

In his boyish arrogance he wrote to Gates on February 22, arraigning him in these melodramatic words:

"Sir, in spite of every consideration, you have wounded my honor, and must make acknowledgement or satisfaction for the injury. . . .

"In consideration of your past connexion, I descend to that explanation with you, which I should have denied any other man."

Continuing, he held Lord Stirling up to infamy and marked him out for punishment:

"The inclosed letters unmask the villain and evince my innocence. My Lord shall bleed for his conduct, but it is proper I first see you." [12]

To this audacious letter from a former aide whose beard had scarcely begun to grow, Gates replied on the following day, quoting extracts from one that he had lately received from Washington. They were to the effect that Conway's disloyal remarks had been communicated to Washington by Lord Stirling, and the earl had learned of them from his own aide, McWilliams, the very one to whom Wilkinson had actually told them when at Reading in October. With this information, Gates then made Wilkinson appear more contemptible than ever by declaring:

"I am astonished if you really gave McWilliams such information how you could intimate to me, that it was possible Colonel Troup had conversed with Colonel Hamilton upon the subject of General Conway's letter." [13]

Wilkinson was now being pilloried for an act not originally serious, but which he had aggravated by continued dissimulation and efforts to throw blame upon a friend who was wholly innocent. In the hope of escape he had led himself into measures of deception, only to find himself held up to the public as an unfaithful subordinate. In this dilemma his judgment proved more immature than at any time before; he seemed to think that a display of physical prowess would exonerate him from previous errors and a lack of moral courage. In keeping

[12] To Gates, Feb. 22, 1778, in *Ibid.*, 385–386.
[13] Gates to Wilkinson, Feb. 23, 1778, in *Ibid.*, 386–387.

with the thought, he sent Gates the following note by Lieutenant-Colonel Burgess Ball of the Virginia Line on February 23, 1778:

"SIR,

"I have discharged my duty to you and to my conscience; meet one tomorrow morning behind the English church, and I will there stipulate the satisfaction which you have promised to grant." [14]

Although commissioned officers were forbidden to engage in duels with their companions in arms, many did so. If any were killed, their deaths might be attributed by the attending surgeons to natural causes: cholera, heart-failure, and the like. For obvious reasons, challenges sent from junior to high-ranking officers were frequently ignored. Field officers could not afford the time or risk to meet every disgruntled subaltern who wanted to salve his pride by taking a shot at his commander. Washington fought no duels, and he advised Greene against yielding to challenges. Putnam had his own original way of bringing the artificial fashion into disrepute. Once he went out to meet his antagonist with his time-worn musket chock-full of slugs. On sight of him, he began firing without form or ceremony. Immediately "Old Put" was the only one left on the "field of honor." On another occasion Putnam agreed to meet a paroled British officer. At the rendezvous the officer was requested to give proof of his valor by sitting beside Putnam on a barrel to which a slow fuse was attached. As it burned nearer and nearer, the swashbuckling Britisher visioned himself being blown to eternity; unable to sit longer, he moved to safe distance. Putnam then remarked, he need not hurry—the barrel was filled only with onions.[15]

Gates had no saving sense of humor like the doughty Connecticut patriot; he agreed to meet Wilkinson for a duel at eight o'clock on the morning of the 24th of February. Pistols were the weapons agreed upon. When Wilkinson was in his quarters preparing to leave for the rendezvous, he learned that Gates was near by and wanted to see him. The two met in an adjacent street, where Wilkinson was received with tender embarrassment. Together they walked along in silence until beyond the buildings of York. Then Gates burst into tears, took him by the hand, and feelingly avowed:

"I injure you, it is impossible, I should as soon think of injuring

[14] *Ibid.*, 388.
[15] Truman, *The Field of Honor*, 441–442, 547–548.

my child . . . besides there was no cause for injuring you, as Conway acknowledged his letter, and has since said much harder things to Washington's face." [16]

At this time Gates was about fifty and Wilkinson something over twenty. Although Gates showed kindness of heart on various occasions, one wonders if he actually made such humiliating efforts to conciliate. The story is Wilkinson's, written ten years after the death of Gates, whose memory was perhaps more cherished by a few manumitted slaves than by all of his countrymen. Apparently Gates did not think the duel of enough importance for him to leave an account of his own.

At this turn of events, Wilkinson was both satisfied and flattered. He arranged with Gates to resume his duties as secretary for the Board of War for a few days and then take a short leave to settle matters with Lord Stirling at Valley Forge. He did not get there as quickly as one might have expected. Ann Biddle was at Lancaster, and here "a fortnight flitted away like a vision of the morn." [17] Only a single shadow darkened his path. A certain Dr. Craik on Washington's staff told him how deeply a number of senior officers resented his recent promotion. All along Wilkinson had known that several had strenuously opposed raising him to the grade of brigadier-general; he had thought of them only as "hardy old fools" moved by envy and ambition.[18] Now he could not entirely ignore them; they might make his prospective visit to Valley Forge embarrassing when he was eager to impress Washington favorably. He could see that, as secretary of the Board of War, his higher rank was not essential; the main thing was that Congress had paid him a signal honor, the token of which was of little consequence to one who was already a colonel and only turning twenty-one. He might easily give up his brevet; he therefore sent in a letter resigning it on March 3, 1778.

About two weeks later Wilkinson reached Valley Forge. Although in a mood to send Lord Stirling a "perempt^y message," he yielded to the better counsels of Colonel Moylan and Colonel Clement Biddle, his future brother-in-law. Acting on their advice, he dispatched a note on March 18 requesting a statement that the information about Conway's letter was merely a piece of conversation "passed in a private

[16] Wilkinson, *Memoirs*, I, 388–389.
[17] *Ibid.*, 391.
[18] *Ibid.*, 389–390, and Wilkinson to Wayne, Nov. 27, 1777, Wayne Papers (Hist. Soc. of Pa. Library), Vol. IV.

company during a convivial Hour." Lord Stirling immediately complied. He also went on to say that he had never mentioned the remarks imputed to Conway until lately when a certain gentleman asserted openly that Wilkinson had denied ever telling them; thereupon he had written to Wilkinson for an explanation, only to get no reply.[19] Wilkinson's letter of February 4 may not have come into his hands; it may have never been posted, it may have been lost along the way. On the other hand, the copy that Wilkinson sent to Congress on February 22 was received on the following day.[20]

As the matter now stood Wilkinson had deceived Gates, and Stirling had deceived Wilkinson. Yet each had reason for forbearance, and harmony had been temporarily restored between them. Gates had also settled his difficulties with Washington, but only after showing himself more untruthful than either of the other two.

In an unskillful effort to save himself and Conway, Gates had declared that the alleged statement was "in words as well as substance a wicked forgery." When informed that it had come into circulation through Wilkinson, Gates wanted him punished for committing "a crime of the first magnitude," one that "involves with it the consequences of positive treason." In this strain he wrote to Washington on January 23, nearly a month before he and Wilkinson went out to fight but embraced instead.[21] In reply Washington ignored Wilkinson's "heinous" offense. He suggested that Conway should employ his "rich treasures of knowledge and experience" to better purpose; he declared him a man "capable of all the malignity of detraction, and all the meanness of intrigue, to gratify the absurd resentment of disappointed vanity, or answer the purposes of personal aggrandisement and promote the interest of faction." If a person like this had been guilty of only a harmless letter, why, he sensibly asked, was it not immediately exhibited?[22]

The question was too hard for Gates. And in face of so withering a denunciation of the miserable Conway he thought it best to give over the attempt to defend him further. He showed his willingness to place all responsibility on Conway when he replied:

"I heartily dislike controversy even upon my own account and much more in a matter wherein I was only accidentally concerned."[23]

---

[19] To Stirling, Mar. 18, 1778, in Wilkinson, *Memoirs*, I, 391–392.
[20] To Pres. of Congress, Feb. 22, 1778, Papers of the Cont. Congress.
[21] Gates to Washington, Jan. 23, 1778, Wilkinson, *Memoirs*, I, 398–401.
[22] Washington to Gates, Feb. 9, 1778, in *Ibid.*, 401–405.
[23] Gates to Washington, Feb. 19, 1778, in *Ibid.*, 407–408.

With Gates's further assurance that he had no offensive views in the matter, Washington expressed a willingness "to bury the incident in silence, and, as far as future events will permit, oblivion." [24] The exchange of letters then ceased, and the two resumed their former relations. Incidentally Conway gave up the ways of conspiracy. He became contrite and asked pardon as well as he could after John Cadwalader, an ardent supporter of Washington, had shot him in the mouth during a duel on February 22, 1778.

Nor was the story yet complete. While at Valley Forge as a dinner guest at Headquarters, Wilkinson was allowed to read the correspondence that had passed between Washington and Gates. Learning in this way what Gates thought of him before the day of their reconciliation, Wilkinson became abusive of both him and Conway in conversation with the commander-in-chief. He knew that sooner or later stories would be carried back to those whom his remarks concerned; then Gates's recently forgiving attitude might turn to vindictive hate. Evidently it would be no longer prudent to retain his place at the elbow of the man whose powers of retaliation might prove too potent to combat successfully. To Henry Laurens, President of Congress, Wilkinson dispatched this unbecoming letter on March 29:

"SIR,

"While I make my acknowledgments to Congress for the appointment of secretary to the board of war and ordinance, I am sorry I should be constrained to resign that office; but after the act of *treachery* and *falsehood* in which I have detected Major-General Gates, the president of that board, it is impossible for me to reconcile it to my honor to serve with him." [25]

Wilkinson could never control his fluency. His pen never wavered, however erroneous his judgment might be. The ease with which he talked and wrote, joined with hasty decisions and a comic-opera sense of honor, had led him into one error after another. The only thing he could do was to escape service under a man whom he had publicly abused. If he did not do so, Gates might part company with him in a more embarrassing way.[26] As events turned out Congress ac-

[24] Washington to Gates, Feb. 24, 1778, in *Ibid.*, 408.
[25] To Pres. of Congress, Mar. 29, 1778, in *Ibid.*, 409–410.
[26] Clark to Stirling, Jan. 15, 1778, and Wilson to Gates, Feb. 21, 1778, in Burnett, *Letters of Members of the Continental Congress*, III, 40, 142.

cepted his resignation but directed that his letter be returned as "improper to remain" upon its files.[27]

After resigning, Wilkinson had no regular employment in the Army until he became clothier-general on July 25, 1779.[28] He doubtless hated to be put on the shelf. In this dreary period of the Revolution, few opportunities for distinction existed, especially for one whose rank was high, and who had lately lost a great deal of public confidence. The British were reorganizing their forces, and the Americans were waiting until French aid should lend strength to their weakening cause. On June 18, 1778, the British evacuated Philadelphia. Washington pursued them, fought the battle of Monmouth, was defeated, and became inactive at White Plains. Tories and Indians laid waste the fruitful Wyoming Valley of Pennsylvania, and in November the luckless farmers of central New York were treated to another dreadful visitation of Iroquois torch and tomahawk. Not until months later did Sullivan come and reach new levels of cruelty and destruction in his punishment of the Indians. In other sections the war continued to drag indecisively on. In none of these operations did Wilkinson share—perhaps because those who might have given him employment had plenty of assistants whom they could wholly trust.

Although Benedict Arnold was in charge of the military defenses of Philadelphia, Wilkinson could expect nothing from him because of their open rupture during the Burgoyne campaign. At this time Arnold was setting the pace for unbecoming extravagance, lavishly entertaining alike both his Whig friends and those who had received British officers before Sir William Howe had left the city with his Knights of the Blended Rose and the Burning Mount. Continental money was daily diminishing in value, and those who possessed it spent with reckless abandon. At one dinner the bill for pastry alone was reputed to be $3,888; at another, the guests had the choice of one hundred and sixty dishes. Those whose incomes were small felt the pinch of penury. Timothy Pickering, secretary of the Board of War, said it was impossible to live on his salary of $14,000. It could not have gone far when his indifferent house cost $4,000 a year, $1,600 was asked for a suit of clothes, forty dollars for a hat, and twenty-five dollars for a pair of shoes. At about the same time flour sold around ninety-five dol-

[27] Ford, *Journal of the Cont. Congress*, X, 297.
[28] To Jay, July 25, 1779, Papers of the Cont. Congress.

lars a hundredweight, and butter ranged from two to three dollars a pound.[29]

The poor suffered greatly. Wilkinson was a member of a committee from the Middle Ward to help raise money to relieve their distress. Like many others, he must have found living difficult, although he seems to have had a little income from his family and may have added to it by doing odd jobs for his future father-in-law, John Biddle, or other Philadelphia patriots who returned home and resumed their commercial activities. Never idle, he was assiduous in his courting, availed himself of the opportunity to become a Mason, and took part in the social affairs of his friends.

During the summer of 1778 Wilkinson went to bear witness for his former commander, General St. Clair, who was brought to trial in the "New Dining Room near Baron De Kalb's quarters" at White Plains, New York, on charges covering neglect of duty, cowardice, treachery, shamefully abandoning Ticonderoga, etc. Gates came and offered testimony for him on the 29th of August. Wilkinson turned up at about the same time.[30] Within a few days the smoldering hatred between the two burst into flame. Apparently "the hero of Saratoga" made remarks reflecting upon Wilkinson's conduct at the duel at York during the previous February. Highly incensed, Wilkinson sent him a challenge, which was duly accepted. Colonel Tadeusz Kosciuszko acted as a second for Gates; John Barker Church, son-in-law of General Schuyler, did the same for Wilkinson. According to agreement, the principals met near Harrison, Westchester County, New York, on September 4, 1778. At the first order to fire Gates's pistol flashed in the pan, Wilkinson fired in the air; at the second, Wilkinson fired, Gates refused to do so; at the third, Wilkinson again fired, again Gates's pistol flashed in the pan. Thrice Gates had posed as a target without making any efforts to defend himself. "Honor" was satisfied, the seconds interposed, and the principals shook hands. Gates declared Wilkinson had "behaved as a gentleman" at York, and a paper to that effect was signed by Kosciuszko and given to Church. Asking for it long enough to make a copy, Kosciuszko refused to return it until Church had furnished Gates with a similar statement signed by Wilkinson. Next day they all assembled at St. Clair's headquarters

[29] Stone, "Philadelphia Society One Hundred Years Ago," in *Pa. Mag. of Hist. and Biog.*, III, 362–393.
[30] "The Trial of Major General St. Clair," in *Collections of N.Y. Historical Society*, XIII (1880), 1–171.

to settle this new cause of dispute. Here Wilkinson said he would not prostitute his honor by giving Gates a certificate of gentlemanly conduct; on the contrary, he called him a rascal and coward, and challenged him to another bout with arms. Gates ignored his abuse and paid no attention to his request for a certificate, duel, or anything else. There the matter stood. The principals were as badly off as ever; they had gained nothing except in mutual hatred.

To have witnesses for St. Clair's defense turn out to be comic opera performers lent new interest to the drab round of court-martial proceedings. The end was not yet. Both Kosciuszko and Church took up the wrangle where their principals had left off. It concerned the bedeviling certificate. Daily their anger grew. When summoned to give testimony for St. Clair, they had scarcely entered the courtroom before they made for each other with sword and pistol. Some one yelled for the guard. When it came tumbling in Church made for his horse and rode away like the wind; he was determined not to be taken in hand as a civilian for disturbing an army tribunal. Kosciuszko did not pursue; he gloated on his fanciful victory, making much of the ignominious flight of his enemy.[31]

A long time had elapsed since any one had come and stirred up as much trouble in camp as Wilkinson had done. Oddly enough, it seemed not premeditated; it was just a result of his flamboyant and thoughtless manner. In the real business for which the Court had summoned him, he showed ability and judgment. On September 7, he appeared as a witness for St. Clair. He endeavored to show that the General had taken pains to learn of the British as they advanced, and that when once the decision had been made to abandon Ticonderoga, the retreat had been managed with energy and intelligence. On September 29 St. Clair was acquitted of all charges "with the highest honour."[32] His chief fault was ignored—that he had delayed the evacuation until part of his force was taken and most of his supplies were lost. The authors of the charges fashioned them to conform with the opinion of the public, who overestimated the importance of Ticonderoga and believed that it should have been held. Obviously the prosecution could not center its case against St. Clair on his delay in doing what politicians had demanded should not be done

---

[31] For an account of Wilkinson's second duel with Gates, *vide New York Packet* (Fishkill, N.Y.), Sept. 17, 24, Oct. 8, 1778; *Continental Journal and Weekly Advertiser*, Nov. 12, 1778; *Mag. of Am. Hist.*, VII, 65, VIII, 368.
[32] "The Trial of Major General St. Clair," *loc. cit.*

under any circumstances; it had to concentrate on other things that would stifle the popular outcry although they might not be susceptible of proof.

Shortly after St. Clair's court-martial, that of General Schuyler occurred. Though Wilkinson was Schuyler's friend, his service had not been so long and intimate with him as with St. Clair. Perhaps his testimony was not needed at this second trial; acquittal seemed to be a foregone conclusion. Presumably he would have been a witness for Schuyler if requested, no matter how eager he was to return to Philadelphia and be with his betrothed, Ann Biddle.

She was the daughter of John Biddle, a well known and respected business man of Philadelphia. For a long time he had kept the Indian King hostelry on Market Street, where he bore an enviable reputation for the care of travelers. His tavern was an orderly one, without liquor after eleven at night. If a guest desired even more quiet, the obliging host sometimes tried to find a place for him in a private house.[33] He was a courteous, kindly Quaker who, marrying Sarah Owen on March 3, 1736, lived happily with her until her death thirty-seven years later.[34] Although fighting was against his creed and he had prospered when England ruled the Colonies, he espoused the Revolutionary cause and gave both money and service to its support. His two sons, Owen and Clement, made similar decisions. Clement, born May 10, 1740, served at Trenton, Princeton, Valley Forge, Brandywine, and Germantown, and acted as commissary-general of forage under General Greene.[35] Owen, three years older, was for a time one of his deputies in the forage department and served as a member of the Board of War, but was more interested in religion and natural philosophy. Scarcely were the British out of Philadelphia before he and David Rittenhouse, the celebrated astronomer and mathematician, were peering through a telescope at an eclipse of the sun. After the war, Owen became deeply penitent for having borne arms and humbly asked to be restored to the fellowship of Friends.[36] While he wrestled with problems of religion, his eldest sister Sarah turned to worldly things and people. She lived for nearly fifty years and married three times, her third husband being Rudolph Tellier, a Swiss of social prominence and charm. Lydia, the youngest of the

---

[33] "Diary of Daniel Fisher," in *Pa. Mag. of Hist. and Biog.*, XVII, 263–278.
[34] *Pa. Mag. of Hist. and Biog.*, XIV, 203, XIII, 178.
[35] *Autobiography of Charles Biddle*, 420–423.
[36] H. D. Biddle, "Owen Biddle," in *Pa. Mag. of Hist. and Biog.*, XVI, 299–329, and S. W. Pennypacker, *Historical Biographical Sketches*, 84.

five children, was attractive like her sister but died before any of the others—seven years after she had become the wife of Dr. James Hutchinson in 1779. He married again, continuing a career of unusual distinction until he gave up his own life for the sake of others during the great epidemic of yellow fever in 1794. Even after the passing of Lydia, the Biddles, especially Ann, held the doctor in affectionate regard.[37]

Ann possessed her share of the family's strength of mind and character. She was an engaging, sprightly Quakeress who could easily arouse in others "a courting distemper." Just when she first stirred Wilkinson with her bright glances and pleasing ways, records do not reveal. It may have been when both were in their teens and he was studying "physic and surgery" in Philadelphia. From then on he visited the city whenever opportunity offered. Maids like her were rarely found. Accustomed to associating with people of ability and means, she had their good manners and character, easily making friends wherever her footsteps turned. In later years many paid tribute to her loveliness. In her youth her hair and eyebrows were dark and abundant, her features attractively cut, and her figure slender and gracefully formed. Well educated for a woman of her time and enjoying acknowledged position, it was very natural that she should become the fiancée of a brilliant and aggressive young man who moved in the same social circles and subscribed to the political faith of her father and brothers. Always active and strenuous in the pursuit of what he wished to possess, Wilkinson quickened his courtship after resigning from the Board of War, and on November 12, 1778,[38] the two were married in Christ Church, Philadelphia.

Ann had chosen one of the "world's people" for her husband, and her family had violated the rulings of the Quakers; therefore the ceremony was performed in a church whose faith Wilkinson and his relatives favored. It had been built before the French and Indian War through the efforts of many distinguished people. Afterwards, several additions modified its general plan. Franklin and others made possible a steeple and a chime of eight bells that rang in pleasing tones on days of piety. Within, the kindly rector preached to his congregation from a wineglass pulpit, his vestments and the chancel flooded with light that entered through a beautiful Palladian window

---

[37] Hay, "Letters of Mrs. Ann Biddle Wilkinson," in *Pa. Mag. of Hist. and Biog.*, LVI, 33–55.
[38] *Ibid.*, 34.

Major-General James Wilkinson
from a miniature by Gilbert Stuart.

*Courtesy of the owner, Captain Theodore S.
Wilkinson, U.S.N.*

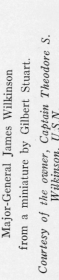

Mrs. Ann Biddle Wilkinson.

*Miniature owned by Mrs. V. G. Crockett,
Los Angeles, California.*

cut in the rear wall. Only a few hundred of the faithful could find
room within the nave and balcony. Even if they were wont to listen
intently to this able, godly man, at times some must have glanced
thoughtfully at the graceful columns, elliptical arches, and harmonious blending of Greek designs that gave beauty to the holy place.[39]
It was befitting that here the charming Ann Biddle should make
her vows upon her marriage day. Records do not reveal who sat
with friendly interest and saw the ceremony through; maybe most
of the Biddles, the amiable Dr. Hutchinson, a few army friends, and
some of Wilkinson's relatives from the Patuxent.

Just where the newly wedded pair immediately established themselves is not certain; temporarily they lived in Philadelphia, possibly
with Ann's father, who seemed to think well of his recently acquired
son-in-law, and who perhaps furnished him with some kind of employment. At odd times, Wilkinson widened the range of his acquaintance, attended Blue Lodge No. 2 of the Masons,[40] and cultivated his cronies in the Army. Ann joined him in social pleasures.
To her must be attributed a good deal of the popularity that he enjoyed. She seemed not to be greatly disturbed at being read out of
Friends' Meeting on December 25, 1778, because she had been married contrary to "the good Order" of their discipline.[41] This Christmas Day token of godly displeasure might have been taken more
deeply to heart if her father and brothers had not already trans-
gressed the Quakers' rules of conduct.

Such a program of life did not satisfy Wilkinson, always restless to take a personal part in the most absorbing events of the day.
To him the Army offered the most popular and extensive source of
agreeable and remunerative work. Once in uniform, he had never
been content out of it. He therefore maintained his contacts with the
service, hoping that his discreditable connection with the Conway
Cabal would be forgotten, and that a position might be found where
he could exercise his old-time rank in a position of commensurate
importance. He did not seek aid from Benedict Arnold, his former
commander, who was then in military control of the city; in fact, he
offered to furnish Joseph Reed, President of Pennsylvania, with evidence of the General's dishonesty.[42] He turned rather to Greene, St.

[39] Cousins and Riley, *The Colonial Architecture of Philadelphia*, 219–221.
[40] Perry to Hay, Dec. 5, 1931, in files of T. R. Hay.
[41] Hay, "Letters of Mrs. Ann Biddle Wilkinson," in *Pa. Mag. of Hist. and Biog.*,
LVI, 34.
[42] To Reed, May 30, 1779, *Pa. Archives*, VII, 149.

Clair, and Washington for a sympathetic consideration of his cause. His efforts were, of course, strongly supported by the Biddles and his own influential connections in Maryland.

On July 25, 1779, Wilkinson enthusiastically accepted the position of Clothier-General, which had been offered him the day before.[43] His predecessor, James Mease, had been eager to retire as early as September 19, 1778, in order to escape an investigation of his alleged incompetence and dishonesty. Mease and Arnold, after the retaking of Philadelphia, had collected clothing from loyalists and patriots alike, often without paying for it, and had then disposed of what they wished for private gain. Congress took no immediate steps to accept the resignation of the Clothier-General or bring him to trial, although soldiers could not leave hospitals or perform their routine duties because they had so little to wear. While the army was thus suffering, civilians, in general, were comfortably clad.[44]

By the following summer of 1779 Congress was ready to make a change. Peter Wikoff and Persifer Frazer were in turn offered the position and declined; because one, perhaps both, felt that the annual salary of $5,000 in depreciated currency was wholly inadequate.[45] Wilkinson, as third choice, declared that nobody except himself would take over the work.[46] He might have added that he was only too happy to be back in the Army with its lengthened horizon of opportunity.

His new duties were enough to challenge his ability and zeal. He acted under the direction of the Board of War, of which Timothy Pickering was then president. Sometimes it made purchases and called on him to act as distributing agent; on other occasions, Wilkinson bought on his own account after Congress had examined his estimates and approved of what contracts should be executed. In addition, different states were called upon for supplies, in each of which a deputy clothier was stationed to collect and care for what it would furnish. The amount and kind from this source were not satisfactory; the states were much more concerned in looking after their own local troops than in contributing to a general fund that had been dubiously administered. More than once agents of the Clothier-

---

[43] To Jay, July 25, 1779, Papers of the Cont. Congress.

[44] Thian, *Leg. Hist. of the Gen. Staff of the Army of the U.S.*, 288, 293; McKee, "Service of Supply in the War of 1812," in *Quartermaster Review*, Jan.–Feb., 1927, p. 15.

[45] Thian, *op. cit.*, 297, and Frazer to Congress, July 19, 1779, Papers of the Cont. Congress.

[46] To Samuel Huntington, Nov. 4, 1780, Papers of the Cont. Congress.

General found themselves bidding against representatives from the states for identical supplies. No matter how variegated the garments, shoes, blankets, etc. acquired through this triple-headed system, Wilkinson was expected to distribute them through his regimental deputies in a manner that would avoid dissatisfaction. These administrative defects, a scarcity of materials, and a lack of adequate transportation had caused more complaints against the clothing department of the Army than against any other before Wilkinson took office.[47]

Fortunately for his reputation, he began his new duties in the summer, so that he had a few months to fill his magazines for the coming winter. Never very accurate in routine work, and probably imagining that he should be concerned with more important tasks, he asked the Board of War for additional clerical assistance for himself and his deputies. This request was refused because of a lack of legal provision. During the same summer, warrants aggregating $300,000 were issued in his favor for general purchases, and he needed several assistants in order that a proper record of disbursements might be kept.[48] At the same time he was enjoined to write "the most pressing letters to the Executives of the several states" earnestly requesting their immediate exertions in collecting "supplies of clothing for the troops of their respective quotas." [49] To discharge his duties more effectively, Wilkinson frequently left Philadelphia to visit the Army at such places as West Point, Newburgh, and Morristown. When cold weather set in, the troops were probably better clothed than during the previous year, although the whole system was so defective that no pronounced improvement obtained. Supplies were scant, local credit exhausted, and purchases abroad at reasonable rates were not easily made. When cloth, leather, etc. existed in any quantity in Philadelphia or elsewhere, there state deputies gathered and bid against each other, paying from a common fund that Congress had appropriated. When a state furnished its troops with clothing, it was indifferent about making a report, in order that more might be drawn from the general supply. When near a magazine, detachments often got special issues irrespective of the amount of their allowance. On some occasions the members of

---

[47] Thian, *op. cit.*, 293–296; Wilkinson to Samuel Huntington, Nov. 4, 1780, in Papers of the Cont. Congress; Washington to Stirling, Sept. 28, 1779, in Force, *Transcripts.*

[48] To Board of War, Aug. 12, 1779, Papers of the Cont. Congress; Ford, *Journals of Cont. Congress*, XIV, 983.

[49] Peters to Wilkinson, Aug. 16, 1779. Wilkinson Papers (Chicago Hist. Soc.), Vol. I.

the Board of War appeared to order, and on others to make, these issues for purely personal reasons. Soldiers far from bases on difficult winter service and in great need had to wait until the short-term, seven-months men drew their bounty clothing before leaving for home. Simultaneously deputies grew rich because of the bonus of one-half per cent on expenditures given them in addition to their pay. A similar perquisite was allowed to the Clothier-General.[50]

Wilkinson in an able letter to the Board of War on November 10, 1780, described these and other defects of the system and urged that they be corrected. He declared that when he had taken charge the department was in utter confusion, and that, although he had tried his uttermost to carry out the established procedure, the very nature of the work had baffled his efforts. The Board of War considered his letter and recommended to Congress a number of significant changes. Among these were abolition of deputies in the several states in order to eliminate competition for supplies; setting up a more highly centralized and adequately staffed office of control; doing away with special issues except in unusual cases; and providing for a more frequent and responsible system of accounting for clothing and funds. Congress accepted most of the Board's suggestions and made some changes of its own; but not all of them became a matter of law until June 18, 1781.[51] In the interim Wilkinson had resigned, leaving his successor, John Moylan, to profit by these improvements in less difficult times.

A variety of reasons prompted Wilkinson to resign. In the August following his taking office he purchased what was known as the attainted estate of Joseph Galloway, situated eighteen miles from Philadelphia and five miles from Bristol and containing four hundred and forty-four acres of good land on which dwelling houses and barns had been erected. The purchase price was £4,600, Continental money, all of which, except the initial payment of £1,150, fell due on November 3, 1779. His newly acquired estate was called Trevose.[52] Supervision of its pasture and farming land, cattle, fine horses, and distillery absorbed a good deal of time; but it was the kind of work that he enjoyed, and to which he had been bred. Being a clothier-general was different; he never had had a bent for the details of

[50] Wilkinson to Samuel Huntington, Nov. 4, 1780, Papers of the Cont. Congress; Thian, *op. cit.*, 292.

[51] Thian, *op. cit.*, 238, 319–321, and Wilkinson to Samuel Huntington, Mar. 27, 1781, in Papers of the Cont. Congress.

[52] *Pa. Archives*, 6th Series, XII, 159–160, and XIII, 180.

business. When the novelty of his position wore off, he found his duties irksome and neglected them. When his salary was reduced to $2,500 and not promptly paid, he had additional reasons for a lessening of zeal.[53]

He also had a large circle of friends, to whom he never begrudged a large share of his time. In fact, he was unhappy unless he frequently mingled with them at Trenton, Morristown, and elsewhere. While master of a dancing assembly in Philadelphia during 1780, he arranged the programs, helping in giving the dances such patriotic names as "The Defeat of Burgoyne," "Clinton's Retreat," "The Success of the Campaign," etc. He or an assistant provided the guests with folded billets, each containing a number; thus partners were selected and kept the whole evening through. When the music struck up it was he who called the dancers in their turns.[54] He liked these parties; often he was the central figure in them. No matter if they were woodenly methodical, they furnished opportunity to do a little casual strutting in gorgeous uniform and to listen with seeming nonchalance to bits of flattery that came his way. He was brilliant, well connected, and twenty-three; and whether in town or in camp he moved restlessly along the paths of pleasure with brother officers and friends.

After Washington had approved Wilkinson's appointment, he seemed nettled when he learned that his new Clothier-General had turned play boy, spending most of his time in Philadelphia rather than near the headquarters of the Army, where the duties of his office could be most effectively discharged. Repeatedly Washington called on him to establish himself close at hand and pay more attention to his business. Expostulation proving ineffectual, the Commander-in-Chief wrote to Congress, asking that its authority be brought to bear on this negligent official.[55] That Wilkinson made scarcely more than a pretense of meeting the wishes of his general suggests an indifference to continuing in office. If some of his Maryland friends had praised the fairness with which he distributed clothing,[56] doubtless there were others whose complaints were loud

---

[53] Act of Cong., Nov. 4, 1780, in Ford, *Journals of Cont. Congress,* 1018–1021, and Wilkinson to Pres. of Congress, Mar. 21, 1781, in Papers of the Cont. Congress.

[54] Scharf and Wescott, *History of Philadelphia,* II, 909.

[55] Washington to Stirling, Sept. 28, 1779, in Force, *Transcripts;* Washington to Wilkinson, Mar. 24, 1781, Papers of the Cont. Congress.

[56] Md. Delegates to T. S. Lee, in Burnett, *Letters of Members of the Cont. Congress,* V, 332.

and frequent. He usually resented criticism, especially when the system under which he worked, rather than himself, was at fault. He preferred service with combat troops to duty in any form with the service of supply, probably because he lacked the business experience necessary to cope with the problems that made life miserable for the quartermasters and commissaries of the Revolutionary Army. When he found his salary reduced as well as too often in arrears, himself hamstrung by vexatious regulations, and the Commander-in-Chief exasperated with his conduct, he decided once more to slough off his responsibilities by resigning. On March 27, 1781, by the hand of Thomas McKean, a friendly member of Congress, he proffered his resignation in a letter without rancor, expressing the hope of future employment where he might be of service. He did not fail to set forth clearly his reason for giving up his post:

"I should be wanting in Personal Candour and in Public Justice if I did not profess that I find my Mercantile knowledge, *on thorough* examination, inadequate to the just Conduct of the Clothing Department, under the proposed establishment." [57]

Nevertheless, he strongly believed that his work had been performed with honor to himself and benefit to his country, and so informed Congress in a letter of the 10th of April.[58] He realized equally well that the odds were too great against him for any sort of vindication. To a friend he wrote:

". . . a slight knowledge of the Temper of this country must convince the difficulty, if not improbability of obtaining a public opinion against the infallibility of General Washington, consequently an impeachment of his justice, be it ever so well founded or ever so ably supported would excite nothing more favorable than derision & contempt, and would be esteemed a sort of impiety." [59]

Wilkinson was evincing better judgment than he had shown during his wrangle with Gates. The proof of it lay in gracefully resigning when Washington and others found fault with his services. Giving up uncongenial work seemed not to disturb him; he merely regretted that he had been unable to use his late office as a means of obtaining another for which he was more adequately fitted.

After severing his connection with the Army, Wilkinson lived during the next two years at Trevose and Philadelphia, looking after

[57] To Samuel Huntington, Mar. 27, 1781, Papers of the Cont. Congress.
[58] To Pres. of Cong., Apr. 10, 1781, *Ibid*.
[59] To McKean, Apr. 8, 1781, McKean Papers.

his growing family and rather unremunerative estate. About the time of his resignation Ann had borne him their first child, John Biddle Wilkinson. The infant was named after his grandfather, who chose him as a favorite and delighted in having him about. Even when John grew older and learned to "write prettily," he remained the old merchant's favorite. Before he had abandoned his hobby-horse and had begun to ride like his friend Philip Nolan, he would bedevil the younger brothers who competed for the place at Grandfather Biddle's knee. If the dignified Quaker frowned disapprovingly when little John aped his father and swore lispingly at toy soldiers, it was always with an indulgent twinkle in his eye. Nothing so delighted the boy as a return to Philadelphia from Kentucky and lording it over the host of young cousins who overran the house and garden where his mother had spent so many days of happiness.[60] She was devoted to her family and relatives. The Biddles were numerous and returned her affection. They lived comfortably and in an even-tempered way, and she and her husband fitted easily into their wholesome program of life.

On occasions Wilkinson visited his army friends scattered in the neighborhood. Sometimes he did volunteer staff duty for the ablest of Washington's generals, Nathanael Greene, who held him in high esteem and regretted that his talents had been lost to the service.[61] More frequently he was found in the camps of the Pennsylvania militia at Trenton, Newton, and places near by. In the course of time he and Joseph Reed, President of Pennsylvania from 1778 to 1781, became intimate friends. When Reed was accused of having intrigued with the British for the purpose of changing allegiance, Wilkinson and officers at Camp Newton evinced their faith in him by signing an "Address of Confidence" during September, 1780. When the charges were revived by General Cadwalader in the early part of the following year, Wilkinson was the moving spirit in obtaining a similar testimonial from those about Philadelphia; possibly still another originating in the vicinity may be credited to his authorship.[62] These tokens of friendship were appreciated by the Pennsylvania patriot, who felt that he could trust Wilkinson implicitly. Every so often Reed stopped at Trevose, where Ann's eldest sister,

[60] For remarks on John Biddle Wilkinson, see Hay, "Letters of Mrs. Ann Biddle Wilkinson," in *Pa. Mag. of Hist. and Biog.*, LVI, 33–55.
[61] Greene to C. Biddle, June 29, 1780, in Reed, *Life and Correspondence of Joseph Reed*, II, 469.
[62] *Reed Papers*, IV, 94; *Pa. Packet*, June 5, 16, 1781; *Pa. Gazette*, June 27, 1781.

Mrs. Shaw, twice a widow, often visited. In the company of this interesting woman the President found it possible to forget for a while the recent loss of the wife who left to his care a brood of five small children. With the ripening of their friendship a marriage seemed probable until Reed appeared to lose interest. Wilkinson took him strenuously to task, the breach being healed only after Reed had made proper explanations and Mrs. Shaw had shown eagerness to be rid of such a volatile suitor.[63] Her antipathy toward marriage was evidently not general or long sustained, for in a few years she took a third husband, Rudolph Tellier, President of the Swiss Confederacy, and went to Switzerland to live. The other two in the tripartite affair quickly resumed their previous friendship.

Reed's assistance was of undoubted aid when Wilkinson embarked in politics. The Army may have appealed to him more, but reëntering it with the same rank that he had previously enjoyed was next to impossible, especially since he had lately angered Washington, and other officers to whom he might appeal, like St. Clair and Greene, were passing through an eclipse or were so busily engaged in distant theaters that they could do nothing for him. There were, moreover, few bright days for the patriots in the period between the beginning of 1780 and the surrender of Yorktown. Wilkinson, like many others, at times despaired of the success of the patriots' cause. With little hope of his country's independence and with his finances in a sorry state, he turned to politics as to an interesting haven where he could better weather his troubles. At least it furnished employment, added something to his income, and gave him a certain amount of honor and influence.

On October 10, 1781, Wilkinson was elected representative to the Pennsylvania Assembly from Bucks County; and he took his seat at the meeting that convened soon afterwards. In this first term he was not connected with matters of consequence; he was evidently serving an apprenticeship. Nevertheless, he was made a general of the militia and assigned as "Brigadier and Adjutant General," continuing at the same time to hold his seat in the Assembly, to which he was reëlected in the autumn of 1782.[64] With a growth of expe-

---

[63] Wilkinson to Reed, Jan. 15, 16, 18, 1783, and to Nichols, May 2, 1782, in Miscel. Papers, Hist. Soc. of Pa. Library.

[64] *Pa. Archives*, 6th Series, II, 162–163; *Pa. Gazette*, May 29, Oct. 10, 1782; *Colonial Records of Pa.*, XIII, 289.

rience he began to play a determining rôle and was placed on several committees of importance.

In spite of heartening success in politics Wilkinson was not satisfied. He knew that its rewards were few, slowly obtained, and often worth little. His personal debts were accumulating; [65] Trevose was advertised for sale, and the coming of peace seemed only to have ushered in chaos. The West, particularly Kentucky, held out promise of better things. Wilkinson determined to try his fortune there. Before the year 1783 had ended he was at the Falls of the Ohio, stirred with a desire to own adjacent stretches of forest and meadow. Daring spirits had already settled on choice parcels that they had acquired with land warrants, either purchased directly or acquired by virtue of service in the Revolution. Wilkinson eagerly joined this vanguard of soldiers and speculators. In December, 1783, he made entries for tracts of land near the present cities of Louisville and Lexington.[66] The next month he made arrangements for two valuable cargoes of merchandise to be sent down the Ohio for his disposal. Before long he resigned as brigadier-general of the Pennsylvania militia. He was definitely taking root in the new country of Kentucky. In this general section and the Southwest he was destined to spend most of the remaining years of his life.

[65] To Lee, Jan. 10, 1782, Wilkinson Papers (Chicago Hist. Soc.), Vol. I.
[66] Jillson, *Old Kentucky Entries and Deeds* (Filson Club Publications, No. 34), 160; Jillson, *The Kentucky Land Grants* (Filson Club Publications, No. 33), 253.

CHAPTER IV

MERCHANT–POLITICIAN OF KENTUCKY

AFTER the Revolution many adventurers, bereft of all but the spirit that had brought them to America and accomplished their national independence, turned their faces toward the Appalachian Mountains and crossed over into a newer land that was famed for fertile soil and abundant water. To them the French interpretation of Ohio, as the country of the beautiful river, was not unknown. Soon hardwood cabins sprang up where clover fields had blossomed and great elm and hickory trees spread their cool, green branches. Louisville, Lexington, and Harrodsburg gave promise of becoming important centers of frontier trade. The fame of George Rogers Clark and his trail-blazers, peace with England, and the lure of commerce and land speculation led many to settle upon the hunting grounds over which the Indians had long roamed without molestation. Incensed at this intrusion and the loss of their game, the savages began to plunder and despoil, torturing and killing whoever fell into their truculent hands. The pioneers in the District of Kentucky could not cope with such acts of barbarity; they had no power to call out the militia and no money for arms, ammunition, and supplies. In final despair they began to abandon their clearings and seek safety within the shadow of poorly constructed and scantily garrisoned blockhouses. Such refugees soon sank into "poverty and indolence" and were ever ready to inveigh against their own state of Virginia and the federal government, both of which they believed should render them aid. Their wretchedness became more acute during the extremely severe winter of 1783–1784. Even at New Orleans the cold was so intense that jams of ice prevented any one from crossing the Mississippi for five days.[1]

In spite of the fact that Kentuckians were afflicted with trouble, many immigrants came to their country hoping to profit from the

---

[1] Christian, *James Wilkinson and Kentucky Separatism, 1784–1798*, 1–7; Alexander Breckinridge to John Breckinridge, Mar. 4, 1784, *Breckinridge Papers*, Vol. II.

gifts with which Nature had blessed it. James Wilkinson was among those who arrived in 1783. He was no aimless drifter; he was an accredited representative of the substantial firm of Barclay, Moylan & Co. of Philadelphia. Although his particular business was to dispose of limited quantities of general merchandise—salt, calicoes, corduroys, chintzes, crosscut saws, liquors, etc.[2]—his vision was not limited to these petty things. This one-time brigadier at twenty years of age was dreaming of a more spectacular career in the rapidly changing West, where Louisville and New Orleans could afford him a better opportunity for a hasty rise than did those drab conservative cities of the Atlantic seaboard.

Even his most unfriendly critics believed that Wilkinson was a man to be reckoned with. He was, as a contemporary politician saw him, "A person not quite tall enough to be perfectly elegant, compensated by symmetry and appearance of health and strength; a countenance open, mild, capacious, and beaming with intelligence; a gait firm, manly, and facile; manners bland, accommodating and popular; and address easy, polite and gracious, invited approach, gave access, assured attention, cordiality and ease. By these fair terms, he conciliated; by these he captivated." [3]

Wilkinson had a mind of many facets, but none was of great brilliance. His knowledge, neither accurate nor deep, was varied and pretentious and satisfied the ordinary frontiersman. Doctor, lawyer, schoolmaster, merchant, chief—he played the rôles of them all and a half-dozen others besides. When a midwife was needed he stood by; when neighbors required a physic he prescribed—salts, tartar, laudanum, and blistering "plaisters" were some of his favorite remedies; and hence Charles Scott, a friend of Revolutionary days, was urged to have a "snug little apartment" of them when he came to Kentucky. He was also asked to bring along vegetable seeds; for Wilkinson, like many others, enjoyed seeing things grow and having turnips, cabbages, and melons to supplement his frontier fare.[4] He greatly treasured a little book that Abercrombie had written on gardening, and took pains that it should not be lost while he was out on a trip trying to outdo the peddlers who had cut into the profits of his Lexington store.[5]

[2] To Shiell, July 4, 1784, in *Ky. State Hist. Society Register*, XXIV (1926), 260.
[3] Marshall, *The History of Kentucky* (1824 ed.), I, 165.
[4] To Shiell, July 4, 1784, in *Ky. State Hist. Society Register*, XXIV, 259–260.
[5] To Shiell, March 31, 1785, in *Ibid.*, 265–266.

Sometimes he traveled with a mule and a horse or two, eating his own bacon and biscuit to avoid the "damn'd Tavern keepers," exchanging gossip, retailing his wares, and keeping his eyes open for a trade in real estate.[6] He declared that he knew more about western lands than "any Christian in America." He may have been right. Anyhow, his personal and broker holdings were large, and he was able to supply anything from town lots to tracts of 60,000 acres.[7] When sales in merchandise and real property declined he took a hand in politics and in fighting the Indians. Like most Kentuckians, he had a relish for both, well satisfying the public demand for a vigorous leader and a wily and hardy advocate. More fluent than others, he was ever ready to take time out for contention and dispute. In the tangled skein of western surveys and business methods, Wilkinson was always able to unravel himself, and this faculty proved reason enough for others to turn to him in times of perplexity.

By nature he was a gregarious soul, generally to be found in the midst of things. He may have wanted to make his home at Louisville, where the Falls of the Ohio caused a natural interruption to river traffic and were proving an important inducement to settle.[8] Nevertheless, he determined to reside where his expenses were less, land holdings greater, and business prospects more immediately encouraging. At Lexington he began to exchange calico and blankets for lumber and labor, and by the last of July, 1784, the building of his "mansion" was well under way.[9] It was a place of size, although not so pretentious as the one that he erected at Frankfort, occupied for a while, and then sold to Andrew Holmes.[10] Returning to Lexington, he lived there for several years, offering frontier hospitality to those who might come his way. His house there had a hall large enough for brother politicians to gather in, rooms numerous enough for the privacy of his family as well as for secret interviews with friends.

It is true that some Kentuckians openly shunned him—Humphrey Marshall, for example, that bitter, combative young lawyer whom Wilkinson had publicly snubbed, and, perhaps, privately blackballed

[6] To Shiell, in *Ibid.*, 262.
[7] To Hutchinson, June 20, 1785, in *Pa. Mag. of Hist. and Biog.*, Apr., 1888, pp. 56–61.
[8] To Miró, May 24, 1790, A.G.I., Seville, *Papeles de Cuba*, leg. 2374.
[9] To Shiell, July 20, 1784, in *Ky. State Hist. Society Register*, XXIV, 262, and Innes Papers (Library of Congress), Vol. XXIII, *passim*.
[10] Hay, "Letters of Mrs. Ann Biddle Wilkinson from Kentucky," in *Pa. Mag. of Hist. and Biog.*, LVI, 35–36.

for membership in the Political Club, a local organization of considerable importance. It included a number of Wilkinson's friends, chief of whom was Harry Innes. He had come to Kentucky in 1785, when thirty-three years of age, and quickly identified himself with the movement for statehood and better defense against the Indians. In spite of opposing the ratification of the Constitution, he was appointed Judge of the United States District Court of Kentucky in 1789, an office that he held until his death in 1815. He handled most of Wilkinson's legal business, proving himself a genial friend as well as a reasonably able advocate. Partly because of this close connection with his client, Innes was finally charged with a dishonorable connection with Spain, but he proved able to clear himself. The charges were prompted by those who in 1806 and 1807 had brought Benjamin Sebastian to book because he had been receiving a Spanish pension. Without evincing any marked talent, Sebastian tried to be preacher, lawyer, judge, and merchant at one time or another. He met with better success in wheedling money out of the Spaniards. On one occasion when Wilkinson feared for his life, he recommended him as his natural successor in hoodwinking the dons at New Orleans. John Brown, abler and stronger in character, had a less detailed knowledge of Wilkinson's schemes of intrigue. The two were of the same age, and worked harmoniously together in politics. Brown was one of Kentucky's first senators, and from the seat of government often informed Wilkinson of federal affairs. From Caleb Wallace, Samuel McDowell, and less important figures in the legal fraternity of the District, Wilkinson kept posted on local matters. Once in a while General Charles Scott of the militia coterie came to visit him, guzzling for a while and expatiating upon ways to defend the settlers. No matter who came and talked with Wilkinson at Lexington or Frankfort, all agreed that something must be done to relieve the unfortunate conditions that were spreading gloom throughout Kentucky.

Indians were then roaming through the forest and blue-grass meadows, killing cruelly those who had come across the mountains and built their cabins in fruitful valleys. Richmond, five hundred miles away, could not readily aid the scattered immigrants; and hence they had to depend on their own methods of protection, which were often illegal and frequently disturbing to the authorities in Virginia. As the Kentuckians became more numerous, they sensed their own strength and felt that they should no longer compose a mere district, but that they deserved to become a state of the Confederation—an idea that was publicly discussed in a meeting held at Danville during the last days of 1784. Since nothing decisive was done in this First Assembly, it was thought better to call another, which almost every one hoped would be endowed with full legal powers to act.[11]

During the early months of 1785 the menace from Indians was not alone in disturbing the thoughts of the people: a rumor circulated that Congress was planning to abandon for twenty-five years all claims to navigation of the Mississippi in return for commercial advantages that Spain offered the seaboard states. A treaty of this kind would close the most natural and profitable route of trade to those who lived along the "western waters." Now more than ever Kentuckians laid plans for autonomy. Wilkinson keenly shared their hopes, although not as one of the members of the Second Assembly, which was called to meet during May, 1785, for initiating the legal machinery for separation. Friends like Harry Innes and others, however, were present, and these doubtless gave expression to ideas like his own. Certainly the two addresses adopted revealed his thoughts: one was entitled "To the Honorable General Assembly of Virginia," and petitioned for separation; the other, "To the Inhabitants of the District of Kentucky," gave forceful reasons for requesting it. Both are reputed to have been written by Wilkinson, a belief that gains strength with time.[12]

If he was the author, they mark his first important contribution to the politics of the District. Soon another followed. In August, 1786, a Third Assembly was called; the Second did not have enough authority to carry through what it had begun. Wilkinson was a delegate from Fayette County; once more he made articulate the hopes of his followers; again the settlers of Kentucky were addressed, and again Virginia was petitioned. The case was clear for those who would see it. Soon the state legislature made reasonable terms for separation in what is known as the "First Enabling Act." Some were satisfied, but others grew restive because a Fourth Assembly became necessary before further action could be taken.[13]

[11] McElroy, *Kentucky in the Nation's History*, 117–118.
[12] *Ibid.*, 118–125; Littell, "Political Transactions in and Concerning Kentucky," in Filson Club Publications, No. 31, pp. 62–66.
[13] McElroy, *op. cit.*, 125–130.

Wilkinson led those who wanted to do quickly what in a legal way required considerable time. He harped on dangers from Indians and the need for immediate independence. This was a much more aggressive and artful program than that which was advanced by his opponent, Humphrey Marshall, who advocated leaving the whole matter with the Assembly.[14]

Wilkinson was a hardy campaigner and pressed his arguments with spirit. On one occasion he confessed to speaking three and a half hours and quickening all his friends with pleasure. He wrote and told about it with more than frank complacency:

"I pleased myself, &, what was more consequential, every Body else, except my dead opponents—these I with great facility turned into subjects of ridicule and derision. I have experienced a great change since I held a seat in the Pennsylvania Assembly. I find myself much more easy, prompt, & eloquent in a public debate, than I ever was in private conversation, under the greatest flow of spirits." [15]

Perhaps Wilkinson had improved, for no record exists that as a Pennsylvania lawmaker he had been able to anger the dead with his eloquence. Granted that his oratorical power was unique, this gift alone would not account for the winning of all his votes. Some of his critics have suggested more earthly reasons. He knew "the way to men's hearts, was *down their throats*. He lived freely and entertained liberally. If he paid for his fare it was well for those who furnished it; if he did not, it was still well for himself and those who feasted on it. He surrounded himself with the idle young men, of both town and country, who loved him dearly; because they loved his beef, his pudding, and his wine. They served to propagate his opinions, to blazon his fame, to promote his popularity, and to serve him in elections; objects of primary consideration with him." [16] Where places were unfavorable to him, these friends had a way of helping his cause. Wilkinson was not to be denied. He was elected to the Fourth Assembly, which did not meet as early as expected because so many of its members were absent on an expedition against the Indians.

When it finally convened in January, 1787, more than fear of the savages worried those gathered at Danville. Virginia had passed

---

[14] To Hutchinson, Aug. 16, 1786, in *Pa. Mag. of Hist. and Biog.*, XII, 64.
[15] Marshall, *op. cit.*, II, 243.
[16] Marshall, *op. cit.*, I, 244-245.

the "Second Enabling Act" postponing separation until January, 1789. Hence Kentuckians had so far accomplished nothing, could hope for nothing until two years had passed. Divested of their authority, they angrily returned to their homes, although not without first unanimously passing a resolution to abide by the act. Neither Wilkinson nor other members were ready to go beyond the provisions of law.[17]

Meanwhile word had come that Jay's treaty with Spain had been secretly approved. John Brown, Benjamin Sebastian, Harry Innes, and others were bitter in denunciation and recommended that delegates assemble again at Danville. They did so in May, 1787, only to adjourn quickly because they learned that this disturbing story about the Mississippi was untrue. Nevertheless, they clearly saw that little help could be expected from a federal government which was daily becoming more contemptible in the eyes of those who knew it best, and that their own state of Virginia was so limited in its powers and so concerned with its own interests that they must depend upon their own efforts to secure protection, establish law and order, and gain a natural outlet to the sea for their growing commerce and trade. There appeared to be a very natural remedy: Kentucky should become independent and make her own terms with those whom she could. However inviting this plan, it did not have enough supporters to obtain immediate and controlling action;[18] instead, a Fifth Assembly was called to meet in September. Wilkinson became a candidate and was duly elected, but never appeared to claim his seat.

The newly elected assemblyman had gone on a more distant mission involving both business and politics. If the governments of Virginia and the Confederation could do nothing for two years, maybe more, Spain, with all her procrastination, offered a better field of effort. At least friendly overtures from her might arouse such fears in the States that they would not suffer the district's alienation without trying to meet its legitimate demands.

In 1784 Spain had closed the Mississippi to Americans.[19] As a result, settlers in the West could no longer profitably dispose of their tobacco, hams, skins, and flour at New Orleans and return home overland with bulging pockets, or else travel by sea with their coveted pieces of eight to Philadelphia where they might buy dry goods,

[17] Bodley, "Introduction" to Filson Club Publications, No. 31, p. xii.
[18] McElroy, *op. cit.*, 134.
[19] Whitaker, *The Spanish-American Frontier, 1783–1795*, 69–74.

hardware, fine liquors, and firearms for sale along the Ohio. If these articles were purchased, they had to be carried across the Alleghenies, to Pittsburgh, at a freight rate of about seven cents a pound, then loaded on flatboats for Louisville or some other frontier settlement.[20] For entrepreneurs this business was heavily fringed with profit; for the pioneers it helped to overcome a dearth of hard money and an uncomfortable lack of manufactured things.

Wilkinson was not slow to understand the possibilities of this three-cornered trade; but he realized that its success lay only in the acquiescence of the Spaniards. Hence, in order to learn more through personal reconnaissance, he approached the governor of Virginia and also the Spanish minister to the United States for passports down the Mississippi.[21] Failing in both cases, he then tried to win the favor of Francisco Cruzat, commandant of the fort at St. Louis, by informing him of how a Spanish merchant at Vincennes might obtain satisfaction for goods that had been seized by certain freebooters under George Rogers Clark. At the same time he told of a meditated attack on Natchez under the auspices of a certain Colonel Green.[22] Such advice and warning were to have their price. By the middle of May, Wilkinson was writing to ask Cruzat for a passport, while he was even then at the mouth of the Ohio. He was reasonably sure that if he went farther he would not be impeded.[23] Nor was he disappointed. At Fort Panmure, Natchez, he was welcomed. When he left, a letter went forward to Esteban Miró, the Spanish governor at New Orleans, stating that a United States brigadier-general was on his way thither with interesting news and a bargeful of merchandise for disposal.[24] The gift of a pair of blooded horses to one in authority at Natchez may have given zest to hospitality and stimulus to friendly words of introduction.[25] At each opportunity Wilkinson intrenched himself in good will, pushing on from point to point in full belief that he could sweep aside any barriers that might be raised by Spanish machinations.

[20] From 1797 to 1801, the freight rate on government supplies from Philadelphia to Pittsburgh was six to seven cents a pound. Possibly before then it was somewhat higher. *Expenditures for the Military and Naval Establishment by the Quarter-Master and Navy Agents, 1797–1801. Passim.*
[21] Whitaker, "James Wilkinson's First Descent to New Orleans in 1787," in *Hispanic American Historical Review*, VIII, 85.
[22] *Ibid*, 91–93.
[23] *Ibid.*, 86.
[24] *Ibid.*, 94–96.
[25] *Appleton's Cyclopaedia of American Biography*, VI, 511.

Confident of success, he came to New Orleans for the first time on July 2, 1787.[26] The city then numbered 5,388 inhabitants, while 37,243 were scattered through Louisiana and West Florida. Within New Orleans flourished a mixture of races. The French were the first Europeans. Then came the Spaniards, who had held the reins of government since 1769.[27] A few Englishmen were there for business reasons. Negro slaves, already numerous, were destined to increase rapidly. Sometimes Indians came and went on peaceful missions of trade, for fears of them had long since been removed.

The lineaments of this assorted population, though decidedly French, were not cut with a cameo's distinctness. In general, however, it was as unmistakably French as the swelling hills that rise out of the morning mist in the valley of the Rhone. Everywhere were courtly ways and the old love for household gods. French of high degree set the pattern for humbler folk. Neither the crassness of the frontier nor the deviltry of their enemies could turn them from their masses or detach them from their allegiance to the ways of the Capetians. They filled their interludes of leisure with dancing, high gaming, and tranquil drinking, and from the fish, fowl, and vegetables of the neighborhood they evolved a delectable cuisine.

Many a flatboater loosened his belt as he lingered over gumbo, calas, and vintages from across the sea. His eyes might rest enchantedly upon powdered Frenchwomen, sweeping by in their intriguing finery; or if not, on some of those "ladies of joy" who, denied their silks and plumes by Miró's decree, still made merry at quadroon balls.[28] Then perhaps, he would ruefully think of his horny-handed spouse and her homespun gown. If he became sluggish in the sale of his goods and cared less and less that the water receded from the willows where his flatboat lay tied, there were no antidotes in his creed for sins such as his. For him no requiem would be chanted, for him no prayers would be offered by faithful priests in far-off cathedral places; yet all too often he adopted the Frenchman's vices with the vigor and enthusiasm of a pioneer.

In New Orleans, Wilkinson came into contact with a people whose language he did not understand, whose religion he never highly regarded. But with his gifts of friendliness, contagious confidence, and apparent sincerity he was soon on easy terms with the Spanish officials,

---

[26] Miró to Valdez, Sept. 25, 1787, A.G.I., *Estado,* leg. 16.
[27] Fortier, *History of Louisiana,* II, 119.
[28] Gayarré, *Spanish Domination,* 179.

especially Esteban Rodríguez Miró who had been appointed governor of Louisiana after helping the Spaniards wrest the Floridas from the British during the American Revolution. Miró was thirteen years older than Wilkinson, had married a sprightly Creole, and entertained with easy hospitality. He spoke French, knew a little English, and was well acquainted with the country and people over which he ruled. Though whole-heartedly loyal to the King, he was wisely generous to the people of Louisiana and the neighboring Indians and Americans. Knowing the deep wounds on the hearts of some of his subjects, he hoped that time and considerate officials would heal them, that even the execution of prominent Frenchmen for alleged conspiracy by his predecessor O'Reilly would be forgotten. Never especially aggressive, and without marked independence, he was still able to rule Louisiana with comparative success for nine precarious years prior to January 1, 1792.[29] Eager to supplement his inadequate salary of four thousand dollars a year, he soon lent ears to Wilkinson's tales of easy wealth, believing him highly agreeable, refreshing, well educated, and possessed of uncommon talent.

Besides his own personal gain, Miró may have calculated that friendly relations with Wilkinson served the best interests of the Spanish government. Louisiana and the Floridas were regarded as barriers for other possessions in America, and both of them had to be maintained against the raids of irresponsible Indians and the increasing encroachment of lawless Americans. The administration of these two provinces was costly, the Spanish government usually incurring an annual deficit of half a million dollars. There were few or no Spanish immigrants in either; Spain could not supply the settlers already there with the kind of articles they wanted, and the things that they produced—furs, lumber, tobacco, and rice—had no continuing market in the mother country. The colonial government was based on the theory of extreme centralization. Each town was controlled by an army officer who was often guilty of petty graft and exasperating tyranny. This condition was frequently made worse by his appointments being made on some other basis than genuine fitness for the positions. Though not of outstanding ability, Miró united in his person both civil and military authority. All of his subordinates used him as a channel of communication on important matters of imperial concern; in a similar way he forwarded his own

---

[29] For data on Miró, see *Dictionary of American Biography*, XIII, 35.

requests and recommendations through his superior, the captain-general of Cuba, to one of the Crown's ministers on colonial affairs.[30] Answers were long in arriving, and sometimes the conditions that they were designed to remedy had already passed. In the eyes of the turbulent and unconventional Americans living along the borders of Louisiana, the Spaniards were procrastinating, evasive, bigoted, tyrannical, and usually dishonest.

The backwoods children of "Ol' Man River" had many grievances against them. Especially were they incensed that "His Most Catholic" Majesty had cut them off from the sea and that their Atlantic kinsmen were callous to this strangling of western trade. The coonskins and wool-hats of Kentucky and Tennessee looked upon the uninterrupted navigation of the Mississippi as their natural right; they also visioned New Orleans as a prize that was priceless and easy to obtain. To the Spaniards they were the incarnation of Goths and Vandals.

Hence, as Wilkinson shuttled back and forth between his boats and the government house, he scattered veiled hints as to what American upcountry men might do in case they were not prudently handled.[31] It would not be good policy to offend their leader; better, perhaps, to give him a hospitable reception and allow him to dispose of his cargo. Nor was fear the only basis for appeal: New Orleans and the Spaniards needed many products from the interior. And Wilkinson convincingly outlined plans for advancing Spanish interests in Kentucky; the details were given in an essay of about seventy-five hundred words, commonly known as the "First Memorial."

It was presumably a true picture of conditions in Kentucky; in reality it was purposely colored to win the Spaniards' fancy. It stressed the indifference of eastern states to the welfare of western settlements, and the consequent discontent that had been created. Forces were making for a western Confederation; Congress would not, or could not, put them down. To promote disunion and ultimate alignment with the Crown, he advised Spain to retain control of the navigation of the Mississippi and grant the privilege of downriver trade to only a distinguished few. These favored sons of her adoption would in return convert others to her allegiance. Then, if western settlers were not completely detached, at least the number of them

---

[30] Whitaker, *The Spanish-American Frontier*, 7–23.
[31] M. de Villars to General and Intendant of Santo Domingo, Sept. 26, 1787, in Whitaker, "James Wilkinson's First Descent to New Orleans in 1787," *Hispanic American Historical Review*, VIII, 97.

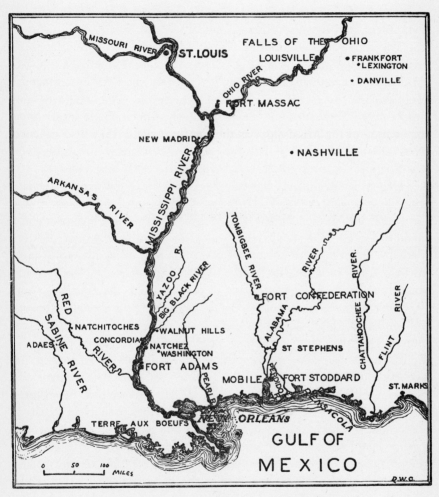

Map of New Orleans and the lower Mississippi.

loyal to Spain would be sensibly increased. In time a barrier would be raised against American aggression. By inference Wilkinson would be the Spanish agent in Kentucky. But let Spain beware; she might incense these western settlers until they united with the British in the Northwest to secure by force what could not be gained by friendly methods.[32]

Here was an apparition that caused the Spaniards to quake. Louisiana was loyal but defenseless. Therefore when Wilkinson asked to ship, duty-free, to New Orleans fifty to sixty thousand dollars' worth of Kentucky produce, he obtained consent. Fear and eagerness for profit induced this favorable decision. Miró was to become a silent, though deeply interested, party in the business of buying tobacco in Kentucky at two dollars and selling it at nine dollars per hundredweight at the King's warehouses in New Orleans.[33]

Wilkinson not only delighted the Spaniards with a chance of profit, he gratified their weakness for empty forms. He wrote out and signed what has been commonly considered as an oath of allegiance to the King of Spain. Almost as a matter of routine those who came down the Mississippi with merchandise were accustomed to doing so in order to please the Spaniards whose favors they sought.[34] Wilkinson, like others, went through this meaningless gesture. Unlike them, he wrote out a form of his own in which he gave reasons for his changing allegiance; but, schemer that he was, he never once directly avowed that he had abandoned his own country and sworn fealty to Spain. Nevertheless, the equivocally worded document passed muster with the Spaniards and for over a century was kept secret from Americans. As to his other political ruminations, the "liberal and gentlemanly" Miró was urged to bury them in "eternal oblivion." [35]

But at the same time the Spanish governor was enjoined to keep his memory keen concerning certain disreputables who might come down the river while Wilkinson was on his way home: "Patrick Joyes, an Irishman . . . a Fool and a Knave, and an abominable liar"; Maurice Nagle, another Irishman, "without principle or property"; William Dodge, a third Irishman, "an artful, subtle scoundrel, in desperate circumstances." However, the rogues were not all Irish-

[32] Filson Club Publication, No. 31, pp. cxix–cxxxvii.
[33] Wilkinson, *Memoirs*, Vol. II, Appendix, Deposition VI; Clark, *Proofs*, Appendix, Note 1; Whitaker, *The Mississippi Question*, 33.
[34] Wilkinson to Innes (no date), in Verhoeff, *The Kentucky River Navigation* (Filson Club Publications, No. 28), 224.
[35] For declaration, see Filson Club Publications, No. 31, pp. cxxvii–cxxxix.

men, for the Tardiveaus were always either drunk or deceiving themselves. Brodhead was "as unprincipled a Scoundrel as ever went unhung," and a bastard in the bargain.[36]

With this fling at his enemies, Wilkinson was ready to leave New Orleans and begin the detailed work of promoting his own interests at the Spaniard's expense. In the light of his subsequent activities, he must have hoped that Spain would keep the Mississippi closed while she left him a monopoly of trade in payment for his pretended efforts at promoting a conspiracy that he hoped, and must have soon realized, would never be consummated. His was an artful program, altogether unhampered by any ethical idea.

Miró could not have been entirely duped by political forecasts that had their origin in greed. He, too, had an ulterior motive. Wilkinson might prove to be of distinct value as an informer from Kentucky and as a vigorous promoter of desirable immigration into Spanish territory. The governor, besides, may have had a vision of Louisiana revived and strengthened with the consequent growth of his own political reputation and personal fortune. Whatever each saw in the other, it was enough to call forth mutual protestations of friendship when Wilkinson left New Orleans on the 16th of September, 1787.[37]

By this time Wilkinson had created the impression that he was eager to induce the people of Kentucky to seek the benefits of Spanish rule. After repeated assurances of his great affection for Miró and deep admiration for the "personal charms" of the governor's consort, Wilkinson took ship; and by the 20th of September had reached Balize, where he was soon on friendly terms with the Spanish officer in command. Once in the Gulf the weather was rough and he suffered his usual seasickness. Off the coast of Cuba he transferred to a swifter vessel headed for North Carolina, arriving at Wilmington on the 4th of November. About three weeks later he was in Richmond, then perturbed by two bitterly hostile factions: one ardently desired the adoption of the new federal Constitution; the other, which Wilkinson immediately espoused, violently opposed it.[38] Governor Randolph thought that his animosity arose from a belief that Congress would surrender the Mississippi.[39] He did not know that Wilkinson had lately advocated this very measure when he had written from New

---

[36] To Don Andrés, Aug. 1, 1787, A.G.I., Seville, *Papeles de Cuba*, leg. 2373.
[37] To Miró, Sept. 16, 1787, A.G.I., Seville, *Papeles de Cuba*, leg. 2373.
[38] To Miró, Sept. 16, 20, 1787, Mar. 16, 1788, A.G.I., Seville, *Papeles de Cuba*.
[39] Bodley, "Introduction" to Filson Club Publications, No. 31, p. xliv.

Orleans to St. Clair, governor of the Northwest Territory, recommending the acceptance of the Gardoqui Treaty.[40] To hold to the same faith in Virginia meant political suicide; Wilkinson accordingly changed. He was aware also that his peculiar plans would flourish best while Kentucky was in ferment and no federal government existed strong enough to give protection and compel obedience. To most of the settlers along the Ohio, an active and adequate government connoted few or no benefits, only taxes and unwarranted curtailment of individual liberty. Therefore by inveighing against the Constitution he would simultaneously serve his purposes and win a following.

It was not alone his "Old Hobby" politics that had drawn Wilkinson to the Virginia capital; he had important personal business to transact. He was interested in lands along the Ohio. Friends could tell him how warrants for them might be advantageously obtained; he knew better than almost any one else what tracts were desirable for purchase. For past and future speculations in Kentucky he had to make reports and draw up agreements satisfactory to his associates.[41] Thus a month passed before he was ready to resume his journey. This delay prevented him from making a visit to Mount Vernon as he had expected; the best he could do was to express his regret and send Washington some Indian fabrics as a slight token of esteem. Unwilling to miss news from the Southwest, Washington sent a Colonel Fitzgerald to travel a part of the way with him. The weather was bad and the snow deep in the Alleghenies, and Wilkinson did not reach the Monongahela until January 12, 1788. Ice was breaking up in the Ohio about a hundred and twenty miles below Fort Pitt, and so he hastened thither to take a boat for Kentucky. After a narrow escape from drowning and constant suffering from bitter cold, he reached his "Mansion" on the 24th of February, 1788.[42]

Here Wilkinson, the far traveler, found happiness at his journey's end; for his was an attractive, affectionate family and one that he loved well. His wife, Ann Biddle, was dowered with Quaker charm and beauty. Her head was small but with fine-cut features and a wealth of dark brown hair; her eyes were large and met one's own in serene, level glances. There was something of determination in

---

[40] To St. Clair, July 4, 1787, *Northwest Territory Papers*, L.C.

[41] Clark, *Proofs*, Notes, 27, 28.

[42] To Miró, Mar. 16, 1788, A.G.I., Seville, *Papeles de Cuba*, leg. 2373; Christian, *James Wilkinson and Kentucky Separatism, 1784–1798*, 122–126.

her lips, thin and tightly closed, and much of grace in the movement of her slender figure. Not a child of the wilderness but of gentle lineage, she knew the sweet ways and quiet manners of good people. Without the strength, yet having the spirit, to withstand hardships, she had come from Philadelphia in 1784, bringing with her their two boys, John and James Biddle. John was then only three; James was a year or two younger; Joseph Biddle was to be born in 1785. Another child came four years later, but was destined to live only a short while.[43]

The care of these three youngsters bore heavily upon a mother so frail, especially since she tried to rear them not as backwoods children but like their Pennsylvania cousins. Even the essentials were difficult to secure for them. They were forever "treading out" their shoes, and replacements were hard to get, sometimes came in wrong sizes, or two of them for the same foot. And when they wore their clothes thin, cloth was dear and mending was not easy for her weary, weakened eyes. When the boys were ready to begin reading and writing, she engaged the best tutor available, although he was more of a simpleton than a scholar. Often her kindly father in Philadelphia, John Biddle, sent tea, coffee, and sugar—articles common enough along the Atlantic but scarce in Kentucky. And sometimes came things for which she so often longed—glistening china, lustrous garments, and gloves to cover her roughened hands.

She was one who would look her best in the presence of her hero. The confidence she had in him, many others shared. Even then Kentuckians were diverted with the pageantry of his success: four glistening horses drew his splendid coach, followed by a retinue of slaves. Underlings stood by and "chortled" at the rumors of his opulence. Truly he had done great things, this affable, open-faced, masterful man. In a few months he had accomplished what neither Virginia nor the federal government had been able to do in years. He had wheedled out of the Spanish government a sort of private trading concession that permitted him to navigate the Mississippi and granted him the privilege of selling tobacco and beeswax, apples and butter, and other interior products, all duty-free at New Orleans. He announced himself ready to buy tobacco at the current price of two dollars per hundredweight, perhaps higher.[44] The long desired millennium was arriving, and Wilkinson had fathered it!

[43] Hay, "Letters of Mrs. Ann Biddle Wilkinson from Kentucky," *Pa. Mag. of Hist. and Biog.*, LVI, 33–55, *passim*.
[44] McElroy, *Kentucky in the Nation's History*, 133; Wilkinson, *Memoirs*, II, 115–116.

Backwoodsmen saw in Wilkinson a person who accomplished things immediately helpful. They liked him because he worked at concrete things and rode straight to popular objectives. They were his friends because he mixed with them readily, spent freely, talked convincingly, and entertained lavishly. Here was a man favorably known by most of the leading people of his section. In 1788 none loomed larger on the Kentucky horizon than did this Wilkinson, who so successfully practiced the theories of Machiavelli.

Wilkinson lost no time; he took immediate steps to maintain his valuable connection with New Orleans. No sooner was he back in Kentucky than he sent Richard Thomas posthaste with letters to Innes. The judge read them with interest and sat up most of the night preparing papers that he and Thomas would take back at the crack of dawn. Arriving at Lexington, Innes immediately went into consultation with Wilkinson. Thomas and others were left in the hall to make the best of their own society, along with a bottle of spirits. Wilkinson's hospitality and the promise of a job kept Thomas about the place until nearly the 1st of March. Then he and two companions were sent on a trip to New Orleans as messengers for Wilkinson. In their canoe was loaded a trunk stuffed with papers that were to be delivered to certain Spaniards at Natchez and New Orleans. In case there was any danger that the papers might fall into improper hands, they were to be destroyed without delay.[45]

Such emissaries were something more than common report had them, heralds of Wilkinson's safe return who would explain the delay of promised tobacco shipments. Documents in a mud-spattered trunk, if all went well, were to bring Miró new visions of commercial gain and expanding empire.[46] Even as the governor read, the messengers stood waiting to plunge again into the wilderness. Several weeks later, in April, they were returning, carrying letters carefully wrapped in oilcloth and securely fastened to their waists. Ostensibly they were written by Daniel Clark, Sr.,[47] and perhaps some of them were. At least one was from Miró, regretting that no answer had yet come to the "First Memorial," but expressing delight at the good news that Wilkinson's letter had told and reciprocating the affection that it fulsomely expressed.[48]

About the middle of June, 1788, Major Isaac Dunn appeared in

[45] Deposition of Richard Thomas, Aug. 3, 1812, Innes Papers, Vol. XXII.
[46] To Miró, Mar. 16 (?), 1788, A.G.I., Seville, *Papeles de Cuba,* leg. 2373.
[47] Statement of Joshua Barbee, Innes Papers, Vol. XXII.
[48] Miró to Wilkinson, Apr. 11, 1788, A.G.I., Seville, *Papeles de Cuba,* leg. 2373.

New Orleans. He was one of Wilkinson's old-time Revolutionary friends and a sort of business associate. Within a few days he was writing back that others had been granted passports to bring tobacco down the river but they were to be charged a duty of 25 per cent and to be denied the use of the King's warehouse. This distinction, he added, constitutes our particular favor and "you cannot be at a loss to know where a participation of Profits is expected, & where it is due." [49]

Money was a sure means of holding Miró's attention and obtaining a continuance of trade dispensations. Wilkinson had other ways too. On May 15, he wrote that Virginia's jurisdiction over Kentucky would cease January 1, 1789; those to whom Miró's offer had been communicated, were filled with "keenest joy"; as soon as some form of government could be organized in Kentucky, agents doubtless would be appointed to treat of the "union in which we are engaged." From Congress he anticipated no trouble, for it lacked both money and power, and the new federal government, of course, would remain contemptible for years. Then he added, if Mr. Daniel Clark, Sr., would help in sending him merchandise, such trade would tie Kentucky to New Orleans rather than to cities across the Appalachians.[50] Miró thought well of the scheme, and advanced Wilkinson and Clark, Sr., $6,000 to help in their upriver shipments.[51] Beside this important favor, a certain D'Arges was forbidden to work as Spanish agent in Kentucky. Wilkinson was left with a free hand.[52]

But these turns of good fortune were counterbalanced by losses in tobacco. Much of it had arrived in bad condition: 15,000 pounds was an entire loss and 80,000 more was of poor quality. Only 118,000 pounds had been received and paid for. In addition, he was warned not to ship more than two hundred hogsheads, about 200,000 pounds, for the ensuing year, including all then on the way. The governor explained that he had already received more than the King allowed and that the Louisiana crop would more than supply his current needs.[53]

Apparently money accruing to Wilkinson was deposited with the

[49] Dunn to Wilkinson, June 15, 1788, Wilkinson Papers, Vol. I, Chicago Historical Soc.

[50] To Miró, May 15, 1788, Pontalba Papers, No. 10; extracts in Fortier, *A History of Louisiana*, II, 134–136.

[51] Miró to Wilkinson, Aug. 6, 1788, A.G.I., Seville, *Papeles de Cuba*, leg. 2373.

[52] Miró to Wilkinson, Apr. 11, 1788, *Ibid.*

[53] Miró to Wilkinson, Aug. 6, 1788, *Ibid.*

firm of Clark & Reese. By July they had credited him with $9,835.50. Thus he was able to return $3,000 that he had borrowed from them; Major Dunn received $3,389; several small bills were settled, and there still remained to be sold eight hogsheads of tobacco and an unknown quantity in bulk.[54] The major had not had so much hard money in his keeping for a long time. Disappointing as business was, it was improving. Those who had tasted the sweets of profit, now (August 7, 1788) were ready for a new commercial agreement, and so the principals—Daniel Clark, Sr., Wilkinson, and Isaac Dunn— organized a sort of trading company for the purpose of developing the Kentucky and New Orleans business. Clark, who had apparently invested the greater capital, was to have double the profits of the other two equal shareholders.[55]

With the help of a $6,000 loan from Miró, they were soon outfitting and stocking a bateau that bore the ironical name of *Speedwell*. It was designed for upriver trade, and involved an outlay of some $21,000. The crew were lazy and made slow progress against the current of "Ol' Man River." By the time they had reached the Ohio, winter had come, and before long the *Speedwell* was caught in the ice and sunk with its cargo of brass candlesticks, barrels of coffee, sugar, "rheams of paper," pieces of Irish linen, cases of fine wine and potent brandy.[56] Those concerned suffered not only immediate loss; they realized that they had failed in the larger undertaking of turning the western settlements from the Philadelphia market to that of New Orleans. If they had succeeded there might have been some chance that Louisiana and Kentucky would coalesce their interests; and Miró, the patron of the enterprise, might have beheld the ripening of his plans. From the failure it became evident that the frontiersmen along the Ohio would continue to obtain their religion, their medicines, their luxuries, and their hardware, as well as their government, from the same places as before.

Major Dunn did not accompany the *Speedwell*. He returned home via Philadelphia in order to purchase supplies for the Lexington store. Once in the East, he made a trip to Rhode Island to visit his family; and, while passing through New York, he fell in with Gardoqui, minister of Spain. Gardoqui seemed to be full of promises

---

[54] Clark, *Proofs*, Notes, 55.
[55] *Amer. State Papers, Miscel.*, II, 123–124.
[56] Clark, *Proofs*, Notes, 30, and Inventory of the *Speedwell*, A.G.I., Seville, *Papeles de Cuba*, leg. 2373.

and good humor. With easy nonchalance, he spoke of granting land and passports, and even belittled Miró's powers, while he waxed eloquent over his own beneficence.[57]

Soon Dunn was crossing the mountains to tell Wilkinson all that he had seen and heard. Speedily he had come, yet more speedily he was told to retrace his steps and to make use of the apparent generosity of Gardoqui. He was to get a grant of 600,000 acres on the Yazoo and the Mississippi for the joint ownership of himself, Wilkinson, Benjamin Sebastian, and John Brown.[58] Compliance on Gardoqui's part would of course frustrate Colonel George Morgan and his magnificent plans for colonizing in Spanish territory. Dunn failed to obtain pay for the information that he gave; and, on one pretext or another, the patent was refused, although Wilkinson declared that his time, his business, and his political character had been sacrificed for the mutual welfare of Kentucky and Spain.[59] Gardoqui did not even defray the cost of Dunn's trip East.[60] From this quarter all hopes of lands, gold, or Spanish favors quickly passed.

In another quarter they were stronger. Unlike Wayne, of a few years later, Miró seemed to value Wilkinson's "damned long letters," which were usually in cipher, filled with rumors, gossip, and political cogitations, sometimes documented even with newspaper clippings and extracts from friends' correspondence. Wilkinson had acquired some skill in propaganda; he knew how to ballyhoo himself into Kentucky prominence, and now he saw to it that the people of Louisiana learned of his success. Nor did he ever oppose the current of Miró's ambition; he was able to tell him tales pleasing but untrue, because of peculiar conditions in Kentucky.

During his absence in New Orleans the Fifth Assembly had met and decided unanimously for separation, adopting a petition for admission to the Union and securing appointment of John Brown as a delegate for delivering it to Congress. By the next summer Brown was writing to his friends that New England opposed their plan through fear of an increase in strength of the southern delegation. The same cause, he suspected, would operate in the future; certainly nothing could be done immediately—the new federal government had to become effective. Under the circumstances he advised Kentuckians

---

[57] To Miró, Feb. 14, 1789, in Gayarré, *Spanish Domination*, 240–247.
[58] Petition of Wilkinson and others to Gardoqui, Jan. 15, 1789, Gardoqui Papers.
[59] To Gardoqui, Jan. 1, 1789, in Gayarré, *Spanish Domination*, 247–248.
[60] To Miró (undated), A.G.I., Seville, *Papeles de Cuba*, leg. 2374.

to declare their independence. Dismayed with such disappointing news, the Sixth Assembly convened at Danville on July 28, 1788. It lasted for only a few days but paved the way for the Seventh, which expected to meet in November and hoped to achieve Kentucky's entrance into the Union, obtain unrestricted navigation of the Mississippi, and set up a constitutional government for the district.[61]

Playing upon Miró's ignorance of existing politics, Wilkinson solemnly assured him that he found all men of the first class in the district, save Colonels Marshall and Muter, decidedly in favor of separation from the United States and ultimate alliance with Spain. Then, with easy grace in lying, he added that Caleb Wallace, Harry Innes, and Benjamin Sebastian vigorously advocated a prompt separation from the American Union.[62] Miró was duped, and interpreted the liberal grant of powers to the Seventh Assembly as if they were designed to promote the rapprochement of Spain and Kentucky.

Until the Assembly met in the fall, Wilkinson was busy with his own affairs, turning tricks only now and then that might help in his intrigues with Spain. During October a certain Colonel John Connolly left Detroit, apparently bent on obtaining a favorable adjustment of old land claims in the neighborhood of the Falls of the Ohio. When he arrived at Louisville in November, Wilkinson "insinuated" himself into his confidence, and learned the real object of his journey. Connolly confessed being an agent of Lord Dorchester, who he declared would furnish pay, clothing, and equipment for 10,000 men if they would join with the British and seize Louisiana. Additional assistance would be given by a fleet based on Jamaica and operating against the Balize. For Kentuckians who would join in the enterprise honors were to be bestowed liberally. Any "Rank or Emolument" [63] Wilkinson might ask for himself was to be granted. Soon Miró's ears were filled with this harrowing tale. To allay the governor's fears, Wilkinson wrote that he had secretly set a reputed assassin upon Connolly and had beheld his headlong departure from Kentucky—only an armed escort had saved him from death. Wilkinson, as a civil magistrate, had furnished this protection, thereby gaining Connolly's gratitude and promise of information concerning Great Britain's future designs against Spain. Once back in Canada,

---

[61] McElroy, *Kentucky in the Nation's History*, 136–138.
[62] Bodley, "Introduction" to Filson Club Publications, No. 31, p. lii.
[63] To Miró, Feb. 12, 1789, A.G.I., Seville, *Papeles de Cuba*, leg. 2373.

Connolly supplied data for an estimate of conditions in the Northwest Territory. Lord Dorchester came to sensible conclusions; he did not yield to advice contained in a paper that was entitled "Desultory Reflections by a Gentleman of Kentucky." It suggested that Great Britain "should employ the interval [of unrest along the Ohio] in forming confidential connections with men of enterprise, capacity and popular influence resident in the Western Waters." [64] The "Reflections" seem to have been Wilkinson's composition. Unlike his "First Memorial" written for Miró, they resulted in no tangible returns. Even so, Wilkinson could feel elated because of his last bit of scheming; he had improved simultaneously his standing with Spain, the United States, Great Britain, and Kentucky, and at a time when their interests in many respects were diametrically opposed. He had set himself up as a clearing house where national secrets would be sold for money or perquisites. If he had none to suit the purchaser, his fluent pen would quickly supply the deficiency. In his program of deception his casual disregard for truth and his singular ability to detect the weaknesses of others were invaluable aids.

Equally skillful tactics were employed in local politics. Although the Court party was not popular with the people of Kentucky, Wilkinson accepted its backing and was the only one of its candidates who was elected to the Seventh Assembly from Fayette County. His success arose partly from personal popularity, dubious methods, and reiterated promises to comply with the wishes of his constituents. When the Assembly convened on November 3, 1788, Wilkinson was its dominant figure, emphatically telling its members that United States treaties and Spain's objections thwarted their navigation of the Mississippi, and that the government could not reasonably be expected to aid them. "The way to obtain it," said he, "has been indicated in the former convention, and every gentleman present will connect it with a declaration of independence, the formation of a constitution and the organization of a new State, which may safely be left to find its own way into the Union on terms advantageous to its own interests." As he concluded, Wilkinson—looking at John Brown, who had lately talked with Gardoqui—remarked that there was one among them who had important information. Brown, how-

---

[64] Enclosure in a letter of Dorchester to Sidney, Apr. 11, 1789, Canadian Archives, Colonial Office Records, Series A, XLI, 283, printed in Brown, *The Political Beginnings of Kentucky*, 245–246.

ever, would make no disclosures, merely stating that if they were unanimous, everything was in their reach.

Thus runs the story of the assembly's proceedings according to Humphrey Marshall, who was a deeply prejudiced person blatantly hostile to Wilkinson. Therefore it cannot be entirely accepted. Although Wilkinson no doubt wanted Miró to believe that he was advocating the program of which he was accused, he knew that its realization would be opposed to his own personal interests and against the views of many of his constituents. He clearly saw that few or no rewards would come to him for hatching conspiracy in Kentucky; nevertheless he left no stone unturned to make Miró believe this was the prime aim of his efforts. With this deception in mind, he asked permission to read an essay that he had composed concerning the Mississippi. In twenty or more pages he described Kentucky's resources, now valueless because the inhabitants had no easy water route to the open sea. He reminded his hearers that they had been on the point of seceding when Congress once threatened to abandon for twenty-five years their natural claims to navigate the Mississippi. If Spain would not yield now to their contention, England was ready to help them. Those present were stirred with his words and gave him a vote of thanks for the interest that he had evinced for the "Western Country," but still they hesitated to take decisive action. They even tabled John Brown's motion, which declared that the people of Kentucky wished to separate from Virginia and become "an independent member of the federal union." A resolution calling for popular instructions and another assembly proved more acceptable. Wilkinson fathered it and was happy to see it unanimously passed.[65] The state of unrest along the Ohio would continue—a condition that he might employ to very personal advantage.

Once the assembly had adjourned, Wilkinson told of its proceedings in a way that suited his purpose. Both Miró and the Kentuckians thought his essay was identical with the "First Memorial" that he had written in New Orleans during the hot summer days of 1787. Hence Miró concluded that Kentuckians were throughly acquainted with his henchman's plan of separation and were eager for it. This misconception was intensified when he learned that Brown's motion had failed and that of Wilkinson had been passed without a dissenting vote. To deceive more, Wilkinson wrote Miró on Febru-

[65] For the proceedings of the Seventh Assembly, see McElroy, *op. cit.*, 138–141.

ary 12, 1789, stating that the Seventh Assembly had agreed unanimously that, should Virginia refuse separation to Kentucky or should Congress fail to support free navigation of the Mississippi, then the people would be invited to set up their own government. This was a whole-cloth prevarication, more than welcome in a Spanish market. Finally, the governor was urged to close the Mississippi, although Wilkinson had spent most of his energy in Kentucky demanding that it be opened! [66]

As a political chameleon Wilkinson was peerless. When circumstances demanded, he changed the color of his faith; in Kentucky he was one person; in New Orleans, another. Whether here or there, he appeared to be in entire accord with those whom he would influence, employing their weaknesses to serve his ends. "Some men," he said, "are sordid, some vain, some ambitious. To detect the predominant passion, to lay hold and to make the most of it is the most profound secret of political science." It was this kind of creed that he practiced when he wrote Miró in 1789 that he had become a "good Spaniard." [67] No matter, Miró diplomatically accepted him as such, and Wilkinson reciprocated by addressing him as "the friend of my bosom."

During the winter of 1788–1789 Wilkinson could ponder how cleverly he had deceived the Spaniards for the benefit of himself and his countrymen. Kentuckians were not concerned with his methods while they enjoyed prosperity at the expense of their enemies. Only a year had passed since he had spread tales of selling tobacco in the New Orleans market while he himself had furnished the means of sending it thither. When he had embarked in politics, Kentuckians had listened to him eagerly and taken his directions as obedient children. He was a newly found favorite, although he had not yet obtained the philosopher's stone for turning their possessions into gold. What if a few boats had gone down the river under his auspices, why worry if their cargoes had failed to bring expected returns? If some began to lose faith in his vision of opulence, many others still came and sat beside his open fire and helped consume his brandy and Madeira when nights were long and cold.

When their visits were returned, Wilkinson, showed no misgivings, then or thereafter; on the contrary, there was something of a swagger and a strut to match the right royal waistcoat and the pair of heavy

[66] To Miró, Feb. 12, 1789, in Gayarré, *Spanish Domination*, 223–240.
[67] To Gardoqui, Jan. 1, 1789, in Fortier, *A History of Louisiana*, II, 141–142.

silver buckles that Miró had sent him as a "regalos." [68] Young and resourceful, Wilkinson was a man who could play the game with Spanish diplomacy. He had discovered gold in the hills; he would work his claim with borrowed pick and pan. He would go to New Orleans when the ice began to disappear from the river; spring, for him, would be a propitious season.

There were good reasons for the trip. It was in keeping with Ann's character to urge her husband to go. She and the children could now be left behind in relative safety. Her loyalty would recall his successes, while she knew that misfortune had come when he had been forced to turn his business over to agents. His family no longer prevented his going.

Politics was at a standstill; nothing decisive could be expected in the district until the new federal government became operative with respectable powers. After the Articles of Confederation had been discarded, Virginia realized that Kentucky could not meet the conditions that she had previously imposed; hence the "Third Enabling Act" was passed on December 29, 1788. Two of its provisions caused great discussion: one called on the prospective state to share Virginia's existing debt; the other abridged sovereignty until certain surveys and land titles were completed. So bitter was the opposition, especially to the second of these provisions, that when the Eighth Assembly met on July 20, 1789, it vigorously protested in the hope of a more generous act. [69] Until Virginia could pass the liberal Fourth Enabling Act six months later, nothing much could be done. Wilkinson had few opportunities at the time to promote his intrigue against Spain; in fact, a display of too much zeal might hurt his reputation.

On the other hand, his presence was needed to revitalize Miró's interest in their mutual plans so that grants, loans, and pensions would be forthcoming. It behooved him to bewitch Miró and the Spaniards again with the icon of conspiracy, especially when Kentucky was farther from Spain than ever before. In his delusion, Miró was hoping for Wilkinson to come as a public character some time in April, 1789. [70] If he thought that Kentucky would then be in a mood to listen to overtures from Spain, he was in abysmal ignorance concern-

[68] For these articles see Miró to Wilkinson, Aug. 6, 1788, A.G.I., Seville, *Papeles de Cuba*, leg. 2373.
[69] McElroy, *op. cit.*, 142–144.
[70] Gayarré, *op. cit.*, 212.

ing the state of public opinion along the Ohio. If Wilkinson could dupe him into believing matters of this kind, he might deceive him in other things of consequence. It was the psychological time to act. Any day an answer might come to the "First Memorial"; he had better be in New Orleans to soften its rigor or to extend the range of its benefits.

Besides, it was high time to thwart the plans of a certain Colonel George Morgan who was suing for Spanish favor. He cherished an entrancing plan of founding a Utopia on 2,000,000 Spanish acres that lay in the southeast corner of what later was to become the state of Missouri. The capital city, New Madrid, was to be the metropolis of the West; it was to be located beside a lake of purest water and have magnificent avenues shaded by uncut forest trees. In so lovely an environment there were to be churches for the pious and schools for the enterprising; the poor were to be no longer poor, but to have land for the asking. The government would be of the people's making, and prosperity was not to be clouded with taxes. The West was agog about this hoped-for paradise, and many were already traveling thither as quickly as they could.[71]

Wilkinson, too, felt the urge to travel. He was restless to be on the way to New Orleans. He wanted to go, not as a catchpenny merchant, but as a wholesaler on a scale such as the Southwest had never seen. He advertised right and left for the Kentucky produce desired for his cargoes. Through the payment of a few dollars and hearty promises of more, his purchases mounted. Goods that had lain about in warehouses for years were bought at fancy prices. Tobacco, flour, and land values rose; through his aid, prosperity was flowing into Kentucky through a Spanish channel.[72] For the transportation of his purchases, twenty-five boats were built, some of which were armed with cannon. With their protection, along with that of one hundred and fifty virile spirits who composed the crews, the fear of Indian attack was removed.[73] Even the Spaniards might not be so stony-hearted with all these stout oak boats tied up along the river bank and scores of backwoodsmen clambering out of them. To avoid civil tumult, Miró might be induced to propitiate their wily leader with extensive purchases. Surely he would not anger the Goths

[71] Saville, "The Founding of New Madrid," in *Mississippi Valley Hist. Rev.*, June, 1932, pp. 30–56.
[72] James, *The Life of George Rogers Clark*, 396–397.
[73] *American Museum*, V, 209.

knocking at the gates of his city, now just beginning to rise from the ashes of the great fire of 1788.

During June, 1789, the spectacular Wilkinson set foot in New Orleans again. Miró was friendly; the two lived together in the same house and joined in the courtesies of friendship.[74] Although Miró appeared to believe distorted tales about Kentucky politics, Wilkinson was not confident of the future. The Court had sent a disquieting answer to his "First Memorial" of 1787. By its order, he was no longer to enjoy a monopoly of trade on the Mississippi; the waters of the river were to be opened to all those who paid a duty of 15, in some cases 6, per cent. Nor was he to be the sole arbiter of immigration. Those who gave evidence of becoming bona-fide settlers were to be granted lands, commercial privileges, and religious toleration. In short, Spain hoped to cajole her neighbors into friendship by a plan directly opposed to that of Wilkinson's apparent program. She would pay no money for hatching revolution in Kentucky. Whatever was to be done in the future, must be accomplished by methods that would not compromise the Crown.[75]

Apparently Spain was inclined to favor the plans of Colonel George Morgan, who had recently visited the city to obtain the backing of Miró for the promises of Gardoqui. With his apparent honesty and liberal plans of colonization, he had allayed the distrust of the governor.[76] But he was wholly unable to overcome the bitter opposition of Wilkinson, who had referred to him as a speculator twice bankrupt and governed by the "vilest self-interest." Statements like these were not as true as the prophecy that he offered: that Morgan's colonists would retain their prejudices, unite with their countrymen across the river, and later embroil Spain with the United States.[77] And the Spaniards accepted the prognosis without waiting fifty years for the Texas Revolution and the Mexican War to verify it. For these and other less apparent reasons, the Morgan grant was ultimately canceled.

Wilkinson met with better success; his tobacco business was in the heyday of prosperity. During the early part of 1789 he had received large sums of money for his shipments to New Orleans. Up to the 1st of May his gross sales amounted to $16,441. After getting

---

[74] To Gayoso, July, 1789, A.G.I., Seville, *Papeles de Cuba,* leg. 2373.
[75] Whitaker, *The Spanish Frontier, 1783–1795,* 101–102.
[76] Saville, *loc. cit.*
[77] To Miró, Feb. 12, 1789. A.G.I., Seville, *Papeles de Cuba,* leg. 2373.

the net balance of $6,251, Captain A. B. Dunn took it to the East and turned it over to his brother, who was then Wilkinson's partner.[78] Again Spanish dollars enriched the circuit of trade between Louisville, New Orleans, and Philadelphia, and caused it to burgeon with profit.

After Dunn left, Clark and Rees found little to do for their merchant friends. Not until Wilkinson arrived in June did business pick up. By August 29 his credits aggregated $21,632; by September his net balance had dwindled to $48, so many disbursements had been made.[79] On September 18 the connection with Clark and Rees was dissolved. Wilkinson acknowledged a debt to them for their share in the *Speedwell* speculation, as well as another sum of £318, Virginia currency, due the firm of Craig & Johnson.[80] The first of these obligations he planned to liquidate by early shipments of tobacco, while the second was left apparently to time and circumstance for adjustment.[81]

Thus Wilkinson dropped his former business associates, except Miró, and trimmed his sails to changing wind. After a disappointing reply to his "First Memorial" had come, he industriously prepared another. Inasmuch as easy immigration to Louisiana had been decreed, Wilkinson now declared himself an ardent advocate for its prosecution; in place of stirring up revolution in Kentucky, he urged that "secret and indirect" agencies should be set in motion for its separation and its independence from the United States. He would build up Kentucky as a barrier state, bind her to Spain by ties of mutual advantage. Both Great Britain and the United States should be thwarted in their efforts to gain her friendship and alliance. New Orleans should be made a free port. There the West would then dispose of its products, making the city renowned for prosperity. If Spain did not adopt a plan like this, she might expect the overrunning of Louisiana and the ultimate loss of Mexico. Whatever the program, Wilkinson would need money, about seven thousand dollars, to sustain his efforts in propagating the ideas of Spain. If the sum were not forthcoming, Miró could expect no help from him except "prayers and good wishes." Mindful perhaps of the Crown's late decision to open the waters of the Mississippi to any one on terms of 15 and 6 per cent, he requested as a personal favor that the Spanish

---

[78] Clark, *Proofs*, 33, and Notes, 28.
[79] Ibid., *Notes*, 32.
[80] *Amer. State Papers, Miscel.*, II, 123–124.
[81] Clark, *Proofs*, 33–37, and Notes, 30 and 31.

government buy, duty-free, two hundred more hogsheads of his tobacco at eight dollars per hundredweight.[82]

Wilkinson knew well how to win favor; on critical occasions with Miró he was never too easily compliant nor too hardy in opposition. He wanted to get the maximum benefit from the conditions Miró and the Court had imposed.

To facilitate the work of "secret and indirect agencies," Wilkinson submitted to the governor a descriptive list of twenty-two persons whom he recommended for a yearly pension from Spain. The rate of payment was to be in proportion to the importance of the individual concerned, ranging from six hundred to a thousand dollars; the whole amount involved, $18,700. Among those to be bribed in such a fashion were John Brown, "member of Congress," Isaac Shelby, "man of fortune and great influence," and Caleb Wallace, "a judge." Even the "Devil's own," Humphrey Marshall, "a villain without principles, very artful, and could be troublesome," was to get six hundred dollars for helping along the cause of Spain.[83] Being called a "villain" would hardly have bothered Marshall, but his pride must have been blasted had he known that his arch enemy classified him as only important enough for the minimum bounty.

To have one's name on the list was no index of dishonesty, only an indication that Wilkinson considered the person worth mentioning to Miró. Wilkinson planned to be the chief beneficiary, for he was to be the dispenser of Spanish dollars, while he would leave Miró with an account increasingly difficult to explain. Although there were plenty of reasons to deter Miró from making so extensive a raid on the royal treasury, he did give Wilkinson $7,000 with the understanding that should the Spanish Court fail to allow it as pension money the amount would be repaid.[84] As both men had expected, no objection was made to this advance payment.

Although the loan itself was enough to repay Wilkinson for his trip to New Orleans, he had accomplished much more during those dazzling summer days in the South. He had sold much of his tobacco at eight dollars per hundredweight and had induced the governor to continue the rôle of patron saint to the wholesale grocery business. He had tested Miró's warming friendship by presenting a "Second

[82] Shepherd, "Papers Bearing on Wilkinson's Relation with Spain (1787–1789)," in *Amer. Hist. Rev.,* IX, 748–766.
[83] *Ibid.*
[84] Whitaker, *The Spanish-American Frontier, 1783–1795,* 117.

Memorial" and accompanying it with plenty of verbal advice. With Miró an apparent convert to his schemes, Wilkinson believed that the psychological moment for his departure had come.

About September 18 he left New Orleans, in spite of incomplete settlements for his yearly shipments. Urgent reasons existed for hastening back to Kentucky if he expected to send down many hogsheads of tobacco or impress Miró with his work in the field of intrigue. The overland route home, although several weeks quicker than that by the Atlantic Ocean and the Ohio River, was menaced by Indians and full of hardship.[85] He chose the former in spite of fears and misgivings. Sickness overtook him on the way, and he stopped a few days with his friend Gayoso de Lemos, Spanish governor of Natchez. There his visit was marked by an improvement in health and the acquisition of a cane that he openly purloined from his host.[86]

Wilkinson's traveling companion was Philip Nolan, a typical goodman Friday, who had come out of nowhere to Wilkinson and the West, and who passed a dozen or more years in bright adventure before losing his life and his ears to the Spaniards in 1801.[87] For his strength, faithfulness, and his knowledge of the Indians he was invaluable to the varied schemes of his ubiquitous patron. Current gossip along the route to Kentucky told how Nolan could lift a sack containing $2000 with one hand from the back of a mule, and carry it into the house.[88] Apparently there were enough silver dollars in the baggage of the two travelers to prove this feat of strength to anyone who might be doubtful. Taming drunken Indians was another one of Nolan's accomplishments. Several times while in the Southwest Andrew Ellicott, official Surveyor of the United States, was to call on Nolan for help against the savages and he was to give it in full force and with high satisfaction. Nolan was, in fact, one of those capable assistants that Wilkinson frequently selected to send on missions of difficulty and importance. In return for his help, Wilkinson paid him well, trusted him implicitly, and treated him as a member of the family.[89]

By November the two had gone as far north as the Cumberland River. Here Wilkinson dispatched a letter to Gayoso in which he stated that "the Convention" had adopted "my policy"; he also de-

[85] To Gayoso, Aug. 5, 22, 1789, A.G.I., Seville, *Papeles de Cuba*, leg. 2373.
[86] To Gayoso, Oct. 12, 1789, *Ibid*.
[87] Brown, *History of Texas*, I, 38–41.
[88] Deposition of Evan Jones, *Amer. State Papers, Misc.*, vol. 2, p. 81; Clark, *Proofs*, Notes, 6.
[89] To Miró, May 25, 1790, A.G.I., Seville, *Papeles de Cuba*, leg. 2373.

clared that the question of the navigation of the Mississippi was a matter that would be settled in Madrid, for no Spanish minister was to be near Congress in the future.[90] If the Eighth Assembly that met in Danville, July 20, was "the Convention" referred to, its chief work consisted in petitioning Virginia to alter the terms on which Kentucky might change from a district to a state.[91] Legislative action of this kind may have been part of Wilkinson's elastic program, but it certainly did not compass the whole of it. Gayoso was far from the theater of affairs, and Wilkinson could easily impose on his ignorance.

Once more in Lexington, Wilkinson could not profit from politics as he had done before. The end of hesitancy and turmoil had almost come. He perceived that Miró was beginning to doubt whether any section of the United States would ever become a part of the Spanish domain, a conclusion certainly warranted by circumstances. During December, 1789, Virginia had enacted the Fourth Enabling Act, which proved wholly acceptable to the Ninth Assembly meeting in the following July. The 1st of June, 1792, was selected as the date when Kentucky's separation should occur. Necessary details were adjusted in a subsequent meeting known as the Tenth Assembly, and the day on which Kentucky was lost to Virginia she became a state of the Union.[92]

It took no political clairvoyance to forecast in 1790 that this event would happen. Wilkinson knew that he could not continue to interest Miró in their original scheme of winning Kentucky; hence, while attempting other means for continuance of favor, he bent every effort to get what he could from the dispensations that he already enjoyed. He had sent five hundred hogsheads of tobacco to New Orleans the previous year; he now planned to send a thousand. If he were successful the *Speedwell* account could be liquidated and his personal fortune stabilized. His scheme was to sell the planters' tobacco on commission. They were to assume the hazards and the expense of shipping and were to receive two-thirds of the rise over and above fifteen shillings per hundredweight, the minimum price expected at New Orleans. Wilkinson and Peyton Short, his associate, were to have the other third.[93] Miró was importuned to admit all the tobacco that he could in "his Majesty's Store"—a favor that

[90] To Gayoso, Nov. 10 (?), 1789, *Ibid.*
[91] Littell, "Political Transactions in and Concerning Kentucky," in Filson Club Publications, No. 31, 109–110.
[92] McElroy, *op. cit.*, 143–146.
[93] Wilkinson and Short to Planters of Kentucky, Dec. 19, 1789, Durrett Collection, Univ. of Chicago.

would give Wilkinson a distinct advantage over his competitors and increase the chances of a gratifying profit.[94]

Wilkinson's finances were in a bad way; he was bending every effort to improve them. The money that he had brought back with him from New Orleans was not nearly enough to meet his personal wants and business obligations. He anxiously waited for the coming of John Ballinger, a messenger of his, from the lower Mississippi. Finally he arrived on Christmas Day, 1789, bringing two muleloads of silver.[95] The amount was much less than the sum Wilkinson had counted on. The same might be said of his creditors, whose hopes of hard money had been greatly inflated by the rumors that Ballinger had brought more than enough for all. Perhaps some did not even get their proportion; Wilkinson's papers were in confusion. Major Isaac Dunn had been his bookkeeper, and recently he had committed suicide, driven to desperation by the acts of his wife and the state of his finances. His death, as Miró was told, entailed a burden of $10,000 on Wilkinson.[96]

The estimate was perhaps exaggerated. Wilkinson was appealing to a source from which he expected financial aid, although he realized that efforts to get money from the Spaniards were seldom successful and frequently met with embarrassing investigations. At this very time he was aware that a belief was growing that his dealings with the Spaniards were not honest. To Miró, he confessed:

"I have the best authority to say that my connexion with you is strongly suspected by the Congress, & they have spys [sic] on my motives in this country.

.   .   .   .

"I am narrowly watched by the servants of General Washington."[97]

To prevent any disclosures the governor was enjoined to "suffer no American to leave the Province by sea, because that will open a direct correspondence with President Washington who I am satisfied must have a spy in New Orleans."[98]

Suspected by many persons, Wilkinson took great pains that incriminating letters to and from him should be written only in code.

[94] To Miró, Apr. 30, 1790, N.A.C., *Papeles de Cuba*, leg. 2.
[95] Deposition of John Ballinger, in Clark, *Proofs*, Notes, 6.
[96] To Miró, May, 2, 1790, A.G.I., Seville, *Papeles de Cuba*, leg. 2374; *Kentucky Gazette*, June 27, 1789.
[97] To Miró, Jan. 26, 1790, A.G.I., Seville, *Papeles de Cuba*, leg. 2374.
[98] To Miró, April 3, 1790, *Ibid.*

An English pocket dictionary furnished the key; one was sent to Miró with elaborate instructions how to use it. Today the Spanish archives reveal how sense was extracted from an apparent jumble of numbers and letters. Secretaries, doubtless, groaned at the task of decoding and translating the long, verbose communications that the governor received from Wilkinson, who was seldom noted for his brevity. Even though guilty of this failing, he did have the ability to write with spirit, particularly when his interests were at stake. He did not waste words when he wrote to Gayoso on February 6, 1790:

"Let me conjure you to be rigid in exacting the 15 p.c. duty [and] every other charge as it will have a happy effect. But we shall never be able to accomplish any thing very important on the subject of immigration until the present injudicious system is destroyed, & the commercial privileges confined to actual settlers only." [99]

When his boats were preparing to move southward he wrote again with even more vehemence: "for God's sake cut off the commercial intercourse with this country it utterly destroys all our plans & views, & if not immediately checked may eventually ruin Louisiana." [100]

In other words, rivals were cutting into a monopoly that Wilkinson wanted to maintain unbroken. He tried constantly to show that dispensations for himself and rigorous exactions from others would best promote the interests of Spain. According to his reasoning, enemies were to be created outside of the royal domain so that many loyal subjects would settle within it. Emigrants from a dismembered Union would cross the Mississippi and lay the foundation of empire, furnishing a sturdy bulwark against intrusion of their own kinsmen. Such a miracle might be achieved by using this suggested prescription:

"In any accommodation which may occur the [Spanish] minister should keep his eye steadily to one object, that is to render the treaty as oppressive to this Country as it may be beneficial to the Atlantic Cities; this would cherish the seed of disunion implanted here, excite immigration to Louisiana and support all our plans." [101]

To what an end Wilkinson might have come, had Kentuckians known that he advocated the most irksome sections of the Jay-Gardoqui treaty that the West detested!

Miró did not subscribe wholly to this program that was inspired by

---

[99] To Gayoso, Feb. 6, 1790, *Ibid.*
[100] To Miró (?), undated, *Ibid.*
[101] To Miró, (undated), *Ibid.*

self-aggrandizement. He did not care to surrender any of his power as arbiter of the use of the Mississippi except in accordance with the orders of the Crown. He did not dare disobey them unless he could offer results well justifying his action. Certainly Wilkinson had not done enough for the general good of Louisiana to enjoy special privileges. On the other hand, the governor did not care to be so unbending toward the backwoodsmen that they, alone or in concert with others, would make a trial of strength against the weakened defense of the province.

If Wilkinson and Miró differed on some things, they were in hearty accord when competition from an unexpected quarter threatened the success of their personal schemes. In 1790 the United States government attempted to establish a satisfactory overland route from Kentucky to New Orleans. Wilkinson learned of the plan, and wrote Miró to set the Creeks on the makers of this new line of communication. Soon the members of Major Doughty's reconnoitering party were attacked, and a few of them had need of the shrouds that had been carried along for gifts to the Indians.[102] The major, a Revolutionary friend of Wilkinson, escaped, and consequently the Northwest was blessed with the Doughty peach instead of the South with a Doughty Highway. Discouraged by this initial failure, the government lost interest in a road to New Orleans.

Those who would go South with slaves and chattels found travel by the Mississippi the only satisfactory route, no matter how disagreeable the Spaniards and their regulations might be. There were many immigrants, for in 1788 Spain had made much easier the conditions of settlement.[103] Wilkinson learned about those going from Kentucky and often gave them personal letters of introduction to Miró; it was understood that, unless the governor received a private communication at the same time, the bearer was not to be seriously considered. Many besought Wilkinson for the open sesame. Ezekiel Forman with his thirteen children and sixty-five slaves and other dependents wanted to settle near Natchez; one James Walsh was eager to start a "manufactory" of cotton, hemp, and flax; and one Forde had invented a steamboat and was ready to build a working model of it at New Orleans. Such were a few of the prospective settlers of Louisiana.[104]

[102] To Miró, Feb. 4, 1790, *Ibid.*
[103] Whitaker, *The Spanish-American Frontier, 1783–1795*, 101–102.
[104] To Miró, Feb. 22, Apr. 18, 29, Dec. 17, 1790, A.G.I., Seville, *Papeles de Cuba*, leg. 2374.

Spain wanted to know about these individuals who were filtering into her domain; but she was more interested in Wilkinson's confidential information concerning the great land companies that were working to acquire magnificent holdings on the lower Mississippi for extensive colonization. In method these companies were none too squeamish; they might easily prove themselves troublesome to their neighbors; and servants of the Crown were inclined to look askance and shrug their shoulders when the names of these real estate pirates were mentioned.

The South Carolina Yazoo Company was true to type. Wilkinson first heard of it in the early spring of 1789 when he was preparing to leave for New Orleans. Thomas Washington, a Charleston promoter of dubious honesty, wrote and told him that he and others had purchased some 3,000,000 acres near the mouth of the Yazoo River from the Choctaw Indians; they believed that Georgia would give title for £100,000, and that a part of this amount might be paid in public securities. Wilkinson was asked to join in the venture.[105] Thinking that some connection with it might be personally profitable, he quickly replied, outlining a few of the requisites of success. He felt sure that several men of "talent and sagacity" ought be selected to act as agents; he suggested that he was well qualified to treat with Miró.[106] After offering his services for this purpose, he wrote to Miró, declaring that the Yazoo settlements might be annexed easily to his Majesty's domain and the leader of the whole project delivered into his hands.[107] The governor evinced no enthusiasm; he asked Wilkinson to make plain to the promoters that any settlement on the lands contemplated would be considered as an act of hostility. Wilkinson suggested that capital be made of the company's "Needy adventurers and Gentlemen of Rank," provided they settled as "aliens of Congress" and "close auxiliaries of Spain"—a condition that the directors, as he said, had willingly accepted. He therefore advised Miró to seize this glorious opportunity to show the King "your zeal for his interest and your ability to serve him." [108] Turning disgruntled Americans into presumably loyal subjects of Spain was a piece of political magic

---

[105] Washington to Wilkinson, Feb. 21, 1789, A.G.I., Seville, *Papeles de Cuba,* leg. 2373.

[106] To Moultrie, Huger, and others, Jan. 4, 1790, A.G.I., Seville, *Papeles de Cuba,* leg. 2374.

[107] To Miró, Jan. 20, 1790, *Ibid.*

[108] To Miró, May 20, 1790, *Ibid.*

of which nobody except Wilkinson would have had the temerity to boast. Beside fathering this miracle, he further declared that he had prevented a settlement at Walnut Hills, an act that would have been dynamic with trouble. In his process of effort he had spared neither himself nor his purse; he therefore wanted a loan of $10,000 to sustain his dwindling finances.[109] Miró did not yield to his devious reasoning or pay immediate attention to his venal request; his opposition to the South Carolina Yazoo Company was as unyielding as before.

Thereupon Wilkinson changed his tack, and bent his efforts to ruin the organization. He advised Miró that St. Clair, Governor of the Northwest Territory, had no relish for the plans of these real estate swindlers, for he wanted immigration into the lands north, not south of the Ohio, and was therefore hoping that Spain would incite the Indians against the Yazoo settlers and the United States would wink at this piece of scurvy trickery.[110] To meet any such situation James O'Fallon, the company's western representative, proclaimed that he and his associates were entirely prepared; he glibly talked of two thousand settlers, and half that number of accompanying troops made up of all branches of the service.[111] His blatant threat to Spain disturbed Miró, who had no desire for belligerent immigrants, especially when relations between England and the United States were critical, and he made redoubled efforts to resist their intrusion.

By this time Wilkinson had a very personal reason for actively helping to accomplish O'Fallon's ruin. From John Brown, member of Congress, he learned that an embarrassing story was being circulated in the East; it declared that "an influential American has been engaged in trade to New Orleans and now acts the part of secret Agent for Spain in Kentucky and is employed by that Court through Miró for the purpose of effecting a separation of Kentucky from the Union." This interesting bit of news originated in a thirty-page letter that O'Fallon had written to President Washington on September 30, 1790.[112] Wilkinson knew that he was the one described. In an outburst of anger, he swore to hang O'Fallon, that "son of Lucifer," on tenterhooks; he would ruin that renegade "whose voice was like unto the roaring of a lion and whose uplifted arm was like the Thunder

[109] To Miró, May 4, 1790, *Ibid.*
[110] To Miró, July 2, 1790, *Ibid.*
[111] *Kentucky Gazette*, Feb. 26, 1791; James, *The Life of George Rogers Clark*, 404.
[112] Brown to Wilkinson, Feb. 10, 1791, A.G.I., Seville, *Papeles de Cuba*, leg. 2374.

of Jove"; he would rid himself of that hack of a doctor whose conduct was "consecrated to villanies of the blackest dye," and who had been guilty of "transcendent turpitude" while under his own roof, "cherished by his family" and professing attachment "to him and his interests.[113] Wilkinson was getting a bit of his own medicine in something larger than homeopathic doses.

Wishing to get O'Fallon out of the neighborhood before he learned anything more, Wilkinson wrote him an anonymous letter. It informed him that while Congress was considering his September letter to the President, another written by him to Miró on July 16 had been introduced. As a result of the second, Congress had directed the President to issue a warrant for his arrest, and John Brown was hourly expected with full authority to carry it out.[114] Not so easily duped, O'Fallon wrote to Wilkinson asking him to inform the author of the anonymous letter that no decision had been reached on the "expediency or inexpediency of the advice." He also remarked that "much must come out of" the investigation before Congress.[115] In other directions Wilkinson succeeded better. He had one of his henchmen insinuate himself into the company and bring about the protesting of one of O'Fallon's bills at Charleston. The artifice was deeply embarrassing to O'Fallon, strutting about in fine feathers with his newly acquired bride—no less than the fifteen-year-old sister of General George Rogers Clark.[116] Life became more complicated for him when the federal government, on learning of the company's warlike preparations for taking forceful possession of Spanish territory, issued a proclamation warning all those involved to desist.[117] Preparations dwindled away, and before long the South Carolina Yazoo Company was just another great real estate venture that had failed. O'Fallon sank into insignificance, and Thomas Washington was later hanged as a counterfeiter.

Wilkinson's part in the whole affair had a definite motive; he wanted pay for his services. His finances were in a bad way, and he hoped Miró would come to his rescue. His latest speculation in tobacco during 1790 had failed to recoup his blasted fortune or still the demands of his creditors. It had been undertaken with several asso-

---

[113] To Gayoso, Feb. 24, and Miró, Mar. 19, 1791, *Ibid*.
[114] To O'Fallon, Mar. 31, 1791, *Ibid*.
[115] O'Fallon to Wilkinson, Apr. 10, 1791, *Ibid*.
[116] To Miró, Mar. 17, 1791, *Ibid*.
[117] Haskins, "The Yazoo Land Company," in *Amer. Hist. Assn. Papers*, V, 395–437.

ciates and had been dogged with misfortune from the very beginning. One of their boats sprang a leak and sank. Three others grounded in the Kentucky River and could not start out in June with the rest. From New Orleans came word that only 262,000 pounds had passed the royal inspection, out of 551,000 sent; 40,000 was still to arrive. Contingent expenses proved nearly the same as if all of the tobacco had been profitably sold. In the end, Wilkinson found himself six thousand dollars in debt during the winter of 1790–1791. In this dilemma he wrote a circular letter to his creditors, asking them to refrain temporarily from pressing their claims.[118]

Miró's anger added to the burden of adversity. He was vexed because excessive tobacco shipments had flooded the market and because Wilkinson's business transactions were not in harmony with ideas set forth in his "Memorials." He, therefore, advised Wilkinson to leave off his mercantile operations and to devote himself exclusively to the interests of Spain, suggestively adding that in her service would be found abundant reward.[119] Miró had the acuteness to realize that Wilkinson would never become important through trade, and that his efforts to become the "Willing of the West" would only mar his usefulness as an agent of the Crown.

In spite of the governor's advice and his own previous failure, Wilkinson, in 1791, made one more effort to ship tobacco to New Orleans. His companion in the enterprise was Hugh McIlvaine, whose name was to cover the first one hundred and eighty hogsheads, as well as others, that were to be shipped down the river. In this way Wilkinson would appear not to run counter to the wishes of Miró. According to the articles of agreement, McIlvaine was to receive the tobacco in New Orleans and there make a sale of it; while Wilkinson was to assume all the risk and receive a big slice of the profit. There was money to be made if the Spaniards could be brought around by some "political molasses." Miró was about ready to leave for Spain; the incoming governor might prove to be less experienced, and might succumb to the tactics of these two confederates. Nolan also was in New Orleans to help them, particularly to protect his patron's interests against McIlvaine's sharpness. But again Wilkinson's schemes failed; the

---

[118] Wilkinson to Rees and Clark, May 20, June 20, 1790, *Amer. State Papers, Miscel.*, II, 121–122; Miró to Wilkinson, Sept. 2, 1790, A.G.I., Seville, *Papeles de Cuba*, leg. 2374; Wilkinson to La Cassagne, Jan. 20, 1791, Durrett Collection, Univ. of Chicago.
[119] Miró to Wilkinson, Sept. 2, 1790, A.G.I., Seville, *Papeles de Cuba*, leg. 2374.

Don Francisco Louis Hector, Baron de Carondelet de
Noyelles, Seigneur d'Haine Saint Pierre.

*From a painting owned by the Duc de Bailen, Madrid,
and reproduced in Fortier, "A History of Louisiana," II,
152.*

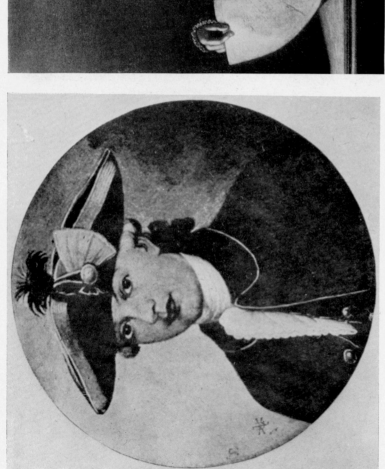

Don Esteban Miró.

*From a portrait owned by Louisiana State Museum. Courtesy of its
President, James J. A. Fortier.*

last great speculation in some 400,000 pounds of tobacco proved disastrous.[120]

By this time Wilkinson was near the brink of ruin. To be sure, Miró had advanced him $7,000 in 1790 with the understanding that it would be repaid in case the Court would not agree to credit it as pension.[121] Even this amount was not enough to meet his mounting obligations. During the winter of 1791 he tried to dispose of his Frankfort estates. Finally a certain Andrew Holmes proved a purchaser, and the proceeds were largely used to satisfy the claims of insistent creditors.[122] Wilkinson was eager to close out his business interests as soon as possible, so that he might leave Kentucky with a good name for honesty and fair dealing. On October 22, he had been commissioned as lieutenant-commandant of the 2nd United States Infantry, and he knew that he would soon be ordered to Fort Washington for duty.[123]

To his friend Judge Innes he entrusted the liquidation of his affairs, and to him he wrote:

"I pray you, my friend, to say that I have left (if you think as I do) sufficient property to discharge my debts and that I am determined to do this at any sacrifice.

. . . .

"I think it will be most proper for you to advertise for my debts, and direct my debtors to make payment. There is much confusion in my books and papers, but yet under such an explanation as I can give, justice may be done." [124]

Wilkinson's creditors were to be satisfied. His lands were put on the market; carriages, horses, oxen, mules, the old family phaeton, and a lot of odds and ends were ordered sold. Harassed as he was, he still made effort to show himself a "man of honor," even if he had failed in commerce and trade.

Though Wilkinson could vision the pathway to great riches, what he actually beheld was in a darkened light and without sharpness of detail. Only in his political relations was he ever able to follow suc-

---

[120] Agreement between Wilkinson and McIlvaine, Mar. 17, 1791, Innes Papers, Vol. XXIII; Wilkinson to Short, Dec. 15, 1791, Innes Papers, Vol. XXIII.

[121] Miró to Wilkinson, Sept. 2, 1790, A.G.I., Seville, *Papeles de Cuba*, leg. 2374.

[122] To Short, Dec. 15, 1791, and Articles of Agreement between Wilkinson and Short, Jan. 28, 1792, Innes Papers, Vol. XXIII.

[123] Heitman, *Historical Register and Dictionary of the United States Army*, II, 1037.

[124] To Innes, Feb. 29, 1792, Innes Papers, Vol. XXIII.

cessfully a tortuous and ill defined course. Constantly occupied with a wide variety of interests, he could not concentrate his energies on the tasks of a merchant, and so he stumbled in pitfalls that a more careful person might have avoided. His mind was not accurate or deep enough to give precision to the preparation and execution of plans. Unwilling to go through the grinding toil of money grubbing, he still wanted to cut a smart, gay figure in the world of opulence; often he flung his dollars about in abandon, creating for himself a momentary paradise of illusion. His trait was very human and made for friends, but it was contrary to successful business and a long continued confidence of the public.

As a politician he was clever, ambitious, and always engaging. He did not suffer from the Puritan handicaps of exact honesty and bigoted piety; with pleasing habits of manner and mind he could fit himself nicely into an environment peopled with Spanish officials. Where the defense of Louisiana against the rapidly increasing Anglo-Saxon population was difficult, where there was neither money nor means to defend the colony, the Spaniards turned to the indirect methods that they had long practiced. Wilkinson was paid to help; more frequently he helped himself and the United States. He intrigued, sometimes with, often against Spain, and masterfully, for the furtherance of his own interests.

For several years he had harped loudly on conspiracy in Kentucky and the district's rapprochement with Spain. When Miró realized that Kentucky was destined to become a state, when the profits from tobacco had begun to dwindle, Wilkinson changed his tactics and grew boisterous about dangerous emigrants and filibustering expeditions from the upcountry. Whether he chose these or other subjects, they were all vibrant with meaning to the Spaniards; and, in proportion to their fears, they paid him well. From them he gained a pension and perquisites.

Kentuckians, however, were the chief beneficiaries of the deceptive schemes that he practiced from 1784 to 1791. He opened their eyes to the value of New Orleans trade. Others had preceded him down the Mississippi but none had ever returned with loads of Spanish dollars to distribute among the men of the backwoods. Hard money was what they needed to pay onerous federal taxes and buy the luxuries of the East that they coveted—money that the Spaniards supplied under Wilkinson's aegis in exchange for tobacco, tallow, hams, and beef. Such trade, according to one estimate, was worth $3,500,000 annually to growers of Kentucky tobacco alone.[125] The farmers, no longer confined to a local market, were able to extend the range of their planting and, from the sale of their surplus, to enjoy prosperity.[126] When once they had tasted of it, they were more unwilling than ever to surrender the navigation of the Mississippi in return for the benefits that the Spaniards offered their kinsmen along the Atlantic seaboard. When the federal government threatened to ratify such a one-sided treaty, Kentuckians were incensed at the sacrifice of their interests. Wilkinson fed their anger and so directed their efforts that the East grew fearful that they might withdraw from the Union. Partly to prevent such an event the government insisted on free navigation of the Mississippi; and the Spaniards, ever mindful of fears that Wilkinson had helped to arouse, thought best to grant this privilege in 1795, before it might be wrested from them. In these antecedents of the treaty of San Lorenzo, Wilkinson played a determining rôle, which, contrary to his expectations, had helped more the general good of his countrymen than his own personal fortune. He was not a genuine but a fortuitous patriot.

[125] McDougall MS, in Lexington, Ky., Library.
[126] Verhoeff, *The Kentucky River Navigation,* 270.

CHAPTER V

A RISING OFFICER OF REGULARS

WILKINSON'S business transactions in New Orleans, when conducted on an equal footing with competitors, had proved neither remunerative nor especially suited to his taste. In that murky underworld of Spanish politics and commercial bootlegging into which he had ventured, his more powerful rivals were nullifying his best efforts. By 1790 stark bankruptcy impended. His prospects, but recently so verdant, had withered until there remained only his rather dubious claim to a two-thousand-dollar pension from the Spanish authorities. If he were to remain on the Castilian pay roll, he had to impress the dons with his undiminished influence with the solons at New York and Philadelphia. Looking to his friends, he was encouraged by the example of those whom he perceived to be enjoying the fruits of federal office while at the same time they diligently and profitably tilled the fields they had secretly sown. Once again in the government service, he himself might cut an important figure in the West, keep his name untarnished, and still retain what was profitable in the Spanish connection.[1]

Wilkinson's honest faith in his talents as a military genius suffered no diminution when he doffed the uniform. His rapid rise during the Revolution had convinced him that opportunity was his only need. When, in 1790, war seemed imminent between England and Spain, he wrote to Miró from Kentucky, urging him to authorize the enlistment of a thousand American riflemen who were to be commanded by ex-Revolutionary officers and employed in defense of Spanish Louisiana.[2] Although the expected clash failed to materialize, it was still possible to fall back on the ever-present Indians as available

---

[1] Innes, Brown, Muter, Wallace, and Sebastian all held federal offices. See Bodley, "Introduction" to Filson Club Publications, No. 31, p. lxix.

[2] To Miró, Aug. 27, 1790, A.G.I., Seville, *Papeles de Cuba*, leg. 2374.

opponents. Exception would, of course, have to be made in the case of the Creeks in the Southwest. They were enemies of the United States but allies of Spain. Therefore a Spanish agent had better win a military reputation by fighting others.[3] In the Northwest lay his opportunity. Here existed a chronic state of savage warfare that Wilkinson urged should be ended. Frontiersmen held a similar opinion; they hailed with delight a foray against their old enemies, especially when it was financed with federal funds. The fact that the Indians would be aroused to greater activity, and the President embarrassed in his future negotiations, cast no shadow on the Roman holiday that Wilkinson planned for himself and his followers. His own reputation had to be enhanced, and the government's efforts employed where Spanish interests would not be jeopardized.

To introduce his program, Wilkinson wrote to General Josiah Harmar, then ranking federal officer in the Northwest, asking for advice and aid against Indians who were attacking boats near the mouth of the Scioto. Hundreds of immigrants were sweeping down the Ohio in flatboats, bringing all their household effects, as well as a great deal of merchandise to barter or sell. On these hardy pioneers the Indians levied a heavy toll of scalps and booty. And the forty-three hundred Americans who were already scattered in lonely groups on the lands north of the Ohio often saw their cabins burned to the ground and their women and children brutally murdered.

By the summer of 1790, Washington had decided upon a more militant policy in the Northwest. General Harmar was selected to lead a punitive expedition against the Miamis. Though brave and competent during the days of the Revolution, he never understood the ways of the savages or the frontier. During the last week of September a force of 1,453 men set out from Fort Washington under his command. The Indians fell back before his advance without making resistance. He destroyed five villages, burning log houses, wigwams, and many acres of ripening corn. Incensed by the loss of their food and shelter for the winter, the Indians attacked an isolated detachment of Harmar's force, completely routing it. A few of its 320 regulars showed that they knew how to die, but the militia demonstrated that they were cowardly and could not be trusted. The whole campaign was just another sorry exhibition of incompetence. Harmar made what explanations he could to a board of inquiry and

[3] To Miró, Apr. 29, 1790, A.G.I., Seville, *Papeles de Cuba,* leg. 2374.

was given in turn a few daubs of whitewash.[4] Its members may have believed that his failure was due to the "ignorance, imbecility, insubordination and want of equipment of the militia" [5] rather than to his own lack of capacity.

Wilkinson's moment had evidently arrived. Bravely he piped that "the voice of all ranks called him" to lead a thousand volunteers on a punitive expedition without further delay. "All obstacles," he said, "arising from the inclemency of the season, from Frost, from Ice & Snow, from deep and Rapid Rivers," would yield to his transcendent powers of leadership.[6] As the winter wore on, however, his ardor appears to have cooled. Certain matters at first regarded as insignificant became portentous. Congress evinced only slight enthusiasm in support of his proposals. He wrote that the command was actually offered to him; but when the time came to accept or decline he obeyed the dictates of prudence and refused it.[7]

Charles Scott, a former brigadier-general of the Continental Army, and lately a member of the Virginia Legislature, accepted the appointment as a four-dollar-a-day brigadier to command the expedition. Wilkinson went along as second-in-command. On the 19th of May, 1791, they assembled eight hundred one-month volunteers at the mouth of the Kentucky River. Four days later they crossed the Ohio on their way to the Wabash country. Before many days Wilkinson had a brush with the Indians, his battalion shooting up five canoe loads of refugees from a village that Scott had attacked. Ordered to search for a reputed river crossing, and to round up the fugitive savages on the far side, he met with no success. On June 2 he retraced his steps and started during the morning with a detachment to capture the village of Kethtipecanuck on Eel Creek. Unimpressed by the melodious name of the place, his volunteers committed it to the flames, and joyously slaughtered any of the fleeing inhabitants they could catch. On the third day, highly satisfied with his accomplishments, the colonel returned to headquarters to report what he had done.

In such touch-and-go methods both Wilkinson and his men delighted. By the end of June the volunteers were back in Kentucky,

---

[4] For an account of the Harmar Expedition, see *Amer. State Papers, Mil. Aff.*, I, 20–36, and Harmar to Sec. of War, Nov. 4, 1790, *Amer. State Papers, Indian Aff.*, I, 104–105.

[5] Burnet, *Notes*, 105.

[6] To Miró, Dec. 17, 1790, A.G.I., Seville, *Papeles de Cuba*, leg. 2374.

[7] To Miró, Feb. 14, 1791, *Ibid.*

eager to spread the word of their prowess on campaign.[8] Scott wrote handsomely of his second-in-command's efficiency, and Wilkinson spoke very well for himself. He told of the villages he had burned, of the acres and acres of growing corn that he had destroyed, and mentioned with favorable emphasis the thirty-two warriors he had slain, "chiefly of size and figure." He numbered among his captives the Indian Queen Thunderstruck, her daughters the Princesses Speckled Loon, Swift Waves, and Clearwater, with fifty-four others of lesser rank. Among the prisoners whose origin was unmarked by distinction were certain aboriginal ladies known as Striped Huzzey, Eat-all, and Beaver Girl.[9] Additional satisfaction was to be derived from the very moderate cost of the expedition. Only about twenty thousand dollars of federal funds had been expended, and the casualties mounted to a total of five men wounded.[10]

Colonel Wilkinson assumed that his apprenticeship as an Indian fighter had been honorably concluded. He was ready for independent service. St. Clair was urging another punitive expedition; the Kentucky Committee agreed and selected Wilkinson to command it.[11] He gathered five hundred and thirty-two rank and file at Fort Washington and started with them for L'Anguille, a village about one hundred miles distant. August 1 was the date of their departure; within twenty days they had destroyed the village named as their objective, cut down four hundred and thirty acres of corn, and taken a few prisoners. They might have done even more, according to Wilkinson's report, if his men had not wearied and the horses become footsore while floundering in mud and swamps for four hundred and fifty-one miles.[12] The raid had no decisive effect other than to arouse the exasperated Indians to greater violence. But Wilkinson had added materially to the kind of reputation that made for preferment.

The Secretary of War, Henry Knox, flatteringly acknowledged his services. Said he: "I have, by this post, instructed Major General St. Clair to thank [you], if he had not already performed that pleasing duty, in the name of the President of the United States, for the zeal, perseverance and good conduct manifested by you in the Command of the expedition, and for the humanity observed towards

---

[8] Scott to Knox, June 28, 1791, and Wilkinson to Scott, June 2, 3, 1791; in *Amer. State Papers, Indian Aff.*, I, 131–133.

[9] Scott to Knox, June 28, 1791, in *Ibid.*, 131–133.

[10] Knox to Scott, Mar. 9, 1791, and Scott to Knox, June 28, 1791, in *Ibid.*, 131–133.

[11] Smith, *The St. Clair Papers*, II, 222–223.

[12] To St. Clair, Aug. 24, 1791, in *Ibid.*, 223–239.

the prisoners whom you captured; and also to thank the officers and privates of volunteers, for their activity and bravery while under your command; and to express the hope that you and they may enjoy in future, entire peace, as a reward for your services." [13]

Wilkinson saw that the situation was developing according to his estimate. As early as the 14th of April he knew that a considerable force was to be led against the savages by General St. Clair, his former Revolutionary commander, now governor of the Northwest Territory. Influential Kentuckians disapproved of St. Clair's selection. They said he had no proper appreciation of their needs, nor did he possess the knowledge and experience to fit him for Indian warfare. Why, they protested, remove the conduct of the operations from Kentuckian control? Why employ improvised regulars instead of expending good federal money on good Kentucky volunteers? [14] Wilkinson himself shied at the notion of taking any part in the expedition. He felt "damn skittish" when his own reputation was at stake and might be injured through the fault of others. Harmar's record had been blighted; Scott was little more than a voluble politician, and should St. Clair fail it was reasonable to suppose that the government would see in Colonel Wilkinson the man of promise.

On October 22, 1791, recognition was accorded his services. The President appointed him "Lieutenant Colonel Commandant" of the Second United States Infantry.[15] Wilkinson attributed this honor to his influence in Kentucky and to the relative success of his campaign against the Indians.[16] There is no doubt that he had a numerous following in the blue-grass country and the administration coveted its favor. Judge John C. Symmes thought that a better choice would have been hard to make; Wilkinson seemed to him peculiarly well fitted for such a commission:

"I take him to be a temperate man of considerable talents. He has youth, activity, ambition, bravery of clear understanding, and ever since I have been in this country, he has always intimated to me that a military life was what he was anxious to attain to. He has one advantage beyond many other men who might be appointed to the command in this country. In him are found those talents which will render him agreeable to the regular troops, and at the same time that his

---

[13] Knox to St. Clair, Sept. 29, 1791, in *Amer. State Papers, Indian Aff.*, I, 182.
[14] McElroy, *Kentucky in the Nation's History*, 156.
[15] Wilkinson's commission, Johns Hopkins Univ. Library.
[16] To Carondelet, Dec. 15, 1792, A.G.I., Seville, *Papeles de Cuba*, leg. 2374.

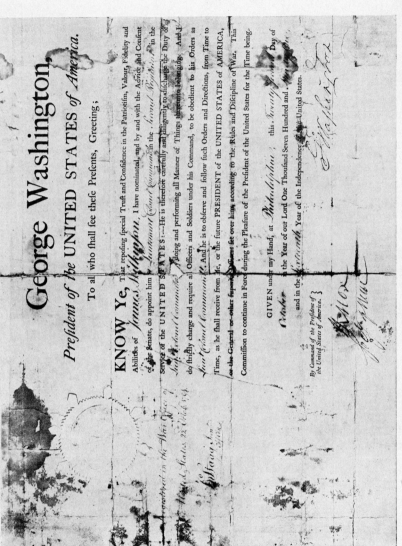

George Washington,

President of the UNITED STATES *of America.*

To all who shall fee thefe Prefents, Greeting;

KNOW Ye, That repofing fpecial Truft and Confidence in the Patriotifm, Valour, Fidelity and Abilities of *James Wilkinson,* I have nominated, and by and with the Advice and Confent of the Senate, do appoint him *Lieutenant Colonel Commandant in the Second Regiment* in the Service of the UNITED STATES:——He is therefore carefully and diligently to difcharge the Duty of *Lieutenant Colonel Commandant* by doing and performing all Manner of Things thereunto belonging. And I do ftrictly charge and require all Officers and Soldiers under his Command, to be obedient to his Orders as *Lieutenant Colonel Commandant.* And he is to obferve and follow fuch Orders and Directions, from Time to Time, as he fhall receive from Me, or the future PRESIDENT of the UNITED STATES of AMERICA, ~~or the General or other fuperior~~ Officers fet over him, according to the Rules and Discipline of War. This Commiffion to continue in Force during the Pleafure of the Prefident of the United States for the Time being.

GIVEN under my Hand, at *Philadelphia,* this *Twenty Second* Day of *October* in the Year of our Lord One Thoufand Seven Hundred and *Ninety Four,* and in the *Nineteenth* Year of the Independence of the United States.

G Washington

By Command of the Prefident of
the United States of America. }

Henry Knox

Regiftered in the War Office ?

the United States 22 Octr 1794.

J. Wagner
Office

familiar address and politeness render him very pleasing to the militia of Kentucky by whom he is much respected and loved, and on this body of militia the United States must very much depend in their future operations against the Indians; they are nigh at hand, and they are mostly riflemen." [17]

Modesty did not deter the newly appointed lieutenant-colonel from believing and repeating to his friends the opinions of the judge. To some of them he secretly confessed that there might be another interesting reason for his selection. It might have been made in order to separate him from his pursuits in New Orleans.[18] As a government agent he would come under the surveillance of the "Father of his Country." And his knowledge of the devious ways of the Spaniards might well prove priceless to President Washington and his colleagues, struggling as they were to unravel a tangled skein of affairs at home and abroad. Perhaps some of Wilkinson's supporters indicated to the powers that were, what a help he might be in solving diplomatic riddles. Washington may have listened to their suggestions and determined not to separate him from those mysterious "pursuits in New Orleans." It was conceivable that he might prove more useful as a sort of federal stool-pigeon.

In accepting his commission on the 5th of November, 1791, Wilkinson was required to subscribe to the following oath:

"I do solemnly swear to bear true allegiance to the United States of America, and to serve them honestly and faithfully, against all their enemies or opposers whomsoever, and to observe and obey the orders of the President of the United States of America, and the orders of the officers appointed over me, according to the articles of war." [19]

Wilkinson was a presumptive subject and an actual pensioner of the Spanish Crown, but he did not hesitate to take this oath. He entered the service, as he says, because his need for "Bread and Fame" was great.[20] He knew that the Spaniards paid well and they would appreciate him more as an army officer. To ingratiate himself with Carondelet, he wrote to him in December, 1792, bidding him make use of the opportunity offered by an "incompetent Secretary of War," "an ignorant commander in chief," and a "contemptible"

---

[17] Symmes to Dayton, June 17, 1792, in Miller, *Cincinnati Beginnings*, 196.
[18] To Carondelet, Dec. 15, 1792, A.G.I., Seville, *Papeles de Cuba*, leg. 2374.
[19] Callan, *Military Laws of the United States*, 89.
[20] To Peyton Short, Dec. 28, 1791 (not sent), Innes Papers, Vol. **XXIII**.

Union.[21] And this advice was given after he had been raised to a brigadier's rank and was junior in the service only to Wayne. In December, 1791, he had written to Miró, giving conventional reasons for becoming an officer and hinting of his rapid rise. "My private interests," he explains, "the Duty which I owe to the Country I live in, & the aggrandizement of my family have determined me to accept the appointment, & it is most probable, as soon as St. Clair is known of that I shall be promoted the chief command." [22]

The resentment against St. Clair had been rapidly growing. His task was to perform not only the duties of governor of the Northwest Territory but those incident to his position as commanding general of United States troops north of the Ohio. The frontiersmen were "disgusted & inflamed" because St. Clair had been selected to lead them against the savages. They were not confident of victory with him; they bitterly assailed the policy of the federal government that had made him their principal defender. Wilkinson wrote to Miró, declaring that he would capitalize this division of opinion for his own and the Spaniards' benefit.[23]

In 1791 St. Clair's military reputation received its *coup de grâce*. During the fall of the same year he started out with a motley collection of untrained troops to punish the Indians in northwestern Ohio. By October they had reached the neighborhood of Fort Jefferson and were heading for the Maumee country. Progress was extremely slow. In ten days his men had covered only twenty-nine miles. St. Clair was afflicted with gout and burdened with years; weakened with colic and asthma he lacked the physical power to command. His men were sick and ignorant, poorly fed and clothed, and the trail over which they marched was rough and swept by a cutting wind.

On the 3rd of November the army reached a branch of the Wabash River, near the site of the present city of Fort Wayne, Indiana. It was bitterly cold, and the bedraggled troops, utterly exhausted and with their morale at the lowest ebb, pitched their tents almost wherever they could. Military precautions against surprise were neglected; the militia bedded down across the creek and at a distance from the regulars; the sole outpost was a mile away in the dense brush. Throughout the night the Indian hordes covertly encircled the camp, a thousand fierce warriors led by the ferocious Simon Girty ("the

[21] To Carondelet, Dec. 15, 1792, A.G.I., Seville, *Papeles de Cuba*, leg. 2374.
[22] To Miró, Dec. 4, 1791, *Ibid.*
[23] To Miró, June 20, 1790, *Ibid.*

Great Renegade"), Little Turtle (the Miami chief famed for his oratory), and perhaps Tecumseh, younger than the other two, but far superior to them in appearance and organizing skill. Indian volleys drove the panic-stricken militia into the hastily formed ranks of the regulars. For a brief space those "hirelings of the gutter" and "sweepings of the street" rose to full stature of heroic men. Sporadic firing temporarily halted the advancing savages, but from behind trees, bushes, and rocks they poured in an accurate and deadly fire on the confused and milling ranks of the Americans. St. Clair was no craven; eight bullets pierced his clothing, one his whitening hair. Officer after officer was picked off, and of the soldiers not more than six hundred remained on their feet. Retreat—on the part of the militia a headlong flight—was the sole recourse. The rout was "pitifully complete." No battle ever fought before by an American army had equaled it in its measure of defeat. Of the Indians not more than a hundred and fifty fell; nearly half the Americans lay dead upon the field, two-thirds of their total number were casualties. By nightfall the demoralized remnants of the army staggered into Fort Jefferson. They had covered in their race for life the twenty-nine miles that had taken them ten days to make on their forward march. The wounded and captives were left behind to be torn limb from limb by the frenzied savages. The luckless women who had followed the column perished in miserable agony; huge stakes were driven through their writhing bodies that fiends had first defiled.[24]

In January, 1792, Wilkinson took a detachment and gave burial to some of the fragments that littered the field of battle.[25] Two years later Major-General Wayne, marching to the Miami country, covered many whitening bones and then pressed on to exact an indemnity of blood.

Sinister rumors circulated about "the great defeat." The *Western World* declared that one Sweezey had informed the Indians where to attack St. Clair's troops, and broadly hinted that Wilkinson had put him up to it. The *Palladium* made use of the same article on August 21, 1806. Neither paper was above stretching a story to satisfy partisan purposes. The tale is little worthy of belief; it appeared

[24] "Unveiling of Fort Recovery Monument," in *Ohio Archaeological and Hist. Quarterly*, July, 1913, 420–424; St. Clair to Sec. of War. Nov. 9, 1791, in *Amer. State Papers, Ind. Aff.*, I, 136–138; McMaster, *History of the People of the United States*, III, 43–47.
[25] Miller, "History of Fort Hamilton," *Ohio Arch. and Hist. Society Pub.*, XIII, 102.

fifteen years after the event and at a time when a host of manikins was assailing Wilkinson's crumbling reputation.[26]

As a matter of fact, the Indians' reconnaissance was continuous and thorough, and there was no need to tell them just when and where to attack. On the other hand, the Americans had only the information acquired from desultory patrolling, and even this was not acted on at critical junctures. On the night of the 3rd, General Richard Butler, whose heart the Indians ate next day, failed to tell St. Clair that the camp was surrounded and that an attack might be expected, although Captain Slough, leader of a patrol, had brought in a report of this kind.[27]

In contrast to St. Clair's disastrous campaign, Wilkinson's August foray against the Indians now stood forth brilliant and convincing; and as a lieutenant-colonel of regulars, during the succeeding fall and winter, he showed great enterprise and spirit. To many he was the man who would rid the West of an Indian menace. Washington, impressed by his apparent capacity and past performance, generously commended him:

"General Wilkinson has displayed great zeal and ability for public weal since he came into the service. His conduct carries strong marks of attention, activity, and spirit, and I wish him to know the favorable light in which it is viewed." [28]

Others like John C. Symmes and Harry Innes along the Ohio, John Brown and Jeremiah Wadsworth in Congress, and Henry Knox of the Cabinet, all held Wilkinson in high esteem.[29]

By the interposition of friends and an ostensibly good record, Wilkinson was made a brigadier-general on March 5, 1792, when Congress increased the Army by three regiments and made somewhat better provision for its equipment and keep.[30]

Only out of sheer necessity had the government taken such steps for national defense. Most people, raucous and blatant with an excess of democracy, still declared a standing army a potential source of

[26] McElroy, *op. cit.*, 160–161.

[27] "Major Denney's Journal," in Smith, *The St. Clair Papers*, I, 174.

[28] Washington to Knox, Aug. 13, 1792, in Ford, *Writings of Washington*, XII, 158.

[29] Symmes to Dayton, June 17, 1792, in Miller, *Cincinnati Beginnings*, 196. For Innes' opinion, see Innes Papers, Vol. XXIII, *passim;* for Brown's, *Appleton's Cyclopaedia*, I, 402; for Wadsworth's, Wilkinson to Wadsworth, Sept. 18, 1792, Wilkinson Papers, L.C.; for Knox's, Knox to St. Clair, Sept., 1791, in *Amer. State Papers, Ind. Aff.*, I, 182, and Knox to Wilkinson, Jan. 4, 1793, Wilkinson Papers, Vol. I, Chicago Hist. Soc.

[30] Heitman, *Historical Reg. and Dic. of the U.S. Army*, II, 1037; Act of Mar. 5, 1792, in Callan, *Military Laws of the United States*, 92–94.

tyranny. To them, whatever bore earmarks of authority was inconsistent with their ideas of liberty. Hence, anything like the British Army, with its formalism and subordination, represented the worst concomitants of a system that they had fought eight years to abolish. In addition, hasty-pudding volunteers and militia considered themselves better than regulars at Indian fighting and were always greedy for the hard money of the federal treasury.

It was in this army that enjoyed so little popular esteem that Wilkinson was to spend the best years of his life. His first station was Fort Washington, which had been built at Cincinnati in 1789. Three years later, the town, confident and vulgar, contained about nine hundred people and two hundred frontier houses. Building lots sold at from thirty to sixty dollars each; two years later prices had jumped, ranging from one hundred and fifty to four hundred dollars for those desirably situated. Everyday articles of dry goods and hardware were plentiful and brought only small profits to the merchant who bartered them across the counter. Meat was generally abundant, particularly that which the hunters brought in from Kentucky across the river. In 1795 wild turkeys could be purchased at from twelve and one-half to twenty-five cents apiece, pork at from fifty to seventy-five cents per hundred pounds. At the same time powder brought a dollar to a dollar and a half for a single pound, and salt from six to seven dollars a bushel. Imported liquor was high, but that of local manufacture cheap and easy to obtain. Along the river were several taverns and dramshops, and here those who would, might spend their time in idleness, drunkenness, and "carnal sin." Although Fort Washington soldiers might get fifty lashes for mixing in civilian brawls, they kept at their deviltry; perhaps they instinctively felt that they were keeping fit for the Indians, who often came close in to kill and steal. The savages did not greatly fear the sallies of the diminutive garrison of about two hundred men.[31]

In 1792 this small number could scarcely be expected to guarantee peace to a rapidly expanding neighborhood, especially when their days were filled with routine tasks and the hard labor common to the frontier. Fort Washington was a piece of their handiwork; and its red-painted walls rose luridly above the lower level of the town to still the fear of determined attack. Its well made bastions and sturdy

[31] "Narrative of John Heckewelder's Journey to the Wabash in 1792," in *Pa. Mag. of Hist. and Biog.*, XII (1888), 34–54; Cist, *The Cincinnati Miscellany*, II, 53–54, 65.

palisades were manned by hardy soldiers, versed in the use of four-
and six-pound cannon. These guns seldom thundered at an enemy,
but civilians often heard them boom in salute to a distinguished visitor
or in honor of an Indian chief who had died while a guest of the garrison.

Beyond the stockade were long, low buildings for the Army's
artificers, mechanics, washerwomen, etc. Near by, potatoes, pumpkins,
turnips, and corn were growing. There, too, perhaps were four-
o'clocks, petunias, periwinkles, sweet williams, and roses, gorgeous
in patchwork of color. In the gardens a few summer houses were
built; Wilkinson's, of course, was the most pretentious.[32]

More distant, lay fields of hay and grain. Fort Washington, like
other posts of the time, probably grew its own winter feed for horses
and pack mules, and men from the garrison did the harvesting. Toward
sunset a sentinel might hear the sound of small iron bells; then he
knew that the oxen drawing huge loads of hay, were approaching,
quickening their sluggish steps in their hunger for fodder or pumpkins.
If a private soldier had been on this haying detail, he possibly might
have earned an extra dime for his day of labor. Since his Army pay
came only three or four times a year, he lived on loans at pawnbroker's
rates, if he had any money at all for himself. In 1790 his pay was
reduced one dollar per month for clothing and hospital stores; [33] the
rest, two dollars, represented the current price of a few pounds of
coffee or a good-sized jug of whisky. Against this modest amount
were entered deductions for loss of equipment or bills to the trader.
Only a super-Caledonian could save money under such conditions.
Sometimes the soldier put a few small coins into his purse by plying
a trade or craft. If he could qualify as carpenter, axman, wheelwright,
or saddler, he might earn a little extra; a trifle might be picked up also
by hunting. Deer, buffalo, beaver, and bear skins all had value, and
could be sold, in case he did not need them for his own bed or shirt
or breeches.

In 1790 the yearly clothing allowance of a soldier consisted of
one hat, one coat, one vest, two pairs of woolen overalls, two pairs
of linen overalls, four pairs of shoes, four shirts, two pairs of socks, one
blanket, one stock and clasp, and one pair of buckles.[34] Underclothes
were not supplied; nor were breeches, which were usually made of

[32] "Narrative of John Heckewelder's Journey, etc.," *loc. cit.*
[33] *Annals of Congress*, 1st Congress, 1789–1791, II, 2281–2284.
[34] Act of Apr. 30, 1790, in Thian, *Leg. His. Gen. Staff U.S. Army*, 328.

FORT WASHINGTON

ERECTED 1790 IN CINCINNATI.

on the ground now occupied as 3d Street, East of Broadway

From a painting by H. W. Kemper.

Courtesy of Public Library of Cincinnati.

leather. Blue and buff were the predominating colors. The uniform was better suited for ceremonial occasions than for work; hence hunting shirts, linen overalls, and coats and caps of individual design were worn by the soldiers on active campaign. Little clothing, less soap, plenty of hard work, and few facilities for bathing explain why the soldier was dirty. His long hair he frequently dusted with flour, or anointed with bear-grease. Nevertheless, with frequent inspections, he was usually cleaner than the ordinary frontiersman with whom he rubbed elbows.

On the other hand, ordinary laborers generally had better food than that provided soldiers. The ration consisted chiefly of whisky, meat, and flour, often varying greatly in quality and amount, according to the honesty and ability of the contractor, who was a person outside the control of the Army. Sometimes fresh beef was supplied, cattle being driven along the line of march and slaughtered when supplies were low. At other times salt pork, frequently unfit to eat, was issued. If the contractor wished, he made the flour into bread; otherwise, soldiers did their own baking. They usually did so in groups of six. First the flour was kneaded in one of the large iron pots of the company; then the dough was worked into a ropelike shape and wound on an iron rod that was kept turning over the fire. When baked, it was cut into pieces, and sandwiches were made with the meat that had been roasted in the meantime. On the march, soldiers usually got one hot meal out of three. When they went into evening camp they cooked their supper, along with breakfast and dinner for the following day.[35] Rum, brandy, or whisky when available was dealt out daily at the rate of one-half gill per man. When service was uncommonly hard or deserving of great approbation, a double quantity might be the reward. No vegetables were regularly issued until after the War of 1812. Sometimes turnips, cabbages, beans, and pumpkins were raised in the company gardens; and, if the sick were lucky, they might have a little rice and wine to offset the drastic dosing and bleeding of the doctors.

The soldiers' small pay, poor clothing, and indifferent ration made an appeal to only a very few. Of these many were from Ireland and Germany,[36] where living conditions were hard; a few were Americans,

[35] Williams, "Expedition of Capt. Henry Brush," in *Ohio Hist. Miscellanies*, No. 1, pp. 30–35.
[36] See the deserter list of Capt. Rudolph's Company, in *Augusta Chronicle and Gazette of the State*, Feb. 25, 1792.

veterans of the Revolution, whose senses were quickened at the sound of a trumpet or the sight of colors—for the most part aimless drifters in need of food and shelter. Recruiting parties were accustomed to sounding their fifes and drums just around the corner from brothels and alehouses. Gathered from sources like these, recruits often lacked both physical and moral stamina, and a heavy burden rested on their officers to make them decent and reliable soldiers.

The Army was a hard school in which rewards were few and punishments severe. Sentinels could not sleep nor soldiers desert in the face of Indian attack; whatever the cost, disintegration and massacre had to be avoided. For such offenses, fifty or a hundred lashes were the fewest that might be expected from a court-martial. Before the culprit was drummed out of camp, he might have his head and eyebrows shaved, a rope tied around his neck and a "D" branded on his forehead. If what he had done was peculiarly heinous, troops might be paraded during the morning to witness his death at the hands of a hangman or a firing squad. Johnson, O'Brien, Gill, Trotter, and others apparently left the Army after the manner of Danny Deever.[37] To catch a deserter, scouts were enjoined to trail him and claim the forty-dollar reward for bringing back his head, which might be placed later on a pike where the soldiers would see it and be warned.[38]

For offenses less serious, punishments were proportionately severe. Poor John Grimes got a hundred lashes for returning to camp drunk and carrying along with him a few drams of whisky for future use.[39] Sergeant Ogden fared no better when he stole from a storekeeper and lost the goods in gambling.[40] When Solomon Brewer, a trader, let soldiers in late, gambled with them, and sold liquor, he was drummed out of camp and had tied around his neck a dirty pack of cards.[41] Samuel Farwell made a somewhat similar exit; he had labeled upon his back, "The just reward of cheating and gambling," [42] because he had swindled a certain Sergeant Healy out of ninety-five dollars. A pair who went absent for twenty-four hours were leniently dealt with: five days to miss their gill of whisky and five days to wear coats

---

[37] *Wayne's Order Books*, VI, 21, and III, 132.
[38] To Armstrong, May 11, 1792, Miscellaneous Papers, N.Y. Public Library.
[39] *Wayne's Order Books*, III, 136 ff.
[40] *Ibid.*, VI, 60.
[41] *Ibid.*, VI, 119–120.
[42] *Ibid.*, VI, 130.

wrong side out.[43] Presumably they were then drawing all of their ration and had the clothes that were due them.

The officers of these men were not always the best. Gentlemen in commission often received their appointments for political rather than military accomplishments. Capacity was not the ruling guide for selection. In disgust, Wilkinson declared that of the 1st Regiment some officers were peddlers, others drunkards, and nearly all of them fools. There were some who had gone little past the horn-book, a few could scarcely sign their names.[44] Ignorance was, in fact, general; labor, often continuous; and liquor, universally potent. In this narrow, hard world, Wilkinson bore sway over officers and men, often ingratiating himself through his fluency and charming manners, occasionally arousing their inveterate hate on account of innovations introduced for the good of the service.

Most of his first year as an officer, Wilkinson spent at Fort Washington, the largest Army post in the Northwest; other forts, like St. Clair, Knox, and Hamilton, were in the process of construction. He often corresponded with, and sometimes visited, Captain John Armstrong, who had been the commanding officer at Hamilton since the fall of 1791. Here a stout fort had been built from forest timber by a few skilled laborers working with indifferent tools. In spite of Indians who scalped and stole, winter stores were laid by for man and beast. The grass in adjacent meadows was cut, and a hundred tons or more of hay were ricked high in rounded stacks. Quarters were made comfortable so that Wilkinson might be properly cared for whenever he chose to come. A huge cellar was dug and provided with a four-hundred-gallon cistern designed for a cooler and fish pond. One day in a spirit of bedevilment, Lieutenant Gaines withdrew the plug; as punishment he was made responsible for keeping the cistern filled for a month. The task may not have been wholly distasteful if it gave the lieutenant access to the ten gallons of port and fine brandy that the General sent to Captain Armstrong shortly after being asked for radish seeds. The liquor may have been sent to stifle further requests for seeds; in any event it was doubtless acceptable.[45]

Like all commanders of frontier posts, Armstrong had to be something of a gardener. He raised green peas in abundance and had

[43] *Ibid.*, III, 167 ff.
[44] To Wadsworth, Sept. 18, 1792, Wilkinson Papers, L.C.
[45] For the relations of Armstrong and Wilkinson, see scattered letters in *The Cincinnati Miscellany*, Vols. I and II.

strawberries too. When he invited Wilkinson to come and dine with him, he thoughtfully added that if only a cow were made available, they might enjoy berries and cream.[46] Since the General and his wife had made possible the planting of his garden, the invitation very naturally followed. As a further mark of courtesy, he sent Mrs. Wilkinson a note of appreciation and a welcome frontier gift upon St. Patrick's Day. In quaintly gallant words he wrote:

"Unacquainted with the etiquette of addressing a lady, I have hopes, the language of my profession will not be offensive to the companion of a brother officer. Be pleased therefore, Madam, to accept the thanks of my family, *alias the mess*, for your polite attention in sending us garden seeds, etc., and should we be honored by a visit from the donor, the flowers shall be taught to smile at her approach, and droop as she retires. We beg you to accept in return a few venison hams, which will be delivered you by Mr. Hartshorne, they will require a little more pickle and some nitre." [47]

During the winter of 1792 Wilkinson fell out with Armstrong, whom he charged with trying to get a sick leave, although apparently hale and hearty. He declared the captain was also guilty of fraud and peculation.[48] In disgust with the service, Armstrong resigned early in 1793. Continuing to live in the Northwest, he enjoyed the benefits of public office and a worthy reputation for honesty. In time he and Wilkinson became reconciled.

The General determined to make Fort Hamilton his headquarters when Wayne came West to assume command. He liked the post with its many conveniences. In his opinion the neighborhood was an "interesting, captivating" place, giving "abundant sport for Dog and Gun" and furnishing a plentiful supply of "Fish, Fowl and Wild Meats." He relished a piece of venison washed down with cool Madeira or made piquant with "tomato essance" obtained from his friend Winthrop Sargent, secretary of the Northwest Territory, only six hours distant by post messenger. From the same source came fine melons, which with cabbages, turnips, beans, and other homely vegetables permitted a fare of rude plenty.[49]

The two men, so different in character, managed to maintain the outward forms of friendship, but little more. Sargent was frequently

[46] Armstrong to Wilkinson, June 1, 1792, *Ibid.*, I, 30.
[47] Armstrong to Wilkinson, Mar. 17, 1792, *Ibid.*, I, 210.
[48] To Wayne, Nov. 1, 1792, Wayne Papers, Vol. XXII.
[49] To Sargent, Sept. 27, 1792, Sargent Papers.

wanting arms, escorts, and transportation. These could not always be easily supplied, and Wilkinson would sometimes offer his instructions as an excuse for denial. On the other hand, it was Sargent's aid that was invoked when Lieutenant William Henry Harrison, later President, gave a lashing to some artificers who claimed they were not subject to military control. The culprits wanted to make much of the matter through the medium of "guard-house" lawyers. The secretary helped to frustrate their efforts. Wilkinson, on his part, recognized that the lieutenant had exceeded his authority and took steps to prevent a recurrence of similar errors.[50] Harmony had to exist between civil and military authorities.

Wilkinson indicated one way to maintain amicable relations. For the important people of the community he often acted as an engaging host in a lavish and attractive manner. One of these occasions is thus described in the *Kentucky Gazette* of May 26, 1792:

"On the first of the month being the anniversary of the *Titular Saint of the Nation* [St. Tammany], the day was celebrated with much harmonious festivity in a Wigwam prepared for the occasion on the margin of the Ohio in front of the Garrison. Our Commandant, Wilkinson, with his amiable Lady and a small, but genteel female group, the Secretary of this Territory, Judge Symmes, the Superior Judges and Justices of the County of Hamilton, the principal officers and most respectable citizens sat down to a most sumptuous dinner at 3 o'clock, where the following toasts were drank [*sic*] under the discharge of many cannon. (1) North American Nation; (2) Washington; (3) The Congress; (4) The Atlantic States; (5) The Western Settlements; and eleven others of a similar nature, 16 in all."

Under the influence of the "16 in all" the Indians must have been temporarily forgotten. As it actually was, peace had to be maintained with them until negotiations were settled in Philadelphia, in spite of the fact that they had become more brazen after St. Clair's defeat. Wilkinson would have curbed their murder and rapine with seven hundred and fifty mounted men and nine companies of infantry.[51] His plan was to institute a short, aggressive campaign like the one in August of the year before. It would never have achieved lasting results, although Wilkinson's reputation among regulars and volunteers might have been enhanced before the arrival of Major-General Wayne,

[50] To Sargent, June 2, 1792, *Ibid.;* Sargent to Wilkinson, June 4, 1792, see Carter, *Northwestern Papers,* III, 376–378.
[51] To Knox, Sept. 17, 1792, Wayne Papers, Vol. XXI.

now near Pittsburgh. It might have made the people almost entirely forget Charles Scott, a militia general, whom Wilkinson considered a rival—"a poor old wretch . . . galled and chafed with jealousy and impatience of office." [52] Wilkinson was restive because he could not enhance his own reputation in a way that he wished while opportunity offered.

Instead, he had to build up a machine that Wayne was to use in winning permanent peace. He often rose at five o'clock in the morning and was busy at army administration. He built Fort St. Clair, about twenty-five miles west of Dayton, Ohio, and supervised the strengthening of Hamilton, Knox, and other places; improved the system of communication between them; laid by large supplies of grain and fodder for the animals; saw that his men were sometimes paid and better provided with clothing; and made war on peculation, drunkenness, insubordination, and other vices, common to an army of the frontier.[53] For such good work he merited and received the thanks of Henry Knox, the secretary of war.[54]

Meanwhile, no offensive measures against the Indians were permitted, for peace negotiations were simmering around Niagara. In 1792 General Putnam came West, spending the summer and autumn in the Ohio country in the hope of stopping outrages against immigrants and settlers. Wilkinson supported schemes of conciliation and limited his men to defensive measures. When chiefs came to Fort Washington he gave them clothing and stuffed them with food. They liked sitting at the same table with their white hosts, being sandwiched in between them, and eating out of the same bowl. And if one of them died perchance from overeating or drinking, Wilkinson laid him away with military honors in the cemetery of the post. Here old Nawiatchtenos was interred, much to the resentment of white men who twice dug him up and placed him upright in the street. Finally he was lastingly buried at about the same time that news was brought of the treacherous murder of Colonel John Hardin, who had been sent under a flag of truce to confer with the Miami tribes.[55]

The killing of a peace commissioner was not the only indication of the Indians' desire for war. At daybreak on the 6th of November,

[52] To Innes, Feb. 29, 1792, Innes Papers, Vol. XXIII.
[53] For Wilkinson's work before Wayne's arrival, see *The Cincinnati Miscellany,* Vols. I and II, and the following papers for the years 1792 and 1793: Innes Papers, Wayne Papers, Sargent Papers, and Wilkinson Papers (Chicago Historical Soc.).
[54] Knox to Wilkinson, Jan. 4, 1793, Wilkinson Papers, Vol. I, Chicago Historical Soc.
[55] "Narrative of John Heckewelder's Journey, etc.," *loc. cit.*

1792, a detachment of Major John Adair was attacked near Fort St. Clair, suffered fifteen casualties, and lost most of its horses. The fort commander gave no aid to the hard-pressed pack train, pleading, in extenuation of his cowardice, that he had been ordered to limit himself to defensive measures. Adair did not criticize this disgraceful act in his report to Wilkinson; he merely told of his losses and the action of his men in a few simple words:

"I can with propriety say, that fifty of my men fought with a bravery equal to any men in the world, and had not the garrison been so nigh, as a place of safety to the bashful, I think many more would have fought well.

. . . .

"I am sorry I cannot send you better news." [56]

Stirred by this Indian outrage, Wilkinson still had to stay his hand until the means of peace were exhausted. He became more discontented daily. The drab round of Army routine irked him. In his restless way he wanted to do something calling for a fanfare of trumpets and applauding audiences. Uxorious man that he was, he greatly missed his "beloved Ann" and the romping boys. His wife had left in the early summer of 1792 for the East, where she expected to visit relatives and place James, John, and Joseph in school. Arriving at Pittsburgh in July, she and the children had been politely helped on their way through the courtesy of Wayne. The dashing young lieutenant, William Henry Harrison, acted as her escort to Philadelphia.[57] In a few months Wilkinson began to miss her keenly. In his own words, her absence was "Hell on earth" for him; nothing could repay for a year's separation. Hurry her back, his friends were bidden; meanwhile he was "panting, sighing, dying for her embrace." Send her to me or give me plenty of Indian fighting.[58] Being without humor, he did not sense the odd turn to his words, but doubtless Ann correctly understood what he meant to say.

During her absence, as well as before, he was harassed with financial troubles. He had entered the Army burdened with debts, and his efforts to recoup his losses through further speculation only increased them. His last great venture in tobacco during 1791 had proved a disastrous failure; and his partner of the previous year, Peyton Short,

[56] Adair to Wilkinson, Nov. 6, 1792, *Amer. State Papers, Ind. Aff.*, I, 335.
[57] Wayne to Wilkinson, July 7, 1792, Wayne Papers, Vol. XX.
[58] To Wayne, Sept. 17, 1792, Jan. 14, Mar. 27, 1793, Wayne Papers, Vols. XXI, XXIV, XXV.

"embarrassed, perplexed with Duns and applications," called on him for aid.

"To save me in this hour of extreme distress," said he, "I now call upon you by every principle that ever warmed an honest heart. Both God and man can witness that you now have it in your power. I beg, entreat, and conjure you to avail yourself of the happy occasion. Lay aside for a moment those prejudices wh. I must suspect have been artfully insinuated into yr. bosom—embrace the offer made you by Mr. Holmes." [59]

Wilkinson did accept the offer on January 28, 1792. By the terms of it Short secured most of the proceeds from the sale of some real estate and chattels in Frankfort, while he assumed, on his own part, a number of Wilkinson's debts.[60] This arrangement did not pay Wilkinson's most pressing obligations. "Distressed and unfortunate" as he was, he made efforts to meet them by sending one hundred dollars of his Army pay to Innes for the benefit of his creditors, and soon added another eighty dollars for the same purpose. Eager to maintain the judge's friendship, he offered to give him "uncontrolled power over my whole property in your own language." He wanted, as he said, to "remove the shackles which oppress my spirit and sit heavy upon my soul." [61] In November, 1792, he sold Louisville property, amounting to £830, to La Cassagne.[62] During the following January he turned over his interest in about 150,000 acres to Benjamin Sebastian, who in turn assumed responsibility for some more of his debts.[63]

If he could only continue to wheedle money out of the Spaniards and salvage something from his Kentucky holdings, he might again enjoy comparative affluence. On February 1, 1792, Carondelet wrote that the Court had granted him an annual pension of $2,000, which was to be retroactive to January 1, 1789.[64] In the summer, $4,000 was sent him as an ostensible tobacco balance through the medium of La Cassagne.[65]

In return for this retaining fee, Wilkinson was liberal in advice to the Spaniards. Of course, as an Army officer, he could not give any

[59] Short to Wilkinson, Dec. 20, 1791, Innes Papers, Vol. XXIII.
[60] Agreement, Wilkinson and Short, Jan. 28, 1792, *Ibid.*
[61] To Innes, Apr. 10, 1792, *Ibid.*
[62] Indenture of Wilkinson and La Cassagne, Nov. 12, 1792, Durrett Coll., Univ. of Chicago.
[63] Indenture of Wilkinson and Sebastian, Jan. 29, 1793, Innes Papers, Vol. XXIII.
[64] Carondelet to Wilkinson, Feb. 1, 1792, A.G.I., Seville, *Papeles de Cuba,* leg. 2374.
[65] Wilkinson, *Memoirs,* II, 119.

active assistance. No longer engaged in business, he revamped his philosophy of deception; he urged that Americans be given a free port on the Mississippi and that merchandise be made as cheap for them in New Orleans as in the East. Thereby the West might be detached from the Union and enticed into an alliance, a result that would be highly desirable in view of the prophecy that he made— inevitable war with Spain in a few years. To prevent invasion of Louisiana, he suggested the creation of strong barriers along its frontiers. Carondelet appeared to accept most of this advice at almost face value. Gayoso was not so easily misled, although he did believe that the United States would ultimately break up into three distinct confederacies, and in the western one of them he thought Wilkinson might play the rôle of a George Washington.[66]

Fascinated with prospect of his own greatness and covetous of Spanish treasure, Wilkinson wanted to continue in the service of both countries. He was hopeful that his intrigue might remain undetected through an elaborate use of codes and trusted agents. While he was commanding general along the Ohio, he could do almost as he pleased; and few would have the temerity to question his acts. When Wayne came to take active command, it would be a different story. Wilkinson would then be just another ranking subordinate, unable to go where he wished and subjected to a measure of surveillance. Hence, he warned his New Orleans accomplices to cover his tracks, while he himself determined to tread more warily than ever before.

[66] Wilkinson to Carondelet, Dec. 15, 1792, and to Gayoso, Dec. 21, 1792; Gayoso to Wilkinson, June 20, 1793, A.G.I., Seville, *Papeles de Cuba,* leg. 2374.

CHAPTER VI

BAITING A GENERAL AND HOODWINKING
A BARON

WHEN spring began to melt the river ice, Wayne started his men loading the ninety-five boats that the Legion had built during the winter before. He was preparing to move down the Ohio to the country that the Indians had menaced since the defeat of St. Clair. During the month of May, 1793, a thousand men or more debarked a mile below Fort Washington and raised their tents on the high ground near by. Hobson's Choice was the name of their newly made camp—no other site was available in a neighborhood flooded with heavy rain. Wayne had come to bring peace to the frontier, through negotiation or the sword.[1]

Wilkinson ruefully considered his prospects. Now his activities would be more closely supervised, perhaps considerably curtailed, and he would have fewer opportunities to enhance his own reputation or build up a personal following. There, too, was more of a chance that his intrigues with Spain might be discovered. Wayne had already shown disapproval of some of the things that he had done in the Army. There was the case of the soldier, Reuben Reynolds, whom Wilkinson had dispatched, under the guise of a deserter, to gather information about the designs of the Indians. Setting out some time in May, 1792, he had visited various tribes from Mackinac to Montreal and, for reasons not equally clear, passed through Vermont and gone to Philadelphia. Finally he had turned up at Pittsburgh, where Wayne treated him roughly and regarded his story lightly.[2] Soon nearly everybody knew what Reynolds had been up to; his career as a secret service agent was ended. Wilkinson was angry and humiliated; he foresaw that his devious methods would not find favor with the direct-dealing

[1] Boyd, *Mad Anthony Wayne*, 258–259.
[2] Davis, "Three Islands," in *Michigan History Magazine*, XII, 513–553.

Wayne. Serving under such a general would be intolerable; he thought of demanding relief as commander of the line from Fort Jefferson on;[3] he was almost ready to resign from the Army.

But the notion proved only a passing one. Maybe Mrs. Wilkinson, now returning from the East in the van of the Legion, helped him reach a more sensible decision. Usually she made thoughtful his whimsical judgment. And she also brought the good news that Knox thought well of his work.[4] Her presence alone was enough to induce content.

They settled at Fort Hamilton—a favorite station of his. Here he spent the early summer of 1793 training troops and laying in supplies against the prospect of a forward movement. Work, though constant, was pleasant: Ann was about, and his men were healthy and ready to reënlist.[5] Peace was also possible if Beverly Randolph, Timothy Pickering, and Benjamin Lincoln were successful in their negotiations with the Indians on the shore of Lake Erie.

After hearing of their failure during September, Wayne was given permission to advance.[6] Wilkinson was not eager for an offensive at this later date, for over three-quarters of his men at Fort Hamilton were on sick report and he himself was abed with the colic. Ann not being well, some safe and comfortable place had to be provided for her.[7] Generally, too, he had been more successful at diplomacy than at tactics; and the Spaniards, knowing the Army was fully occupied in the Northwest, would have less fear of American aggression and slighter desire for his aid and advice. For Wilkinson the world was out of joint. To Innes he dismally croaked: "I feel for our country, I feel for Kentucky which will again be covered with opprobrium. I feel for my brethren in arms and if I had not the firmest reliance in the protection of Heaven I should feel for myself.

"The volunteers may go to damnation and stay at home for all we care, we can do better without them. When crossed, perplexed, disappointed and perhaps deserted what will we say—rather what not say."[8]

---

[3] To Wayne, May 18, 1793, Innes Papers, Vol. XXIII.
[4] Knox to Wilkinson, May 17, 1793, Durrett Coll., Univ. of Chicago.
[5] To Wayne, various dates, July, August, and September, 1793, Wayne Papers, Vols. XXVII, XXVIII, XXIX.
[6] Boyd, *op. cit.*, 261.
[7] To Wayne, Sept. 30, 1793, Wayne Papers, Vol. XXIX; to Innes, Oct. 3, 23, 1793, Innes Papers, Vol. XXIII.
[8] To Innes, Oct. 3, 1793, Innes Papers, Vol. XXIII.

"My General treats me with great civility, and with much professed Friendship, yet I am an O, for he conceals his intentions from me, never asks my opinion, & when sense of Duty forces me to give it, he acts against it." [9]

Bilious colic and stubborn influenza had made him morose. Sick, jealous, and ignored, he found fault with almost everything that Wayne did. He foresaw his own recovery just about in time to get his brains knocked out by the savages. To him such a personal calamity was only a part of the general ruin that his "blockhead" commander was fathering. [10]

In spite of Wilkinson's jaundiced estimate, Wayne was laying the basis of lasting peace. He was methodically accomplishing the conquest of the Indian country. During the early days of October he and the Legion encamped six miles north of Fort Jefferson. Soon blockhouses and stout walls rose to give security and comfort to those who would winter there. Wayne called the place Greenville in honor of his old-time friend General Nathanael Greene. [11] The Indians looked on and were disturbed at this sign of permanent occupation; but, heartened by the British, they still refused peace, picking off stragglers and attacking wagon trains whenever opportunity offered.

Wayne's work was slow, expensive, and without spectacular features; but it was almost wholly devoid of chances for failure. Knox's habitual warnings against a defeat like that of Harmar or St. Clair had produced effect. Wayne appreciated his great responsibility.

Wilkinson did not rise to share it by rendering loyal support. Though giving his service grudgingly, he was clever enough to avoid an open breach at this time. He was ruled almost exclusively by considerations of personal advantage and consequently inspired little confidence in those superiors who knew him. Though a petulant critic in private, he was publicly courteous to Wayne in official relations. On occasions he went even further than routine duties demanded. Wayne had been kind to Mrs. Wilkinson. Often he was asked to dine with them. One of these invitations is dated December 20, 1793. Simple and direct, it reveals Wilkinson at his best, and Ann as a true daughter of the peerless host of the Indian King Tavern. It reads like this:

[9] To Innes, Oct. 23, 1793, *Ibid.*
[10] To Innes, Oct. 23, 1793, *Ibid.*
[11] Boyd, *op. cit.,* 264.

"Mrs. W. ventures to hope your Excellency may find it convenient & consistent to take dinner with Her on the 25th inst. with your suite, & any eight or ten gentlemen of your cantonment you may think proper should attend you; she begs leave to assure you the Dinner shall be a Christian one, in commemoration of the Day, and in Honor of Her Guest, and on my part I will promise, a welcome from the Heart, a warm fire, and a big-bellied Bottle of the veritable Lachrymae Christi. We pray you answer." [12]

A glowing fire, fat bottles, and friends have often made endurable the pitiless hardships common to the winning of a great frontier. Wayne was convivial, but his sense of duty was keen and his regard for Wilkinson slight. Instead of traveling south to Fort Jefferson, he and Captain Burbeck and eight companions started north on the 24th of December, planning to establish themselves on the site of St. Clair's defeat. Here, after many skulls had been cleared away, a camp was pitched, the beginning of Fort Recovery.[13]

Thoughtful chiefs grew fearful when they saw its bastions rise in the heart of their country. They now could count Forts Recovery, Greenville, Jefferson, and Washington stretching on an almost straight line to the south; they already knew that presiding over them was an iron-willed man whose eyes were seldom closed. When spring and summer came they might expect an invasion of their rich and long-held lands of the Maumee and Auglaize; Wayne, as rumor ran, was working out the details of just such a campaign.

Wilkinson, as second in command of the army, bent his energies to the same task; but he still maintained his connection with the Spaniards and enjoyed the fruit of their bounty. This dual rôle seldom disturbed his casual conscience. On December 4, 1791, shortly after accepting his commission, he had written to Miró and asked for ideas on the *"principal subject,"* the alignment of Kentucky with Spain, urging that letters in reply be in cipher, "much perplexed," and directed to Judge Innes or Clement Biddle.[14]

Meanwhile Francisco Louis Hector, Baron de Carondelet, had become governor of Louisiana on December 30, 1791, and on him fell the burden of answer. He had only a commonplace mind with which to solve the complicated problems of his extensive province. Soon Wilkinson had a reply that was thoroughly satisfactory; he was

[12] To Wayne, Dec. 20, 1793, Autograph Letters, II.
[13] Boyd, *op. cit.*, 266.
[14] To Miró, Dec. 4, 1791, A.G.I., Seville, *Papeles de Cuba*, leg. 2374.

granted an annual pension of $2,000 retroactive to the first of the year 1789, and was asked in what way he wanted the money sent. Of course, $7,000 was to be deducted—the amount that Miró had previously advanced as a loan.[15]

Some time during the year 1792, $4,000 was secured from the Spaniards by the Frenchman, La Cassagne, postmaster, gardener, and general rich man about Louisville, who in turn remitted it to Wilkinson on the 4th of August.[16] This was $3,000 more than was actually due at the end of the year; but opportunities for remitting so large an amount were infrequent, and the General had repeatedly voiced his great need. He declared that he ultimately received only $2,600. The balance of $1,400 may have been thriftily assumed by La Cassagne, to whom he was indebted from time to time.[17]

From money like this Wilkinson could not abstain. On the contrary, he tried to evince such zeal for the service of Spain that Carondelet would be deeply impressed and the pension money continued, perhaps even doubled. Again he confessed his faith and offered advice. He declared: "I have not abandoned those views, principles and attachments which I professed to Miró." He added that he foresaw no immediate peace with the Indians, for the secretary of war was incompetent and the commanding general ignorant. Besides, "intestinal discord," quarrels, disunion, etc. throughout the United States "renders [sic] the whole weak and contemptible, the occasion is favorable to Spain and you know how to improve it."[18]

From these alleged conditions, Carondelet hoped Spain would profit, perhaps securing Kentucky, even though she had become the fifteenth state on June 1, 1792. In this mistaken conception he revealed little knowledge of the Union or the character of the western people. His credulity and ignorance were a fertile field of exploitation; and Wilkinson made the most of both, suiting his advice to those whom he would beguile. Often when engaged in a competitive struggle for Spanish trade, he had urged that the Mississippi be closed to all foreigners except a favored few. Now, no longer in business, he declared that Kentuckians should be given a free port and that merchandise should be made as cheap for them in New Orleans as in the

---

[15] Carondelet to Wilkinson, Feb. 1, 1792, *Ibid.*
[16] Wilkinson, *Memoirs*, II, 119.
[17] Statement of Wilkinson account (undated), A.G.I., Seville, *Papeles de Cuba*, leg. 2374.
[18] To Miró, Dec. 15, 1792, *Ibid.*

East. Possessed of an excellent market for buying and selling and a natural highway thither, they would then gravitate toward Spain; they might even become her ally in a war that seemed inevitable with the United States. To be ready for such a struggle Spain should, of course, strengthen her river defenses.[19]

To the thoughtful, preparedness was wiser than trying to extend dominion through liberality to the Kentuckians. However, the former plan was expensive, and Spain did not care to lavish more funds on a province that had proved only a liability even if there was real prospect of its being invaded.

Danger of invasion soon became obvious. On March 9, 1793, Napoleon had declared war against Spain, and, without delay, tried to foment rebellion in her far-flung colonies of America. The Spanish masters of Louisiana trembled; they realized that the French at New Orleans yearned to be once more under the flag of their ancestors. Perhaps they might join with those hardy Americans of the backwoods, always ready for a fight, especially if there was a chance to wrest New Orleans from the Spaniards.

When Genêt, the French minister to the United States, arrived in Charleston on April 8, 1793, he quickly provided the Georgia frontiersmen with means to raid East Florida, and simultaneously laid plans for an expedition to attack Louisiana from the north. George Rogers Clark thought he could take New Orleans with 800 men. Genêt agreed, and appointed him "major-general of the Independent and Revolutionary Legion of the Mississippi." Washington in a few months proclaimed neutrality, Jefferson warned, and Genêt was recalled. Then Clark realized that France, like his own country, paid little for what he had already done.[20]

Though the enterprise failed, its preparation filled Carondelet with fears. Wilkinson made capital of them without delay. He urged the governor to strengthen his defenses against the possible coming of the Kentuckians, now keen for plunder and eager to navigate the Mississippi in their own right. He had bribed, as he says, the real leaders away from Clark's bandits and thereby saved New Madrid and St. Louis as Spanish possessions. Money was needed; in fact, he expected to spend from $6,000 to $10,000, and so he asked that $4,500 be sent him by the bearer. His own pension should be raised

---

[19] To Gayoso and Carondelet, Dec. 21, 1792, *Ibid.*
[20] James, *The Life of George Rogers Clark,* 408–427.

to $4,000 a year, for it was "absolutely necessary" to leave the Army and devote himself exclusively to the interests of Spain. But, said he, "do not believe me avaricious as the sensation never found place in my bosom. Constant in my attachments, ardent in my affections, and an enthusiast in the cause I espoused my character is the reverse." [21]

With the ever gullible Carondelet apparently accepting these self-made credentials as true, Wilkinson continued to emphasize his interest for Spain by harping on filibusters and Mississippi navigation. On the last day of April he wrote that he was employing a stool-pigeon to learn about Clark's plans, which, he added, were designed to drag the United States and Spain into war. Spain, he advised, had better court peace through negotiation, insisting on the exclusive right of navigating the Mississippi. If Congress agreed to such a monopoly, this would result in the "summary and infallible mode of accomplishing our wishes"; Kentucky would immediately apply for "the protection of Spain or England." To prevent an alliance with England, the Spanish minister at Philadelphia should have $200,000 for bribe money. Wilkinson, of course, would help in its correct distribution.[22]

As spring turned into summer, Wilkinson still continued his intrigues against the Spaniards, although much of his time was consumed in preparing his men for the long expected campaign against the Indians. He liked neither Wayne nor his methods; in fact, he had written to Knox directly charging his commander with incompetence. Under such a general, dangerous service had no personal appeal. Again he thought of resigning, but doing so would not enhance his prestige among the Spaniards, even less among his companions now on the eve of battle. After all, the Army did furnish a livelihood, and he was always in need of a dollar.

As usual, he was spending a good deal faster than he earned. In early March he had paid $800 to Harry Innes and Benjamin Sebastian through Michael La Cassagne, that thrifty Frenchman who had received $4,000 for him from the Spaniards in 1792. In May and June he had to meet $900 more in drafts drawn in favor of Major Thomas Cushing and others.[23] His Army pay of $104 per month could not liquidate obligations like these. He had to look about for other sources of income.

---

[21] To Carondelet (undated), A.G.I., Seville, *Papeles de Cuba,* leg. 2374.
[22] To Carondelet, Apr. 30, 1794, *Ibid.,* to same, June 20, 1794, A.H.N. *Estado,* leg. 3898.
[23] To La Cassagne, Mar. 11, 12, 1794, Innes Papers, Vol. XXIII.

On June 15, he wrote to Innes and asked if he knew the whereabouts of Henry Owen, that Irish soldier of fortune who was well acquainted with Spaniards of importance. He was just the man for a difficult mission and was one of the few that had an intimate knowledge of the General's intrigues. Wilkinson, now believing that he had "a magic wand at which all my difficulties are to vanish," wanted to employ him and a certain Captain Collins to help loosen the Spaniards' purse strings. They were both to go to Natchez and New Orleans bearing letters full of ruses for extracting pieces of eight from Carondelet, the governor of Louisiana. One scheme, previously referred to, involved furnishing the Spanish minister at Philadelphia with $200,000 which Wilkinson offered to distribute so that the Kentuckians would no longer desire to invade Louisiana or secure an alliance with England. They were the "dregs of society" or renegades from across the mountains and would listen readily to his plans, if paid. For several distinguished men in the West he needed immediate cash, were they to accompany him to a conference at New Orleans in November. He added that there were some sixteen Army officers, from major to lieutenant, who would like to enter the service of Spain. Naturally he counted himself in the number. They might prove valuable. Could the matter be arranged? Personally he had shown great zeal for His Majesty's interests; he had papers to prove that he had expended $8,640 in breaking up the contemplated expedition of George Rogers Clark against New Orleans. In view of this outlay and what was due him as pension, he asked that $12,000 be sent him in two amounts equally divided between Henry Owen and Captain Collins.[24]

Carondelet replied on the 6th of August. Yes, Wilkinson could help by dispensing the money that Spanish agents would send from Philadelphia. Besides, his own expenses to the November conference would be paid, as well as those of two others, Innes and Sebastian, for example. The Army officers, he warned, could not be taken care of, for that would only make others jealous. The General's pension might be increased to $4,000, that is, if the governor had anything to do with it. As a final piece of good news, the letter added that Henry Owen was being sent with $6,000, and, if directions to the contrary were not received, Collins would soon follow with a similar amount.

[24] To Innes, June 15, 1794, Innes Papers, Vol. XXIII; to Carondelet, June 20, 1794, A.G.I., Seville, *Papeles de Cuba*, leg. 2374.

Of the $12,000, $4,000 was to be credited as pension; the rest was reimbursement for the Clark business.[25]

Some time in August, 1794, Owen left New Orleans. Though a resourceful fellow, he needed help with so much specie; hence for greater safety it was sent in a Spanish vessel as far as New Madrid. Here it was packed in three small barrels, transferred to the galiot *Flèche,* and carried to the mouth of the Ohio, where Lieutenant Langlois, the officer in charge, left Owen, turning over to him the money and providing him with six oarsmen and a pilot called Pepillo. Owen did not travel far before the crew murdered and robbed him.[26] When he failed to appear, Wilkinson grew anxious and wrote to find out what had become of him. The worst was learned when three of the culprits were arrested and taken to Frankfort and confined in a house near Lewis' Tavern. Here they were interviewed by Innes and several others.[27] To try them then and there required evidence and might reveal important secrets; besides, a question of jurisdiction was involved. Judge Innes thought best to send them to Fort Washington, with the idea, perhaps, of the Army handling the case or giving Wilkinson an opportunity for personal investigation. The General did not care to have them about; they might talk too glibly; so he hustled them back to the Spanish commandant at New Madrid. On the way they were seized by a certain Major Doyle, of the Army, who was then commanding at Fort Massac and did not seem to like Wilkinson. Once more they were sent to Frankfort, where they were finally discharged for lack of evidence.[28]

About the same time that Owen was leaving New Orleans, Wilkinson was moving north to make war on the Indians. During the winter of 1793–1794 they had come to Greenville and discussed peace, but they were only a few and not representative of all the tribes. Those present were unwilling to return all their white captives—a condition for further negotiation. On February 10 they were heartened by the speech of Lord Dorchester, Governor-General of Canada, who told them that the British were on the eve of war with the Americans and expected to seize the land that was held in violation of the treaty of 1783. In April the Indians saw soldiers of the Crown erect a sturdy

[25] Carondelet to Wilkinson, Aug. 6, 1794, A.H.N., Madrid, *Estado,* leg. 3898.
[26] Deposition of F. Langlois, Dec. 29, 1808, *Amer. State Papers, Miscel.,* II, 81–82.
[27] Thurston to Innes, Dec. 28, 1810, Innes Papers, Vol. XXII.
[28] Affidavit of Thurston, Feb. 20, 1811, *Ibid.;* affidavit of William Hubble, James Hampton, and Ambrose White, *Ibid.,* Vol. XVIII.

fort at the foot of the Maumee rapids, and believed they had won powerful allies. They were happy, too, that the trader, Colonel Alexander McKee, was close by and could supply them with plenty of powder and ball. They saw their crops growing lush in the river bottoms and realized these soon would be burned unless the progress of the Americans was stayed.[29]

Blue Jacket, bitter with grievances, stirred the young braves with ideas of attacking Fort Recovery. They eagerly joined him in an enterprise that offered chances of good rations, horses, and blankets. On June 30, 1794, a band of a thousand or more were lurking in the tall grass a few hundred yards from the fort, waiting for a convoy returning to Greenville. Scarcely had the wagons rattled through the gates and headed southward, before the Indians opened fire, killing or wounding most of the officers and men and chasing the rest of them back to the cover of the stockade. Surrounding the fort, they fired into it all day long, hoping to exasperate the defenders, now half casualties, into a sally. Failing in this, they waited until the middle of the misty night and then tried to crawl forward until they could climb the wooden walls; but the sentinels were watchful and the attackers met with a stinging repulse.[30]

Such was the answer of the Indians to the white men's proposals of peace. Wayne now determined to let them have war, as they had chosen. On July 24, Major-General Charles Scott reached Greenville with the militia. With these reinforcements the Legion began the advance two days later.[31]

Of course Wilkinson was along, jealous of Wayne and peevish because few of his ideas had been adopted. Some of these had been expressed in a letter of the 10th of May. Wayne had replied three days later, stating among other things that the use of mounted volunteers had been anticipated as early as the 24th of March, but that he did not want them until the "avaricious" contractors had improved his supplies and transportation. When both were bettered, then he could give directions where the volunteers should join him; and he hoped that Wilkinson would then help him in accelerating their movement forward.[32] Wilkinson was angry because of an insinuation that he had not accumulated enough provisions at the head of the

[29] Boyd, *Mad Anthony Wayne*, 267–271.
[30] *Ibid.*, 273–278.
[31] *Ibid.*, 280.
[32] Wayne to Wilkinson, May 13, 1794, Wayne Papers, Vol. XXXIV.

line.[33] He also believed that he could advantageously employ the volunteers immediately. Wayne did not want them until everything was ready; he did not expect them to act as an independent body striking the enemy when and wherever they chose; they were not to enjoy federal pay without giving him aid in the way that he wanted it. He was not eager for superficial popularity and success; what he sought was a lasting peace, and he was carefully making preparations to obtain it. As might have been expected, Wilkinson found fault with such plans: the expense was excessive, the campaign was progressing too slowly, the volunteers were shabbily handled, etc.[34]

He felt peevish and humiliated because Wayne had sometimes ignored him. He was fearful that he might become a subordinate under Major-General Charles Scott of the volunteers, who, "though a fool, a scoundrel, and a poltroon," might secure the chief command in case Wayne were incapacitated.[35] Some time in April, Scott had visited Philadelphia, and while there had praised the work of Wayne that others had criticized.[36] Wilkinson knew only too well who these critics were, and he was resentful because any one had tried to confute them. To the stigma of incompetence Scott had added the sin of being a partisan of Wayne.

Fortunately for all concerned, Wayne, in spite of an old and often painful wound, continued as the commanding general of the advancing army. For nearly two weeks after leaving Greenville, it met with no resistance. It marched at the "usual velocity" of twelve miles a day through "Marassies," "Thickets almost impervious," "Defiles and beads of nettles more than waist high & miles in length." Mosquitoes were everywhere, water was scarce and heat intense. The men saw few hostile signs, and each day ended the same: they "beat their drums," "blowed" their trumpets and went to bed.[37]

On August 7 the Legion arrived within six miles of the Auglaize villages. Wilkinson would have attacked them immediately and thus

[33] To Wayne, June 8, 1794, Gratz Collection.
[34] To Innes, Oct. 23, 1793, Feb. 10, 1794, Innes Papers, Vol. XXIII.
[35] To Wayne, June 8, 1794, Gratz Collection; to Innes, Innes Papers, Vol. XXIII, Jan. 2, 1795, *et passim*.
[36] Scott to Wayne, Apr. 20, 1794, Wayne Papers, Vol. XXXIV.
[37] Clark, *Journal of General Wayne's Campaign;* Boyer, *A Journal of Wayne's Campaign;* and Wilkinson to John Brown, Aug. 28, 1794, in *Miss. Valley Historical Review,* June, 1929, pp. 81–90.

ended the war, as he thought; Wayne preferred to wait until more of the Indians had assembled. When he had come to the confluence of the Maumee and the Auglaize, he halted in this choice spot for eight days. Here fish and game were plentiful and the men found forage for their horses and ate greedily of the vegetables growing in the abandoned gardens. Wayne coveted the land and determined to hold it. Without delay he set his men to cutting timber for his latest stronghold, which was to bear the name of Fort Defiance. While at this task he sent a message to the Indians, making them again an offer of peace. In a few days an answer came, bidding the invaders halt for ten days; then they would learn if peace or war was to be their portion. Time was needed for the warriors to gather. Wayne understood, and resumed the advance.[38]

By the 18th his men had reached the head of the Rapids of the Maumee River. At the foot of them, ten miles distant, the Indians had pitched their camp about the British fort. For two days the Legion was busy building an earthwork, where all except the equipment for battle was stored. On the 20th, stripped for a fight, the men again took up the march. At about ten o'clock that morning they came to an opening in the woods where once a tornado had passed. Trees had fallen in a network of intricate patterns, and in this tangle of timber the Indians lay hidden, eagerly waiting for the moment of attack.

When Wayne's advance guard of volunteers approached, they met with a withering fire and retreated in confusion; but the regular light infantry re-formed and counterattacked. General Scott was ordered to move up on the left and fall on the Indian flank. The center and right rapidly advanced, driving the savages back two miles in less than an hour. Once through the forest and in the cornfields and prairies beyond, the Legion cavalry readily broke down any further resistance. Some of the fugitives made for the British fort, but they found the gates closed and had to continue their headlong flight to other places of refuge.

Major William Campbell was unwilling to give shelter to his would-be allies and risk war with the United States. He could salve his pride only by demanding an explanation of Wayne, who sent in turn an even more insolent reply. To anger the British more, he advanced within range of their guns and laid waste the land that they

[38] Boyd, *op. cit.*, 279–286.

had cultivated. The Indians now had proof that they could no longer expect aid from the British as once they had hoped.

Moreover, casualties, though not extremely heavy, were enough to lessen the Indians' faith in their prowess. Wayne generously estimated that there were 2,000 warriors at Fallen Timbers, and that they suffered twice his own losses, which he reported as 133 dead and wounded.[39] The Indians still had their main force; but they had lost the will to fight, they had begun to sense the power of Wayne and the futility of further resistance. He had invaded their best lands, cut down their crops, and burned their long-established villages. Wherever they threatened, he seemed to build a fort and place a garrison, and neither one nor the other could they take or surprise. Fallen Timbers was merely another convincing token of the irresistible advance of the white men into the lands north of the Ohio.

Wilkinson did not consider the battle of great importance, although he relished the praise that came to him for his action in it. Wayne, usually appreciative of good work on the part of subordinates, did not depart from his custom in his report to the Secretary of War:

"There were, however," said he, "some whose rank and situation placed their conduct in a very conspicuous point of view, and which I observe with pleasure, and the most lively gratitude. Among whom I beg leave to mention Brigadier General Wilkinson and Colonel Hamtramck, the commandants of the right and left wings of the legion, whose brave example inspired the troops." [40]

Hamtramck was that sturdy, combative Frenchman who sat on his horse like a frog. Praise to him was also sweet. In return for it he gave good and loyal service.

Wilkinson was different. On the very day that the official report on the battle of Fallen Timbers was composed, he wrote John Brown, senator from Kentucky, a letter that was filled with strictures on the conduct and capacity of Wayne. As he went on to say, Wayne lacked both resolution and enterprise; he was ignorant and liked to gasconade; he neglected his wounded, kept his men poorly supplied, and was indifferent to public expense. The same results, Wilkinson

[39] Wayne to Sec. of War, Aug. 28, 1794, *Amer. State Papers, Ind. Aff.*, I, 49. For other accounts of Fallen Timbers, see Wilkinson to John Brown, Aug. 28, 1794, in *Miss. Valley Hist. Rev.*, June, 1929, pp. 81–90; Clark, *Journal of General Wayne's Campaign*; Boyer, *A Journal of Wayne's Campaign.*

[40] Wayne to Sec. of War, Aug. 28, 1794, *Amer. State Papers, Ind. Aff.*, I, 49.

believed, might have been achieved by 1,500 volunteers in thirty days.[41]

A month and a half later, in October, he was even more caustic in a letter to Innes. "I am," said he, "well satisfied that such feeble & improvident arrangements, and such guardless & disorderly conduct was never before witnessed in any military corps of six months standing—Yet the specious name of Victory & the gloss of misrepresentation, will doubtless gild the Character of our Chief—For my own I am content, conscious as I am, that I have in several instances partially saved my country, and having extorted applause from my most bitter enemy, and the most finished scoundrel on Earth."[42]

By November he had lost all judgment and restraint in discussing the campaign. In another letter to Innes:

"The whole operation presents us a tissue of improvidence, disarray, precipitancy, Error & Ignorance, of thoughtless temerity, unseasonable Cautions, and shameful omissions, which I may safely pronounce, was never before presented to the view of mankind; yet under the favor of fortune, and the paucity & injudicious Conduct of the enemy, we have prospered beyond calculation, and the wreath is prepared for the brow of the Blockhead."[43]

In December, Wilkinson characterized Wayne as "a liar, a drunkard, a Fool, the associate of the lowest order of Society, & the companion of their vices, of desperate Fortunes, my rancorous enemy, a Coward, a Hypocrite, and the contempt of every man of sense and virtue."[44]

Apparently Wilkinson overlooked such obvious blemishes as being short-tempered and having the gout. Nevertheless, they were probably very important to Wayne even if Wilkinson did not think them worth mentioning.

Wilkinson's railing, almost wholly untrue, strikingly contrasted with the opinion of the people, whose enthusiasm had been deeply aroused by the victory of August 20. In December, 1794, Wayne and his men received the thanks of Congress.[45] This commendation was not undeservedly given. The Legion had labored unsparingly in the erection of forts across the length of a hostile country. These, with

---

[41] To John Brown, Aug. 28, 1794, *loc. cit.*
[42] To Innes, Oct. 13, 1794, Innes Papers, Vol. XXIII.
[43] To Innes, Nov. 10, 1794, *Ibid.*
[44] To Innes, Dec., 1794, *Ibid.*
[45] Boyd, *op. cit.*, 303.

lines of communication between, it continued to hold against frequent attack. In a trying campaign, it had decisively defeated the Indians in battle; and from them had wrested the control of the Northwest for the first time. Peace had not been definitely established; but the memory of Fallen Timbers, the hunger of hard winter days, and Wayne's indomitable will were destined to accomplish the treaty of Greenville within a year.

Against such a successful person, Wilkinson would have difficulty in proving his jealous and ill founded indictments. On December 5, 1794, he received a letter from Henry Knox, Secretary of War, in answer to two of his own that had been written in June and July making five general charges against Wayne and requesting a court of inquiry covering his own conduct. Wilkinson was told that he might have his inquiry if he chose, but that the charges would have to be more specific before they were considered further. A copy of them, Knox significantly added, had been forwarded to Wayne, who duly received them some time in January, 1795. He straightway pronounced them "as unexpected as they are groundless, and as false as they are base and insidious; and had I not known the real character and disposition of the man, I should have considered the whole as the idle Phantom of a disturbed immagination [sic]." [46] If guilty of them, Wayne declared, he himself ought to be hanged.[47] Just what they stated is not easily ascertained; the letters containing them seem to have been lost or destroyed. Not unlikely Wilkinson expressed in some of them his belief that Wayne was arrogant and overbearing toward his subordinates, notoriously wasteful of government funds, and contemptuous in his treatment of the volunteers. After the battle of Fallen Timbers, Wilkinson's strictures were equally violent but less open and more extended in scope. Among other things he declared that Wayne had failed to take all the prisoners warranted by that victory, he had pursued a line of march which was "improper and absurd," and his battle formations were wholly preposterous. In his official correspondence, Wilkinson changed the character but not the number of charges. Unfortunately they have not been found in their final form.[48]

[46] Wayne to Butts, Jan. 29, 1795, Wayne Papers, Vol. XXXIX.
[47] Hamtramck to Wilkinson, Aug. 29, 1796, Wilkinson Papers, Vol. I, Chicago Hist. Soc.
[48] Belli to Wilkinson, May 16, 1796, *Ibid.;* Day to Wilkinson, May 23, 1796, *Ibid.;* Blue to Wayne, Jan. 8, 1796, Wayne Papers, Vol. XXXIX.

Seeing that Knox would not countenance any underhand methods to ruin a rival, Wilkinson temporarily changed his tactics, especially after Fallen Timbers, when the star of Wayne was in the ascendant. It might prove highly embarrassing to attack a general who could, if he chose, retaliate meanly. Accordingly on January 1, 1795, he wrote Knox a "public letter" to this effect:

"My Lips are now Sealed, my Pen is dismissed from depicting well founded grievances, and I implore Heaven that the painful office may never be forced upon me." [49]

Apparently Wilkinson was willing to bury the hatchet.

But next day, in a letter to Knox marked "private," he disclosed his real thoughts. Toward Wayne and Scott he showed no change of heart. Wayne, he declared, knew nothing about the action of the right wing at the battle of Fallen Timbers; in fact, he had not even come near his ranking brigadier during the whole engagement; hence the official report covering that part of it was just about as applicable as "the battle of the Kegs." Doubtless Scott's version would have proven even less satisfactory. When Wilkinson thought he might possibly have to serve under such "a worthless old scoundrel" as the latter, he declared this would be "the most agonizing mortification" of his life.[50]

Lately Scott had been circulating the story that Knox was eager to have Wayne in command so that he would not be persecuted by Wilkinson's "damned long letters." [51] This gossip quickly gave offense to Wilkinson, who was never able to save himself through a sense of humor. Because of his exaggerated sense of honor, he was readily offended and quickly stirred into action. Often in mad moments he flung caution to the winds and attacked with vigor and vengeance. Then he was easily vulnerable but none the less dangerous to those who had aroused his anger. Only enemies with a real stomach for fighting and a hatred to strengthen their arm had spirit to challenge his strength.

Wayne did not do so immediately. Though acquainted with Wilkinson's treachery, Wayne may have decided that the wisest procedure was to ignore it temporarily. Certainly it was not because he was noted for his patience and his willingness to conciliate. He

---

[49] To Innes, Jan. 1, 1795, Innes Papers, Vol. XXIII.
[50] To Knox, Jan. 2, 1795, *Ibid.*
[51] Wilkinson to Innes, Jan. 2, 1795, *Ibid.*

must have realized that this was no time for factional fights. He could well recall how investigations and courts-martial had nearly wrecked the Army during critical days of the Revolution. So far he had succeeded only partially in the mission assigned him; more important work was ahead. Congress was in session and hopefully watching developments in the Northwest. In a way, Wayne himself was on trial, and he could not afford to jeopardize his own and his country's interests by spending his energies in bringing disloyal subordinates to book, particularly when they had a strong following and charges against them would be difficult to prove.

Wilkinson was, therefore, left free in his efforts to injure the reputation of Wayne. He wanted his own to grow by contrast. Both faced the recurrent danger that one of them would lose his commission in case Congress should decrease the Army. In February, 1795, its members were debating this very question. Madison, among other Virginians, favored a reduction. To him the Army was expensive and a constant menace to the liberties of the people; if it had to exist, its functions should be confined to protecting the frontier.[52] Fisher Ames of Massachusetts was of contrary opinion, for he knew that the use of militia in the past had only tended to increase expenses and prolong the period of war.[53] Wayne, according to Wilkinson, was guilty of the "pious fraud" of trying to save the Legion by withholding news of a favorable turn in negotiations with the Indians until after Congress had adjourned. If once the prospect of peace were certain, support for the Army would weaken.

Wilkinson might not have made this imputation of trickery had he shared in the preliminaries of the treaty of Greenville; apparently he was engaged in only a few routine duties of minor importance. At the time Wayne declared Wilkinson "had no command in the Army, and if he had any modesty he would resign"; [54] he considered him a "vile assasin," an agent of British and Democrats of Kentucky to dismember the Union, the "worst of all bad men." No wonder he swore to resign his commission if Wilkinson continued in the service.[55]

Openly ignored and given little work to do, Wilkinson was left largely free to follow his own peculiar bent. Like most persons in

[52] Madison to Jefferson, Feb. 15, 1795, in *Letters and Other Writings of James Madison* (Worthington ed.), II, 35–36.
[53] Ames to Dwight, Feb. 3, 1795, in *Works of Fisher Ames*, I, 166.
[54] Certificate of J. M. Scott, Jan. 8, 1796, Wayne Papers, Vol. XLIII.
[55] Wayne to Knox, Jan. 29, 1795, *Ibid.*, Vol. XXXIX.

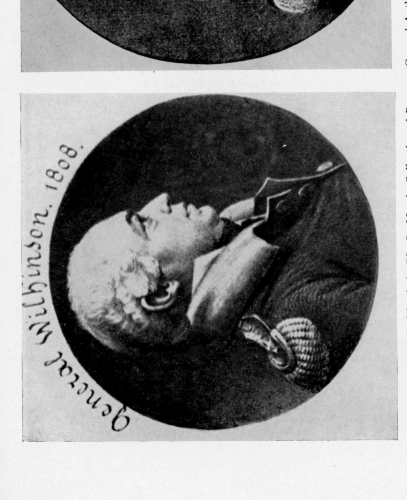

From a portrait by St. Memin in *The St. Memin Collection of Portraits*, p. 33 of plates.

General Anthony Wayne from a portrait by Edward Savage in the New York Historical Society.

Courtesy of the Librarian, Alexander J. Wall.

the West, he had not been able to refrain from trying to make a fortune in real estate. At one time while living in Kentucky, his personal and joint holdings had been counted in thousands of acres; but many of these had been sold in the last few years to pay different persons for losses that they had suffered in his tobacco transactions. To Peyton Short, former business associate, he still owed three thousand dollars. In 1795 Wilkinson was "tampering" with him through an agent who was authorized to pay one-third of the amount as total settlement. Of course, as he wrote Judge Harry Innes,[56] the ruse was to be kept as silent as the grave.

The Judge had handled all of the General's legal business for several years. When debtors failed to make their payments or titles were clouded, he brought suit for his client. As often as requested, he arranged for the sale of large or small tracts to raise funds for meeting the demands of insistent creditors. He prosecuted some for knavery in land deals. One of them was Humphrey Marshall, who had lied about the title and quality of land sold to Wilkinson. The case was decided in the General's favor during 1793. From then on Marshall voiced his hatred without restraint or regard for facts. In November, 1795, Wilkinson believed that he and the "Old Harredan [*sic*] the Widow Todd" were attempting to vilify him through the agency of one Percival Butler.[57] He retaliated in characteristic fashion. Within a few months, during January, 1796, Marshall, as a newly elected senator from Kentucky had to suffer the humiliation of defending himself from charges of "gross fraud" and "perjury" that Muter, Wallace, and Wilkinson had formulated and forwarded through the governor of Kentucky. By a vote of eight to sixteen, the Senate permitted Marshall to retain his seat.[58]

Legal services, such as Judge Innes rendered, were expensive, and the transactions that they involved required considerable capital. As a good liver and a free spender, Wilkinson had to have more than his Army pay. He had a hankering for speculation, for, beside being a field for daring ventures, it sometimes disclosed a short road to affluence. He did not seem to have trouble in finding some one to share in his enterprises, inasmuch as they frequently presented alluring prospects of gain and he usually lived up to his own part of the bargain. Often leading men in the West and East were his associates.

[56] To Innes, Mar. 17, 1795, Innes Papers, Vol. XXIII.
[57] Wilkinson to Innes, Nov. 28, 1795, *Ibid.*
[58] *Amer. State Papers, Miscel.,* I, 141, 144.

On October 18, 1796, he and John Brown, a senator from Kentucky, signed a bond to Innes for $4,000, one-half of which was to be paid within a year.[59]

Maturing accounts like this one, Wilkinson might be able to meet, if the Spaniards continued to provide him with funds. And this they appeared willing to do. Late in August, 1794, Captain Collins, Wilkinson's agent, had begun preparations for leaving New Orleans for Kentucky with $6,334 that Carondelet was sending. After a number of delays he took the route by sea instead of the more direct one that the unfortunate Owen had followed the year before. He arrived in Charleston safely with the money but was somewhat the worse off because of a stormy autumn voyage.[60] From there he made his way to Pittsburgh, where he remained until the weather made travel safe down the Ohio. On April 3, 1795, Wilkinson was expecting to see him in a month; a week later he arrived, but with only a part of the original sum. A thousand dollars had been frittered away; $2,500 had been invested without authority in land around Fort Pitt; $334 was paid over to Collins as a carrying charge; only $2,500 remained—this, at least, was the way that Wilkinson would have the Spaniards cast up his account.[61]

While Wilkinson was anxiously waiting for the coming of Collins, arrangements were being perfected for a conference with the Indians at Greenville. During the winter of 1794–1795, some of their chiefs, hungry like their lean horses, had come and talked and eaten with Wayne. They had agreed to an armistice and planned to gather again in larger numbers for discussing the conditions of peace. In midsummer they came, about eleven hundred strong; but it was not until August 3, 1795, that the treaty of Greenville was formally signed. By its terms the Wyandots, Shawnees, Delawares, Miamis, and other tribes of the Northwest ceased making war and agreed to evacuate all but the upper third of the Ohio country less certain parcels of land about Chicago, Detroit, and a few other places. Thus for a time they desisted from robbing and killing those who would settle in a long disputed area, and the United States, relieved of a great burden of defense, was better able to defend her rights against those who held dominion along her borders.[62]

[59] Bond of Wilkinson and Brown, Oct. 18, 1796, Innes Papers, Vol. XXIII.
[60] Collins to Clark, Mar. 10, 1809, *Amer. State Papers, Miscel.*, II, 84.
[61] To Gayoso, Apr. 3, Nov. 1, 1795, A.G.I., Seville, *Papeles de Cuba*, leg. 2374.
[62] Boyd, *Mad Anthony Wayne*, 305–322.

Close by was Canada. England, an old and powerful enemy, possessed it; but she had lately given tokens of friendship in the Jay treaty, which the Senate had grudgingly ratified on June 24, 1795. It said nothing about impressment, little about trade; boundaries, damages, and debts were to be arbitrated, and the fur posts along the Great Lakes were to be evacuated within a year.[63] Such terms indicated a rapprochement that other powers beheld with jealous concern.

Spain was one of these. Although a traditional enemy, she had become an ally of England on May 25, 1793. To her, Protestant doctrines were somewhat easier of acceptance than the democratic principles that France had adopted and was endeavoring to spread. From this mismated alliance of three years, Spain profited little on the Continent of Europe; within the United States she saw her ally indirectly help toward stabilizing conditions along the Ohio.[64] Once peace and unity obtained in this area, Spain would find increasingly difficult a continued monopoly of the Mississippi and the defense of her possessions along its lower reaches. Consequently her agents at New Orleans viewed with alarm the turn that events were taking during the summer of 1795.

They tried to revive their old scheme of breaking up the Union, centering their efforts on Kentucky, whose citizens were now exasperated with excise taxes and the apparent failure of federal diplomacy to secure navigation of the Mississippi. To promote discord in the West, Carondelet had written to Wilkinson on August 6, 1794, asking that Benjamin Sebastian, Harry Innes, and others come to New Madrid and confer with certain Spanish officials on matters of mutual interest.[65] By July 1, 1795, the governor felt sure that through the means of private discussions they would be able to reach an agreement concerning the Mississippi in fewer months than Congress had taken years.[66] Fifteen days later he wrote that commissioners must come "indubitably prepared to treat," and that he would recompense them liberally with pensions. If negotiations proved successful Wilkinson himself might aspire to the same position in the West that Washington had attained in the East. On the same date, July 16, he also wrote to Sebastian, requesting again that those who were to

---

[63] Channing, *History of the United States*, IV, 137–138.
[64] Bemis, *Pinckney's Treaty*, 191 *et passim*.
[65] Carondelet to Wilkinson, Aug. 6, 1794, A.H.N., Madrid, *Estado*, leg. 3898.
[66] Carondelet to Wilkinson, July 1, 1795, A.G.I., Seville, *Papeles de Cuba*, leg. 2374.

act as delegates be properly empowered as his own Spanish agents would be. He suggested October as the time for meeting and that the general plan be discussed with leading men in Kentucky.[67]

Soon Innes and William Murry met at the house of Colonel Nicholas, and there Sebastian showed them the letter that he had received. Then the four of them composed a reply. They evinced willingness to attend a conference, for they realized that the navigation of the Mississippi was of supreme importance to their section and, if it were not secured, peace could not long be maintained. However, they declared their inability to come except in a private capacity.[68]

On October 3, 1795, Thomas Power arrived in Cincinnati bringing letters of "greatest importance." Wilkinson had known him for several years as a confidential agent of Spain whose "ruling passion" was traveling. The two held several nocturnal conferences in Wilkinson's quarters. Power remained in the neighborhood until the 14th, and then left with letters for Gayoso de Lemos, Spanish governor at Natchez.[69] These, with others that Wilkinson wrote to him shortly afterwards, urged a cash gratuity of $20,000 and an increase of his pension, liberal payment of those who should attend the conference, and secret strengthening of Spanish defenses along the Mississippi. Should the need arise, Spain should be ready to supply Kentucky with 10,000 stands of arms, a field train of brass ordnance and accompanying ammunition. War, however, was not desirable; it would prove better to increase indulgences to the western people until peace was established in Europe. Then, as he apparently wished Gayoso to infer, the United States would have greater difficulty in finding an ally to support her claims. He declared the Army would soon be reduced, if he had his way. He pertinently advised that the whole matter should be kept secret; disclosure would mean the sending of a federal army corps to the Mississippi. He might have added that Kentucky would have been thrown into tumult and that he and his friends would have suffered unmeasured embarrassment.[70]

During December, Power got in touch with Sebastian, and the two made their way to the mouth of the Ohio, where they were to meet

[67]Carondelet to Wilkinson, July 16, 1795, *Ibid.* Carondelet to Sebastian, July 16, 1795, Bodley, "Introduction" to Filson Club Publications, No. 31, p. lxxx.
[68] Bodley, *op. cit.*, lxxxi–lxxxiii.
[69] Deposition of Power, Mar. 18, 1809, *Amer. State Papers, Miscel.*, II, 86–87.
[70] To Gayoso, Nov. 4, 11, 1795, A.G.I., Seville, *Papeles de Cuba*, leg. 2374; Whitaker, *The Mississippi Question*, 212–213.

Gayoso. Here they discussed Carondelet's chimerical scheme for Kentucky's seduction. Innes, Nicholas, and Murry were not present; for one reason or another they had thought best not to go. Since Gayoso could come to no agreement with the ex-preacher and lawyer without cases, they decided to go to New Orleans and lay their differences before Carondelet. They arrived there about the first of the year 1796. In February the governor received the text of the Pinckney treaty. It gave to the western people all they wanted concerning navigation of the Mississippi, but Carondelet still clung to the infatuation of winning their allegiance to the Crown.[71]

Sebastian was paid $4,000, and Power was given the job of carrying more written and verbal messages to Wilkinson. They remained in New Orleans till about the last of March, and then left together, returning to Kentucky via the Atlantic and Philadelphia. On the 19th of May, Power again reached Cincinnati. From this place he wrote and asked permission to visit Fort Greenville for the purpose of delivering some "segars" and other gifts to Wilkinson. His request was granted, and before long he was at the fort, where he remained a week. Thus he had full opportunity to deliver in person important dispatches from New Orleans and talk over with Wilkinson the aid Spain might give toward promoting the separation of the western country from the United States.[72] They were discerning enough to know that an objective like this could not be achieved, but both wanted to line their own pockets; and so they colored their reports in a way best suited to make Carondelet believe that his scheme was entirely feasible. The governor was no match for this parasitical pair; at this very time he was paying handsomely for wholly imaginary services.

Power brought the exhilarating news that $9,640 was being sent up the Mississippi by Carondelet for Wilkinson. Thereupon Wilkinson dispatched him to get it. Bound on this errand he set out for New Madrid. On reaching there he had difficulty in obtaining the money, because Wilkinson had refused to give him a written order for it. To make matters worse, a certain Elisha Winters, of the town, wrote and told Wayne of its coming. In the hope of avoiding a disaster like that of Henry Owen, the money had been packed in barrels of sugar and coffee. So hidden, it had passed safely up the river, even es-

[71] Bodley, *op. cit.*, lxxxiii; Bemis, *Pinckney's Treaty*, 345–347.
[72] *Annals of Congress*, 11th Cong., Part 2, pp. 2313–2323.

caping detection when a Lieutenant Steele of the Army searched the boat that bore it. This piece of international discourtesy Wilkinson endeavored to make much of while on a later visit to Philadelphia. Knowing the need of haste, Power plied his men with whisky to give zest to their rowing. Arriving at Louisville, he had the cargo landed safely and then hastened to Cincinnati to inform Wilkinson, from whom he received directions to deliver the money to Nolan, who had recently returned to Kentucky from Louisiana. The barrels were carried to Frankfort and opened in the store of Montgomery Brown. Nolan took $9,000, while Power retained $640 as payment for expenses. When a report was made to Wilkinson, he said "it was well." [73]

Wilkinson might have said the same thing about his success as a Spanish agent for the preceding six years. In 1790 Miró had advanced him $7,000.[74] Since accepting his commission in the Army, he had received $4,000 through La Cassagne in 1792; $12,000 had been sent him in 1794 by Owen and Collins, of which he had probably received half; and lately Nolan and Power had delivered $9,000 more. Therefore by the end of 1796 Spain had disbursed, at least, $32,000 for Wilkinson's alleged services for the Crown. Of this amount he received approximately $26,000. Since his venality was never long disturbed by pricks of conscience, so large a sum must have made bearable what, as he confessed, was his "villainous confidential connexion with Spain." [75]

In the future the Spaniards were not to yield so readily to requests for pay. The Pinckney treaty had placated most of their enemies in the West, and Wilkinson could no longer picture them as Vandals eager to plunder a Spanish domain. He would, of course, try to create bugbears out of boundary disputes, prospects of an English alliance, or the Burr conspiracy, but fears would not be engendered that were productive of great financial reward. The heyday of bribes, gifts, pensions, and perquisites was coming to a close. They would continue only in a very modified way, for Spain was growing poorer every day.

Wilkinson could not even feel sure of his pay as a brigadier-general in the Army. Through the work of Jay, Pinckney, and Wayne our

---

[73] Deposition of Power, Mar. 18, 1809, in *Amer. State Papers, Miscel.*, II, 86–87.
[74] Miró to Wilkinson, Sept. 2, 1790, A.G.I., Seville, *Papeles de Cuba*, leg. 2374.
[75] To Gayoso, Apr. 7, 1795, *Ibid.*

relations with England, Spain, and the Indians had all been improved during the critical year of 1795. Peace in the West, from Canada to the Gulf of Mexico, was nearer realization than it had been for a long while. The immediate need for an Army was not so apparent as before. Its reduction was therefore espoused by some who were prejudiced and shortsighted and others who courted popular favor by curtailing federal expenditures.

Wilkinson knew that a "Grand Committee of the Union" had favorably reported a bill on March 25 that involved cutting down the Army and abolishing the grade of major-general.[76] Later he was informed by Jonathan Dayton, a congressman from New Jersey, that the Senate favored retaining the higher grade but abolishing that of brigadier-general.[77] It is significant that Wayne had been in Philadelphia since the first of April, enjoying there and elsewhere many marks of popular esteem. On June 7 Wilkinson learned that both houses had come to an agreement on the size of the Army but none could be reached about which of the two grades in question should be eliminated.[78] Finally a law was passed on May 30, 1796, providing for the retention of both, a diminished strength for the Army, and abolition of the legionary organization. The changes were to become effective October 1.[79]

Wilkinson might congratulate himself that he had been neither deranged nor eliminated. He could attribute his good fortune more to the work of some of his friends and a belief among the discriminating that the integrity of the Army should be preserved than to any helpful, friendly influence that Wayne, while in the East, had exerted. Less than a year had passed since he had stated publicly that Wilkinson, being without a command, ought to resign.[80] Wayne knew the source of disloyal and subversive influences in the Legion and the author of the charges against him that Washington was then endeavoring to find out the best way to handle. He was also acquainted with Power, whom he considered both a spy of Spain and a friend of Wilkinson. So suspicious had he become of the Spaniards that boats coming from the lower Mississippi were ordered searched. In short, Wayne had good reasons for wishing to be rid of his second

[76] To Innes, Apr. 16, 1796, Innes Papers, Vol. XXIII.

[77] Dayton to Wilkinson, May 20, 1796, Durrett Coll., Univ. of Chicago.

[78] Belli to Wilkinson, June 7, 1796, *Ibid.*

[79] Callan, *Military Laws of the United States,* 83–84; Ganoe, *The History of the United States Army,* 103.

[80] Certificate of J. M. Scott, Jan. 8, 1796. Wayne Papers, Vol. XLIII.

in command. If he had been more of the type of an Andrew Jackson, he would have done so in spite of political obstacles.

In this struggle between the two, Wilkinson was cleverer, and usually more indirect, in venting his spite. Two days after Wayne's departure for the East in February, 1796, he had declared in a general order his "Determination to inculcate, to enforce and to maintain a Uniform System of Subordination and Discipline through all Ranks, without Partiality, Prejudice, Favor or Affection." In this "Arduous undertaking" he called on his "Officers one and all for their aid and cooperation." [81] Thus was the Army to be remade according to Wilkinson standards. By implication, it was no longer to suffer the deterioration that had existed during the days of Wayne's command.

This unbecoming declaration added nothing to the reputation that Wilkinson now appeared so eager to improve; perhaps it made others less appreciative of the good work that he had actually accomplished and expected to perform. Forts that Wayne had recently built and those that the British were to evacuate, all were subject to his orders. When Captain B. Shaumburgh was sent to arrange the details for the surrender of Detroit he was instructed to arouse no discontent among the inhabitants but to assure them that the government would promote their happiness. He himself was bidden to be discreet, live quietly, and make no promises.[82] One could little improve advice like this. Major H. Buell was told to move to Fort Wayne until supplies were on the way. For this newly made fort, Wilkinson arranged for 12,000 pounds of flour, asked Wayne for proper artillery and ammunition, and warned against peculation of soldiers' clothing and Indian annuities that were soon to arrive.[83] In another area Colonel Hamtramck was urged to conciliate the savages and economize on supplies.[84]

Thus did advice and arrangements run concerning rations, shelter, and protection of the scattered garrisons in the great Northwest. As a soldier of experience Wilkinson understood the difficulties of the task and his own personal responsibility as commanding general. Goaded by professional pride and nettled with jealousy, he was keen to give proof of work well done when once Wayne had returned and demanded an accounting.

[81] Boyd, *Mad Anthony Wayne*, 331–332.
[82] To Shaumburgh, May 27, 1796, Miscellaneous Papers, N.Y. Public Library.
[83] To Buell, May 10, 1796, to Butler, June 20, 1796, *Ibid.* Wayne to Wilkinson, Apr. 1, 1796, Wayne Papers, Vol. XLIV.
[84] To Hamtramck, June 30, 1796, Miscellaneous Papers, N.Y. Public Library.

In June, 1796, he arrived after four months' leave in the East. Wilkinson wanted to go there himself, possibly in the *Federal,* the government barge offered for the purpose.[85] Two generals were one too many in the Northwest; one could look after the routine work of the Army without the other's help. The frontier could spare him, Philadelphia beckoned. He and Ann had not been there for several years; now they could make a visit in comfort on the money that Power had brought. Soon another President would be elected, a new administration inaugurated. It was well to know those who were to sit in the seats of the mighty. In the late Army reorganization, he had escaped elimination only by a hair's breadth; next time he might not be so fortunate. Wayne had told his own story of the campaign; the time was ripe for another version that would invigorate the reputation of Wilkinson, on which lengthening shadows had been lately cast.

To some Wilkinson gave his own specific reason for going. He told Innes that he wanted to defend his own name "against a variety of foul and infamous imputations," to support his "allegations against Wayne," and to vindicate the "Conduct & the Character of many of my friends in Kentucky." [86] Perhaps the "infamous imputations" concerned his intrigues with the Spaniards; they may have referred to his connection with the case of Robert Newman. For some time before the battle of Fallen Timbers the British had been trying to induce men in Wayne's army to desert and join them. Acting as a stool-pigeon for Wayne, Newman became friendly with those suspected of British leanings and obtained from them, in the name of Wilkinson, "sundry papers under seal." After reading their contents, Wayne ordered Newman to carry them to the British at Detroit. He did so, but on returning to Pittsburgh, he was put in irons and brought to Greenville, where he was held in confinement until the treaty of 1795 had been made with the Indians. He hoped for reward but obtained little. Wayne's aide, who acted as intermediary, spent the money instead.[87] Such, at least, is the story as told by Obadiah Newman, a brother of Robert; found among the former papers of Wilkinson, it is probably favorable to him.

The exact part Wilkinson played in the affair is not clear; that

[85] Boyd, *op. cit.,* 332.
[86] To Innes, Sept. 4, 1796, Innes Papers, Vol. XXIII.
[87] Deposition of Obadiah Newman, July 13, 1796, Wilkinson Papers, Vol. I, Chicago Hist. Soc.; *Memoirs,* II, App. XLIV.

imputed to him was sinister enough to cause the greatest personal anxiety. For several days he was incapable of "eating or drinking." He tried to confuse the real issue by making much of "the violated seal." [88] If the evidence forwarded to Philadelphia had indicated his collusion with the British or Indians, he never would have escaped merited punishment at the hands of Washington or Adams. Wayne certainly was in no mood to minimize any incriminating details when he wrote or talked to the Secretary of War. Wilkinson may have been employing dubious methods, but it was unlikely that he was guilty of treachery. He may have been up to one of his old tricks, using real or pretended deserters to obtain information that he wanted. Wayne had shown displeasure with Wilkinson for sending Reuben Reynolds on a somewhat similar mission during 1792; he would scarcely countenance a repetition of the same methods without his consent only two years later. Wayne liked to spend secret service money in the way that he chose; obviously he did not want it diverted into channels that would benefit a rival.

Holding the purse strings was a privilege worth having, and serving as a commissioner to the Indians increased an officer's pay at the rate of eight dollars a day. These, with other perquisites and honors of the commanding general, Wilkinson coveted and was determined to have. By a vigorous counter offensive he expected to save himself and ruin Wayne. His principal weapon consisted in the charges that he had previously preferred, somewhat modified by conditions that had arisen since the battle of Fallen Timbers. Thomas Cushing, a stanch friend, carried letters including them to the Secretary of War, remaining in Philadelphia for a while and inform-ing Wilkinson what Wayne and his staff were doing.[89] Until his departure for the East, Wilkinson searched far and near for evidence that would injure Wayne; he also took steps to prevent his own reputation from being assailed.

He was afraid that his intrigues with the Spaniards might be dis-covered. During the autumn of 1796 he wrote to Gayoso de Lemos that he was planning a trip to the East to "belie Wayne's slanders" and make an international affair of Power's mistreatment. Along with such an avowal went this request: "For the love of God, my friend,

[88] Hamtramck to Wilkinson, Aug. 29, 1796, Wilkinson Papers, Vol. I, Chicago Hist. Soc.; Turner to Wilkinson, Feb. 19, 1796, *Ibid.*
[89] Cushing to Wilkinson, June 4, 1796, *Ibid.*

enjoin greater secrecy and caution in all our concerns; never suffer my name to be written or spoken." He added that the suspicion of Washington was wide awake, and that he wanted his correspondence placed beyond the reach of treachery.[90]

Simultaneously he urged Carondelet to observe all secrecy in writing, and so to distort Spanish accounting that moneys remitted in the past would appear as tobacco balances legitimately due him. He also asked that Power, provided with plenty of papers, meet him in Philadelphia. Power's case might be the means of "disjoining" the Pinckney treaty. By such means Wilkinson hoped to dissipate rumors of his dishonesty that came from New Orleans; then he could better discharge his confessed mission in the City of Brotherly Love: "to keep down the military establishment to disgrace my commander and secure myself the command of the Army." [91]

In early autumn Wilkinson left Fort Washington and began his passage up the Ohio. Wayne remained behind, performing the duties incident to an army widely scattered along an Indian frontier. Broken by hardships and wounds in the service of his country, he, too, was soon to start upon an even longer journey. His strength was failing and his days were few. Shortly after reaching Presque Isle he sickened and died. While cold December winds blew strong his comrades buried him in the frozen earth beside the flagpole of the fort. Young "Jackie" Wilkinson had already traveled to that same "fearsome country" during the autumn.[92] Thus within a short while Wilkinson was to find that death had robbed him of his eldest son and destroyed his bitterest rival. A new chapter in his career was opening; his visit to Philadelphia was to mark its beginning.

[90] To Gayoso and Carondelet, Sept. 22, 1796, A.G.I., Seville, *Papeles de Cuba,* leg. 2375.
[91] To Carondelet, Sept. 22, 1796, *Ibid.*
[92] Butler to Wayne, Oct. 19, 1796. Wayne Papers, Vol. XLVII.

CHAPTER VII

THE NEW GENERAL–IN–CHIEF INSPECTS
AND DISPOSES

DURING the last days of September, 1796, several boats were being prepared at Fort Washington for passengers who expected to travel to Pittsburgh. Since the signing of the treaty of Greenville, Indians had become less hostile and travelers might use the river with relative safety, although they had to suffer many discomforts. Only the best keel boats had separate cabins for men and women and fireplaces that furnished means for heating and cooking. No matter how watchful, pilots could not always escape running into sawyers, planters, and shoals. Barring common accidents and attacks from savages en route, not more than ten to fifteen miles could be counted on as the average upstream distance that might be covered in a single day; and such progress was always accomplished at the price of great labor with cable, oars, and sail. To cover the round trip from Cincinnati to Pittsburgh in four weeks required both luck and skill. In 1794 Winthrop Sargent consumed twenty-eight days in actual travel on the upstream leg of the journey.[1]

Wilkinson made it in about ten days less when he set out on or about the 3rd of October, 1796.[2] He was accompanied by Mrs. Wilkinson and Master Joseph Biddle, who was now almost eleven, a connection or two of the Harrises, and presumably several officers and soldiers who were using this opportunity to go East before the coming of winter.[3] Already maple leaves were yellowing and little patches of corn and pumpkins that pioneers had planted were covered with hoarfrost during some of the early mornings. Perhaps Biddle—for so his mother called him—welcomed a buffalo robe or bearskin thrown over him when night winds blew cold across the surface of the river,

[1] Bond, *The Civilization of the Old Northwest*, 351–361.
[2] Wayne to McHenry, Oct. 3, 1796, Wayne Papers, Vol. XLVI.
[3] To Innes, Sept. 4, 1796, Innes Papers, Vol. XXIII.

although his father had seen to it that their cabin was new and comfortable and spacious. He was accustomed to travel, knew the things that made it easier, and usually provided them for his family and friends. Like many others of the frontier, he was generous, too; and when he reached Pittsburgh on the 20th of October, he offered his boat to Andrew Ellicott, who was then planning to descend the river to survey the boundary line in accordance with the provisions of the Pinckney treaty.[4]

The Wilkinsons remained in Pittsburgh only long enough to visit a few of their friends and secure transportation. They were eager to be off; crossing the mountains was difficult when snow began to fly, and they all yearned to see John and James, who had been in Philadelphia since 1792 for schooling.[5] The General had additional reason for haste; he wanted to make sure of his own professional future while there was opportunity. But before starting they were stunned by distressing news. John, who used to read so prettily and write amazingly well, had been stricken, perhaps with yellow fever, and had died while they were moving slowly up the Ohio.[6] In the presence of such a disaster there was nothing they could do; they could only hold him closer in memory and keenly recall the love they bore him or perhaps break down in sorrow beside a newly made grave on some dreary autumn day.

Under this burden of grief, they reached Philadelphia, which was still enjoying intervals of Indian summer. Senators and representatives were returning to the city in anticipation of the second session of the Fourth Congress. Wilkinson had a number of friends among them. Some time before coming East he had written Jonathan Dayton, an associate in land speculation and now speaker of the House, about renting a place for Mrs. Wilkinson and the family.[7] John Brown had been a full-fledged senator from Kentucky since 1793; Aaron Burr, from New York, was enjoying an even longer period of similar service. Besides, James McHenry, Secretary of War, and John Adams, President-elect, seemed favorably inclined toward Wilkinson; even Washington himself, now eager for retirement, had given tokens of appreciation for good work accomplished in the Northwest. On the other hand, there was Humphrey Marshall, senator from Kentucky

[4] *The Journal of Andrew Ellicott*, 6.
[5] Wayne to Wilkinson, July 7, 1792, Wayne Papers, Vol. XX.
[6] Butler to Wayne, Oct. 19, 1796, Wayne Papers, Vol. XLVII.
[7] Dayton to Wilkinson, Mar. 16, 1796, Wilkinson Papers, Vol. I, Chicago Hist. Soc.

since 1795, who harbored bitter memories of lawsuits and investigations and was ready to employ almost any means to bring humiliation upon his old-time rival. Andrew Jackson and Wade Hampton were also in Congress, but at this time their hatred of Wilkinson, if conceived, was not so violent as in later years.

Wilkinson appreciated that these friends and enemies of his could make or mar his future through Army legislation; he also knew that his record was subject to attack from several angles. He realized it was Wayne's privilege to forward to the War Department all matters that might arouse suspicion in his own mind about the character of his second in command. Wayne had apparently done so, perhaps acquainting a few in Philadelphia with some of the facts relating to Robert Newman and the $9,640 that had come up the Mississippi and been turned over to Nolan. Being partially acquainted with Power's rôle in the transfer of the money, Wayne had ordered him arrested on the eve of Wilkinson's departure for the East.[8] If the public once learned of what was going on, Wilkinson would immediately lose his precarious hold in the Army and wholly unfit himself for a continuance of Spanish favor. It therefore behooved him to proclaim loudly his innocence and to offer every proof that he could muster for his defense. Not knowing the direction Wayne's counterattack might take, he had to buttress himself against every possibility by securing helpful evidence and friends whenever either could be found.

To this difficulty was added an even greater one; he could not foresee what events were in the making and how they might directly affect him. A new President was soon to be inaugurated; but he was not well supported, and the Vice President was of opposite political faith. The recently made treaties with England and Spain had not yet become fully operative, and no one dared prophesy that they would be faithfully fulfilled. France, angry ever since Washington's declaration of neutrality, constantly irritated the United States and soon would precipitate a naval war. England, no longer friendly with Spain, had begun war against her, and soon Spaniards in Louisiana would be fearful of an invasion of their province by British subjects from Canada and American allies from the upper Mississippi. Under these conditions Wilkinson could not tell what to do for himself or

[8] Wayne to McHenry, Oct. 3, 1796, Wayne Papers, Vol. XLVI.

for the interests that he secretly served. To Gayoso he wrote on
November 6:

Point out with precision, the object to be pursued, and if attainable,
you shall find my activity, exertions equal to your most sanguine expectations;—but involved as I am in uncertainty, it is impossible to act with energy or even propriety.[9]

In such a quandary, Wilkinson felt that Philadelphia offered an
unequaled point of vantage from which to observe the important events
of the day. It was winter, and a return journey to the West would be
full of hardship for himself and family. He also wanted to be on
hand when Wayne arrived to answer the charges that had been preferred. The defense, however, never told its side of the story. Wayne
failed to come; ten days before Christmas he died at cheerless Presque
Isle. Wilkinson then realized that to assail the memory of the dead
would merely detract from his own reputation, and hence he concen-
trated on offering evidence that would render his own character in-
vulnerable. Believing that an inquiry would be favorable to him in
its conclusions, he conferred in January with James McHenry, the
new Secretary of War, about the prospect of having one.[10] The Secretary, being naturally averse to wrangling and perhaps believing in
Wilkinson's innocence, suggested that the whole matter be dropped.

Shortly afterward, on the last day of the Fourth Congress, the
grade of major-general being abolished, Wilkinson found that he had
to content himself with the same rank that he had held since March 5,
1792. Although he was now General-in-Chief with greater powers
and larger responsibilities, his pride was hurt and his hopes disappointed because Congress had not seen fit to promote him. Its action,
however, was not based entirely on personal hostility or distrust, for
there existed a deep-set and far-reaching desire to reduce the Army.

The incoming President, John Adams, appeared friendly. On the
4th of March, 1797, Wilkinson sat in honorable place among the
august few and saw him take the oath of office. In less than a year
afterward he was to receive further proof of the Executive's regard
in the form of a courteous letter expressing esteem for his services and
skepticism about the stories of his intrigues.[11] Adams, himself the

---

[9] To Gayoso, Nov. 5, 1796, A.G.I., Seville, *Papeles de Cuba*, leg. 2375.
[10] To Adams, Dec. 26, 1797, in Wilkinson, *Memoirs*, II, App. XXXVIII.
[11] Adams to Wilkinson, Feb. 4, 1798, in Wilkinson, *Memoirs*, II, 154–156.

frequent victim of unjust rumors, was loath to punish another unless the evidence was beyond question; he knew that, in the bitterness of party strife, slander was a common weapon for ruining an adversary.

A few weeks after the inauguration, Wilkinson left Philadelphia and traveled to Pittsburgh with his family. After making them comfortable at this place, he set out to inspect the scattered posts in the West and to arrange for a few changes in the location of troops. By the terms of the Jay and Pinckney treaties, England and Spain had agreed to evacuate certain areas, and in them the United States was now obliged to take over the duty of maintaining law and order. On Wilkinson fell the task of disposing of the Army in diminutive detachments and preventing them from lapsing into ignorance and vice because of long isolation and the weakness of those in immediate command.

He inspected Fort Washington and found out that officers were violating conventions with concubines and soldiers had too many washerwomen to suit regulations; cards and dice were also being used in quarters for sinful purposes. Backgammon was regarded as better amusement for soldiers. At Detroit he tried to stop drunkenness and improve discipline. Lydia Conner, a camp follower, and William Mitchell, a sutler, were found guilty of selling liquor without permission; both were sentenced to be drummed out of the fort and through the town to the accompaniment of the "Rogues' March." They had to make their unhappy exit, joined hand in hand, with two bottles suspended from each of their necks, and were forbidden ever to return. On July 4, 1797, the date set for the execution of a deserter, Wilkinson exercised clemency, and ordered that the culprit "be conducted to the standard where kneeling and grasping with his right hand, his left uplifted, he is to renew the oath of fidelity to be administered by the Judge Advocate. He is then to be reconducted to the main guard, discharged from confinement and from the corps." One can speculate how fervently such an oath was taken upon that summer day. Rulings were also made concerning the allowance of rations: children of the Army were to have one; suckling infants none, but their mothers one and a half. Presumably another order was issued when weaning was reached. Often the ranks had been thinned because men had been detailed as "hunters, fishermen, hostlers, Gardners, fatigue men, scullions, etc. at the expense of the meritorious soldier and to the great injury and disgrace of the service." Such lawless impositions were therefore strictly prohibited.[12]

But to such routine matters Wilkinson was not entirely confined. He kept a meteorological journal at the fort and another when he went to Mackinac, both of which he later gave to the American Philosophical Society.[13] He often conferred with Colonel Hamtramck, who, as commanding officer at Detroit, was kept busy settling quarrels between Indians and the frontier riffraff and trying to prevent American soldiers from deserting into Canada. The British observed the dwindling of the garrison with satisfaction. Wilkinson had long held a strong dislike for them, and now it was greatly increased on hearing that they were furnishing asylum for army renegades.[14]

Wilkinson was therefore more than willing to comply with the wish of the Secretary of War, to resist the intrusion of the British in any attempt that they might make to pass through federal territory for an attack on Louisiana. The possibility of this invasion worried the Spaniards; they suspected that Americans, stirred with bitter memories of overbearing dons, might join with the British and revel in a heyday of vengeance. The prospect of what this mismated alliance might do, filled Carondelet with fear. It was increased still more when he realized the violent opposition of the Americans to imperial delay. He had recently received instructions that were to incense John Adams and many a backwoods trader.

In such an extremity Carondelet sent Thomas Power as his agent up the Mississippi to interview Wilkinson and other prominent characters in the hope that they might be induced to further the interests of Spain. The governor seemed to harbor the notion that the restless spirits of the West might be duped through fair promises into becoming submissive subjects of the Crown or invincible warriors for the winning of a fantastic empire. In all the arrangements planned, Wilkinson, of course, was to be an important figure. If he were unmoved by enticing tales of conspiracy he might at least be influenced to prolong the days for the Spaniards to hold the lower Mississippi against the assaults of the British from Canada or of Americans angered at continued deception and delay.

[12] G.O., Fort Washington, May 22, 1797; G.O., Detroit, July 4, 20, Nov. 3, 10, 1797, in War Dept., Adj.-Gen.'s Off., Old Records Bur.
[13] *Early Minutes of the American Philosophical Society*, Dec. 7, 1798, and Dec. 6, 1799.
[14] To Wayne, July 12, 1797, Wilkinson Papers, Vol. I, Chicago Hist. Soc.

Power left New Orleans during the summer of 1797 with authority to offer $100,000 to those who would start a revolution in Kentucky and Tennessee. He was to tell them of a new Spanish province to be carved out of the country lying east of the Mississippi and stretching from the Ohio to the Yazoo. Wilkinson would be the military personage in this princely domain. When once the revolution was under way an equal amount of money and the requisite munitions of war would be forthcoming. As success gave play to imagination and effort, more territory might be acquired, the trans-Mississippi West might be won, a realm that kings might covet—all to be ruled in harmony by Spaniards and Americans beneath a flag of their own choosing.[15]

When Power had reached Natchez on his journey north he told Gayoso this opium dream of empire. Although the governor proved rather unbelieving, he did furnish a little money to help pay expenses for traveling farther and planting seeds of conspiracy in Tennessee and Kentucky. Not dismayed, the ubiquitous Power continued on his way. He was soon writing Carondelet that Wilkinson, George Rogers Clark, and others, whom the common folk would blindly follow, were devoted adherents of Spain, and that they could not afford to reject the flattering offer to be made them. He could ill afford to tell the truth. An interview with Benjamin Sebastian, one of Spain's most trusted pensioners, failed to kindle any enthusiasm. The ex-preacher thought the time not ripe for such a project, although Power sought his support by promising him that those who lost their position on account of Spanish affiliations would be fully indemnified. He also added that the boundaries of Kentucky as the nucleus of a newborn state would be greatly enlarged. Nevertheless, Sebastian showed little interest; he merely promised to discuss the matter with his friends and let Power know the result; he also expressed a willingness to visit New Orleans for a conference, should this be desired.[16]

Power had accomplished nothing so far in an area that he had stated would listen greedily to his plans. Pushing farther north, he was destined to meet with even greater apathy. On the 16th of August he reached Detroit. Wilkinson was absent at Mackinac. About a fortnight later the General returned, burning to know the news from

[15] Carondelet to Power, May 26, 1798, *Amer. State Papers, Miscel.*, II, 102–104; Ellicott to Pickering, Nov. 14, 1797, in Matthews, *Andrew Ellicott*, 161–163; Cox, "Wilkinson's First Break with the Spaniards," in *Biennial Reports Archives and History West Va., 1911–1912, 1913–1914*, pp. 49–56.
[16] Cox, *loc. cit.*

New Orleans but realizing that if he received Power enthusiastically all the tongues in the neighborhood would be set wagging; he therefore ordered him held in nominal arrest in officers' quarters under directions to prepare for returning to New Madrid immediately. To further increase the impression that he cared nothing for Spanish overtures, he detailed Captain Shaumburgh with several men to see that Power was hustled on his way under guard.[17] By this trick no one could halt and search him for suspicious papers. Wilkinson also wanted Carondelet to know as quickly as possible that the British were not planning to invade Spanish territory via Mackinac, and that, if by any chance they did so, he would effectively stop them. He wished the Spaniards to think that his expectation to protect them from the north was a matter of his own volition, not induced by orders of the Secretary of War to prevent violation of neutral territory.[18] According to the route Power was compelled to travel, he would have opportunity to see how Wilkinson was shifting troops, apparently for meeting any such threatened invasion. If he had been allowed to go by Cincinnati and Louisville as he wished, he might have heard a different story; but Wilkinson was deaf to entreaty, writing Carondelet that his emissary was receiving every facility for a speedy return.[19]

Carondelet must have been gratified to learn that affairs were turning his way in one quarter, even if in another failure attended the plans that he cherished. He expressed the hope that Wilkinson would not insist on too hasty an occupation of Walnut Hills, Natchez, and other places, in spite of the fact that Andrew Ellicott was growing angry at delay and had accused Gayoso of stirring up the Indians to prevent the surveying of our southern boundary line. Counter accusations had followed, then "swearing and indecent words." To keep the peace, Carondelet requested Ellicott's powers be circumscribed to the limits of his commission. Wilkinson apparently did nothing to restrain him or prevent Captain Guion from continuing on with his men to Natchez.

Nor was Power able to suborn the General into supporting the plan that he had already unfolded to Sebastian and others in Kentucky, although Carondelet gave promise of great reward:

[17] Power to Gayoso de Lemos, Dec. 5, 1797, *Amer. State Papers, Miscel.*, II, 107–109.
[18] To Carondelet, Sept. 4, 1797, A.G.I., Seville, *Papeles de Cuba*, leg. 2375.
[19] To Power, Sept. 5, 1797, *Amer. State Papers, Miscel.*, II, 105; to Carondelet, Sept. 4, 1797, A.G.I., Seville, *Papeles de Cuba*, leg. 2375.

"You will have the Grant you solicit in the Illinois Country, and you ought to depend upon an annual bounty of four thousand dollars which shall be delivered to you at your order and to the person you may indicate." [20]

In spite of such a retaining fee Wilkinson would not share in Power's chimerical project. He explained, as others had done, that the western peoples, now enjoying the navigation of the Mississippi, had no special reasons for leaving the Union. He also added that his honor and position would not allow him to continue his former connection; in fact, he had gone so far as to destroy his cipher and previous correspondence with the Spaniards. In keeping with this apparent determination to serve only his country, he now advised them to carry out the treaty as they had agreed to do; but he also remarked that he might become governor at Natchez, and there opportunities might be found for making new plans. Wilkinson did not wish to break entirely his contact with the Spaniards; hence he did not fail to ask Power about the $640, which they still presumably owed him. The answer was disappointing; Power said that he had not cared to risk bringing the money along.[21]

Shortly after this interview with Power, Wilkinson made preparations to leave Detroit. At one time he thought of accompanying troops to Kaskaskia in order "to keep our neighbors in check, to countenance our friends, and confound the Banditti"; [22] but after Winthrop Sargent arrived there and established tranquil conditions, he decided to make directly for Pittsburgh. For nearly two months he was traveling four hundred miles across snow-covered country, sleeping under canvas in the open with the temperature frequently around zero.[23] One of those with him was ex-Senator Mitchell's son, a likable boy, worth taking under one's wing according to Wilkinson's notion. Kindnesses of this sort might be bountifully returned by the old gentleman himself. Another companion was Little Turtle, a chief who wielded great influence among the Indians.[24] His good will meant present safety for the travelers and valuable help in any later negotiations with Indians of the Northwest. Wilkinson accordingly treated him with consideration. Shortly after the middle of December, when the detachment reached Pittsburgh, he wrote a very courteous letter to his brother-in-

[20] Carondelet to Wilkinson, Apr. 20, 1797, A.G.I., Seville, *Papeles de Cuba*, leg. 2375.
[21] Power to Gayoso, Dec. 5, 1797, *Amer. State Papers, Miscel.*, II, 107–109.
[22] To Sargent, Sept. 6, 1797, Sargent Papers.
[23] *Gazette of the United States*, Dec. 16, 1797. L.C.
[24] To Pratt, Dec. 27, 1797, Pratt Papers.

law, Owen Biddle, suggesting that Little Turtle be introduced to the Philosophical Society when he made a visit to Philadelphia to see the President. In the same letter were some very thoughtful observations about Indians in general:

"My late intercourse," he wrote, "with various tribes and nations, from this neighborhood to Lake Superior, convinces me that the corruptions of the Savages, are derived from those who stile [*sic*] themselves Christians—because, the further they are advanced from communications with white people the more honest, temperate, and industrious I have found them.

.   .   .   .

"If this people are not brought to depend for subsistence on their fields, instead of their forests, and realize ideas of distinct property, it will be found impossible to correct their personal habits, and the seeds of their extinction already sown. must be matured.

.   .   .   .

"The experiments heretofore made to reform the Indian character, have not been well adapted to the object. Our missionaries have in general been narrow minded, ignorant, idle, or interested, and have paid more regard to forms than principles. The Education of Individuals at our Schools, have [*sic*] turned out the most profligate of the nation to which they belonged.—Speaking once to George White Eyes [a Miami chief], who was I believed educated at Princeton, respecting the incorrigible attachment of the Indians to savage life, he replied to me: 'it is natural we should follow the footsteps of our forefathers, and when you white people undertake to direct us from this path, you learn us to Eat, Drink, Dress, read and write like yourselves, and then you turn us loose to beg, starve or seek our native forests, without alternative and outlawed by your society, we curse you for the feelings you have taught us, and resort to excesses that we may forget them.'

"A great source of my present happiness is the conviction that I have deserved and enjoy the confidence and the friendship of the Indians N.W. of the Ohio." [25]

Wilkinson wrote with uncommon truth on that Christmas Eve of 1797. It is regrettable that he did not employ enough of his masterful energy and cleverness to win over the leaders of his country into adopting the ideas that he had so clearly expressed. His own reputa-

[25] To Owen Biddle, Dec. 24, 1797, Collection T. R. Hay.

tion and that of the federal government in the treatment of its Indian wards would have been greatly enhanced. As it was, the American Philosophical Society thought well of him, making him a member on January 19, 1798.[26] Unfortunately Wilkinson could not hold grimly to a group of theories over an extended period; he discarded them as a skillful opportunist when they became too bitterly opposed, or when he was too busily engaged to rise up in their defense. Just then he felt no inclination to go to Philadelphia and help Little Turtle champion them.

He did not care to take the 297-mile journey across the mountains just after completing one even longer and more dangerous; he was comfortable at his present station and nothing much could be gained by visiting the seat of government, where he might be coldly received. Like Hamilton and Washington, he did not have a very high opinion of the ability of the Secretary of War, James McHenry. To the General he was a "mock minister," who did not answer official correspondence and would make the Army the victim of ignorant and untimely experiments.[27] He therefore thought better to stay at Pittsburgh, a sort of halfway station between the western posts and the important cities of the East. In this location he could readily receive and transmit orders. Meanwhile he endeavored to make the place worthy of the station of the general-in-chief. Quarters were papered and painted and plastered. Bundles and boxes of household supplies were sent to him from Philadelphia to make his quarters comfortable for his family and guests. A pipe of wine was hauled over the mountains, followed by kegs of different sizes, and these helped to make merry the long winter evenings.[28] Friends came and went, doubtless happier because of the easy hospitality of the Wilkinsons. Ann welcomed them. She was now in good health and the full enjoyment of her husband and the two boys. It was years since all of the family had been together for such a long time. The General hated the idea of separation, and hence made arrangements for them to accompany him when he started for the Southwest in the summer of 1798.

Many things were calling for his presence there. Indians, land speculators, British agents, and French sympathizers were proving frequent disturbers of the peace. The Spaniards looked kindly upon some of them, hoping that they might be an indirect means of dis-

[26] *Early Minutes of Amer. Philosophical Society,* Jan. 19, 1798.
[27] To Pratt, Dec. 27, 1797, Pratt Papers; to Sargent, Jan. 3, 1798, Sargent Papers.
[28] *Expenditures in the Naval and Military Establishments . . . 1797–1801,* 34, 35, 38, 233, 234.

rupting the Pinckney Treaty. Over part of this troubled area Winthrop Sargent was preparing to preside, for he had received his commission as governor of Mississippi Territory on May 28, 1798. Wilkinson planned to travel down the Ohio, perhaps with him, and give support to the civil government soon to be organized. The two had known each other since the Revolution. Although they had occasionally disagreed as to the limits of civil and military authority, they had a number of friends and several interests in common. Each wanted to build up the West with hardy immigrants; each tried to plant in its nourishing soil the fruits and vegetables older countries had long enjoyed. In March, Wilkinson had written to Sargent asking for some Alpine strawberry seed; a month later he was forwarding to Sargent a shoot of the "Antwerp raspberry," worth twenty guineas as his letter ran.[29]

If Sargent received this expensive gift, he probably never enjoyed its fruit, for he was usually moving from place to place, trying to maintain law among the settlers and keep peace among magistrates who complained that Army officers were disregarding civil authority. Wilkinson promised to bring to account any such offenders in his own command. At the same time he requested Sargent to furnish him with the names of any British subjects enjoying federal office in the Northwest. They, of course, should be removed before an investigation was made.[30] As he thought on those of double allegiance, his own dealings with the Spaniards came to mind. On the selfsame day that he wrote to Sargent, the following lines were sent to Gayoso:

"Observed everywhere, I dare not communicate with you, nor should you try to do so with me; [Humphrey] Marshall has attacked my honor and fidelity. You should not trust the western people, because some are traitors. Fortify your frontiers well. While I remain as at present all is safe. Have buried my cipher, but I will recover it. You have many spies in your country. Do not mention me nor write my name. I implore you in the name of God and our friendship. Fort Pitt, fifth March."[31]

There was reason for anxiety. Bitter enemies of the General might find opportunities to read the letters that passed to and from him over the long distance from Pittsburgh to New Orleans. The use of codes might delay, but did not always prevent, disclosure of im-

[29] To Sargent, Mar. 24, Apr. 23, 1798, Sargent Papers.
[30] To Sargent, Jan. 3, Mar. 5, 6, 1798, Sargent Papers.
[31] To Gayoso, Mar. 5, 1798, A.G.I., Seville, *Papeles de Cuba,* leg. 2374; and Cox, *op. cit.,* 54.

portant secrets. Less chance of discovery lay in personal conferences between those who would engage in intrigue. If anything of
consequence was to be attained, Wilkinson had better go to Natchez,
where his presence was needed as commanding general of the Army
and he would be in a more convenient position for extracting money
from the frequently credulous Spaniards.

About the first week in June the Wilkinsons left Pittsburgh, and
by the 14th they had reached Cincinnati, where the General remained
over a month engaged in routine work of the Army and in settling
difficulties between Indians and lawless whites.[82] He soon knew what
was going on in this section; perhaps the $100 that he spent for secret
service made talking easier for those who had things to tell. A similar amount of federal funds went to pay a messenger who brought
news and letters from the country of the lower Mississippi. To ingratiate himself with the savages, he had a great dinner—an $85 one
—for chiefs of neighboring tribes. His friend Little Turtle was
present, and he and four of his associates so enjoyed this gesture of
hospitality that they lingered a month and were boarded at public
expense.

They liked liquor, which was generously supplied. The tavern
keeper had reasons for being agreeable—possibly thrift and fear. He
presented a bill for boarding Little Turtle and his associates that included the following items:

	Dolls	Cts
June 25th　1798　To Boarding 5 Indians 4 weeks @ 4 dollars per week	80	
Boarding one Indian 2 weeks @ 4 dollars per week	8	
28 quarts of wine equal to one quart per day @ 1.50 p. q.	42	
14 quarts of Brandy equal to 1 pint per day @ 2.00 per qt	28	
1¾ quarts of Gin equal to 72 gill per day @ 2^D per qt	3	50
8¾ quarts Bounce equal to ½ pint & ½ Gill per day @ 1^{D}50^{cts}	13	12½
Dollars	174.	62½[83]

[82] To Jacob Reed, June 24, 1798, Gates Papers.
[83] Bill of William Austin, in Gratz Coll.

Little Turtle had already experienced a bit of the General's kindness and the government's munificence at Pittsburgh. There his heart had been gladdened by the gift of seven shirts, a pair of boots, a plated bridle, two pots, and some firearms. Besides, wine and brandy were his for the asking. The liquor may help explain why his favorite musical instrument needed repair. Nor had Mrs. Little Turtle been entirely forgotten during those days. She had been wheedled into complacent grunts by a present of twelve and one-half yards of calico and two pairs of black silk gloves, appropriate finery for covering her swarthy figure and calloused hands when winter winds were strong and cold.[34]

Wilkinson understood these children of the forest and, like Jefferson, felt that the cost of stuffing them with food and decking them out in gewgaws was nothing to compare with the expense and horror of an Indian war. Along with methods of conciliation, he simultaneously quickened their fear and admiration by dazzling parades and the salvos of many guns. At the same time he tried to prevent the whites from cheating them in trade or settling upon lands reserved to them by treaty. At Fort Washington, as in other cases, his efforts met with success, and toward the end of July he was ready to resume his journey to Natchez in one of the government barges.

His family did not accompany him. It was better for his wife and boys to remain behind, for he could not feel sure just what accommodations might be obtained for them in the lower country, where yellow fever had recently appeared and various endemic diseases prevailed. During the first days of August he reached Fort Massac, situated near the juncture of the Ohio and the Mississippi. Nine years before, he had passed this point en route to New Orleans with great cargoes of Kentucky tobacco; now he had a flotilla of nearly thirty boats filled with armed men for taking over the forts that the Spaniards had promised to surrender. From an entrepreneur who had awakened the West to the great profits from down-river trade, he had become the chosen instrument of his government for sweeping aside the barriers that hindered its natural flow. Thoughtful persons could readily foresee that the Army's coming was a mere prelude to the further extension of federal domain. In five years Louisiana

[34] *Expenditures in the Naval and Military Establishments . . . 1797–1801*, 203, 204, 219, 222, 264.

would be taken, and before Wilkinson's death the American invasion of Texas would be well upon its way.

Indians, hidden in willows and canebrakes, did not look with friendly eyes upon this roughhewn armada moving sluggishly through the loops and oxbows of the great river that they had long considered their peculiar possession. When the boats drew close inshore at the end of the day, a chain of sentinels was posted on land, spreading fanwise out from the center of the flotilla to prevent the intrusion of Chickasaws and Choctaws. At reveille the outguards were drawn in and a few minutes afterwards the General gave a signal for getting under way. His boat led, followed in turn by the ones used respectively for kitchen, cows, and supplies. Then came the rest, in equal divisions commanded by various officers. Travel was slow, not much faster than the current of the river. The ordinary soldier liked changing station in such a fashion; fatigue details were not large except when a boat ran aground or met with some other disaster. He had a reasonably comfortable place for a bed, although it was commonly closed in. Even if he might have protected himself from mosquitoes he did not dare to sleep in the open; for the dews and night air were regarded as unfailing sources of disease. Although he found swimming refreshing in the hot summer weather, it was permitted only before sunup and after sunset, apparently for reasons of safety rather than modesty.[35]

In early fall Wilkinson reached Loftus Heights; and here, after the boats had been tied up, the men began to establish a camp, which was soon to bear the name of Fort Adams in honor of the President. Wilkinson was in and out as circumstances demanded. He often went up the river to Natchez, a nine-hour trip by boat, to make arrangements for establishing a garrison there and to confer with Winthrop Sargent, Daniel Clark, Sr., and others, on matters of personal and public concern.

The political and economic conditions of the neighborhood had greatly changed since Wilkinson's last trip to New Orleans in 1789. Cotton had displaced tobacco and indigo as the most remunerative crop, and many more planters had drifted down the Mississippi and settled along its banks, finding the rule of the Spaniards easily bearable and the land unusually fertile. With Whitney's invention they now

[35] G.O. Aug. 8, 9, 10, 1798, Wilkinson's Book of General Orders, 1797–1807, W.D., A.G.O., O.R.

had a staple crop yielding exceptional profits. The necessities of life grew abundantly in the rich alluvial soil, which had been acquired often without cost to the owner. Slaves did most of the common drudgery, leaving to their masters a good deal of leisure. The more affluent of the whites usually spent it in politics, entertaining, and the raising of numerous progeny.

In spite of the fact that the country already belonged to the Indians and Spaniards, and that dangerous fevers usually prevailed within its boundaries, many prominent men of the frontier ardently coveted it, not infrequently seeking foreign aid to promote their desires. William Blount, senator from Tennessee, was an outstanding example of the type. During the winter of 1796–1797, Wilkinson and Jefferson had been his dinner guests in Philadelphia. According to the story, John D. Chisholm, a garrulous adventurer from the Cherokee country, was to drop in casually and disclose the schemes that he and Blount and others were forming to win the Southwest from Spain by means of British aid along the coast and active support from Indian tribes of the interior; but, for some reason, he kept his peace and the Vice President and the commanding general of the Army did not become, at least for the time, companions in conspiracy.

However, Robert Liston, the British minister, when acquainted with the freebooter's program, seemed to see enough in it to pay Chisholm's passage to London. While he was sailing to England, Blount was hurrying back to Tennessee and had gone as far as Colonel King's, just south of the Virginia line, when he learned of the special session of Congress that President Adams had called. Under the necessity of returning to Philadelphia, he wrote to James Carey, his one-time subordinate but now an accomplice, who was employed as a federal agent among the southern Indians. The letter, after disclosing encouraging progress of the conspiracy, directed Carey to burn it after reading three times; on the contrary, he became drunk and careless and allowed it to fall into unfriendly hands. It soon became the property of the President, and by July 3, 1797, the Senators knew in what shady transactions their colleague was involved. They took immediate action and expelled him from their body. He then made a headlong flight to Tennessee, where he labored with diminishing success to regain his prestige until he died in 1800.[36]

[36] Whitaker, *The Mississippi Question,* 104–115.

Among the associates of Blount was Zachariah Cox, whose reputation was already soiled from his connection with the "notorious Yazoo Land Grants." When this real estate venture proved abortive he and Mathias Moher became the chief promoters of the Tennessee Land Company, to which the pliant legislature of Georgia had made an extensive grant near Muscle Shoals during January, 1795. After establishing a settlement known as Smithland on the Ohio between the Tennessee and the Cumberland, Cox prepared to descend the Mississippi for the avowed purpose of exploring the country west of it and making a commercial connection in New Orleans. He set out for the South a few weeks after the departure of Winthrop Sargent, the newly appointed governor of Mississippi Territory, and managed to reach Natchez several days ahead of Wilkinson. There his troubles began. On August 18, 1798, seven days after his arrival, Captain Isaac Guion, a trusted officer of Wilkinson, reached town, and about midnight a detail of soldiers surrounded Cox's lodging and took him away to keep company with an odd lot of horse thieves for more than a month.[37]

Wilkinson had written Sargent from Massac recommending such strong-armed action on the basis that "he had taken a position on the lands guaranteed to the Indians by the Treaty of Hopewell,—that he had there assembled, organized, and arranged an armed force, inlisted [sic] for twelve months, and that he had erected Tribunals, which have proceeded to inflict punishments unknown to the nation." Wilkinson further added that against such an armed rabble operating far from the seat of government and opposed by inadequate military forces, it was expedient to act, particularly since a great conspiracy from Georgia to the Monongahela was expected to mature in December. Therefore "we must stifle the monster in Embryo, or extensive Calamities may ensue; Cox's followers begin to doubt his stability, but are reluctant to let go the lure by which he has attracted them— to unmask the Impostor, to dispel his delusions, and to blow up the whole combination, it is only necessary to seize this chief actor and to hold him in safe custody." [38]

Under secret charges, Cox was held at Fort Panmure until the night of September 26. Then he managed to escape by climbing over the walls of his place of confinement while the guard was per-

[37] Cox, "Documents Relating to Zachariah Cox," in *Quarterly Publications of Historical and Philosophical Society of Ohio,* VIII, 31–114.
[38] To Sargent, Aug. 2, 1798, Sargent Papers.

haps intentionally negligent, and Wilkinson and Hamtramck were having a party. Cox did not linger in the neighborhood but traveled south, reaching New Orleans on October 3, and without delay called on the Spanish Governor, Gayoso de Lemos, and told him a story of persecuted innocence. Before his arrival, however, a messenger had come posthaste from Wilkinson, bringing a warning that a leader of bandits was coming to arouse disorder and tumult. Gayoso, there-upon issued a proclamation telling the inhabitants the news that he had received and enjoining them to be on their guard. When Cox put in an appearance, he was not molested in spite of Wilkinson's request that he be arrested and turned over to American authorities. With no treaty of extradition, the Governor, of course, did not comply; the General, in fact, had exceeded his authority and the Secretary of War took him to task for doing so.[39]

When rumors spread north that Cox might return to vaunt his freedom and "rescue his Brethren in confinement," Wilkinson wrote and offered Sargent $300 from federal funds to secure his apprehen-sion. Money bred success; the fugitive was taken in the lower towns of the Choctaws. But here, Samuel Mitchell, federal Indian agent, interposed his authority and dispatched him under guard to Ten-nessee, where he was very eager to be sent. Thus Wilkinson, though chagrined at his failure to bring Cox to book, did feel that he had driven another "disreputable" from the district of Natchez; he was also glad "White the rascal" was off, and would have felt further relieved if "Old Hutchins, the scoundrel" had left with the other two.[40]

Although Wilkinson's strenuous efforts to be rid of Cox may have been inspired by the reasons given to Sargent, others, not openly avowed, may have also influenced his actions. In New Orleans, Cox expected to form business connections, and these might interfere with the General's personal interests there; he also wanted to open up a trade route from the Tennessee and Cumberland rivers directly to the Gulf, a scheme that might complicate federal relations with both Indians and Spaniards. By vigorously suppressing men like Cox, Wilkinson would have a better chance to promote his own ends and advertise his loyalty to the government.

[39] Cox, *op. cit.*, 78 *et passim*, and McHenry to Wilkinson, Jan. 31, 1799, Wilkinson Papers, Vol. I, Chicago Hist. Soc.
[40] To Sargent, Nov. 4, 1798, Sargent Papers; to McHenry, Dec. 6, 1798, Hamilton Papers, Vol. XXXIII.

Knowing that his own reports would not sufficiently impress the administration in the ways that he wanted, he cultivated the friendship of men like Andrew Ellicott and Winthrop Sargent, who were constantly writing to important people in the East. Ellicott had been in or around Natchez since February 24, 1797. Before leaving Philadelphia he was particularly enjoined to keep peace with the Spaniards, an injunction that he tried to observe although his patience was sorely tried. At first Gayoso seemed willing to coöperate. Then, in accordance with instructions from Carondelet, he reversed himself, and placed as many stumbling blocks as possible in the way of those who would execute the provisions of the Pinckney treaty. At one time Ellicott had to look impotently on and see the Spanish cannon remounted in position at the fort from which they had been recently taken and laboriously hauled to the river landing. A few days later Gayoso issued a proclamation declaring that he would not give up the district until he felt sure that land titles would be respected and the Indians pacified. Next, Nolan added to the ill feeling by bringing word from New Orleans that Carondelet had declared: "Lead for the Americans, hemp for the inhabitants." Somewhat later a smallminded Baptist preacher came and, after stirring up tumult in a drunken wrangle, was rightfully thrown in the stocks by the urbane Gayoso. His confinement was considered tyrannical by the already indignant settlers, and Gayoso had to take refuge in the fort to escape their retaliation. From this time until the arrival of Sargent the government rested in the hands of a committee composed of inhabitants of the district.[41]

Thus almost a year slipped by, and Ellicott had nothing to show for his efforts, although he might congratulate himself that he had escaped being tomahawked by drunken Indians and had not succumbed to the fevers of the lower Mississippi. Philip Nolan had often come to his rescue when beset by savages, and Dr. Benjamin Rush of Philadelphia had supplied him with a great quantity of pills for bi-weekly dosing. Ellicott had great faith in them, believing that if he had had enough of them his sickness two years later might have been prevented. These wonder-working pills were made of "calomel and gamboge combined by means of a little soap."[42]

Finally, in January, 1798, Ellicott learned that the Spaniards

---

[41] *The Journal of Andrew Ellicott*, 40–65, 85, 96–100, 167.
[42] *Op. cit.*, 292.

would immediately begin to evacuate Natchez and Nogales. Godoy, having changed his mind, had decided that the treaty should be carried out; and Gayoso became the instrument for making mutually satisfactory arrangements for the establishment of the new boundary line. On the 9th of April, Ellicott left Natchez to begin surveying; [43] for him the most critical days concerning the treaty were past. To be sure, he still had many problems; but with the aid of Wilkinson, now on the way south, they would yield to solution.

Perhaps Sargent, the newly appointed Governor of Mississippi Territory, who arrived on the 6th of August, had an even greater need for the General's active support. Until late in September, Sargent had suffered from ill health; and when he began to improve he was still handicapped by a brittle mind and unbending manner. Meticulous by nature, he could not understand why many showed an easy disregard for law and order. From time to time he sought help from Wilkinson in establishing his new regime. Frequently he asked rations for his assistants and visiting Indians. On occasions he wanted to use some of the public buildings that he thought Wilkinson could spare. As a rule the General complied, but sometimes rather grudgingly.[44] Both men saw that they must, at least, be outwardly friendly if the civil and military governments were to prosper under their direction. Besides asking aid of the governor in cases like that of Cox, Wilkinson did not hesitate to make requests of a very personal kind, going so far as to ask Sargent to write Mrs. Wilkinson a few lines "commendatory of the climate and society" in order that she might hasten to the South.[45] Since the governor liked her, abominated Natchez, and also had a regard for truth, one wonders if he complied, especially at a time when he was recovering from a month's illness and writing Wilkinson to express sympathy for the large number on the Army's sick report. He hated the place worst of all on Sundays, when it was overrun with drunken soldiers, Indians, and negroes. For the purpose of quelling these disturbers he asked aid of the garrison and expressed the hope that if troops were to have whisky they would be prohibited from drinking it within the limits of the town.

[43] *Op. cit.*, 177.
[44] Sargent to Pickering, Sept. 27, Nov. 1, 1798, Mar. 3, 1799, in Rowland, *Mississippi Territorial Archives, 1798–1803*, I, 53–56, 74–76, 111; Wilkinson to Sargent, Oct. 28, 1798, Sargent Papers.
[45] To Sargent, Oct. 20, 1798, Sargent Papers.

In spite of these difficulties the civil government grew in strength, and the Indians gave fewer signs of hostility. The Spaniards procrastinated as usual but showed a willingness to execute their part of the treaty. For the Americans, political conditions had decidedly improved since the early days of 1797. By the time Wilkinson reached Natchez on September 27, 1798,[46] much of the difficult preliminary work had been accomplished; his task was largely to further what had already been started. Being a natural diplomat and enjoying the Army's support, he quickly became a very formidable figure in Mississippi Territory. He liked the orders that he had received to promote peace with the Indians and Spaniards; the idea was congenial to his real temperament and made for his personal advantage.

Andrew Ellicott had similar instructions and was also determined to obey them. While in the Southwest he and Wilkinson were friends. Each visited the other as well as Daniel Clark, who, with his wife, often sent them neighborly tokens of regard. Once Ellicott was favored with a few cows. Before long he was writing a letter asking what had become of the milkmaids.[47] At a later day Wilkinson might have inquired why he asked for such companion pieces when already possessed of Betsy the harlot. But in 1798 Wilkinson and Ellicott were on congenial terms. They were government officials, far from home, and quarreling might defeat their separate missions. They were also about the same age, had come under Quaker influence, and were endeavoring to establish themselves as faithful servants of the Federalist party. Both had relatives and friends among well known people of Philadelphia, and they eagerly looked forward to the day when they could be there again. Each had reached the height of his respective profession, and that fact was enough to excite mutual admiration. Although without a natural bent toward science, Wilkinson respected men like Owen Biddle, Rittenhouse, and Franklin who had won distinction in it. These three, and Ellicott, were all members of the Philosophical Society, an honor that Wilkinson had only lately received.

If such reasons did not induce Wilkinson to show himself friendly, perhaps another, more important than all the rest, determined his attitude—a fear that Ellicott might be a channel through which tales of bribery and intrigue traveled to Congress and the President. In

[46] Sargent to Pickering, Sept. 29, 1798, in Rowland, *op. cit.*, I, 53–56.
[47] Clark to Ellicott, July 21, 1798, Ellicott Papers, Vol. II; Ellicott to Hawkins, Feb. 25, 1798, Ellicott Papers, Vol. I.

fact, Ellicott had already acted on Washington's request; namely, to inform him about certain citizens, particularly Wilkinson, who were suspected of being too friendly with the Spanish government.[48] In the summer of 1797 he had made a report concerning Wilkinson to the Secretary of State.[49] On June 5 he wrote that Thomas Power, an agent of Carondelet, was on the way to the Ohio country with the object of detaching Kentuckians from the Union and of paying a visit "in the first instance" to General Wilkinson, then in Detroit. Toward Power, Ellicott gave no sign of mistrust; on the contrary, he gave him a letter for the General, telling how the Spaniards were thwarting the provisions of the treaty and requesting that an officer of "sobriety, talent and industry" be sent to take command at Natchez. Captain Isaac Guion, certainly of more than average ability and experience, had already been selected for the detail and was traveling down the river to his new station.

In the following November, Ellicott sent even more startling information to Philadelphia.[50] He declared that Wilkinson, John Brown, Sebastian, and La Cassagne were all in possession of "annual stipends" from Spain, and that once in a while others received bribes from the same source. Letters to them were written in cipher and hidden in barrels of sugar. The first object of the conspirators, as he went on to say, was to detach Kentucky and Tennessee from the Union and place them under the protection of Spain. Then was to follow the "great plan"—creation of a new empire with Mexico as its center. Wilkinson was to lead Kentucky troops thither along a route that had been already explored. Spanish officers had agreed to the idea and were trying to cover up their plotting by a pretended zeal for the interests of the Crown. The ubiquitous Power, of course, was the secret disseminator of this conspiracy.

What Ellicott reported, Carondelet was endeavoring, in general, to do. Pickering, the Secretary of State, however, was not stirred into action; he was too practical for that. He knew the West was not in a mood to listen to Power's piping; he knew that Wilkinson could not be convicted of any serious charge on the evidence that had been lately received, even if the Spaniards should be willing to disclose their disreputable diplomacy and testify against him. He therefore

---

[48] Whitaker, *The Mississippi Question*, 280.
[49] Ellicott to Pickering, June 5, 1797, and Ellicott to Wilkinson, June 5, 1797, in Wilkinson, *Memoirs*, II, 164, 168.
[50] Ellicott to Pickering, Nov. 14, 1797, Pickering Papers.

very wisely waited for the turn of events and the receipt of more information.

Less than a year after this last report Wilkinson arrived at Loftus Heights. On October 14, 1798, he visited Ellicott in camp and remained with him for about three days. The General, wanting the good will of his host, tried to make his short stay one of mutual pleasure; he talked a good deal about the "state and situation of the country," and his ideas about both seem to have met with approval.[51] They also discussed and reached agreement concerning two of Ellicott's subordinates. One of them was Thomas Freeman, an assistant surveyor, who was frequently drunk and went absent without leave. He also disturbed others by rehearsing scenes from Shakespeare; he was especially eloquent in the rôle of Falstaff and delighted to brandish a sword.[52] To these rather exhilarating defects he added a seditious correspondence with Captain Guion, whom Ellicott very much hated. Another whom Ellicott thoroughly disliked was Lieutenant John McClary, commandant of the escort, who was charged with being "lazy and under hostile influence." Wilkinson agreed to relieve McClary and to support Ellicott in his charges against Freeman. On October 18, two days after Wilkinson's departure, Freeman was suspended as a surveyor of the United States because of "impropriety" in the discharge of his duties, disobedience, and "inflammatory conversation."[53] "An idle, lying, troublesome, discontented, mischief-making man," as Ellicott would say, no longer had a job.[54]

Now stranded, Freeman had to seek employment, and within less than a month he was talking things over with Wilkinson, who almost immediately sat down and wrote Ellicott a very pertinent letter. In it he said Freeman "has given me a certificate of old Bare Bones to him touching my Spanish Commission, and written me a letter of vindication." There was also included news of more personal importance to Ellicott; Freeman was not planning to prefer any charges unless forced to do so in his own defense.[55] A counterattack of this kind would probably not have been successful, but it might have caused a great deal of trouble for Ellicott. Wilkinson realized his

[51] Ellicott notes, without heading, Ellicott Papers, Vol. I, and Ellicott to Sargent, Oct. 20, 1798, Ellicott Papers, Vol. III.
[52] Drewry, *Episodes in Western Expansion, etc.,* 118.
[53] Ellicott to Sargent, Oct. 20, 1798, Ellicott Papers, Vol. III; Ellicott to Freeman, Oct. 18, 1798, Ellicott Papers, Vol. I.
[54] Ellicott to Mrs. Ellicott, Nov. 6, 1798, in Mathews, *Andrew Ellicott: His Life and Letters,* 160.
[55] To Ellicott, Nov. 10, 1798, Ellicott Papers, Vol. II; to Ellicott, May 8, 1799, *Ibid.*

advantage in maintaining peace between the two; he saw in Freeman a man whom he could use. Within six months he put him on the pay roll in place of William Dunbar, a recent suicide. Employing him, as Wilkinson explained, arose from necessity and meant "no deadening of affection" for Ellicott, who in the meantime had gone to New Orleans and moved eastward to complete the boundary survey. In this new area he and Freeman would not be embarrassed by crossing each other's paths.

Just before leaving the Natchez neighborhood, Ellicott gave proof of his friendship for Wilkinson. On December 16, 1798, he wrote him, in part, as follows:

"I have seen a letter in the handwriting of M. Power dated the 23rd. ultimo in which your name is mentioned in a manner that astonishes me. I dare not commit any part of it to paper but if I should ever have the pleasure of another interview with you I will communicate the substance of it under the injunction of secrecy. If the design of it has been to injure you in my opinion it has failed in its effect for on the most material point I am confident it is false. Any coolness toward him on your side or any indiscreet observations not in his favor to any person whatsoever might excite suspicion detrimental to me in our present situation." [56]

To find out the contents of this astonishing letter was evidently one of the reasons that Wilkinson had visited not only Ellicott but also Stephen Minor during October. Gayoso declared neither trip had been necessary, because such papers, like those belonging to the subscribers of the "great plan," should cause no worry to Wilkinson, Sebastian, or Brown so long as they conducted themselves with propriety. In fact, all the General's original letters, as he said, had been forwarded to Spain; only copies had been retained. [57]

With a persistence that seemed to make no impression, Ellicott forwarded the above information to the Secretary of State on November 8, just as he had done in two other instances during the previous year. Even if Wilkinson did not know what the government was learning about him through this source, he must have known that tales none too flattering to his reputation were being glibly told. On the 19th he wrote to Gayoso:

"My commercial correspondence with New Orleans, and our

[56] Ellicott to Wilkinson, Dec. 16, 1798, Ellicott Papers, Vol. I.
[57] Enclosure from Ellicott to Jefferson, Nov. 8, 1798, Jefferson Papers, Vol. CVII.

personal friendships, have been interpreted into the most sinister designs, and falsehoods and fictions have been invented, from Natchez to Philadelphia, to rob me of my Fame and Fortune." [58]

Granted that Gayoso had no original letters, he could still produce evidence, if he chose, that would be ruinous to Wilkinson. But the General knew that he would not do so, and thereby reveal a seamy side of Spanish diplomacy. He could, therefore, afford to evince little anxiety about Ellicott's letter of December 16. To it the General replied on Christmas Eve. Though baffled by its contents, he would observe "his uniform conduct" toward Power, to whom, as he said, he had written only once privately in the last three years. He revealed no anxiety to see Ellicott soon and learn what could not be safely committed to paper; instead, he merely expressed himself as he might have done to many another of his friends: "To-morrow is Xmas and I wish you were here to enjoy it with us. We shall make the cannon roar and remember our Atlantic friends. I make no doubt you will be better entertained in the gay city of New Orleans." [59]

From New Orleans, Ellicott went to the Floridas. While he was at St. Marks, Madame Portel, wife of the Spanish commandant, told him of Wilkinson's pension money previously sent from New Madrid.[60] At the time he did nothing about this interesting bit of information. Wilkinson was a long way off, and Pickering, the Secretary of State, was not hunting for additional trouble. Being of a pacific disposition, Ellicott had no flair for controversy; perhaps he also realized that there were many others who were tarred with the same stick as Wilkinson. Not until years later did he seem inclined to injure the General with what he had learned.

His information, like most of that published by Wilkinson's detractors, was based on sources not highly regarded. Spanish officials were really the only ones who could produce testimony that would convict him, and they would suffer loss of reputation and probably of office by doing so. Miró, Carondelet, and Gayoso also had other reasons for silence. Wilkinson constantly showed himself friendly and sometimes engaged with them in schemes for mutual profit; but he almost always cut the cloth of his personal enterprises to fit the pattern of orders that he had received from the federal government. Perhaps Washington, Adams, and Jefferson understood his methods, believing that he would

[58] To Gayoso, Nov. 19, 1798, A.G.I., Seville, *Papeles de Cuba*, leg. 2375.
[59] To Ellicott, Dec. 24, 1798, Wilkinson Papers, Vol. I, Chicago Hist. Soc.
[60] *The Journal of Andrew Ellicott*, 238.

never go so far as to commit open treachery, although he might use his office as an aid to fattening his purse. Each of the three Presidents wanted to maintain peace with Spain; and Wilkinson, as an important official in trying times and in critical areas, vigorously endeavored to carry out this phase of their policies.

Ever since arriving at Loftus Heights he had been making a strong bid for Spanish favor. By 1798 the chief barrier to friendly advances had been removed. Carondelet had received Godoy's orders of September 22, 1797, to evacuate the posts stipulated in the Pinckney treaty; and Gayoso, no longer handicapped by conflicting directions, found no particular reason to delay coöperation with the Americans, restless to acquire the land that had been ceded to them. As troops came down the Mississippi, Wilkinson gave assurance that they were designed only for the purpose of peaceful occupation [61] and made satisfactory arrangements for some of them to be supplied over the more convenient routes that lay through Spanish territory. An agreement for the mutual surrender of deserters was also effected.[62] Unfortunately, as Wilkinson thought, it did not include civil offenders like Zachary Cox.

As commanding general of the Army, Wilkinson often tried to return favors that the Spaniards had granted. Once when a Spanish subject, Matías Agustín, sold taffia without a permit to soldiers at three bits a pint, he was sentenced to one hundred lashes and drumming out of camp with two bottles suspended from his neck. After approving the sentence, the General remitted the punishment except dismissal from camp. He justified his clemency on account of the amicable relations "subsisting between his Majesty of Spain and the United States of America," and the consideration due a foreigner of a sovereign power whose good will was appreciated. Of course, he furnished Gayoso with a copy of the court-martial and the remarks justifying such leniency.[63] For this gesture of good will he soon received a letter of thanks from New Orleans.

Gayoso was polite; he was also discriminating. He did not bestir himself to see that the General's pension was paid, and, as Carondelet's successor, his influence might have helped. Although showing to the General and his friends more than conventional interest and re-

[61] To Gayoso, Nov. 19, 1798, A.G.I., Seville, *Papeles de Cuba,* leg. 2375.

[62] To Hamilton, Apr. 10, 1799, Hamilton Papers, Vol. XXXIX; to Hamilton, May 24, 1799, Hamilton Papers, Vol. XLII.

[63] G.O., Loftus Heights, Nov. 19, 1798, Wilkinson's Book of General Orders, 1797–1807, W.D., A.G.O., O.R.; Wilkinson to Gayoso, Nov. 17, 1798, A.G.I., Seville, *Papeles de Cuba,* leg. 2375.

gard, he did not yield to their schemes of personal gain unless the interests of Spain were well served in the bargain. Educated with Englishmen, he understood them and their point of view, although he did not practice their directness in manner or speech. He clothed his words with courtesy and carefully observed the outward forms decreed by Spanish gentlemen.

At times he favored Wilkinson's protégé, Philip Nolan; on other occasions he endeavored to hinder his plans. During the winter of 1796–1797 Nolan had gone north into the general area of Missouri and made a map of the country. When ready to return south he had fallen in with Ellicott, who was happy to add to his party a frontiersman having a large following throughout the Southwest and knowing how to handle both the Indians and the Spaniards. While they traveled together, Nolan learned more about surveying and won from Ellicott lasting admiration. On reaching Natchez, Nolan continued on to New Orleans, where Carondelet became enthusiastic over the news and maps that he brought. Hoping for more topographical data, Carondelet, on June 17, 1797, granted a passport into Texas for Nolan and his followers. Gayoso, although apparently helping the enterprise by furnishing a sextant, was soon regarded by Nolan as an "implacable enemy." Gayoso knew that the adventurer's chief object was to introduce prohibited goods into Spanish territory and to return with horses that he could sell in Louisiana at a handsome profit. He may have suspected that the data wanted by Carondelet would fall into the hands of men like Wilkinson, who yearned for the acquisition of Texas. Possibly Gayoso believed that information derived by these methods did not compensate for the injury done to the interests of Spain; hence, on succeeding Carondelet, he wrote to the governor of Texas and requested that Nolan be apprehended. Nothing was done, and Nolan returned to Louisiana near the end of 1799 and before long was telling stories of Texas that aroused interest from Philadelphia to New Orleans. Apparently neither Nolan nor Wilkinson knew what steps had been taken to thwart the expedition until after Gayoso's death in 1799.[64]

No doubt Wilkinson would have vigorously remonstrated had he known of Gayoso's action. He usually did well by his friends, of whom he had a great number—recipients of his easy hospitality, asso-

[64] Wilkinson, *Memoirs*, II, App. II; Parker, *Philip Nolan and the Forerunners of American Expansion in the Southwest*, 32–40.

ciates in commercial enterprises, and contractors who had profited from government business. These now saw Wilkinson in his prime and without the bitterness of later years. He was jovial, voluble, and successful; his nose was tinged with claret, and his waist had begun to thicken; his eyes were bright, and he talked enthusiastically about whatever caught his fancy. His listeners were usually impressed even if they were not convinced of the correctness of his thesis. He talked of things about which they liked to hear—politics, Indians, arms, hunting, fine houses, and women, too, in a gallant sort of way. He was masterful, and a splendid showman. When he walked, it was with something of a strut; when he rode, his uniform was colorful and his mount was well bred and carefully groomed. Usually he was accompanied by a flashing turnout of officers and men. He was an easy spender of government money, and also of his own. He had exuberant and restless energy, and, although he insisted that his headquarters be provided with conveniences in keeping with his rank, he used them only casually. At Natchez there was a swinging cot with a canopy and mosquito net where he might recline to take his ease after a cup of wine, a bit of venison, and a fragrant cigar; but he did not frequently avail himself of a siesta, because the range of his duties was large and he had the desire to work. He spent hours in travel and writing voluminous letters concerning the units of his widely scattered command. With the rank and file he was not especially popular; they did not care for some of his reforms, and they knew what a tempest he could raise in moments of anger. The wiser ones tried to avoid incurring his ill will. They saw in him a man who was vain, pretentious, and wholly devoid of a sense of humor; they knew that when he took up the cudgels he seldom desisted until amends were made. To force and persistence he added an unrestrained and careless fluency. When once he had put his hand to quill and ink, he did not stop until he believed his case was proved and his enemies had been branded with the names that they deserved.

With Gayoso, however, the General was on pleasing terms of intimacy during the year of 1799. In the spring Gayoso offered Concordia, his country estate near Natchez, for the use of Mrs. Wilkinson and the boys, who were then on the way down the Mississippi under the care of eight sturdy boatmen. The General did not immediately avail himself of the offer. Perhaps he did not like the proposed terms of rent or purchase. Nor could he very well leave Loftus Heights, where he was supervising the expenditure of $80,000 of federal funds on works that he had designed to make Fort Adams invincible. Nevertheless, he expressed a belief that Concordia had as good a title "as any," and that the price asked for it would be obtained in a couple of years. Meanwhile, he would try to find a buyer or suggest means for making it immediately productive.[65] Such was the message that one Joseph Collins presumably bore; he may have proposed also that Concordia be turned over to the General to liquidate pension arrears. A transaction like this might have been hard on Gayoso and a little perplexing to an ordinary bookkeeper, but the Spaniards had a way of their own in the mixing of personal and royal accounts. In addition, Collins was prepared to unfold the details of a speculation in which the Governor, the General, and he might profit. The scheme must have had seductive points, for the promoter had means, a good deal of experience, and was favorably known.

Collins also brought along a little gift to Madame Gayoso from Mrs. Wilkinson: "a few cranberries, a northern berry, valuable for its rarity in this quarter and its fine aromatic flavor when properly prepared." [66] Both the General and his wife found pleasure in such acts of courtesy. Somewhat later they expressed a strong desire to have Gayoso's daughter for a visit. They hoped the rest of the Governor's family would come and stay awhile with them at Bayou Tara, where the General thought of making a home for the summer.[67] Much to the disappointment of them all, his plans went awry. The Secretary of War wished to confer with him, and before long he was traveling to the seat of government as quickly as he could.

[65] To Gayoso, Mar. 15, 1799, A.G.I., Seville, *Papeles de Cuba*, leg. 2375.
[66] To Gayoso, A.G.I., Seville, *Papeles de Cuba*, leg. 2375.
[67] To Gayoso, Mar. 26, 1799, *Ibid*.

CHAPTER VIII

FEDERAL COMMISSIONER IN THE REACH
FOR DOMINION

BY the first part of the year 1799 Wilkinson had completed the work that had fallen to the Army as a result of the Pinckney and the Jay treaties. The administration was eager to learn directly from him just what he had done, and what was the political sentiment in the Southwest, especially since the United States was in turmoil over the Alien and Sedition Acts and was openly threatened by some of the most powerful countries of Europe. France was particularly objectionable. She had demanded loans and adherence to an outworn treaty. Angry at failure, she had then insulted the United States Minister and begun the capture of American vessels upon the high seas. The American reply had been, "Millions for defense, but not one cent for tribute." Measure after measure had been passed, strengthening the harbor defenses and mobile forces. An army of 10,000 men had been authorized, plus an "additional force." To raise and train these new troops was as formidable a task as to employ them properly. Wilkinson was needed to help solve the complicated problem; he was therefore requested to come to Philadelphia without delay. At the prospect of his departure, Ann became greatly distressed and pleaded to accompany him in spite of the fact that the trip would be a trying one for her and the boys.[1] Since he expected to return by autumn he felt that she had better not go, and hence made arrangements for her to stay at Concordia in the care of a certain Mr. Walker, who was employed there as a sort of overseer and general manager. That she might see more clearly the reasons for remaining behind, he wrote to Gayoso requesting:

"Would you take the trouble to point out the dangers and the

---

[1] To Gayoso, March 15, 1799, A.G.I., Seville, *Papeles de Cuba*, leg. 2375.

incommodations of the voyage, it would have great weight with my Ann, and will oblige me, but the thing must appear like a suggestion of your own—you perceive I treat you with the intimacy and unreserve of a Brother." [2]

Wilkinson knew the value of argument originating outside the family circle. Apparently Sargent had helped before; now he called on Gayoso, who could comply with much better excuse.

As a sort of recompense for this favor, Wilkinson declared that he would promote Gayoso's views with "my own court and your ambassador—and nothing will be left undone." [3] About two weeks later he reverted to the same topic and promised that some of the Governor's letters would be faithfully reported to the President with a "viva voce." [4] Since Carondelet had not spoken well of Gayoso, praise from some one else of importance might prove decidedly helpful. Wilkinson also promised that he would defend the clouded title of Concordia "against all the subtilties and chicanery of Lawyers and Judges." [5] Maybe Judge Tilton was thought of; he had come down the river a few months before and had made disparaging remarks about the property.[6]

Meanwhile, yielding to masculine argument, Mrs. Wilkinson and the boys moved to Concordia, and here the General lingered with them for a while. He was very loath to leave them. During the last week in May he wrote Gayoso and explained why he had not reached New Orleans:

"The anxiety of my wife at the idea of our separation, gives us both agony, and so sensibly affects her whole frame, that I shall not be able to tear myself from her as soon as I expected, but yet hope to embrace you around the 1st. proximo." [7]

After arriving in New Orleans, he was still disturbed about her. She was constantly in his mind, and he could not keep from mentioning her in a letter to Ellicott. So it read:

"I left Mrs. Wilkinson with our friend Walker at Concord House, in tolerable health but deep affliction—my own solicitude exceeds anything I have before experienced on Her account and my absence will be shortened by every means in my power. I shall find pleasure

[2] To Gayoso, April 20, 1799, *Ibid*.
[3] To Gayoso, May 1, 1799, *Ibid*.
[4] To Gayoso, May 14, 1799, *Ibid*.
[5] To Gayoso, Apr. 25, 1799, *Ibid*.
[6] To Gayoso, May 14, 1799, *Ibid*.
[7] To Gayoso, May 14, 1799, *Ibid*.

in reporting your progress to the President, and rendering you any service in my power." [8]

Thus both Gayoso and Ellicott were to have a friend at the seat of government. Mrs. Wilkinson and the children were to be the only losers. She was very lonely and had only a few persons in the neighborhood to whom she might intimately turn. She was nearly forty, often indisposed, and within the last few years had suffered the loss of an affectionate brother and her eldest son. Now her husband was on the eve of a long and dangerous voyage, leaving her behind in a sickly climate with the responsibility of caring for two growing boys. She wanted to go with him to Philadelphia, where she had spent her youth and had many friends. There she could find her people, and pass her days in comfort and content.

Although the General had many faults, lack of affection for his "beloved Ann" was not among them. In New Orleans he often thought of her, and on leaving there he wrote Gayoso thanking him for his courtesies and asking that she be his particular care. [9]

While in the city, Wilkinson had been the house guest of Gayoso. Although the Governor possessed only a little real estate and a few slaves and pieces of furniture, his conversation was "easy and affable and his politeness was of that superior cast, which showed it to be the effect of early habit, rather than an accomplishment merely intended to render him agreeable." [10] Wilkinson thought so highly of his culture and character that he had considered sending his eldest son, James Biddle, about fifteen years old, to New Orleans, where he believed that, under Gayoso's tutelage, his morals would be maintained, his manners improved, and his knowledge of the French language increased. [11] The visit was not made, more on account of a change in plans than because of any diminished admiration for his Spanish friends. When his vessel was leaving the river and its sails began to fill with the clean, fresh breath of the sea, he sat down and wrote upon a July morning:

"We are all in health and spirits, eat without allowance and drink your own and Madame Gayoso's health daily." [12]

Three weeks later a robust youngster at Natchez took out his

[8] To Ellicott, June 12, 1799, Ellicott Papers, Vol. II.
[9] To Gayoso, July 4, 1799, A.G.I., Seville, *Papeles de Cuba*, leg. 2375.
[10] *Journal of Andrew Ellicott*, 216.
[11] To Gayoso, Dec. 22, 1799, A.G.I., Seville, *Papeles de Cuba*, leg. 2375.
[12] To Gayoso, July 4, 1799, *Ibid*.

ink and a quill pen and copied down in a roundish, childlike hand the following note that his mother or tutor suggested:

". . . your polite and friendly letter enclosing three from my Father was handed me a few days since by Captain Vidal, for which mamma begs to offer her warmest acknowledgements.

.   .   .   .

"She is indisposed or would have done herself the pleasure of writing your Excellency and Madame Gayoso to [whom] she presents her most affectionate and respectful compliments." [13]

Gayoso did not read the last of these letters, perhaps not even the earlier one; he was stricken with fever, and on the 18th of July his record as Governor was forever closed.

By the 1st of August Wilkinson had reached New York after a tedious journey in a "clumsy ship" from New Orleans. Since his departure from the East in 1797 troubles with France had grown worse and efforts had been made to prepare the Army for any eventuality. For an increased number of federal troops, three major-generals had been authorized. Wilkinson felt badly that he himself had not received promotion, an act that Hamilton had urged but Adams and Washington, whose ears had been filled with tales of Spanish intrigues, seemed unwilling to support.[14]

However, they all knew that Wilkinson's knowledge of the frontier and of Army administration was extensive, and that he should be consulted when important decisions were to be made about either. They, therefore, very seriously considered a long report that he made to Hamilton on the 4th of September, 1799. In it he pointed out that the regular regiments were greatly under their authorized strength, and that many of the officers were absent from their commands. For example, the colonel of the 3rd had not seen his regiment for seven years. Besides, as he said, "the derangement and dispersion of the corps, and the separation of the men that are effective from the officers, and the officers from the men, tear up the fundamental principles of military institutions; they extinguish the pride of Corps, that powerfully operative impulse—they prevent emulation—they perpetuate ignorance—they produce insubordination and indiscipline, and they destroy responsibility, without which all multitudes become mobs, and an army the worst of all." [15]

[13] J. B. Wilkinson to Gayoso, July 24, 1799, *Ibid.*
[14] Steiner, *The Life and Correspondence of James McHenry*, 396.
[15] To Hamilton, Sept. 4, 1799, in Wilkinson, *Memoirs*, I, 442–451.

Such observations deserved and received more attention than those that he made governing the strategic disposition of the Army. In matters of strategy and tactics Wilkinson seldom carefully collected and weighed all the data that were necessary for correct conclusions. When he recommended that Oswego, Fort Fayette, Fort Washington, Fort Wayne, etc., be abandoned and their garrisons be removed farther south, Washington did not concur, partially because he believed that thereby the Northwest might be inadequately protected and the Spaniards disturbed by troop concentrations near their borders.[16] These dispositions, however, would serve to checkmate the French, to whom the Mississippi region was reputed to have been ceded, and would foster any plan of the United States for taking Louisiana and Florida, perhaps "squinting at South America"—a project that was dear to the heart of Hamilton, who hoped England and the revolutionists in the Spanish colonies would join him and his countrymen to promote it. In any such reach for dominion Wilkinson would have an important command; perhaps no one was better acquainted with the territory through which offensive steps would first be taken. However, Washington and others clearly saw that a policy of peace would be better for the interest of the country, and their judgment fortunately prevailed.

After remaining about four and a half months in the East, Wilkinson left Hampton Roads on December 16, 1799, aboard the sloop of war *Patapsco*. During his stay he had visited New York, Trenton, Philadelphia, endeavoring to do what he could to assist in the reorganization of the Army and learn more fully what he was expected to do in the Southwest. He had been told to prepare for recruits coming down the Ohio in the spring to swell his depleted command, to hasten the building of fortifications along the lower Mississippi, and to coöperate with the civil agents in their relation with the Indians. To carry out these injunctions and many others of a routine kind, Wilkinson was bidden to return as quickly as possible. After fifty-five days of almost constant "death-like" seasickness he reached Natchez on February 22, 1800.[17]

There he found all his family in good health. Ann, he described as "blooming still as Hebe and fully qualified richly to repay me

[16] To Hamilton, Sept. 15, 1799, in Ford, *Writings of Washington*, XIV, 204–209.
[17] To O'Hara, Nov. 6, 1799, Vol. LX; to Hamilton, Nov. 7, 12, 1799, Vol. LX; to Hamilton, Nov. 21, Dec. 14, 1799, Vols. LXI and LXIII respectively; to Hamilton, Jan. 20, 1800, Vol. LXVII; to Hamilton, Feb. 25, 1800, Vol. LXIX, all in Hamilton Papers.

for the pains and pangs of absence." [18] He was likewise delighted that the Spaniards appeared friendly. The very day after the General's arrival at New Orleans, the Governor, Casa Calvo, successor of Gayoso de Lemos, called and showed himself inclined to favor arrangements helpful to the American Army. From him Wilkinson subsequently obtained permission for troops and supplies to pass through Spanish territory en route to posts north of the Gulf; each agreed to the surrender of deserters from the other; William Augustus Bowles, a chronic disturber in Spanish territory, was to be put down. Wilkinson went so far as to promise to throw the rogue in jail for a year and fine him $2,000 if he could catch him on American soil.[19] The announcement of this threat, at least, pleased the Spaniards and deterred Bowles from using our territory as a haven of refuge.

With the Spaniards in a mood to meet most of American requests, Wilkinson could delegate his work to another and return to the East, where duties of the Army required his presence. He was also eager to place his sons in the College of New Jersey, at Princeton, and remove Mrs. Wilkinson to a more healthful climate. At Natchez he knew nothing of his own future, but perhaps he might favorably influence it by being near at hand when a new administration was inaugurated. For several years he had cultivated the friendship of Jefferson, who was now in line for the Presidency. It might be well for the General to show a warming or cooling of Federalist sympathies according as he read the political horoscope at the Capital; a wrong kind of partisanship added to reputed Spanish leanings might result in his being supplanted.

Hence, Wilkinson was pleased when he heard that the thirty-two-gun frigate *General Green* awaited him below New Orleans. He accordingly laid plans to leave Fort Adams on May 22, 1800, and hasten to the mouth of the Mississippi for embarking. Just a month later his vessel cast anchor in Havana for a few days. Wilkinson was greatly impressed with the "politeness and urbanity" shown him there. He attended a ball and was delighted with the ladies. He observed, "The lustre of their Eyes, which far exceeded that of their diamonds, quite fascinates me and transported my imagination to Elysium, where I felt myself surrounded by a group of Hyades . . .

[18] To Hamilton, Mar. 24, 1800, Hamilton Papers, Vol. LXXII.
[19] To Hamilton, Mar. 7, 1800, Hamilton Papers, Vol. LXX; to Casa Calvo, Mar. 14, Apr. 24, 1800, both in A.G.I., Seville, *Papeles de Cuba*, leg. 2375.

but of all the Angels, I prefer Donna Antonio." Mrs. Wilkinson was not among the guests; she was deterred by fears of the fever and had to content herself with receiving distinguished visitors.[20]

About the first of July the *General Green* reached Cape Henry, and from there Wilkinson went to Norfolk. He wanted to visit Hamilton and others, who had pressed him with an invitation, but his purse would not permit. He was still waiting for reimbursement of expenditures made for himself and his suite while at New York and en route to New Orleans, something like a thousand dollars. He could think of his own conditions in comparison with that of the high Spanish officials of Havana, his late hosts, who drew $26,000 a year exclusive of perquisites. He did not fail to write Hamilton of their salary and to remark again upon certain Spanish "women of figure": "I defy the most prized mortal to behold them steadily for a second without strong emotions of admiration and desire." In the same letter he remarked that he had sent a box of pecans to the Hamiltons and two small orange stalks to Mrs. Church, daughter of General Philip Schuyler [21]—little acts of courtesy that Wilkinson often practiced.

Without any excuse for lingering on the Virginia coast, the General rode quickly to Georgetown. From here he expected to continue on to Pittsburgh, but, instead, he was detained in the neighborhood until December. On the 6th of May, McHenry had resigned, and no one was immediately available as a successor.[22] Until Samuel Dexter took over the office of Secretary of War, Wilkinson performed a number of its duties. The expansion of the Army had created a great deal of work, and its official papers were in confusion. After arrangements had been completed for administration of the War Department and Wilkinson had seen a few of his old friends, he proceeded to Pittsburgh, the great depot for troops and supplies destined for the Southwest. Once there he began to renovate Fort Fayette as he had done during the winter of 1797–1798: soldiers cleaned, whitewashed, and remodeled the barracks; artificers increased the housing facilities for incoming recruits; here and there masons repaired with mortar and brick; carpenters and cabinet work-

[20] To Sargent, May 20, 1800, Sargent Papers; to Casa Calvo, June 26, 1800, A.G.I., Seville, *Papeles de Cuba*, leg. 2375.
[21] *Expenditures in the Naval and Military Establishments . . . 1797–1801*, 260; Wilkinson to Hamilton, June 29, 1800, Hamilton Papers, Vol. LXXVII.
[22] Steiner, *The Life and Correspondence of James McHenry*, 453–458.

ers united their efforts in making tables, Windsor chairs, and a first-class "necessary" for the General.[23] With driving energy he endeavored to provide the post with these and other improvements; then he laid plans to return to Washington.

Recrossing the mountains in March with his suite, he began to hobnob with members of the new administration. For a long while he and Jefferson had found mutual interest in the Mississippi country. During the winter of 1797–1798 they had seen something of each other when Wilkinson was in Philadelphia. Then the General had talked of the Blount conspiracy; he had also told of Nolan's ventures in Texas, perhaps indicating that others would soon be attempted. Interest once aroused, the General continued to stimulate. Just before leaving Fort Adams in 1800 he had written a letter to Jefferson introducing Nolan, and expressing the hope that "you will find pleasure in his details of a Country, the soil, clime, population, improvements and production of which are so little known to us." [24]

Jefferson doubtless did enjoy the tales that the much traveled Nolan related, tales not merely limited to information about the wild horses west of the Mississippi on which he had asked information. Nolan had another object in mind during that summer of 1800 that he spent in the East: he wanted aid for the conquest of Spanish territory, and hopefully turned to the British minister. But neither from this quarter nor from Jefferson did he obtain any backing. Returning to New Orleans, he and twenty-four of his followers crossed the Mississippi at Walnut Hills on the 1st of November, 1800; and before the end of the following March, the Spaniards had found his camp and brought his career to a grisly close. Negro slaves sorrowfully buried him beneath Texas sod after his body had been mutilated with a cannon ball and his enemies had cut off his ears to send as a gift to the Governor of Texas.[25]

The information Jefferson had gained from Nolan was supplemented and reinforced by Wilkinson during the early months of 1801. He also contributed to the President's hobbies. In January, 1800, Jefferson had asked the General to look after the transportation from New Orleans of "two Indian busts of Palmyra," a gift of

[23] *Expenditures in the Naval and Military Establishments . . . 1797–1801*, 138, 139, 152, *et passim.*
[24] To Jefferson, May 22, 1800, Jefferson Papers, Vol. CVII.
[25] Parker, *Philip Nolan and the Forerunners of American Expansion in the Southwest*, 65–67; Brown, *History of Texas*, 38–41.

a certain Mr. Morgan Brown.[26] When he left there on the 5th of June he was not able to find them; he thought Jefferson had in mind "Italian busts from Palmyra of the Old World." In lieu of them he brought a few "productions of nature and of art with several original modern manuscripts of some interest." To this collection he added other things about two months later: petrifactions, Indian knives, a sketch of settled parts of Mississippi Territory, and meteorological observations by the late William Dunbar, a surveyor recently employed by the Army.[27]

Perhaps Wilkinson was trying to pave the way for his appointment as Governor of Natchez; he would have enjoyed the extra pay, and the Spaniards might have found his rule desirable. If so, Jefferson thought otherwise, and Wilkinson returned to Pittsburgh, the Army paying his tavern bills as he went back and forth. One account in Washington, covering from March 9 to April 10, amounted to $210.35.[28] He was always willing to share his bread with others, never closing his door against those who would enter, no matter if the expense entailed was his or the government's.

After reaching Pittsburgh in April he again was engaged in routine work of the Army and in laying plans for a new road on the American side to connect Lakes Erie and Ontario. He visited Presque Isle, Buffalo, Black Rock, Fort Niagara, and other places, riding hard and putting in long hours.[29] Even if horses cast their shoes, aides grew weary, and wine flowed deep in tavern bowls, the work went on, and Wilkinson could feel that he was accomplishing something worth while.

By June what still remained to be done could be intrusted to other hands. Wilkinson, therefore, prepared to leave for the Southwest, where he and two others had been ordered to make treaties covering boundaries, roads, and trading posts with the Indians below the Ohio. About the first of September he reached the neighborhood of Knoxville, and found the commissioners who were to work with him. One was General Andrew Pickens, now sixty-two years old, whom the Indians called Skyagunsta (Wizard Owl), "the Red Men's friend"; the other was Colonel Benjamin Hawkins, agent for Indian affairs south of the Ohio, "Beloved Man of the Four Nations." [30] Persons

[26] Jefferson to Wilkinson, Jan. 16, 1800, Jefferson Papers, Vol. XVI.
[27] To Jefferson, Sept. 1, Nov. 29, 1800, Jefferson Papers, Vols. XVII, CVIII.
[28] *Expenditures in Naval and Military Establishments . . . 1797–1801*, 223.
[29] *Memoirs*, III, 146.
[30] *Amer. State Papers, Ind. Aff.*, I, 648–649; Pickens, *Skyagunsta*, 125, 158.

better fitted to deal with the savages, it would have been hard to select. Failing to arrange for a meeting with the Cherokees, the three drifted down the Tennessee, and by October 18 had reached Chickasaw Bluffs, near Memphis. Here the long peaceful Chickasaws assembled to listen to the message brought them. On the 24th they agreed to a road through their own territory, thus linking the Miró district of Tennessee with the settlements near Natchez. Travelers using it were expected to be a source of profit to the Chickasaws, who planned to operate the ferries and offer provisions for sale. Perhaps the hope of a little money and the promise of protection by the United States may have influenced the Indians' decision. Certainly the gift of seven hundred dollars in goods helped toward friendly acquiescence.[31]

Successful in their first treaty, the commissioners continued on down the Mississippi to Fort Adams. Here in December the Choc- taws gathered, a "humble, friendly, tranquil, pacific people." They were poor and asked for gifts. Game was no longer abundant, and their way of living had changed. They wanted a set of blacksmith tools; they sought teachers of spinning and weaving for their young women. Instead, they were given hoes, axes, and colorful clothing with a small amount of tobacco and twelve rations apiece to sup- port them on their journey home. Now happy, they agreed to the building of a road from Fort Adams to the Yazoo, accepted the old boundary line as it had existed between the British and them- selves, and professed a willingness that it be clearly marked once more.[32]

However, the work of the commissioners was not yet finished; they still had to deal with the most civilized of the southern Indians, the Creeks, who would not be ready for a conference before spring. In fact, negotiations did not begin at Fort Wilkinson, near Milledge- ville, Georgia, until May 24, 1802. Then Wilkinson and his com- panions were elaborately received in the public square with music and dancing. Two warriors were decked out in white wings, wings of reconciliation with which the commissioners were touched to re- move all grievances of the past. Bows and arrows painted red were broken and cast into a pit and covered with earth and spotless skins. Then three great chiefs came forward and, after wiping the faces

[31] *Amer. State Papers, Ind. Aff.*, I, 648–653.
[32] *Ibid.*, 658–663.

of the commissioners, threw over each a skin without blemish. With the end of these and other symbolic preliminaries, the way was open for embraces of friendship, long addresses, and silent passing of the pipe of peace. For most of May and until the middle of the following month all ate heartily and talked at great length. Finally on June 16 a treaty was signed. The Indians were given something like ten thousand dollars in goods and a promise of annuities; the whites were ceded the lands in Ockmulgee fork. Thus were the boundaries of Georgia moved a little farther westward.[33]

With "the chain of friendships brightened with the Indians" the commissioners departed. Pickens went back to his beloved Tamassee, where he lived in tranquil faith until they laid him in the low red hills that look away to the "Mountains of the Immortal Ones." Benjamin Hawkins remained in Georgia, continuing his association with his Indian friends and compiling three volumes of observations about them. Unfortunately his theories of fair dealing were not held by others, who later, with Andrew Jackson's connivance, wrested from the savages their land and property. Wilkinson remained for a time in the neighborhood, inspiring a belief among the Creeks that they were no longer to be the victims of thieving soldiers or lawless immigrants.

During August he pushed on to Fort Confederation, an important post on the Tombigbee, founded years before by the Spaniards. Here he again met the Choctaws, obtaining from them the land lying between the Tombigbee and the Chickasawhay, an area once acknowledged as British. A black handkerchief, a saddle and bridle, some powder and lead, three rifles, and several yards of cloth for shrouds —these were the gifts that helped turn the treaty on October 17, 1802.[34] By final agreement a new boundary line was to be surveyed and a trading house and a main highway established in the country of the Choctaws. From his camp near the mouth of the Yazoo Wilkinson supervised the work. William C. C. Claiborne, who had recently superseded Winthrop Sargent as governor of Mississippi Territory, thought the General's work "economical and expeditious." The planters, too, were pleased, because more good land of the neighborhood became available for purchase. The Indians expressed no resentment over the loss that they had suffered and were apparently

[33] *Ibid.,* 637, 651, 669, 690, 698; Pickens, *Skyagunsta,* 150–154.
[34] *Public Statutes at Large,* VII, 67, 73; Hamilton, *Colonial Mobile,* 387–388; Wilkinson, *Memoirs,* II, App. CXXIII.

gratified that a trading house was established for them at St. Stephens.[35]

Forts and factories owned by the federal government east of the Mississippi and north of the Gulf were dependent for a majority of their supplies upon the good will of the Spaniards, who controlled the mouths of the Pearl, Mobile, and Apalachicola, rivers that furnished the principal means of transportation to the interior. Wilkinson conferred frequently with the Spaniards, obtaining permission for detachments of the Army to pass through their territory with arms and stores. On the other hand, civilians often found their goods subject to duties that varied with their capacity to pay. The Spaniards believed a limited acquiescence was preferable to unbending resistance. Confirmed opportunists, they avidly seized on whatever offered immediate gain.

In their desire for pelf Wilkinson was not unlike them. He knew that his own profession would never supply the comforts and affluence that he craved; on the contrary, military life was fraught with hardships. Ever since 1797 he had been moving almost constantly; during 1802 and 1803 he is said to have traveled sixteen thousand miles in work for the government.[36] In spite of his hardy constitution he suffered from the chills and fevers of the lower Mississippi. He had no place he could really call home; the very nature of his tasks kept him separated from his family. Ann had been away in Philadelphia since 1800; Joseph Biddle was pursuing his studies at Princeton, and James Biddle, who had been commissioned on February 16, 1801,[37] went wherever the Army ordered him. The General had little to compensate him for the enforced absence of his wife and sons and the frontier privations that he constantly suffered. It is true that the act of March 16, 1802, granted him $225 a month,[38] and that, for a part of the time since 1800, he had received an additional eight dollars a day as an Indian commissioner; but his expenses in the meantime had been heavy, his own private ventures had not been profitable, and the Spaniards who had paid him well in the past were now without funds. Perhaps if Congress kept whittling away on the Army, which now consisted of three regiments and a few engineers, his own

---

[35] To Claiborne, Nov. 11, 1802; Claiborne to Dearborn, Nov. 16, 1802; Claiborne to Dearborn, Jan. 17, 1803—all in Rowland, *Mississippi Territorial Archives, 1797–1803,* I, 552–555, 581.

[36] *Memoirs,* I, vii.

[37] Heitman, *Historical Register and Dictionary of the U.S. Army,* I, 1037.

[38] Callan, *Military Laws of the United States,* 100.

grade of brigadier-general would be abolished. This idea had already been openly discussed. With his tenure of an ill paid and trying office in jeopardy, Wilkinson turned to Samuel Smith, a distinguished Representative from Maryland, and asked aid in being made the governor at Natchez, a little later surveyor-general.[39] In soliciting support for the second of these positions, he wrote a letter to the Secretary of War, who in turn placed on it this blighting superscription: "Such a situation would enable him to associate with Spanish agents without suspicion." [40] Wilkinson was therefore left, as before, to administer the Army.

To perform this task successfully required uncommon ability. Most of the higher officers were aged, ex-Revolutionary soldiers, who had failed to keep pace with the times, partly because they had been confined to the wilderness where their scanty pay allowed them little beyond the necessities of life. Even when they became infirm in mind and body, they still remained in the service, for no adequate provision was made for their retirement. Hence the Army became a sort of almshouse for military ineffectives. These and haphazardly selected younger officers were intensely individual, and frequently were given to bitter wrangling. They obeyed orders begrudgingly, often exhausting every means to evade them. Like the civilian population, they suffered from an excess of democracy, and no matter what steps might be taken to improve the Army, a few recalcitrants were always found.

On April 30, 1801, Wilkinson had issued a general order at Pittsburgh directing that those in the Army cut their hair short.[41] For time out of mind they had been accustomed to wearing it long, tied in a cue, and generously powdered. In preparation for important inspections and reviews, flour and tallow were usually issued to soldiers for dressing their locks, which were bound on a thin piece of wood with a black rosette for officers and a leather thong for the enlisted personnel. Wilkinson considered the cue, especially in a southern climate, a "filthy and insalubrious ornament" that was inconvenient, expensive, and unnecessary.[42] Times were changing in

[39] Samuel Smith to Jefferson, Mar. 20, 1801, June 21, 1802, Jefferson Papers, Vols. CIII and CXXIV.
[40] To Dearborn, May 30, 1802, W.D., A.G.O., O.R.
[41] G.O., Apr. 30, 1801, Wilkinson's Book of General Orders, 1797–1807, W.D., A.G.O., O.R.
[42] To President of Court-Martial, June 1, 1803, in *National Intelligencer*, Mar. 1, 1805.

both dress and politics. It would not be long until taboured shirts, knee breeches, and silver buckles would remain only in memory; the rule of the "rich, well born, and able" was passing to those whose ancestry had been neither distinguished nor affluent. Marks of aristocracy were taboo in France, and the mania to discard them had already spread to our country. Hence Wilkinson issued the cue order with which Jefferson was tacitly, if not openly, sympathetic.

When the order was published at Wilkinsonville, Georgia, all complied except a certain Captain R. Bissell, who in great agony of mind wrote thus to his brother in Connecticut:

"I was determined not to do it (cut my hair), provided a less sacrifice to my feelings would have sufficed, I wrote my Resignation, & showed it, but . . . the Col. was not impowered to accept, nor was the pay Master here, & I found it impossible to undertake a journey of eighteen hundred miles without making a settlement with him. . . . I was obliged to submit to the act that I despised, and if ever you see me you will find that I have been closely cropped." [43]

Perhaps another reason stirred the captain into obedience: he may not have cared to be the only long-haired person to greet General Wilkinson on his arrival a few days later.

There were many others who resented that the "greatest ornament of a soldier should thus be lost." Lieutenant-Colonel Thomas Butler was probably the most cantankerous of them all. He was an old officer of experience and reputation and had a following. Out of consideration for the colonel's health and his personal request, Wilkinson exempted him from the order on August 2, 1801. [44] As a result Butler became arrogant and neglectful of his duties. Wilkinson then retaliated by annulling the exemption, and on June 1, 1803, ordered Butler to be tried at Fredericktown because he had failed to cut his hair and change station and take command of troops at Fort Adams as he had been directed to do. Somewhat later the court came to the conclusion that Butler should comply with the order and be subjected to a reprimand. Wilkinson was incensed at the verdict, declaring it a "misapplication of mercy" little becoming those who had tried the case. Nevertheless, he approved it, and, during February, 1804, ordered Butler to New Orleans. The Colonel failed "to leave his tail behind," as Wilkinson sarcastically observed, and before long was showing himself "more contemptuous and disrespectful"

[43] R. Bissell to D. Bissell, July 9, 1802, Kingsbury Papers, Vol. I.
[44] Gardner, "Uniforms of the American Army," in *Mag. of Amer. Hist.*, I, 490–491.

than ever. In December, 1804, he was informed that he would be tried again; his perversity and insubordination could not be endured. Failing to obtain any help from either Congress or the President, Butler had to face a second trial at New Orleans on July 1, 1805.[45] This time he did not fare as well as before: he was sentenced to a suspension of "command, pay and emoluments" for the space of twelve calendar months. On September 20, 1805, the sentence was approved without comment.[46] Thirteen days before, Butler had died of yellow fever; he had passed to a station where the "superannuated Coxcomb," "the flatterer of Adams and Jefferson," the "vicar of Bray" could no longer disturb.

Army administration was made especially difficult by such officers as Butler. A uniform policy was almost impossible to carry out. Wilkinson was in constant need of tact and judgment in reviewing cases involving senility, ignorance, dishonesty, and downright meanness. He was decidedly better at these routine tasks than at instructing his subordinates in their profession. But he wearied of the daily round of identical duties; he was not methodical, and welcomed changes. He liked being sent on a colorful mission of a quasi-military kind in which he might play a leading rôle. Such a detail was now in the making.

In 1800 the secret treaty of San Ildefonso had been signed, transferring Louisiana from Spain to France. Rumors of the change in ownership soon reached the United States. Fears for what Napoleon might do later were aroused on October 16, 1802, by Morales, Spanish intendant of Louisiana, when he withdrew from the Americans the privilege of deposit at New Orleans. To this disconcerting act was added the rumor that General Victor of the French army was coming with a considerable force to take possession of Louisiana, while Spain, angered at the turn of affairs, was reputed to have plans to prevent its retrocession. Anxious over what the future might hold, the War Department reinforced its garrisons on the lower Mississippi and laid plans for calling out the near-by militia. Meanwhile, Monroe and his colleagues in France were bidden to exert themselves for the purchase of the island of Orleans. They more than succeeded; for Napoleon, changing his plans, sold them, instead, all of Louisiana for the sum of $14,500,000.

To take over Louisiana, William C. C. Claiborne, governor of

---

[45] To Butler, Nov. 25, Dec. 10, 1804, March. 25, 1805, James Brown Papers.
[46] *National Intelligencer*, Aug. 30, Nov. 20, 1805.

Mississippi Territory, and James Wilkinson were appointed as United States commissioners. Neither of them spoke the language nor adequately understood the people with whom they were to deal, but both, besides knowing the country, were easily available and appreciated the honor of their selection. Wilkinson was always ready to leave his Army troubles behind, dispense public funds, and quit the wilderness of fevers, mosquitoes, and dirty Indians and make merry with his friends in the metropolis of the great Southwest. On or about the 10th of December he boarded the *Fair Weather* at Fort Adams and started for New Orleans, accompanied by seventeen other boats and two barges. By the 15th the flotilla had reached a point two miles from the city, and here about three hundred and fifty soldiers, with their four women per company, began to pitch camp.[47] After a round of diplomatic visits, the United States commissioners arranged to take over the province from the French, to whom it had been surrendered by the Spaniards on the 30th of November, 1803.

The day appointed for the ceremony, December 20, dawned warm and bright. With a salute of twenty guns from Fort St. Charles, the American regular infantry and a few artillerists entered the city by the Tchoupitorelas gate and stationed themselves on the river side of the Place d'Armes opposite the Territorial militia and in front of the Cabildo. Within the council chamber of this government building, Pierre Clément Laussat, the French commissioner, appeared with Claiborne and Wilkinson on his right and left, and, after a mutual exchange of credentials, read the treaty surrendering Louisiana to the United States. Then, declaring the transfer effected and his countrymen absolved of their former allegiance, he handed over to Claiborne the city keys adorned with the tricolored ribbons of France. Claiborne now had a turn. Going to the balcony, he addressed the people beneath in words designed to stir their loyalty, promising that the United States would protect them in the full enjoyment of their liberty, property, and religion. As his words ceased, the French flag was lowered, thus ending foreign dominion. As it floated near the ground, members of the escort caught it, wrapped it round their sergeant-major, Legrand, and marched away with beating drums. Then the Stars and Stripes were run up the halyards, six-pounders began to boom, and scattered onlookers threw up their hats and

---

[47] G.O., Ft. Adams, Dec. 8, 10, 1803, and G.O., Dec. 19, 1803, in Wilkinson's Book of General Orders, 1797–1807, W.D., A.G.O., O.R.

yelled. The rest stood by in questioning silence.[48] Within a stone's throw of them the Mississippi flowed majestically to the sea. Perhaps few visioned the magnificent country that it drained or realized that the Union had begun its irresistible march to the Pacific.

If Spain felt resentful that Louisiana had passed to the United States after France had promised to retain it forever, she was still unwilling to risk war for a province that had never paid for its keep. In fact, Casa Calvo, one of the Spanish commissioners, celebrated its retrocession as a national triumph. His ball in honor of Laussat, an archenemy, is reputed to have cost fifteen thousand francs. The one given in return on December 16 was equally splendid. Four or five hundred persons enjoyed Laussat's hospitality, coming and going the whole night through, eating and drinking, gaming and dancing. Not until eight in the morning had the "baleaux and galopede" been danced and the last exuberant guest departed. Then servants began to clear away the debris of the party and to rehang the doors that had been removed to make exit and entrance easier.[49]

Without sufficient personal or government funds, Claiborne and Wilkinson could not entertain on a corresponding scale. What they failed to do in this respect was not offset by the brilliance of their personal accomplishments. The Governor was young and unimpressive, the General was dogmatic and voluble. Of course, the Spaniards were not unaware of these defects, but they also knew that the two commissioners were important in the country bordering the Crown's domain; and for obvious reasons their friendship was valuable. They saw real advantage in refraining from carping criticism. With the rather fussy and ephemeral Laussat the case was different. Neither Claiborne nor Wilkinson could especially promote the interests of France. Laussat, too, had once reveled in dreams of grandeur; he had hoped to be governor of Louisiana, only to awaken and find himself a mere messenger boy of Napoleon. In the bitterness of his disappointment, he was prone to judge others unfairly. Claiborne, he wrote, was extremely ill fitted for his place, and Wilkinson was a rattle-headed fellow, frequently drunk.[50] Claiborne certainly lacked

---

[48] Claiborne to Madison, Dec. 20, 1803, in Rowland, *The Official Letter Books of W. C. C. Claiborne*, I, 307, 309–310; Fortier, *A History of Louisiana*, II, 284–286.
[49] Fortier, *A History of Louisiana*, II, 240–241, 283–287.
[50] Laussat to Decrès, April 7, 1804, in Robertson, *Louisiana Under Spain, France, and the United States, 1785–1807*, II, 53.

experience, but he undoubtedly possessed marked ability and had his country's interests at heart. When Wilkinson grew talkative, Laussat failed to realize that there was still enough behind his façade of chatter to cope amply with any of his visionary projects. Claiborne had a much higher opinion of his colleague even if association with him on the same mission was frequently trying. He liked the General's military arrangement, believing the measures taken to maintain order and support the civil authority had been well conceived.

In fact, Wilkinson did work intelligently to insure domestic tranquillity during this difficult period of transition. He posted guards wherever there offered opportunity of trouble, carefully enjoining them to show themselves friendly and considerate toward the population.[51] Of the eight or ten thousand inhabitants not a few were eager to incite disorder. Spanish and French soldiers, along with their parasites, had plenty of time on their hands for work of the devil. With few exceptions, the Territorial militia and American regulars held them in contempt and welcomed an opportunity to prove their own prowess invincible. Besides, many émigrés had come from the French West Indies, spreading horrible tales of successful servile insurrection. Slaves in Louisiana had become restive, and their masters fearful of what might happen. The time was propitious for trouble. It was the holiday season, when bonds of discipline were customarily relaxed and offering liquor was an accepted rule of hospitality. Especially were wilderness soldiers hungry to feast on the fleshpots in this cosmopolitan city of alluring sin. Once when Wilkinson inspected Fort St. Louis he discovered most of the members of the guard had gone on a bounding spree and those remaining behind were so sodden-drunk that they could not move.[52] Partisans of the old regimes did not fail to point out these lapses on the part of the would-be heralds of the millennium.

The French held closely to their well established customs. Laussat was not averse to their looking derisively upon the ways of the Americans, a rough sort of folk who liked to dance the reel and the jig. The public balls, an institution long popular, proved a source of friction. At one of these on January 8, 1804, an overbearing American threatened an obstinate musician with a cane. Claiborne weakly interposed. When the music struck up a French quadrille, the Americans interrupted, dancing in the English fashion. Angered at

[51] G.O., Dec. 20, 25, 1803, Wilkinson's Book of General Orders, 1797–1807, W.D., A.G.O., O.R.
[52] G.O., Dec. 20, 1803, *Ibid.*

The home of Mr. Duplantier near New Orleans, once occupied as headquarters by
Major-General Wilkinson.

*From William Birch, "The Country Seats in the United States
of North America," 1808.*

New Orleans in 1803.

From a painting in the Pratt Collection.
Courtesy of the Chicago Historical Society.

this breach of decorum, all of the women left the hall while Casa Calvo, playing at cards, looked cynically on.[53]

A fortnight later trouble again occurred when a Frenchman named Gauthier refused to obey the regulations regarding the order of dances. Wilkinson, after having him taken in hand by the guard, tried to allay any resentment by addressing the crowd in a mixture of English and bad French. With the hubbub increasing, the Governor and the General, assisted by their staff officers, gave a spirited rendering of "Hail, Columbia." When this selection failed to calm those present, they launched with equal fervor into "God Save the King." As a counter-irritant, the French struck up "Enfants de la Patrie" and "Peuple Français, peuple frères," ending with a shout of "Vive la République." The waxing of the din marked the waning of the General's zeal. Both he and Claiborne thought best to make a postern exit. After their departure quiet was restored. Next day the Americans gave a "banquet of reconciliation," which the French attended after duly considering.[54] Thus ended the teapot tempest that might have grown into a serious disturbance.

In dealing with these and other embarrassing situations, Wilkinson was more successful than his colleague; perhaps because he was decidedly vigorous in his methods, more widely experienced, and better understood the reactions of the people in New Orleans. With the Spaniards, of course, he had been on intimate terms for years. To them he now turned in order to fatten his purse through a situation created by the acquisition of Louisiana. During February, 1804, Vicente Folch, Governor of Florida, was in New Orleans, enjoying its pleasures and the hospitality of friends. Wilkinson thought him the very one to whom a secret might be told without the aid of an interpreter, for the Governor had shown himself friendly and spoke English fluently. He therefore made an appointment to call and, after obtaining from his host a promise of secrecy, disclosed the object of his visit. It was to induce the Crown to increase his pension to $4,000 a year and to pay up the arrears of $20,000 now due him. In return for such a retaining fee he promised to write out for the Spaniards some helpful reflections. Folch declared that he had no money, but that Casa Calvo had $100,000 for expenses as boundary commissioner. Clearly he was the one to see. But Wilkinson hesitated. He did not trust Don Andrés Armesto, Casa Calvo's

[53] Fortier, *A History of Louisiana*, II, 288–289.
[54] *Ibid.*, 288–291.

talkative secretary and, worse still, a business associate of Daniel Clark, who had the ear of Jefferson. Nevertheless, in spite of the risk, he went, and, after binding Casa Calvo with an oath of secrecy, emphasized his needs and his plan to promote the purposes of Spain. The Governor was caught with the lure and promised him twelve thousand dollars. This amount was not enough for the General; he also wanted to sell sixteen thousand barrels of flour in Havana. In return for such a privilege, he promised to employ his influence to win adherents to the "interests and maxims" of Spain. No answer could be immediately made to this second request, but the money was forthcoming and the General invested it in a cargo of sugar for the eastern market. Meanwhile he had to produce the "reflections." For twenty days he toiled on this high-paid piece of composition, Folch translating each sheet into Spanish as it was finished. Finally the diffuse document, now making up some twenty-two printed pages, was finished and duly forwarded to Someruelos, the Captain-General of Cuba.[55]

For all the good that the "Reflections" did Spain the price was high. Wilkinson was the only one who really profited by them. He advised the Crown to hold on to the Floridas, no matter what claims the United States made to them as a part of the Louisiana purchase. Garrisons should be strengthened to prevent American aggression. In case Spain found herself compelled to yield, she should endeavor to exchange the Floridas for the territory across the Mississippi, even offering to pay the public debt of the United States in addition. Failing in these efforts, she should save what she could of her western domain and wrest from the federal government a solemn agreement that Americans would never attack it, or allow others to initiate movements hostile to her within the boundaries of the States. To carry through any such plans, the General suggested, among other things, that France be induced to support Spain's contentions, plenty of secret service money be expended, the Indians be cajoled into being friends and allies, and the explorers with Lewis and Clark and the settlers with Boone be taken prisoners or forced to retire from Spanish territory.[56]

[55] Folch to Someruelos, Apr. 10, 1804, A.G.I., Seville, *Papeles de Cuba,* leg. 1574; Cox, "General Wilkinson and His Later Intrigues with the Spaniards," *Amer. Hist. Rev.,* XIX (1913–1914), 794–814.

[56] "Reflections on Louisiana by James Wilkinson," in Robertson, *Louisiana Under Spain, France, and the United States,* II, 325–347.

While Wilkinson was telling the Spaniards how to halt the dwindling of their empire, he was writing another edition of the "reflections" for the benefit of Jefferson and his colleagues. It told of the length and breadth, the climate, history, people, and resources of the Louisiana country, which few knew as well as he.[57] Certainly no one employed such knowledge with equal cleverness for personal advantage. He was playing an old trick with minor variations. In 1787 he had duped Miró, receiving a pension and trade dispensations for the writing of a long "memorial." With many of the same data he had won the vote and confidence of many Kentuckians. Playing both ends against the middle was one of the General's favorite games that he had long practiced with success.

Able to do little more in Louisiana at this time, Wilkinson prepared to leave for Washington. Here he might learn what lay deep in the heart of the President—information that he had promised the Spaniards.[58] Jefferson, too, was eager to see him and learn more of the country that Monroe had purchased; he realized that new arrangements would have to be made for the Army in the widened area of the frontier. On his own part, Wilkinson was forever ready to tell of the Southwest, where he had spent years of interesting travel. Like Marco Polo when describing the wonders of Cathay to fellow citizens of Venice, he had a multitude of listeners who hung upon his words. He rather enjoyed the sound of his own voice, especially when he felt that those within its range were being impressed.

He, therefore, felt no reluctance in going North. After making arrangements about a speculation of his in sugar, he drew $3,000 from the assistant military agent at New Orleans on April 24, 1804.[59] The next day he left on the good ship *Louisiana*. For the fourth time since 1796 Wilkinson was on his way to the Capital. From the beginning of John Adams' administration, he had been an active federal agent in the reach for dominion. He had taken over Wayne's work in 1797 and dealt successfully with the Indians of the Northwest, securing from them peaceful consent to the rapid settlement of Americans on the lands north of the Ohio. He had carefully supervised the taking over of the forts that the British had held along the Great Lakes since the Revolution. At these and other strategic points he had disposed his diminutive forces. In the Southwest he

[57] To Dearborn, July 13, 1804, W.D., A.G.O., O.F.
[58] Folch to Someruelos, Apr. 10, 1804, A.G.I., Seville, *Papeles de Cuba,* leg. 1574.
[59] Deposition of William Simmons, *Amer. State Papers, Miscel.,* II, 113.

had performed a somewhat similar service with corresponding success. There many of the difficult details incident to the Pinckney treaty had fallen upon his shoulders. After the surrender of the Spanish forts, he had treated with the Choctaws, Chickasaws, and Creeks, winning from them grants of land and permission to establish roads and trading houses within their territories. Lately he had been an active instrument in one of the greatest real estate deals of which the world holds record. And all the while as immigrants swept north, south, and west into the new territory of the United States, he had scattered little groups of soldiers among them in order to preserve law and order and protect their lives and property from the raids of Indians and renegades. To consult with those who would frame the laws and shape the destiny of the West, growing with almost fearful rapidity, Wilkinson was traveling to the East, where he would linger for a year or more, finally going out, like a Roman proconsul, as Governor of Louisiana Territory.

CHAPTER IX

IN AND OUT WITH BURR

WHEN Wilkinson reached Washington in the summer of 1804, the Democratic-Republicans were strongly intrenched in power. Their leader, Thomas Jefferson, that freckled, sandy-haired, rawboned farmer from the rounded Virginia hills, had proved himself an able and discerning politician since his accession to the Presidency. He loved the soil and the means of living thereby. Not a few of his supporters had the same agrarian bias. Nathaniel Macon, Speaker of the House, enjoyed returning to Buck Spring, his North Carolina estate, where he could ride over his meadow land and watch his thoroughbreds play—thoroughbreds whose birthdays were carefully recorded on the flyleaf of the family Bible. Another plantation statesman was Representative John Randolph of Roanoke, brilliant and venomous, who was at this time loyal to the administration, for as yet he had not gathered together his band of recalcitrant Quids. And of course there was the Secretary of State, "little Jimmy Madison," a distinguished student of law and heir apparent to the Presidency. Scarcely less important was Albert Gallatin, a Swiss, who, although he spoke the language of his adopted country brokenly, acted as Secretary of the Treasury, and was preëminently able in solving its financial problems. Henry Dearborn and Robert Smith, intellectual inferiors, but willing and faithful servants of the party, sat at the Cabinet table as sponsors for the military and naval establishments.

With these helpful subordinates Jefferson had completed more than three years of his first term and was now assured of reëlection, a reward that his accomplishments merited. He had shown himself little of the radical that the Federalists had prophesied; indeed, he had evinced no objection to a continuance of the First Bank of the United States and several other institutions that they favored. He had whittled away at government expenditures until some of the most obnoxious taxes could be abolished and the federal debt gradually reduced; he had established a peace of sorts with the Mediterranean pirates by making use of a navy that he had partially demoralized through his economical measures; among office holders he had built up a strong following by eliminating incompetents or violent partisans of the opposite party; he had magnificently extended the public domain through the purchase of Louisiana from the French and through favorable treaties with the Indians. Those who considered his manifold accomplishments either in a political or in a personal way were duly impressed in spite of Federalist propaganda. Jefferson, in fact, had reached such a high level of esteem that the people were ready to give him whatever he wished. He and his colleagues were fully able to crush any opposition that might rise up against them.

With respect to the Vice President, Aaron Burr, the case was exactly reversed; the people's confidence in him was definitely waning in spite of the fact that his ancestry was of the finest in America and his career had been both successful and distinguished. His father was the Reverend Aaron Burr, who at one time had held the presidency of the College of New Jersey (Princeton). His maternal grandfather was the famous Jonathan Edwards, who, in turn, was the son of the Reverend Timothy Edwards. With prayers and books the formal education of Aaron Burr was abundantly supplied. During the Revolution he had conducted himself with bravery and distinction at Quebec, Monmouth, West Point, and elsewhere. After the treaty of peace he had risen steadily in politics. In 1800 he had tried to become President by taking advantage of the ambiguity brought about by voting for President and Vice President on the same ballot. He erroneously contended that the people had voted for him for the first instead of the second position. Since neither of the two candidates had a majority of electoral votes, the House had to make a choice. After considerable political skirmishing, Jefferson was chosen.

The new President did not fail to remember this piece of chicanery "with disgust and loathing." Before long Burr discovered that he had little to do with the distribution of the spoils of office in New York State; worse still, that they were being used to build up the Clinton faction. Finding himself without party support, Burr ignored its wishes and delayed action on the repeal of the Judiciary Bill—a piece of independence that his Democratic-Republican colleagues never wholly forgave. And again at a banquet given by the Federalists in honor of Washington's birthday Burr proposed a toast, "To the Union of all honest men." Immediately his enemies construed the remark as a veiled attack on Jefferson. Much to Burr's disadvantage, the hostility of the President continued to increase. Finally, to vindicate himself and regain the confidence of the people, Burr became a candidate for the office of Governor of New York State. Many Federalists came to his support, but they were not strong enough to overcome the opposition that Alexander Hamilton and others raised against him. Morgan Lewis was elected, and for years continued to enjoy the favors of the "Virginia dynasty."

It was while Burr was bitter from defeat and incensed at Hamilton that Wilkinson arrived in the East. He and the General had known each other since the Revolution, but although they had met and corresponded during the intervening years they had never been jointly concerned in any great enterprise. During 1799 Wilkinson had visited him in New York; in 1800 Burr had helped place the General's sons in Princeton. Not until May, 1804, did their mutual relations arouse conjectures; then Wilkinson, en route to Washington, sent Burr the following message from Richmond Hill:

"To save time of which I need much and have little, I propose to take a Bed with you this night, if it may be done without observation or intrusion—Answer me and if in the affirmative I will be with [you] at 30 after the 8th Hour." [1]

By then complete darkness would make his visit less easy to detect. He did not wish the story to be spread that he was an intimate of an avowed enemy of the administration, especially when he was trying desperately to curry its favor. Army officers were often sacrificed for partisan purposes. Something more than a mere trivial reason induced him to ask for a night's hospitality, no matter how much pleasure the two might find in exchanging ideas on topics of interest. Few surpassed Burr in a knowledge of current politics in the East; no one equaled Wilkinson's information about the Southwest. In the light of later events, each seems to have obtained help from the other in formulating a plan for their mutual advantage. As usual Wilkinson needed money. The Act of 1802 had reduced his Army

[1] To Burr, May 23, 1804, *American Antiquarian Society Proceedings,* XXIX (1919), 122–123.

pay; the prospect was slight that he might again be an Indian commissioner with an allowance of eight dollars per day; the Spaniards
certainly would give him nothing unless they were put on tenterhooks
and he could pose as their deliverer. Burr, in efforts to revive his
moribund influence, might well be expected to father some extraordinary enterprise in which glittered opportunities peculiarly suited to
the needs of an ambitious politician and a financially hard-pressed
general. Mexico and the Floridas presented a field in which the
adventurous might reap a harvest of glory and gold. If Burr yielded
to prospects in the Southwest, he might unwittingly play a rôle for
the benefit of James Wilkinson, as George Rogers Clark had done
in 1793. His influence as Vice President—such as it was—might
even be exerted to bring about the appointment of the General as
Governor of Louisiana Territory. Together they could see that the
office should not fall into unfriendly hands, particularly if they were
to carry out plans in the West without regard for conventional ethics.
Although they may not have reached any definite agreement on that
spring night, before long they were apparently working toward a
common end.

Following his conference with Burr, Wilkinson continued on his
way, reaching Trenton on the 28th of May.[2] Near by his youngest
son, Joseph Biddle, was attending school at Princeton. During the
early part of June, he arrived in Washington, where, soon afterwards,
he met Baron Alexander von Humboldt, the noted traveler and geog-
rapher. In some respects they were kindred spirits, with data they
were eager to exchange. The General was admirably informed on
the subject of the Mississippi Valley. He had lately delighted Jefferson with the gift of a great portfolio of maps covering it; but he was
not well acquainted with the country beyond that linked the United
States with Mexico. The interest of many Americans had begun
to center in this intermediate area, a sketch of which Wilkinson
obtained from the obliging baron. If he could not use the information just then, maybe it would come in handy later. Mexico lay
ready for conquest; many of the silver dollars that he had most easily
earned and spent had come from that very place.

Although Wilkinson was doubtless fired with enthusiasm to conquer this section of the Spanish domain, he could not afford to offend
the leaders of the Democratic-Republican party. In 1804 the ad-

[2] *True American* (Trenton), June 2, 1804.

ministration's objective was peace rather than war; the appetite for expansion had been temporarily satisfied by the purchase of Louisiana. Therefore, the only immediate outlet for the General's energies was in the performance of routine duties, usually onerous and frequently insistent.

Shortly before the middle of July, Army headquarters were established at Frederick-Town, Maryland, for the summer. Washington was sultry and oppressive. Seldom did a refreshing breeze sweep from the Potomac to stir the leaves in the elm trees beside the White House or raise little whirls of dust along the newly made road leading to the Capital. Mrs. Wilkinson, broken in health, was eager to be elsewhere, and before long she and the General were on their way to Frederick-Town. For a while she stayed at Sulphur Springs near Carlisle, Pennsylvania, in the hope that she might grow stronger. Traveling over the mountain roads was difficult and fatiguing, sometimes dangerous. Once the horses ran away and nearly made an end of both her and the General.[3]

With the coming of cool weather, the Wilkinsons returned to Washington. The General cut a smart, gay figure among those who had left the plantation or countinghouse to make their country's laws in a provincial capital. Idlers along Pennsylvania Avenue often pricked up their ears and craned their necks when they heard a cavalcade approach, led by the glittering general-in-chief riding on a blooded mare that had been groomed until she shone in the wintry sun. It was a sight to stir the imagination of bucolic democrats: his magnificent uniform—of his own designing—his stirrups and spurs of polished gold, his saddle-cloth of leopard's hide with dangling claws. Behind him rode his son and aide, James Biddle, arrayed in almost equal splendor. Smart orderlies brought up the rear, alert to receive the General's bridle reins when he dismounted at "the six buildings," the domicile where he entertained his friends in lavish fashion.[4]

On November 5, 1804, the second session of the Eighth Congress convened. With it began a round of festivities, which Wilkinson always enjoyed. He liked to talk with others beside a flowing bowl and a loaded sideboard. Congressmen listened better that way. He talked to them about Army legislation while he told them of condi-

[3] *Pa. Mag. of Hist. and Biog.*, XLIX, 333–334.
[4] Watson to O'Callaghan, Sept. 20, 1860, O'Callaghan Papers, Vol. XVIII.

tions in the Southwest. He constantly received news from his friends there. One of them, John Adair, frequently wrote to him from Kentucky. A letter of his to the General is revealing. Because the conquest of Mexico by the United States depended upon war with Spain, Adair laments that it is not being waged. He adds that peace has robbed him of more agreeable employment, and that it is now useless to answer the inquiries of Wilkinson. Nevertheless, says he, "the Kentuckians are full of enterprise and although not poor [are] as greedy after plunder as ever the old Romans were. Mexico glitters in our Eyes—the word is all we wait for." [5]

Burr, probably more than Adair, was eager for hostilities to start. The fortunes of the Vice President had been growing progressively worse. When he had asked Hamilton, as the reputed author of a piece of slander, to deny it, no satisfaction was given. An exchange of notes followed. Several times before, Hamilton had thwarted Burr's ambition; now he had begun to vilify him. Thereupon Burr used the conventional method of settlement; he challenged Hamilton to a duel. The two met at Weehawken, New Jersey, in the early morning of July 11, 1804. Hamilton was killed, perhaps without firing directly at his enemy. Although many of Burr's friends rallied to his defense, a general feeling of indignation against him swept over the country. For a while he remained in New York, hoping to weather the storm; then he sought refuge in Philadelphia at the home of Charles Biddle, a cousin of Mrs. Wilkinson and a great friend of the General. Though never brought to trial, he was indicted in New York for sending a challenge and was charged with murder in New Jersey. Following his visit in Philadelphia, he made a trip to Florida. Prospects were not inviting there, and he returned to Washington in time to preside over the United States Senate for the last time.

Burr was forty-nine years old. He could not continue practicing law in New York City, where he had been a distinguished barrister; his estate at Richmond Hill had been sold, and his creditors no longer trusted him; he had no family left except his beloved daughter, Theodosia, married and far away in South Carolina. Forsaken by many Democratic-Republicans and hated by the Federalists, he realized that his political career in the North was ended. Restless and em-

[5] Cox, "Opening the Santa Fe Trail," *Missouri Historical Review*, XXV, 36–37; Adair to Wilkinson, Dec. 10, 1804, Durrett Coll., Univ. of Chicago.

Aaron Burr from a painting by John Vanderlyn in the
New York Historical Society.

Courtesy of the Librarian, Alexander J. Wall.

bittered, he thought of the West, where many had gone, started life over, and won success. There in politics and land speculation he might rise to wealth and eminence. He was no tyro in real estate ventures, and some of the theories of government that had provoked his quarrel with Hamilton were heartily espoused by frontiersmen. Why not investigate this alluring country? Wilkinson was close at hand and knew a great deal about it; and he always liked to talk, almost without end, if his purposes were served. During the winter of 1804–1805, the two apparently agreed on some scheme of mutual advantage. Neither was altruistic enough to allow the other to profit alone; neither gave the other his entire confidence; both were wily associates united by the ties of temporary self-interest.

Wilkinson was the first of the two to get what he wanted. He had come to Washington for a variety of purposes. One of these was always very dear to his heart, that of either making more money directly or procuring a position where better opportunities existed for supplementing his income. Some time before, he had wanted the appointment of surveyor-general, only to have it go to another. Now he was a candidate for a much more desirable post—the governorship of Louisiana Territory. Burr did what he could for him in the Senate. Early in 1805, Wilkinson was appointed to this $2,000 position, thereby uniting in his person the civil and military authority controlling the northern section of the Louisiana Purchase. Dr. Joseph Brown, a brother-in-law of the Vice President, became secretary. Wilkinson now held a point of vantage from which he could promote or ruin any western schemes in which he and Burr might engage.

When congratulated on his success, the General was wise enough not to appear too elated. He said he could tell more about his new position twelve months hence. "In the meantime I can only say the country is a healthy one and I shall be on the highroad to Mexico." [6] In the same letter he remarked that Burr would be in New Orleans in June. Thus did he continue to ponder on Mexico and to keep well informed of Burr's plans.

Burr had not been idle during the winter months. Once having decided to try his fortune in the West, he set to work with cleverness and zeal. The first requirement was money. To get it Wilkinson could offer helpful advice. Although he would endeavor to frustrate any of Burr's efforts to extort it from the Spaniards, he would offer

[6] To Biddle, Mar. 18, 1805, in Cox, *loc. cit.*

no opposition to the trial of any schemes designed to exploit others for the purpose of funds. Whatever Burr got from a new source might be used by them both.

At this time England, no less than Spain, was eager to see the United States weakened. Any plan to effect its division was welcome news to the British minister, Anthony Merry. Early in 1804 he had been approached by Timothy Pickering, Roger Griswold, and other prominent New England Federalists to ascertain what support they might expect in a project of separating their section from the Union. Burr probably knew of their proposals, but he wanted one of his own pattern accepted instead. He therefore suggested that he could induce the states of the West to withdraw from the Union if he were properly supported. Charles Williamson, a British subject, acted as go-between. The overture was so favorably received that Burr himself called on Merry. Instead of disclosing the conquest of Mexico as the main objective, the Vice President stressed his ability to break up the Union if a half-million dollars were placed at his disposal and a British fleet stood by at the mouth of the Mississippi to promote his designs. The credulous Merry, won over by this would-be traitor of high degree, sent Williamson on a special trip to England to obtain approval and necessary funds. He arrived there during the first week in October, 1804.

With these seeds of conspiracy sown and his term as Vice President ended, Burr started for the West in the early part of the summer of 1805. In a cheerful mood he confided to his daughter Theodosia that the object of his journey was "not mere curiosity, or *pour passer le temps*," and that it might lead him to New Orleans, perhaps farther.[7] Farther, of course, meant Mexico. He had maps of the country in his portfolio and had obtained a passport from the Spanish minister, Casa Yrujo, under the pretext that the United States was no safe place for him after the fatal duel with Hamilton. Truthfulness was not a habit with Burr; he told foreigners and his own countrymen what he believed would best promote his own ends. If Mexico were his ultimate goal, Spaniards must be kept unwitting, Englishmen must supply funds and a fleet, and Americans must secretly and adequately prepare.

It was difficult for Burr to assign each of these hostile forces a proper place in his jigsaw puzzle of conspiracy. He had to have a de-

[7] Wandell and Minnigerode, *Aaron Burr,* II, 37.

tailed and personal knowledge of the theater in which he was to operate. On April 10, 1805, he left Philadelphia for the West. Nineteen days later he reached Pittsburgh, where he expected to meet Wilkinson. The General was late in arriving, and Burr drifted on down the Ohio in company with several Army officers detailed for the trial of the long-haired Butler at New Orleans. Shortly afterwards Wilkinson followed in his wake, stopping at Cincinnati to visit his friends, John Smith and Jonathan Dayton, then engaged in a scheme to build a canal around the Falls of the Ohio. While there, he wrote to Adair, regretting that he had been unable to introduce Burr. As a sort of compensation, he promised: "Prepare to visit me and I will tell you all. We must have a peep at the unknown world beyond me." [8]

Continuing on his way, Wilkinson reached Fort Massac, near the mouth of the Ohio, where he overtook Burr, who had delayed awhile at Nashville visiting Andrew Jackson. For four days the two were together. Wilkinson later claimed that they talked of nothing sinister to the Union. However, they must have discussed conditions in the West, difficulties of an expedition into Mexico, probabilities of a war with Spain or England, etc., for these were topics that were then disturbing nearly every restless mind.

Before leaving Fort Massac for St. Louis, Wilkinson lent Burr a helping hand, inviting him to travel to New Orleans in a comfortable government barge that was going down the Mississippi with a small detachment of troops. Burr accepted the invitation as well as a letter of introduction to Daniel Clark, a well known merchant of New Orleans. Such acts of courtesy were common with Wilkinson. Although it was his habit to write in exaggerated phrases, he was canny enough not to disclose the secrets that Burr would tell. The note, in part, requested:

"If the persecution of a great and honorable man can give title to generous attention he has claims to all your civilities, and all your services. You cannot oblige me more than by such conduct; and I pledge my life to you, it will not be misapplied. To him I refer you for many things improper to letter, and which he will not say to any other." [9]

To one of his Spanish friends with important connections in New

---

[8] Beveridge, *The Life of John Marshall*, III, 294.
[9] *Memoirs*, II, Appendix LXXI.

Orleans he wrote another letter of introduction filled with maudlin praise and hints of dark conspiracy. So it ran:

"This is to introduce to you a brave, learned, eloquent, gallant, honorable, discreet [gentleman] rich in the best affections of the human heart—in short a man who has filled the second place, in the Government of the United States with dignity and admiration. Gilberto [Leonard] do you serve this man without saying to my enemies he is my friend, and you may serve me and yourself also. Your strong family connections will be able to promote Col. Burr's views, and so serve the good of their country if they follow his advice and then give him their support, and he will soon send your —— blackguard W.C.C.C. [Claiborne] to the devil." [10]

After helping Burr in this fashion to meet the "correct people" in New Orleans, Wilkinson traveled on to his new station, reaching St. Louis in the latter part of June, 1805. Major James Bruff, who had the military "command in Upper Louisiana and its vicinity," went out and met the General, as requested, a little distance below the town. A gesture of welcome like this was common when a high-ranking officer came to take over a post. According to later testimony, Bruff said Wilkinson wanted to tell him something of great importance, to disclose a "grand scheme," if you please.[11] Although afterwards a blatant enemy of Wilkinson, he never furnished any incriminating details of their first conference. Probably there was none. Wilkinson was old in intrigue; he was not foolish enough to tell secrets of importance to a scarcely known subordinate who was irritated on account of being relieved. More likely, as the General said, his motive in seeing Bruff first was to find out what he could before his arrival concerning the problems that he would have to solve.

Contrary to expectations, and much to the chagrin of Bruff, Wilkinson did not first accept the hospitality of his fellow officers on reaching St. Louis; instead, he took dinner with the leading magistrate of the town, Auguste Chouteau.[12] Wilkinson disclaimed any other reason for his action than that of indicating the superiority of the civil government over the military establishment. From this point of view, his decision was wise and in keeping with Jefferson's practices; it conformed to the President's wish to gain the good will of the French inhabitants. Certainly Chouteau was one from whom

[10] To Leonard, June 9, 1804, A.G.I., Seville, *Papeles de Cuba*, leg. 2375.
[11] Testimony of Bruff in *Amer. State Papers, Miscel.*, I, 571–577.
[12] *Amer. State Papers, Miscel.*, I, 578–584.

this amateur in civil office-holding could learn much of local conditions; he, as well as other prominent men of the neighborhood, held large grants of land from the Spaniards and was enjoying unusual profits from the fur trade. The continuance of their prosperity would depend largely on how the General viewed titles to real estate and what steps he took to control traffic with the Indians. His methods of solving both problems were destined to arouse bitter hostility.

Following an inveterate habit of his own, Wilkinson was soon engaged in speculating with those around him. He had taken the first steps while in the East. One of his officers, Captain John McClellan, could see little to enjoy in a frontier post until it was suggested to him that a few articles taken along to trade for furs would probably yield him a substantial profit. A Baltimore merchant apparently backed him. Wilkinson, acting as a sort of silent partner, helped him circumvent freight charges. The goods were shipped from Baltimore, weighed about a ton, and were valued at $2,500. When they reached Fort Massac they were considered the property of the General but were cared for by the captain. Later they were forwarded to St. Louis and disposed of at a profit.[13]

About a year later, during the summer of 1806, Wilkinson tried to turn a few dollars in real estate. In July he bought about five hundred acres adjacent to the post at Belle Fontaine. The General held on to his land until 1809, finally selling it to the government without profit to himself.[14] In an entirely different quarter he met with no better success. Through Forbes & Co. he had acquired Dauphin Island, at the mouth of Mobile Bay on March 19, 1806.[15] What money or service he gave for the property is not clear. Possibly he had begun to capitalize already on the information that he was sending the Spaniards about Burr.

Never caring to do things in a small way and forever ready to speculate, he burned to do something on a scale that was worth the embarrassing investigation that usually followed. In the North and West the fur trade was yielding handsome returns. In the Southwest the same was true; and, besides, the Spaniards lived in this region. With them he might renew his former relations and develop a remunerative overland trade. By exploring parties he might acquire information that would help himself and simultaneously serve the

[13] Cox, *op. cit.*, 39.
[14] Coues, *The Expeditions of Zebulon M. Pike*, II, 358.
[15] *Amer. State Papers, Claims*, V, 498–499.

interests of the government. He appreciated that Jefferson was eager to learn more about the geography, fauna, and flora of the trans-Mississippi country. He knew that the President had sent out the Lewis and Clark Expedition partly for this purpose during the spring of 1804.

While it was on the way, Captain Stoddard, at Wilkinson's suggestion, had come to Washington with a trunkful of things designed to please the President and whet his curiosity. He brought salt from the river Platte and the headwaters of the Arkansas, and two horned toads from nobody knows where; there were also specimens of iron, lead, and fusible spar gathered from hither and yon. With these were other odds and ends: pumice stone, "plumbago from the Missouri," "Black chalk from the Mandane," a buffalo pelt, and a "cluster of fruit from the cottonwood tree." One of the most important items was a map that the captain carried; it traced the route to Mexico City via San Antonio, Laredo, Monterrey, Saltillo, and San Luis Potosí.[16]

About a year later Wilkinson was ready to revise the map through an Indian chief named Riccari, who went to pay Jefferson a visit. The chief could communicate in eleven different languages by his "Arms, Hands, and Fingers"; in fact, they could be moved with such "ease and velocity" that he found no more difficulty in using them than his tongue. Riccari had traveled widely and could tell about an "aquatic horned animal" and a "drum-beating fish"; he had also "seen and could locate a volcano." [17]

Before long Wilkinson had officers from the Army exploring the wilderness of which Riccari and others had told. One of them was Lieutenant George Peter, whom Wilkinson sent out late in July, 1805, to the Osage Indians, ostensibly to invite them to make a good-will trip to Washington. Pierre Chouteau went along with the lieutenant's party because he was friendly with the Osages and wanted to trade with them, a privilege that the Spaniards had enjoyed alone for several years. As a result of the expedition, more peaceful relations were established with the Indians, Chouteau was soon given a trading monopoly, and a belief was created that troops could make a march from St. Louis to Santa Fe.[18] In a letter to the Secretary of War,

[16] Memorandum of Stoddard for the President (undated), Jefferson Papers, Vol. CXLVI.

[17] To Jefferson, Dec. 25, 1805, Jefferson Papers, Vol. CLIV.

[18] Cox, *op. cit.*, 41.

Henry Dearborn, Wilkinson gave his reasons for believing that it was feasible. He said that the distance to Santa Fe did not exceed nine hundred miles, only one mountain range had to be crossed, and enough food could be obtained along the route to maintain his forces. If war with Spain occurred, he advised seizing the northern provinces of Mexico. In such an event, he would establish a chain of magazines in advance of the main force of two thousand men. If more troops were needed, others easily could be recruited.[19] Thus the General was keeping his eyes open both to military contingencies and to trade possibilities. He could use what he learned for personal as well as official purposes.

From somewhat similar motives, Wilkinson dispatched Lieutenant Zebulon Montgomery Pike in an opposite direction. He left camp near St. Louis, August 9, 1805, for the purpose of strengthening our peaceful relations with the Indians, establishing control over British fur traders, and ascertaining the sources of the Mississippi River. He was also to examine the country with the idea of finding desirable locations for small garrisons designed to maintain law and order.[20]

While Wilkinson was learning to play the rôle of civil governor and trying to gain a more extensive knowledge of Louisiana Territory, Burr was in New Orleans, enjoying the hospitality of many quickly made friends. He had arrived there on June 25, 1805. Prominent people cordially received him. Daniel Clark, to whom he presented Wilkinson's letter of introduction, gave a great dinner in his honor. The Spaniards did not exert themselves to show him courtesies. Casa Calvo complained that the distinguished visitor had treated him rudely; [21] he doubtless heard that Burr harbored a plot against Mexico.

Perhaps Burr did have some agreement with the Mexican Association, a body of about three hundred New Orleans men who wanted to liberate Mexico from Spanish rule. Clark was acquainted with the aims of the Association. Although sympathizing with the down-trodden Mexicans, he had no desire to see their liberation coupled with the separation of our western territories from the Union.[22] If Burr confided in him, he apparently did not suggest treason as he did when talking with Merry. Nevertheless, rumors prevailed that

[19] To Sec. of War, Sept. 8, 1805, Durrett Coll., Univ. of Chicago.
[20] *Amer. State Papers, Miscel.,* I, 944.
[21] Casa Calvo to Wilkinson, July 15, 1805, Wilkinson Papers, Vol. II, Chicago Hist. Soc.
[22] McCaleb, *The Aaron Burr Conspiracy,* 31.

it entered into Burr's plans before his sojourn in the South was ended. Clark wrote and told Wilkinson of what the people were talking.

"Many absurd and evil reports," he said, "are circulated here [New Orleans] and have reached the ears of the officers of the late Spanish Government, respecting our ex-Vice-President. . . . You are spoken of as his right hand man. . . . What in the name of Heaven could give rise to such extravagancies? Were I sufficiently intimate with Mr. Burr and knew where to direct a line to him I should take the liberty of writing to him. . . . The tale is a horrid one, if well told. Kentucky, Tennessee, the state of Ohio, with part of Georgia and part of Carolina, are to be bribed with plunder of the Spanish countries west of us to separate from the Union; this is but a part of the business. Heaven, what wonderful doings there will be in those days. . . . Amuse Mr. Burr with an account of it." [23]

The news was probably far from amusing to Wilkinson. To have his name associated with a plan for breaking up the Union was decidedly disturbing. What would the President think of such an ugly tale about his newly made Governor, his Commanding General of the Army? And this was at a time when Army legislation was pending. How would the officials of Spain react? If they thought him a turncoat, they would never yield to his future requests for pay. Of course, if he could convince them that he was acting as their stool-pigeon, he might bask again in their munificent favors.

While Clark's informative letter was on its way to Wilkinson, Burr was riding north on horses provided by the writer. He stopped first at Natchez, then rode on through four hundred and fifty miles of wilderness to Nashville, where he visited Jackson once more. Then he continued on to St. Louis for a second visit with Wilkinson. Going so far out of his way was not done without calculation. He was eager to talk over conditions in the Southwest; perhaps he wanted to know how the General was getting along as governor. Possibly the position might be suitable for a former Vice President. By September, Burr was in St. Louis, reputedly trying to convert Wilkinson to the idea that the West was ready to revolt. Eager for information, Wilkinson continued to pump him for more. When his guest was ready to leave he furnished him with a letter of introduction to William Henry Harrison, governor of the Territory of Indiana, soliciting aid

[23] *Ibid.*, 32–33.

for the former Vice President in returning to Congress. Burr was ready for anything that would give him a new start in politics. He later enigmatically wrote that he and Harrison had "gone round about" the subject that filled their minds.[24]

Soon afterwards Burr was back in the East trying to obtain financial backing for his nebulous schemes. In spite of not seeing them clearly, he never once lost the trick of human appeal when he described them to others. "The gods invite us," said he, "to glory and to fortune; it remains to be seen whether we deserve the boon." [25] Nevertheless, many did not yield to his blandishments. Merry might have done so, if the British government had not been sufficiently discerning to recall him in June, 1806. Although Burr impressed the dapper, red-headed Marquis de Casa Yrujo, Spanish Minister, with schemes for destroying the Union and promoting the interests of the Crown, those who controlled disbursements from the treasury of Spain were unconvinced and would give nothing toward an enterprise that might be skillfully turned against them. What money Burr obtained came in driblets from contributors who had earned it by penurious effort.

While Burr was thus engaged Wilkinson continued to send out small detachments of his hardiest men to learn more of the unknown country that lay to the west between the headwaters of the Mississippi and the upper reaches of the Rio Grande.

During October, 1805, a month after Burr's visit to St. Louis, he dispatched an expedition under his son, Lieutenant James B. Wilkinson, with orders to ascend the Missouri and establish a fort at the mouth of the Platte River. A prominent local physician, Dr. Andrew Steele, was invited to go along, but he delayed until he was granted permission to carry with him a small stock of goods to trade with the Indians. Soon after the party had started, news circulated that its object was to form an advance post "near the coast of Santa Fe." The story must have been designed for those who were ignorant of geography and the direction of Santa Fe. The lieutenant did not accomplish his mission. About three hundred miles up the Missouri River his men accidentally clashed with Indians. Although only one soldier was killed, the rest were discouraged from going on. By the early part of December, 1805, they were back in St. Louis. The en-

---

[24] Wandell and Minnigerode, *op. cit.*, 47.
[25] *Ibid.*, 81.

terprise had failed, and the General and his son were subject to criticism.[26]

A party under Lieutenant Pike, previously sent out, succeeded better. He traveled through the wilderness until he reached Leech Lake, which he believed to be the source of the Mississippi. In this neighborhood he spent the winter, returning to St. Louis on April 30, 1806.[27] He had ably performed a difficult task; Wilkinson was more than ever convinced of his unusual ability and dependable character.

Because of these qualities, Pike was selected for a more hazardous undertaking, to lead an expedition to the Southwest. Its object was apparently lawful and had nothing to do with Burr's schemes. According to Wilkinson's letter of instructions of June 24, 1806,[28] Pike was ordered to conduct a party of Osage Indians back to their country and to effect a peace between them and neighboring tribes. While in this region he was to reconnoiter the territory drained by the Arkansas and Red rivers, and, if advisable, to explore each stream to its mouth. He was cautioned not to give the Spaniards cause for offense. Dr. John Hamilton Robinson, going nominally as an accompanying surgeon, really went to assume command in case Pike met with disaster. Of course, Santa Fe was to be reconnoitered if possible. Pike understood and, just before leaving, informed Wilkinson of the subterfuge that he expected to employ. In case he encountered the Spaniards, he would pretend that he was traveling to the garrison at Natchitoches but had lost his bearings and would be happy to pay the commandant at Santa Fe a "visit of politeness." If the ruse did not work, he would continue on his way.[29]

The expedition started for Santa Fe on July 15, 1806. It had a fur-trading claim against the Spaniards that it hoped to use for a sort of passport into their territory. Those around St. Louis eagerly gossiped about its object. Timothy Kibby, at St. Charles, had an interesting tale that he adorned with a few Irish embellishments. He was just on the point of learning about a "mysterious secret" that would bring fame and riches to those who shared in it, when the General suddenly became cautious, and would tell him no more. Later, when Kibby, overcome with curiosity, plied Wilkinson with questions, he got nowhere for his pains, learning only that the expedition was of

---

[26] Cox, *op. cit.*, 45.
[27] Coues, *op. cit.*, I, 215, *passim*.
[28] To Pike, June 24, 1806, *Amer. State Papers, Miscel.*, I, 943.
[29] Cox, *op. cit.*, 48.

a "secret nature." [30] This answer kept Wilkinson from being further bedeviled; it also enabled Kibby and others to raise a mountain of conjectures. By not taking the public into his confidence, the General may have better served his own devious purposes and enabled the brave and indomitable Pike to penetrate the wilderness with more safety to himself and his devoted band.

Pike and his men were ill prepared for the long journey that lay before them. No government authority existed for the expedition, and no money was available for incidental expenses. In spite of scant equipment, they arrived at the headwaters of the Arkansas in August. Here Lieutenant James B. Wilkinson was detached with five men on the 28th to explore its lower reaches; by February of the following year, 1807, he was in New Orleans. Meanwhile the rest had continued on. They soon believed that "the grace of God had petered out on the other side of the Arkansas." To make up for a lack of shoes they had to cut up their blankets. On the 3rd of December, 1806, Pike, shivering in his tattered cotton overalls, looked, for the first time, upon the glories of the peak that bears his name. The next month some of his men had nothing to eat for four days in succession. When they entered the Mountains of the Blood of Christ, the weather turned extremely cold, and the feet of two in the party were so badly frozen that they could not walk. In the midst of a snowstorm they were temporarily left behind with a little food. Some time afterwards Pike and his party were overtaken by a body of Spanish troops and carried to Santa Fe, where they remained for a while, and were then sent on to Chihuahua. Again detained, he was finally set free and permitted to return to the United States, arriving at Natchitoches on the 1st of July, 1807.[31]

These expeditions enjoyed Jefferson's personal, if not official, approval. They were favored also by civilians greedy for trade and soldiers who had a lust for adventure. They pointed the way for the development of new commercial interests; they helped to promote peace with the Indians and to establish our national sovereignty over a newly acquired domain; they once more brought Wilkinson into contact with the Spaniards whose favors or fears he might use for personal advantage. Although Burr was not a direct agent in inspiring them, Wilkinson knew that they would bring back information that

---

[30] *Ibid.*, 49.
[31] Coues, *op. cit.*, II, 359–487, *et passim; Dic. of American Biography*, XIV, 599–600.

the former Vice President wanted, and for which he might pay.

Wilkinson achieved distinct success in gathering information of Louisiana Territory through these exploring expeditions. If he had been able to demonstrate executive ability commensurate with his knowledge of the frontier, greater honors would have been his without even the asking. Then he might not have felt the need to curry the administration's favor by posing as the country's deliverer from the conspiracy of Burr. Unfortunately he began quarreling with his subordinates soon after reaching St. Louis. For the most part they were a difficult lot; their aims were usually selfish, and sometimes dishonest. Wilkinson dealt rigorously with them, seldom using the tact that he almost uniformly employed in winning the good will of his superiors.

Within the Army a strong faction of opposition grew up under the leadership of Major James Bruff. Ever since coming to St. Louis, the General had paid him scant attention. Angry and humiliated, the Major had retaliated by repeating Kentucky newspaper stories that charged Wilkinson and Burr with a plot to separate the western states from the Union. Bruff, according to Wilkinson, was a sort of half-breed Yankee, "a damned cunning fellow" whom he did not trust enough for any post of importance. Soon an incident occurred to increase their mutual antipathy. When Bruff complained that the camp site for which Wilkinson had personally contracted was unhealthy and without tactical importance, he received a scathing reprimand in public. When General Miranda sailed in February from New Orleans with an expedition to liberate the South American colonies from Spain, Bruff said Wilkinson was the instigator and abettor of the plot, and had the temerity to tell the General that he would not last six months in the service. Wilkinson was incensed at this "act of sedition." Daring the General to arrest him, Bruff got what he asked for and more. He was tried and found guilty of insubordination, writing letters to Washington disparaging the Commanding General of the Army, and other unbecoming acts. He was sentenced to be deprived of all pay and command for twelve months. The findings, however, were eventually disapproved, and he was exonerated.[32]

In dealing with civilians, Wilkinson met with greater opposition and was less able to cope with it. Although he bore himself with dignity and entertained extensively, he frequently lacked tact in ex-

[32] *Amer. State Papers, Miscel.*, I, 571–585.

ercising his extensive powers. Not only was he Governor and ranking general of regular troops in Louisiana Territory, he was also general-in-chief of the militia and ex-officio commissioner of Indian affairs. In executive matters he was supreme; even in legislative and judicial fields he was able to do almost as he pleased. The law-making power was entrusted to him and three associates: John B. C. Lucas, John Coburn, and Rufus Easton. These three judges were appointed by the President for a term of four years. As an additional duty, they constituted the Superior Court. For executive assistants Wilkinson had five lieutenant-governors or commandants, each presiding over one of the following districts: St. Louis, St. Genevieve, St. Charles, Cape Girardeau, and New Madrid. All of the commandants were Army officers except in the case of the New Madrid district.[33]

At first many thought that Wilkinson would perform his numerous duties with distinction. Gideon Granger, Jefferson's Postmaster-General, considered him "one of the most agreeable, best informed, most genteel, moderate, and sensible Republicans in the nation." [34] Matthew Lyon, a Kentucky Representative, glowed with pleasure over Wilkinson's appointment. To bring it about, General Samuel Smith, a Senator from Maryland and a brother of the Secretary of the Navy, had done all that he could. Jefferson believed the selection well made.

Wilkinson did not measure up to their expectations. The inhabitants who had lived under Spanish rule had enjoyed a long period of "salutary neglect"; they were irritated because of Wilkinson's abrasive regulations. They called him a Federalist, Royalist, Burrite, etc.; they said he had risen to power through a miserable accident. They resented his mandatory ways; they saw no virtue even in excellent orders because of the manner in which some of them were given. Edward Hempstead, a prominent citizen of St. Louis, voiced an opinion that others shared. He said: "From a rank Federalist to a suspected Republican he [Wilkinson] became a bigot and is now a petty tyrant." [35] Samuel Hammond, commandant of the St. Louis district, had personal reasons for animosity. Wilkinson had refused to recognize his company of "Volunteer Riflemen" on the ground that its members were disturbers, malcontents, and, for the most part,

[33] Houck, *A History of Missouri*, II, 382, 401, *et passim*.
[34] Granger to Easton, Mar. 16, 1805, in Scharf, *History of St. Louis City and County*, I, 334.
[35] Houck, *A History of Missouri*, II, 403.

not even citizens of the district; he had openly declared that Hammond's nephew had wantonly murdered a drunken Kickapoo Indian. To make matters worse, the General had tried to reopen the case after the accused had been exonerated.[36] Colonel Seth Hunt, commandant of St. Genevieve, was equally hostile. He disapproved of Wilkinson's appointment and declared it unconstitutional. Wilkinson charged him with fraud in connection with the St. Genevieve lead mines. Hunt went to Washington and, on his return, spread the news that Wilkinson would be supplanted.[37]

The General's relations with most of the legal fraternity were equally strained. They resented his efforts to put James Donaldson on the bench; they hated his meddling supervision. Wilkinson declared that the Superior Court, under the leadership of Meigs, broke down "every barrier of Law & Justice." He called the judge "a poor, pimping, lying, hypocritical Yankee, a coadjutor of the scoundrel Hammond."[38] He would allow none of his mail to pass through the hands of the St. Louis postmaster, who was none other than Easton. With "Lucas and Co." he was on no better terms. He said Lucas hated him "because I do not acknowledge his superiority, because I sometimes wear a cocked hat and a sword, and am fond of a clean shirt, which are Eyesores to him, because my infirm wife rides daily for her Health in a carriage, which he considers aristocratic."[39] No wonder Judges Meigs, Easton, and Lucas exhausted almost every excuse before they obeyed Wilkinson's summons to come and sit with him to make laws for the Territory.

Much care needed to be exercised in writing them. The population was heterogeneous, and the methods of the United States were very different from those of Spain. The period of transition for Louisiana was difficult, especially because of the influx of many people whose aims were often dishonest. Interpreting the law as he understood it, Wilkinson did not hesitate to prosecute offenders. When no place was available for their confinement, he put them in the guard house. Debt-evading rogues, murderers, thieves, and unlicensed, swindling Indian traders, all experienced the sternness of his justice. They deserved little sympathy and received less.

But with those who were endeavoring to meet the rulings of the

---

[36] Wilkinson to Smith, June 4, 17, 1806, Darlington Papers.
[37] Wilkinson to Sec. of War, Sept. 8, 1805, and subsequent dates, W.D., A.G.O., O.R.
[38] To Smith, June 10, Nov. 14, 1806, Darlington Papers.
[39] To Sec. of War. Dec. 31, 1805, W.D., A.G.O., O.R.

federal government on land titles the case was different. Shortly before the purchase of Louisiana many had fraudulently purchased land for which deeds, dated back to 1799 or earlier, were given. To correct this situation commissioners were appointed by Congress to examine titles. All claims not declared by a certain date were subject to forfeiture. As an additional complication, Wilkinson created a surveyor-general who had to certify every claim before it was recorded. The 1st of March, 1806, was set as the last day for recording. The news of these regulations did not reach distant sections until compliance with them was impossible. To make matters worse, the fees for surveying were excessive, the people were generally too poor to pay them, the deputies were few, and St. Louis was a long way off for many who had to go there. The inhabitants bitterly complained of these acts of injustice.[40] Among them was Moses Austin, whose son, Stephen, was later to be associated with Wilkinson in Mexico. They contrasted the easy-going methods of the Spaniards with the unfair conditions that their own countrymen had imposed. Wilkinson was naturally blamed for most of their troubles.

Jefferson had no reason to keep an unpopular governor in St. Louis, but he did need a general in the Southwest where the Spaniards were showing signs of hostility along the Sabine. The President decided to shift Wilkinson to the vicinity of New Orleans, where in a military capacity he might coöperate with Governor Claiborne. According to the orders of May 16, 1806, he was to make this change of station "with as little delay as possible"; [41] nevertheless, he made no apparent effort to hurry on his way. Mrs. Wilkinson was unwell, the climate to the south was especially enervating during the summer, his extra pay as Governor was decidedly agreeable, and he did not relish making war on the Spaniards, least of all in company with Claiborne whom he wanted consigned to the devil. It was not until September 7 that he finally reached Natchez.[42]

Burr had long been planning to journey in the same direction. During the winter of 1805–1806, he had been active in trying to obtain funds from the British and Spanish ministers, as well as from his friends, for a purpose that varied with the penchant of the person approached. According to some reports, he wanted to purchase

[40] M. Austin to Gallatin, Aug., 1806, *Annual Report Amer. Hist. Assn., 1919,* Part 1, p. 97.

[41] McCaleb, *The Aaron Burr Conspiracy,* 121.

[42] *Ibid.,* 122.

400,000 highly desirable acres near Natchez on which colonists might cultivate the rich black soil with profit until the day should dawn for them to advance on Mexico. By midsummer of 1806, he had raised about $50,000 and was writing that his plans were developing according to secret arrangements.[43] Wilkinson, of course, was to share in them, and on the 29th of July a letter in code was sent to him. One copy was dispatched by land; another was entrusted to Dr. Erich Bollman, who was traveling to New Orleans by sea.

Wilkinson eventually received both copies of the letter. What it told was enough to damn Burr with treasonable intentions. Its contents were to the effect that the English would meet them with ships at the mouth of the Mississippi and the United States Navy stood ready to join them—"a host of choice spirits," "a corps of worthies," "the best blood of our country." Money was available, river boats were being built, and depots for provisions were to be established. Burr was leaving for the West in August, 1806. By the middle of November from five hundred to one thousand men would be at the Falls of the Ohio. A month later contingents would be reaching Natchez, where plans might be laid for seizing Baton Rouge or passing it by, according to circumstances. In the entire scheme of things Wilkinson was promised high place, Burr alone would be greater.[44]

While this incriminating letter was on its way, Wilkinson had advanced with a small force as far as Natchitoches and was preparing to resist the Spaniards should they readvance east of the Sabine River. Americans in the Southwest were eager for hostilities. Wilkinson, perhaps, shared their views; but he did not want to wage war alone— he could see only slender prospect of success without the power of the federal government behind him. Running counter to Jefferson's pacifist policies was one of the surest ways of having his own political head fall in a basket. Before leaving St. Louis, he had declared that he did not anticipate war.[45] Nor did Simon de Herrera, the near-by Spanish officer at Bayou Pierre, have a stomach for fighting. He could expect nothing from his lazy, half-mutinous, barefooted soldiers in a one-sided struggle over a questionable cause. Hence he evacuated his position on September 27, and a few days later was encamped west of the Sabine. Wilkinson had apparently wrung from the

[43] Wandell and Minnigerode, *Aaron Burr*, II, 68–78.
[44] Burr to Wilkinson, July 29, 1806, in Beveridge, *The Life of John Marshall*, III, 614–615.
[45] To Smith, June 17, 1806, Darlington Papers.

Spaniards a part of what Jefferson wanted. The terms of agreement were not loudly proclaimed because territory often claimed as part of the United States was abandoned; they stipulated that the Americans would not advance west of Arroyo Hondo. The area between it and the Sabine was to be neutral territory interdicted to the use of both parties.[46]

Before this agreement was made Wilkinson had received Burr's letter of July 29. Samuel Swartwout, accompanied by Peter Ogden, brought it. They arrived at Wilkinson's Natchitoches camp some time during the first ten days in October. For a little over a week Wilkinson marked time; his plan of action was not yet determined. Before he had left St. Louis he knew that he did not stand well with the administration, a piece of bad news Swartwout confirmed.[47] Something had to be done to ward off disaster, to restore himself to political favor. Thinking things over in terms of the past, he found a key. He could recall how in 1788, after becoming a confidant of Colonel John Connolly, who was trying to rouse Americans to join with the British and invade Louisiana, he had gainfully disclosed all of the Englishman's plans to Governor Miró at New Orleans. In 1790, when O'Fallon and his armed colonists were an open threat to Spanish power, Wilkinson played a similar rôle, much to his advantage. When George Rogers Clark leading some motley back-woodsmen would have taken New Orleans for the benefit of France, Wilkinson, writing to Carondelet, told how his own individual efforts had broken up their nefarious project. For this alleged piece of work he was handsomely paid. Surely these leaves in his scrapbook of memory were worth reading when the case of Burr was up for solution. By a single stroke, Mexico, the United States, and the President might be induced to believe that they had been saved from disaster by his forethought and patriotism.

A stool pigeon, however useful, has few admirers. But Wilkinson thought the rewards great enough to repay him for the ignominy of the part. Let Burr's project continue to develop. In fact, he would help advertise its menacing proportions, and then step stoutly forth as the savior of the people from treason and bloodshed. The idea was a piece of sour fruit that naturally grew on the tree of his devious and intriguing past.

On October 20, he took the first steps to promote his scheme.

[46] McCaleb, *op. cit.*, 116–150.
[47] *Amer. State Papers, Miscel.*, I, 539–556.

Writing to the President, he revealed the horrid schemes that his patriotic energies had unearthed. A powerful group of influential characters recruited from the East and the West was bent on an expedition against Vera Cruz.[48] By December they would be in New Orleans; under whose leadership, he was unable to say. Next day he again wrote in language even more lurid. The expedition was pregnant with "stupendous consequences." Again no names were given; he did not want to "mar a salutory design." The West might soon be in tumult; he thought that he had better make what compromise he could with the Spaniards concerning the Sabine border.[49] Wilkinson was skillfully endeavoring to please the Spaniards and to justify his action in creating a neutral ground that was destined to be only a nuisance.

That was not all; he must needs do more. Lieutenant-Colonel Freeman at New Orleans was bidden to be on guard and have his troops in readiness for an emergency that could not then be disclosed.[50] To Cushing he hinted of calamity, great enough to make his gray hairs stand on end: "I perceive the plot thickens," he wrote. "Yet all but those concerned, sleep profoundly. My God! What a situation has our country reached. Let us save it if we can." [51] Five days after this letter another went to Jefferson dated November 12, enclosing a copy of Burr's code communication that had been written on July 29. If Jefferson did not quake with fear, it was not because Wilkinson's words failed to suggest the dire peril with which the situation was fraught. The people were faced, as he said, with a "spectacle of human depravity, to excite our sorrow, indignation and abhorrence"; nothing but peace in Europe could save the country from the possibility of desolation and the government from being shaken to its foundations. There was on foot "a deep, dark and widespread conspiracy, embracing the young and the old, the democrat and the federalist, the native and the foreigner, the patriot of '76 and the exotic of yesterday, the opulent and the needy, the ins and the outs." This all-embracing plot had strong support in New Orleans. He would do everything to demolish it, although his means were deficient and he badly needed reinforcements. He would employ "indefatigable industry, incessant vigilance and hardy courage."

[48] *Memoirs*, II, App. XCV.
[49] To Jefferson, Oct. 21, 1806, Letters in Relation.
[50] To Freeman, Oct. 23, Nov. 7, 1806, in *Memoirs*, II, App. XCIX and CI.
[51] To Cushing, Nov. 7, 1806, *Ibid.*, App. XCIX.

He would glory to give his life for the service of his country. New Orleans, he thought, should be put under martial law, for then he could apprehend or banish the "disaffected." He planned to employ "political finesse," "military stratagem," and "false colors" against his adversaries. He would move against them with secrecy and determination, for there were "more than three desperate enthusiasts" who were ready to assassinate him.[52]

Jefferson was not terrified by this melodramatic letter, but he was impressed. After consulting with the Cabinet he gave directions to stop armed bodies traveling down the Ohio and the Mississippi. Commanders of scattered Army posts were warned to be on their guard; militia were to be called out if necessary. Boats building at Marietta, Ohio, and suspected of being intended for Burr's use, were ordered seized. Wilkinson was to be given unusual powers.[53] Affairs were moving swiftly in the direction that the General wished. He could feel sure of his position for a while at least; the stories that Bruff and Swartwout had spread about some one else commanding the Army could now be ignored.

From another angle Wilkinson planned to make capital out of conspiracy. Not knowing the exact location of Governor Folch of the Floridas, he sent letters addressed to him at both Mobile and Pensacola. He declared "on the honor of a soldier" that he would do his uttermost to protect the dominions of Spain from a band of "lawless" and "intelligent" citizens of the United States. Fully armed, they threatened to take Baton Rouge immediately and ultimately the Mexican provinces. He would employ all the means in his power to avert so dire a calamity and prevent this foul stigma on the name that was American.[54] In Wilkinson's mind was racing the thought that, if there were gratitude, the Spaniards would pay.

In another direction the appeal was equally frightening but decidedly more pointed. To Walter Burling, who had been living near Natchez and acting as a military aide, he intrusted a mission involving extensive travel. He was to go to the City of Mexico, reconnoiter the intervening territory, and try to make a few dollars by speculating in mules. He was also to carry a letter to Viceroy Iturrigaray. It described how Wilkinson had succeeded, at "the risk of his life, fame, and fortune," in preventing the descent of Burr and his bandits upon

---

[52] To Jefferson, Nov. 12, 1806, *Ibid.,* App. C.
[53] Cabinet Memoranda, Nov. 25, 1806, in McCaleb, *op. cit.,* 195.
[54] To Folch, Dec. 6, 1806, A.G.I., Seville, *Papeles de Cuba,* leg. 2375.

the "Coast of Mexico." For the sums expended in the cause of "good government, order, and humanity," he asked reimbursement. One remittance of $85,000 and another of $26,000 would just about repay him. Iturrigaray had already heard of the projected invasion; he felt perfectly able to repel it. He was not easily deceived and had no money to spend. He therefore arranged for the hasty return of Burling, to whom was entrusted a message for Wilkinson thanking him for his efforts and wishing him well in "his righteous intentions." [55] So the long trip yielded only a fifteen hundred dollar bill for expenses, which the United States government subsequently paid.

On November 25, 1806, about a week after Burling had set out on his cross-country journey for real dollars and fictitious mules, Wilkinson arrived in New Orleans. He lost no time in preparing the city against attack. Militia were called out, fortifications repaired, and seamen impressed. He began to clear the city of those "choice spirits" who might thwart his ruthless ways. Unfortunately for himself, Erich Bollman delivered, during December, the other copy of Burr's code letter of July 29. Wilkinson soon had it published and Bollman arrested and thrown into jail. When he sought release through a writ of habeas corpus, Wilkinson, arrayed "in full uniform," went into Court, and made a return stating that the accused had been arrested for misprision of treason. He further declared that he would treat similar cases in the very same way. Samuel Swartwout was duly apprehended; he and Bollman were put on a war vessel and shipped off to Baltimore, consigned to the President. On January 23, 1807, Bollman obtained an audience with Jefferson and filled his ears with tales damning to Wilkinson. Peter Ogden was no luckier than the other two; before long he was forcibly sent to join them in exile. General John Adair of Kentucky fared worse; in 1804, when there was a prospect of invading Mexico, he had written Wilkinson, "The word is all we wait for." He knew too much, and so he was dragged from his dinner by Wilkinson's soldiers, paraded through the streets, held for a time below the city, and finally sent North to face investigation.[56]

No one was certain that Wilkinson's heavy hand would not fall on him as an accomplice in the "machinations against the state." The "hesitant" Claiborne made no assertion of his authority, so the Gen-

---

[55] Iturrigaray to Cevallos, Mar. 12, 1807, in McCaleb, *op. cit.*, 168–169.
[56] Wandell and Minnigerode, *Aaron Burr*, II, 132–146.

eral went unhampered about his purposes. So disgusted was Judge Workman of New Orleans with the utter disregard of legal procedure that he adjourned his court and resigned his office in protest. Wilkinson retaliated by arresting and holding him for trial. He was released only when the federal judge of the district came to his rescue. With weeks passing and still no host of bandits appearing, the people rebelled against this uncalled-for imposition of martial rule. According to a later confession of Jefferson, the General had trodden the law in the dust, set the judges at naught to their faces, and "swaddled" Governor Claiborne "in his sack and laid him to bed like a great baby." [57] The territorial legislature of Louisiana declared nothing but circumstances of extreme danger could justify Wilkinson's violent measures. Such circumstances did not exist. Neither foreign nor domestic enemies were in striking distance of New Orleans. Nor were traitors within the city. In short, Wilkinson's acts were "too notorious to be denied, too illegal to be justified, too wanton to be excused." [58]

While this tempest of indignation was rising against Wilkinson, he suffered a great personal loss. On February 23, 1807, his wife died at the home of Bernard de Marigny, then serving as one of his temporary staff officers. Marigny was a perfect representative of the Creole type distinguished for its "fine living and generous spending." Beneath his roof, ill and beset with trouble, Mrs. Wilkinson had found refuge during the tumultuous days of the Burr conspiracy. She had succumbed to tuberculosis, probably aggravated by the frontier hardships that she had willingly suffered. The General could ill afford to lose her. Her devotion, patience, and charm had always exerted a calming influence upon his boisterous and unstable ways. He and his son James Biddle and many friends sorrowfully buried her at New Orleans. [59]

Though many sympathized with the General in his bereavement, more turned upon him with bitterness and scorn. A tale circulated that he had consorted with one of the better known harlots of the city during the illness of his wife. Copies of notes that passed between the two were published in the *New Orleans Gazette*, [60] after Wil-

[57] Daviess, "View of the President's Conduct During the Conspiracy of 1806," in *Historical and Philosophical Society of Ohio Publications*, X–XII, 126.
[58] Wandell and Minnigerode, *op. cit.*, II, 136.
[59] *Louisiana Gazette*, Feb. 27, 1807.
[60] July 13, 1807.

kinson's departure for Richmond. They smell strongly of forger's ink. They were printed when Wilkinson was no longer in the city, by an avowed enemy, who was not famed for his veracity. Wilkinson was genuinely fond of his wife, and it seems incredible that, while she was at the point of death or shortly afterwards, he would court the bed and caresses of a prostitute. If willing to defy the rules of decency, he was yet shrewd enough to know that he should not increase the tide of indignation against him.

Many openly charged that he had aroused New Orleans to the point of rebellion for no worthy purpose; he had conjured up devils only to have them harmlessly vanish. Burr was by no means the horrible menace that he had been painted; he seemed to be no more than a leader of western immigrants with bucolic intentions. After dispatching the code letter of July 29, he had started on his second journey to the West. Floating down the Ohio, he visited Wheeling, Cincinnati, and other places. At Belpre he spent the night with Harman Blennerhassett, a visionary financial contributor, who hoped to win fame and regal rewards in the conquest of Mexico. With whomsoever he talked, Burr gilded his colonizing of the Bastrop grant with alluring plans of greater adventure. Sometimes they hinted at the conquest of Mexico and the establishment of an empire there; or again they were concerned with the carving of an imperial domain out of United States territory and adjacent provinces of Spain. In spite of the broad range of the appeal recruits and money came slowly. And before long the President's proclamation of November 27 reached the western country. Burr fell under suspicion, and his friends began to suffer misfortune. Blennerhassett's beautiful island home in the Ohio was ransacked by drunken and obscene vandals, none other than Wood County volunteers acting in the name of the law. While in Kentucky, Burr was subjected to a grand-jury investigation, though not otherwise molested. After visiting Jackson again in Tennessee, he assembled his men at the mouth of the Cumberland, and before long they were drifting down the Mississippi, sixty strong in nine boats loaded mostly with farming tools and supplies. On reaching Washington, Mississippi Territory, he had to suffer another grand-jury investigation, although he escaped indictment as before. Unwilling to trust himself to Wilkinson and a court-martial, he abandoned his demoralized companions and fled, only to be apprehended near Fort Stoddard, Alabama, on the 19th of February, 1807.[61]

[61] Wandell and Minnigerode, *op. cit.*, II, 69–170.

On March 26, Burr's guard reached Richmond and lodged him at the Eagle Tavern. Before the month had passed, he was brought before John Marshall, Chief Justice of the Supreme Court, for examination. Finding the evidence insufficient to warrant a trial for treason, Marshall had Burr held only for misdemeanor. In June the grand jury began its investigation. Planters, politicians, backwoodsmen, soldiers of fortune, all came to give their versions and watch the constantly diverting show. "General" William Eaton, dressed up like the lord of a harem, strutted along the streets, full of the story that he had related to Congressmen about the seizure of Washington, the assassination of the President, and insurrection in the West. Commander Truxton was on hand, garrulous as ever when the toddy flowed free. Andrew Jackson, gaunt, masterful and profane, had come to offer what evidence he could for Burr and to damn Wilkinson whenever opportunity offered. Winfield Scott, though no friend of Wilkinson, was convinced of Burr's guilt and wanted him convicted. Spectators on those hot midsummer days had only to twist their necks a little to see one of the Army's great generals of the future high above the rest, ill balanced on the great lock of the courtroom door. Though seats were few on those stifling days, no one was willing to miss seeing the witnesses and hearing the evidence that they offered. On June 13, Wilkinson arrived, stout, red-faced, and a little wheezy, resplendent in the colorful uniform of Commanding General of the Army. He had sailed from New Orleans on May 20, 1807. After debarking from the *Vengeance* at Hampton Roads, he had hastened to Richmond, bent on supporting Thomas Jefferson and vindicating his own honor. He was going to convict Burr, that "little arch traitor," that "damned and pickled Villain," no matter how much time it took before the jury; he was also determined to acquaint the whole wide world with the truth by means of a "book of three hundred pages quarto." [62] In spite of his pretensions, Wilkinson had little valuable evidence to offer except Burr's code letter of July 29. No one seemed to know how it was decoded except John Randolph, and he had no faith in Wilkinson's rendering. He hated the General and wanted him investigated and tried. Just how Wilkinson could describe the contemptuous manner of Randolph as "chaste and delicate," [63] is something of a riddle; possibly he wanted to create the impression that the Virginian had been cowed by the stal-

[62] Wilkinson to Smith, June 20, 29, 1807, Darlington Papers.
[63] To Smith, June 12, 1807, *Ibid*.

wart demeanor of the star witness for the prosecution. Eaton had even less than Wilkinson to offer that was worth considering. Many regarded the pair as just chore boys for Jefferson. Finally the grand jury concluded as Andrew Jackson had previously declared, that "something was rotten in Denmark." It brought in two indictments against Burr on the 24th of June: one charged him with treason, another with misdemeanor.

It was not until August 3, 1807, that the actual trial began. From then until October 20, Burr was fighting his case with the assistance of Luther Martin, Edmund Randolph, and other distinguished lawyers. The prosecution was ably directed by George Hay, William Wirt, and Alexander McRae. After two weeks had been consumed in selecting a jury, the trial for treason began. The crux of the case was concerned with the assembling of armed men on Blennerhassett's island with the idea of descending the Mississippi and seizing New Orleans. A long line of witnesses had their turns, led by the colorful Eaton and the sore-headed Truxton. For the most part, the rest were gardeners and drovers and men of menial station; they told how they had been beguiled into the conspiracy, and the bitter fruit that they had eaten. The total evidence was not enough to show that Burr had borne arms against the United States or given aid and comfort to its enemies. On September 1 the jury reported, finding Burr not guilty of treason.

The trial for misdemeanor then followed. The prosecution endeavored to prove that Burr had planned hostilities against Spain, a nation with which the United States was at peace. Again Hay and his assistants failed. On September 15 the second stage of the prosecution ended with a verdict similar to the one before.

Still unwilling to admit defeat, Hay moved to hold Burr and his confederates for trial in the District of Ohio on the charge of treason. Once more the tedious round of evidence was heard by the imperturbable Marshall. Finally on October 20 he directed that Burr be committed only for misdemeanor because the enterprise of the accused had been directed solely against Mexico. Although put under a $3,000 bond for appearance, Burr was never tried. The prosecution had played its last card and knew that no chance existed of obtaining a conviction.

Wilkinson's part in the trial seemed to hurt his reputation more than that of Burr. His great contribution had been made already; he had been the chief instrument in starting proceedings against the accused. He had no important evidence except the Burr letter of July 29, 1805, a letter that he had altered and not carefully decoded. When plied with questions, he had to admit that for a long period of years he and Burr had corresponded and visited each other when opportunity offered. Both of them had been interested in South American projects, especially the late efforts of Miranda to overthrow the Spanish regime. An opinion seemed to grow that the prisoner and the star witness for the prosecution were tarred with the same stick. The defense tried to use this connection to undermine the confidence in Wilkinson. It tried to show that he was governed by a base desire to stand well with the administration; it elicited the fact that he had often acted without authority and beyond any reasonable interpretation of orders. He soon found himself refusing to answer for fear that he would incriminate himself. He offered document after document to explain why he had done this and that, but those who sat and listened were not wholly convinced. General Van Poffenburgh, as Washington Irving would call him, had plenty of embarrassing moments. Though badgered and harassed by Luther Martin and his colleagues, he stood doggedly by his guns. Nevertheless, the opinion prevailed that he had not met the test for the general-in-chief of the Army, and his country had not been well served by his efforts.[64]

If Wilkinson had failed, so had Burr. The former Vice President might exult over the verdict but not over the result of his trial. From 1807 he was a marked man. People could not forget his great ability as a lawyer, and in later years they would sometimes consult him in difficult cases. But their confidence in him as a great political leader was gone; he would never again enjoy the honors of high public office. The ruin of his reputation had been initiated by Wilkinson; Jefferson and his Democratic-Republican partisans would see that it was thoroughly achieved. Little was left to the "proud pretender" except his evil ways. He continued them as before—seducing women, beating his debts, and planning conspiracies that were never consummated. Wilkinson knew that rewards were due to him for helping to bring a talented super-rascal to book; before long he would be going to Washington to claim them.

[64] For Wilkinson's part in the Burr trial, see *Amer. State Papers, Miscel.*, I, 539–567.

CHAPTER X

A BETTER LAWYER THAN GENERAL

DURING October, 1807, the trial of Aaron Burr in Richmond came to a close.[1] Although partisans of the administration had failed to win a conviction, they had succeeded in so clouding his reputation that he would never again enjoy wide public esteem. Wilkinson had helped them. With the flimsy evidence that he possessed, few could have done better; certainly none but the clever and thick-skinned could have done equally well. For rendering an archenemy innocuous, Jefferson now had to acknowledge a debt to Wilkinson, who, in turn, was in great need of executive support, especially since his performance as chief witness for the prosecution had thrown long shadows on his own honesty and honorable intentions.

Some had thought Wilkinson guilty of misprision of treason. Among these was John Randolph of Roanoke. As foreman of the Burr grand jury he and six others of the sixteen members were eager to press charges against the General.[2] Randolph went so far as to call him a rogue, peculator, and would-be murderer. These were hard words, and Wilkinson was no weakling. Army regulations did not forbid him to demand satisfaction from a civilian in the conventional way.[3] He hastened to send Randolph a challenge, only to meet with a refusal, contemptuous and direct:

"In you, sir, I recognize no right to hold me accountable for my public or private opinion of your character that would not subject me to an equal claim from Colonel Burr or Sergeant Dunbaugh. I cannot descend to your level. This is my final answer." [4]

On December 31, 1807, six days after sending this answer, John

[1] Wandell and Minnigerode, *Aaron Burr*, II, 220.
[2] McCaleb, *The Aaron Burr Conspiracy*, 235.
[3] Callan, *The Military Laws of the United States*, 135, 140.
[4] Bruce, *John Randolph of Roanoke*, I, 314.

Randolph rose in the House and asked an investigation of the report that Wilkinson had corruptly received money from Spain while an officer of the United States Army. In support of his resolution he presented copies of several incriminating letters: one was from Carondelet to Tomás Portel concerning $9,645 sent to the General in 1796; another of the same year was from Wilkinson to Gayoso de Lemos, enjoining "greater secrecy and caution" in all their mutual concerns. To these were added suspicious paragraphs from the correspondence of Thomas Power.[5]

Daniel Clark had supplied most of the information. Though an ally of Randolph, an enemy of the administration, he did not care to testify unless compelled by the House. His own life was soiled with licentious adventures, and he knew that Wilkinson, once his anger flamed, would retail them glibly to all who might be inveigled to listen. He had no relish for what he and Randolph had started; both knew that only a stalwart offensive would save them from the Jeffersonian headhunters with whom Wilkinson was allied. On the 2nd of January, two days after the resolution for an investigation had been proposed, Clark wrote to Power asking for documents that would help the prosecution. A week later, in great ferment of mind, he repeated the request, importuning Power for more data and beseeching him to see Vidal, Gayoso's former secretary, Stephen Minor, one-time agent of Spain, and others before they had opportunity to manufacture evidence for Wilkinson. He feared the storm that threatened to break upon his "poor devoted" head; even then there was talk of expelling him from the House.[6] Though arousing hostility and suspicion, he had not yet submitted convincing proof of corruption; the best that he could do for the time being was to give a written account of Wilkinson's Louisiana transactions as he personally knew them. This he did in a letter to the House on the 11th of January.[7] It hurt the cause of Wilkinson but disclosed to him the main line of attack. Until the receipt of letters from the Southwest, Clark would supply no further evidence for the muckrakers.

Meanwhile Wilkinson would have destroyed their leader; for the second time he sent John Randolph a challenge. With it went a taunting invitation to rise to the level of a gentleman and accept; there was also added the blustering declaration that solely because

[5] *Annals of Congress*, 1807–1808, I, 1258–1262.
[6] Clark to Power, Jan. 2, 11, 1808, Gansevoort Papers, N.Y. Public Library.
[7] *Annals of Congress*, 1807–1808, I, 1387–1391.

he was a Congressman had he escaped being caned like a common rogue.[8] Randolph made no reply; he ignored also Wilkinson's scurrilous handbills scattered in the District of Columbia:

"Hector unmasked: in justice to my character, I denounce John Randolph, M.C., to the world as a prevaricating, base, calumniating scoundrel, poltroon and coward." [9]

On conspicuous street corners and in the lobbies of the Capital's taverns, many stayed their steps to read these ugly words. From then on, posting became a fashion among those who would settle their quarrel with a duel.[10] Not a few Congressmen secretly rejoiced that their colleague had been so thoroughly vilified; they could easily recall the insulting epithets that he had frequently applied to them. They gloated that he could not satisfactorily explain his refusal to fight. Wilkinson was willing to let matters ride, though he perhaps would have preferred an opportunity to kill John Randolph. By his death a wrangle would be ended; many of the followers of Jefferson would breathe with relief. This result was not impossible, for Wilkinson could handle his weapons well.

If Randolph was disturbed by imputations of cowardice, he gave no hint; only when he appeared to have been cleverly thwarted, did he display moments of exasperation. On January 2, Jefferson submitted the whole matter to a court of inquiry, which Wilkinson had astutely requested in order to place his case in the hands of some of his comrades in arms. They would be loath, thought he, to convict one of their own number on the equivocal evidence that an avowed enemy of their profession planned to employ. The detail for the court consisted of three members—Colonel Henry Burbeck, Colonel Thomas H. Cushing, and Lieutenant-Colonel Jonathan Williams.[11] They were all Wilkinson's juniors in rank, and at least one of them, Cushing, had been his stanch friend for many years. They could perceive that their careers might be made easier if Wilkinson were exonerated and retained as head of the Army; they knew also what troubles they would make for themselves if they recommended that the General be tried. Meeting as a court on January 15, 1808, they continued in session for nearly six months.

---

[8] Truman, *The Field of Honor*, 83–84; Bruce, *John Randolph of Roanoke*, I, 314–315.
[9] Bruce, *John Randolph of Roanoke*, I, 315.
[10] Truman, *The Field of Honor*, 83–84.
[11] *Memoirs*, II, 10–11.

John Randolph did not believe this tribunal sufficient; he continued his vindictive efforts to bring the General to book. At his instigation, the President was asked on January 13, 1808, to make an investigation of Wilkinson's conduct and to furnish the House with all available information concerning citizens who were suspected at any time of trying to dismember the Union or of federal officers corruptly receiving money from the agents of a foreign government. A week later he complied with the request in part by turning over copies or extracts of a few letters that Miró, Gayoso de Lemos, Ellicott, and Carondelet had written between 1789 and 1798, all bearing upon Wilkinson's intrigues. Jefferson admitted that pertinent papers were not available, explaining that some had been burned in the War Office fire of 1800 and that others were private or could not be found on account of the faulty filing systems.[12] Such evasions were not surprising. For who could expect faithful Democratic-Republicans to search successfully for documents that would embarrass their party and their chief?

Nevertheless, with a pretense of effort they did manage to unearth a few more documents within a fortnight. One was a letter that Clark had written to the Secretary of War in 1803 telling of the West's wavering allegiance when the navigation of the Mississippi was at stake. In proof of the tale he had then enclosed several letters from Carondelet.[13] By 1808 their significance had passed: the United States had purchased Louisiana, and Wilkinson possessed evidence to establish his innocence.

On April 25, 1808, Clark submitted more damning proof of Wilkinson's guilt. It consisted of six original letters to and from Power revealing the General's receipt of money from the Spaniards in 1796. This correspondence, though not conclusive proof of guilt, was more than enough to generate doubts of his honor and honesty. The last day of the first session of the Tenth Congress being at hand, time did not allow a proper consideration of the letters; they were merely ordered printed and sent to the President.[14] Not until the 7th of November would its members reassemble. Most of them rode away to their homes; they had no desire to spend the dog days in the newly made Capital.

Wilkinson preferred to remain in order to improve his political

---

[12] *Annals of Congress,* 1808, II, 1459, 2726–2745.
[13] *Ibid.,* 2745.
[14] *Ibid.,* 2794–2802.

position and to plead his cause before the court of inquiry. From February 24 to June 25, 1808, he appeared as his own invincible advocate, writing and delivering his defense and sustaining it with fifty-five imposing exhibits.[15] Few could surpass him in the manufacture and presentation of evidence; none could easily withstand his vigorous cross-examination. Randolph and Clark did not appear before the court. They hated the Army, and their evidence was secondary and could be readily obtained from the President. On July 4, 1808, the court made public its findings completely exonerating Wilkinson. It declared that no evidence had been discovered that he had corruptly received a pension or money from Spain, and that, on the contrary, he had behaved "with honour to himself and fidelity to his country." [16] With this turn of good fortune Wilkinson could count on no further investigation until Congress should meet in the fall.

He was now free to apply himself to other matters of official concern. By the act of April 12, 1808, the Army had been increased by five regiments of infantry, and one each of riflemen, artillerists, and light dragoons.[17] As a result, armories had to be enlarged, new depots established, additional officers appointed, and men recruited, organized, equipped, and trained. Feeling the imminence of war, the militia insisted on federal aid. Money was not always available; only advice could be dealt out in any quantity. Wilkinson wrote many a letter, traveled many a mile to carry out the program of defense that he and the administration had adopted.

Though diligent in his work, Wilkinson was not averse to pleasure. He often went to Baltimore, where he had many friends. Women were not least among them. He frequently "inhaled" the perfume from an "all aimable Mademoiselle," a certain "Mrs. T." [18] A rumor went the rounds that he was going to marry her—"an unlicensed, indelicate report." The General was deeply embarrassed because he thought that she might suspect him as the author of the tale.[19] With all his faults he was not the kind to boast of female conquests. Though not unwilling to marry again, he seemed to think the time inopportune. Within a few months his affection became more generalized; he wrote of several women who were the subject of his "matins and vespers." [20]

[15] *Amer. State Papers, Miscel.*, II, 124–126.
[16] *Memoirs*, II, 12–13.
[17] Ganoe, *The History of the United States Army*, 112.
[18] Graves to Wilkinson, May 26, 1808, Wilkinson Papers, Vol. III, Chicago Hist. Soc.
[19] To McPherson, July 18, 1808, *Ibid.*
[20] To Smith, Nov. 2, 1808, Darlington Papers.

They did not resent his attention; he was a high-ranking officer who bore his years with ease and passed gayly among them with a romantic flourish. He treated them as if he were a knight-errant in the days of tournaments and castles.

In his relations with men, he was also frequently governed by artificial rules of conduct. Although less than a year had passed since John Randolph had refused to meet him on the "field of honor," he did not hesitate to seek the same method of redress with another one of his enemies during the autumn of 1808. The person concerned was none other than Robert G. Harper, who had once been a Representative from South Carolina and was soon to be a Senator from Maryland. He was blamed for advising Clark to furnish Congress with papers incriminating Wilkinson. In spite of the fact that dueling was expressly forbidden between those who were in the Army, Major Bissell carried a challenge from "the Commander in Chief of the army, to Capt. R. G. Harper, commanding a company of Volunteer Artillery." [21] On refusing "the only admissable atonement," Harper was posted as follows in a column of the *National Intelligencer* of November 4, 1808:

"To those who know Capt. H. G. Harper, it is unnecessary to say he is a swindler and an alien to honor, but to the whole world it may be necessary to proclaim him for a coward because he has been a bully; and thus to place him below the consideration of every man, who values the character of a gentleman.

"JAS. WILKINSON."

Regulations forbade commissioned officers either to send or to accept challenges among themselves. Disobedience was subject to the penalty of being cashiered.[22] Nevertheless, Wilkinson did as he chose, making his own rules of conduct just as he designed the pattern of his uniform. At this time dueling was not publicly condemned, and Wilkinson knew that he could rely on a measure of popular support. Apparently neither President Jefferson, whose caucus dinners he attended, nor Vice President George Clinton, with whom he was quartered, exerted pressure to make him refrain from trying to fight it out with Harper. Henry Dearborn, Secretary of War, knew of

[21] *National Intelligencer*, Nov. 4, 1808; Callan, *The Military Laws of the United States*, 140.
[22] Callan, *The Military Laws of the United States*, 140.

the wrangle and did not interpose his authority;[23] he was going out of office soon, and had no desire to stir up trouble. There was a rumor that Wilkinson would succeed him.

Jefferson seems to have had other plans for the General. The President, afraid that the Spanish-American colonies would fall into the hands of France or England, looked covetously to the acquisition of the Floridas by the United States. Probably with his knowledge, Wilkinson wrote on August 25, 1808, to Folch, Spanish Governor of the Floridas, suggesting that a convention with the United States would be better than the "galling restraint" that the Emperor of France might exercise. On September 15 he wrote again, recommending to Folch that "your own superior understanding should direct the course you ought to pursue" in the eventuality of Napoleon's success. With this as a prelude Wilkinson could make the administration's policy clearer when he went to the Southwest and was able to talk with the Governor in person.[24]

Until his departure from the East he was busy supervising the Army and laying plans for the enforcement of the embargo along the northern frontier. But he was not detained by duties alone; he wanted to be near by when the second session of the Tenth Congress met, so that he might be in better position to rout any of his enemies who planned the promotion of another investigation.[25] It is significant that they refrained from doing so until he left the Capital in the early days of 1809 for a theater where open hostilities were threatening.

Ever since the summer of 1807, when the *Chesapeake* had suffered twenty-one casualties from the *Leopard's* gunfire, the United States had been on the point of war with Great Britain. In retaliation for that outrage British war vessels had been ordered out of her waters, and her citizens prohibited from intercourse with them. Nevertheless, impressment continued. Still eager to avoid war, Jefferson believed that Great Britain could not afford to lose United States trade, and so the embargo was evolved. Enacted on December 22, 1807, and strengthened by succeeding acts, it continued for over a year.[26] During its operation, the shipment of goods from the United States became almost impossible. Although inhabitants of the West Indies

[23] To Smith, Nov. 2, 1808, Darlington Papers; to Dearborn, Oct. 28, 1808, Wilkinson Papers, L.C.

[24] To Folch, Aug. 25, Sept. 15, 1808, and Mar. 8, Apr. 9, 1809, A.G.I., Seville, *Papeles de Cuba*, leg. 2375.

[25] To Cushing, Nov. 7, 1809, Cushing Papers.

[26] Channing, *A History of the United States*, IV, 379–398.

paid from thirty to forty dollars per barrel [27] for flour, and Canadians yearned for beef from the valley of the Hudson, Great Britain continued her high-handed practices, seizing sailors with equivocal records whenever opportunity offered.

Americans whose livelihood depended on ocean trade could see no virtue in measures of negative defense; they preferred to take their chances as neutrals winning large but precarious profits. On the other hand, western hotheads burned with the idea of invading Canada; they coveted its great domain and longed to separate the Indians from their scheming British friends. Planters of rice, cotton, and tobacco believed that their interests had been crucified through a spineless policy; open belligerence might, at least, save their self-respect and perhaps wring consideration from England.

Thus did the winter of 1808–1809 prove disappointing to Jefferson and his followers. He had failed to counter the cunning of England and France, and he had neither a united people nor an adequate military force to support his endeavors. Through a species of unwarranted economy the Army had been reduced to an authorized strength of 3,350 men; [28] even fewer were actually in the ranks to defend some 7,000,000 people scattered along a frontier from 9,250 to 11,955 miles in extent. [29] It is true, legislation had been enacted on April 12, 1808, providing for an increase of eight temporary regiments—but these could not be recruited and given a semblance of training in less than a year. The dawdling Dearborn, as Secretary of War, had not the temper to inspire and expand what he and the President had demoralized and almost wholly destroyed.

While harried with these problems, Jefferson heard rumors that Great Britain was assembling troops in Canada to send to the West Indies, whence an attack might be launched against Louisiana. [30] Such an operation would tend to neutralize any offensive that the United States might make on the northern frontier. To oppose a British movement of this sort, Wilkinson received orders on the 2nd of December to prepare for the concentration of about 2,000 troops at New Orleans. From the Atlantic seaboard, the Ohio, and the upper reaches of the Mississippi they were to come. Some of them would be seasoned

---

[27] Galpin, "The American Grain Trade Under the Embargo of 1808," in *Journal of Economic and Business History,* Nov., 1929, p. 75.

[28] "Returns of Military Force in 1807," *Amer. State Papers, Mil. Aff.,* I, 222–223.

[29] Calhoun to House of Representatives, Dec. 14, 1818, *Amer. State Papers, Mil. Aff.,* I, 791.

[30] Wilkinson to Cushing, Nov. 22, 1808, Cushing Papers.

veterans, others raw recruits; and Wilkinson's mission was to dispose them in such a manner that "New Orleans and its dependencies" would be "effectively defended." [31]

As usual, Wilkinson had a few axes to grind, and he was in no particular hurry to leave until he had obtained several favors from Dearborn, who was soon to retire. The General met with marked success; his claims for commutation of quarters and sixteen rations per day while at Natchitoches and New Orleans during Burr's conspiracy were officially approved. Both were entirely illegal according to the law of March 6, 1802.[32] Similar allowances were to be his in the future, but this ruling had better color of legality because of the recent act of April 12, 1808.[33] As additional proof of friendship, the General was given permission to draw six months' advance pay, a sizable sum only half of what he had requested.[34] He was also allowed, in spite of the embargo, to put aboard ship fifty barrels of flour and twelve of apples.[35] Such merchandise was readily salable in Cuba and would have the twofold virtue of affording the General a handsome personal profit while at the same time it smoothed the way for Jefferson's overtures to the Spaniards.

It was not until January 24 that he started south in the schooner *Wolf*, accompanied by his staff and the American consul at Havana, a city that they expected to visit before reaching New Orleans.[36] At every port of call he was the central figure in an expensive pageant. A showman *par excellence*, he reveled in the publicity that was eagerly accorded whenever he stepped ashore. All the way down the Atlantic seaboard, salutes, dinners, and crowds did honor to his coming. When the *Wolf* sailed from Annapolis on January 25 the booming of seventeen guns announced the departure of the distinguished passenger. Four days later, at Norfolk, the people turned out as if Washington had returned to them. A great dinner was held with a hundred guests, and to him they drank a flattering toast: "May the brilliance of his achievements be such as to secure him the confidence and support of his present enemies." [37] Unfortunately both his reputation and his

[31] Dearborn to Wilkinson, Dec. 2, 1808, *Memoirs*, II, 324–343.
[32] Dearborn to Wilkinson, Jan. 4, 1809, Wilkinson Papers, Vol. III, Chicago Hist. Soc.; Callan, *op. cit.*, 141–149.
[33] Callan, *op. cit.*, 200–203.
[34] Dearborn to Wilkinson, Jan. 6, 1809, Wilkinson Papers, Vol. III, Chicago Hist. Soc.
[35] Cox, "The Pan-American Policy of Jefferson and Wilkinson," *Miss. Valley Hist. Rev.*, I, 222–224.
[36] *Baltimore Whig*, Jan. 25, 1809.
[37] *Baltimore Whig*, Jan. 30, Feb. 6, 14, 1809.

friends were to dwindle. A truer but less appropriate prophecy was his own offering: "The New World governed by itself and independent of the Old." [38] On his mission, the toast was rather patriotic than diplomatic. The Spanish grandees at Havana evidently read the *Baltimore Whig* and were not pleased to learn that the approaching envoy harbored sentiments hostile to them.

When he came to Charleston it was still winter, although the sun often shone warm and bright along the waters of the Ashley and the Cooper. Few of the near-by planters were then visiting in the city; most of them remained on their own broad acres stretching away to the sea. They liked to enjoy the healthful season in their country houses, which beckoned invitingly at the end of stately avenues of cedar or oak; they had to be present when their negroes were starting spring planting of rice and cotton. Slaves were their instruments of toil, the hall-mark of their prosperity. Whether entertaining in their own homes or sitting in the sanctity of St. Michael's, these rich and often able planters prescribed the amenities of life for those of Carolinian origin. None might safely tell them that slavery, like Wilkinson's mock-heroics and gorgeous manners, was an anachronism; it had entered so long into their economy that they believed it would forever prevail. They hated those who would challenge their erroneous reasoning, just as they despised the crude or ungrateful who found flaws in their gracious hospitality; but they opened their doors wide to those whose lineage was acceptable and whose politics were approved. Wilkinson was one of these. He had long known their kind; Charleston and Charleston manners were to him the Maryland of his boyhood days.

When the schooner came up the Bay on the 17th of February, the wharves were thronged with crowds in hearty welcome. A few days later he was the guest of honor at a large public dinner at which Wade Hampton and other distinguished persons were present. Eighteen scheduled toasts were offered and drunk, not counting several voluntary ones highly flattering to Wilkinson and his hosts.[39] The General delighted in these tokens of esteem; he refused to worry because storms were raging outside the harbor, demurrage was mounting, and a tale was making its way back to Washington that he had called the new Secretary of War a "black-mouthed Federalist." [40]

[38] Cox, *op. cit.*, 222.
[39] *Baltimore Whig*, Mar. 6, 21, 25, 1809.
[40] Cox, *op. cit.*, 223.

After about a week's stay Wilkinson and his staff took passage on the brig *Hornet* to which his apples, flour, and other supplies had been carefully transhipped. In company with the sloop *Centurion* they set sail for Havana, arriving there on the 23rd of March. As Jefferson's minister without passport or portfolio, he was to inform the officials of Spain that the United States sympathized with her struggle for independence and hated to see any of her American possessions fall into the hands of England or France. He voiced official regret that the embargo was proving a hardship to the Spaniards and declared that neither it nor the troop concentration at New Orleans was designed for their injury. Only in case West Florida was used as a hostile base would a movement be made to capture it. Such was his message, embodied in an unsigned statement to Someruelos, who as the Captain-General of Cuba, was not deeply impressed.[41]

On the 2nd of April, Wilkinson departed for Pensacola, where he hoped to see Governor Folch and fill his ears with a similar story of good will. Since the Spanish governor had impolitely taken to the woods, his visitor had no alternative to traveling on to New Orleans.[42] By the 13th of April he was still one hundred miles from the city. Six days later he was there [43]—back in familiar haunts where cronies and enemies were equally abundant.

Some of the "swinish multitude" made sport of his coming, describing it in this wise:

> "Sound the trumpet, beat the drum,
> Tweedle dee and tweedle dum,
> Gird your armour cap-a-pie,
> Tweedle dum and tweedle dee.

"Sweet was the song sung on Monday evening, when it was announced by a herald from headquarters, that his Serene Highness, the Grand Pensioner de Godoy, was approaching the city and that he was to make his triumphal entry yesterday. Great preparations were made for the reception of the grand pensioner. Field Marshall Possum kept a watchful vigil the whole night. Next morning he ordered his military coach and 'with solemn step and slow' he moved to meet his serene highness—in his train were found the alguacil mayor, and a long list of dependents and retainers. It is to be lamented that our sovereign

---

[41] *Ibid.*, 223–224.
[42] To Folch, Apr. 9, 1809, A.G.I., Seville, *Papeles de Cuba*, leg. 2375.
[43] *Memoirs*, II, 345–346.

lord, King Solomon [Governor Claiborne of Louisiana Territory] is settling an affair of honour at Point Coupee, between the parish judge and the parish priest, and could not attend to welcome his serene highness. The army was drawn up in dread array. The military officers paraded—but, alas, there was no militia; carts and mules were still; Kentucky's hardy sons stood wondering in amaze, and asked with an inquiring look 'is this the man who wished to separate the western from the eastern states and sell our country to Godoy?' For once the luckless wights were doomed to disappointment—his serene highness did not make his appearance. The malicious say he was drunk.

"This day as his serene highness approached the city, he was met by a vast concourse of boys, mulattoes, and negroes, who welcomed him with loud and repeated acclamation; and the condescension of his supreme highness was astonishing in returning the salute. When his serene highness entered the city, the bells they rung

> "The pensioner is come,
> um,
> um,
> um,

and the drums re-echoed the joyful tidings. How grand the spectacle! What terror did it carry to the hearts of traitors!

"When his serene highness reached the mansion prepared for his reception, his first care was to call his conscience keeper and go to confession. His next was to convoke his privy council to devise means of future operations." [44]

And of course there was to be a superb dinner; pounds and pounds of beef and ham and vegetables, with plenty of pickles and condiments. Yes, there were also provided bottles, barrels, and pipes of whisky and wine, and enough cigars to provide every person in New Orleans with one. But as the chronicler went on to say, there were no capers provided; the Pensioner meant to cut plenty of them himself. [45]

Doubtless Wilkinson was not the best choice, but some one had to come and try to bring order out of existing chaos. Already about 2,000 troops had straggled into this "graveyard of the Old South," settling down almost wherever they chose and bringing with them an

---

[44] *Federal Republican and Commercial Gazette* (Baltimore), May 30, 1809, quoted from *Pensioner's Mirror* (New Orleans), Apr. 20, 1809.
[45] *Ibid.*

overmastering desire for women and liquor.[46] In days of idleness they soon found opportunity to obtain both. The recently appointed officers, generally ignorant and often indifferent, were not the type to save the enlisted personnel by the exercise of sane control and the imposition of healthful tasks. In consequence soldiers careened along the streets, reveling in acts of deviltry and utterly forgetting the intolerable climate and their own personal hardships.[47] Hospitals were soon filled. By the 16th of April five hundred and fifty-three were sick—almost one-third of the whole command.[48] For the care of these peace-time casualties only two surgeons and two mates were available, and one of the former was confined to his bed.[49] Hospital stores were soon exhausted of the stock remedies for chills and fevers.

New Orleans was no place for the army to remain if it was to be saved from dissolution. Rent and commodity prices were soaring in the city. Many of its leading characters, feeling that their day of vengeance had come, baited the General with ridicule and sneers. Nevertheless, he seemed in no hurry to remove the army elsewhere until the rainy season had abated, although the Secretary of War had directed him to do so in a letter of the 30th of April. He found excuse for delay by declaring that he did not receive it until a month and a half later.[50] Other reasons may have caused his inertia. He was loath to be away from the pleasing companionship of friends. Here lived Celestine Laveau Trudeau, whom he was to marry within less than a year. He had to dispose of some personal merchandise acquired in Havana and some flour that he had shipped contrary to the embargo. Both were guarded by a company of soldiers and housed in a building costing the government $1,800 a year.[51] Of course, he was not reluctant to interview and entertain Folch, who reached New Orleans on the 28th of April.[52] The Governor felt that Bonaparte would triumph and West Florida would fall to the United States. So Wilkinson reported, advising his superiors to send an agent to arrange details for the province's

[46] Wilkinson, *Memoirs*, II, 345–346.
[47] Deposition of Peter, in *Amer. State Papers, Mil. Aff.*, I, 282, and deposition of Dale in Wilkinson, *Memoirs*, II, App. CXI.
[48] *Memoirs*, II, App. CIII.
[49] *Ibid.*, 347.
[50] *Ibid.*, 379.
[51] "Memorandum for Eustis," Monroe Papers, N.Y. Public Library.
[52] Cox, *op. cit.*, 234.

surrender—an act that might be hastened by a monetary gift to its officials.[53] Very naturally, he offered to handle the financial arrangements.

Thus the days slipped by, and search for a new camp site was unreasonably delayed. Not until the 29th of May did Wilkinson believe that he had found one suitable for his purposes, twelve miles below New Orleans and near a settlement of about sixty persons called Terre aux Bœufs. It was situated on the left bank of the Mississippi, at a point where the river makes a great bend, commonly known as English Turn.[54]

Wilkinson later endeavored to justify his selection by quoting the unimpressive opinion of others concerning its salubrity.[55] By the change expenses were cut, but only at the cost of great discomfort and disgust. Slight strategic advantages were obtained, and the Secretary of War had good reason for belief that his orders had been ignored.

Fitting the place for a camp was a task of great labor, particularly in the hot, sultry days of midsummer. A part of the land was covered with heavy grasses, and here and there were gnarled live oaks with spreading, moss-grown branches; the rest was swampy, tropical jungle—willows, cypress, palmettos, brambles. On June 9 Major Pike arrived at Terre aux Bœufs—the selfsame Pike who had blazed a way to the Colorado mountains and who was soon to find his Valhalla beneath the parapets of York. With him were five hundred men, who went to work redeeming the wilderness and kept at it with varying industry until about thirty acres were cleared. A rumor circulated that the owner was being paid high rent for his land and having it improved in the bargain—a story easily believed by those who had long tours of irksome fatigue.[56]

The work of clearing finished, that of drainage began. The camp site lay three feet below the ordinary level of the river, which was only fifty-five yards distant when the waters rose. Hence, the men were quickly making the dirt fly for a huge ditch and numerous laterals to furnish the principal drainage. Tents were laid out in parallel lines about eight hundred yards long. On the sides of the

[53] *Ibid.*, 234–235.
[54] To Eustis, May 29, 1809, in *Memoirs*, II, 358–361.
[55] *Ibid.*, App. CIX, and Claiborne to Wilkinson, July 28, 1809, W.D., A.G.O., O.R.
[56] Deposition of Darrington, in *Amer. State Papers, Mil. Aff.*, I, 282–284; deposition of Parker, *Ibid.*, 284–286; deposition of Delassize, *Ibid.*, 294.

main ditch, where the ground was higher, sentinels walked post and learned the fundamentals of guard duty.[57]

For those who were able to get about, little time remained after routine police and training of the day had ended. What leisure there was, necessarily had to be spent in camp. Getting to New Orleans was not easy. Once soldiers succeeded, they found little in the city for dirty, half-naked bankrupts; consequently they stayed with their kind. In foul weather they found refuge in tents that held a half-dozen apiece; sick and well all kenneled together. Here and there they lay, filthy men in filthy straw. Often rain descended in torrents, coming through well worn tents as through a sieve; nor did improvised wooden floors wholly protect from the rising water or the mud that followed after. When the river was in full flood during July, the drainage ditches, filled with sewage, overflowed and littered the camp with foulness. Flies were everywhere. Sick men neglected all rules of sanitation.[58] When rains ceased and clouds blew away, the grounds steamed and stank under the scorching sun. Nor was there relief from the heat until evening, when leaves began to rustle with the breath of the sea.

When the weather permitted, soldiers found it more to their liking to loiter about beneath the palmetto arbors along the company street. Here they could gossip with the convalescents. Here, too, they could wash down their rancid pork and sour bread with muddy river water or experience for a moment the warming glow of their daily gill of whisky. Toward evening they gathered wretchedly in little groups around the smudge fires in the hope of getting relief from the mosquitoes—a privilege denied to their weakened companions, whose piteous outcries were so often heard from the near-by tents.[59]

Only the sick in hospital were provided with mosquito bars; the cost of them for others could not be met by an unpaid soldier or a saving Secretary of War. At a later day even stables and henhouses in this locality were protected with screening.[60] As a cheaper substitute, a curtain was made for tent entrances; it proved of little value, for sick men were constantly going and

---

[57] Testimony of Backus, in Wilkinson, *Memoirs*, II, App. CVIII; deposition of Beall, in *Amer. State Papers, Mil. Aff.*, I, 278.
[58] Testimony of Backus, in *Memoirs*, II, App. CVIII.
[59] Deposition of Darrington, in *Amer. State Papers, Mil. Aff.*, I, 283.
[60] Wilkinson, "James Wilkinson," in *La Hist. Quarterly*, I, 155.

coming during the night. When the wind blew from the wrong direction, mosquitoes swarmed in fabulous numbers. With them came a nauseating odor. Men had been carelessly buried near by and lay under a few scant inches of loam.[61]

Sickness had become so general that at times some organizations had only five or ten men fit for duty. Improvised hospitals could not receive all those who needed help; many of the sick remained in their own company tents and were attended by their well-wishing but ignorant comrades. Medicines were insufficient and not of the right kind. Patients received little attention; there were too many for the few surgeons and mates, who were often seriously sick like the rest. Several civilian physicians were employed, and even a line officer, with a little knowledge of medicine, was drafted for hospital service. Efforts to salvage those stricken with fever and bowel complaints were not successful. From June 10 to September 14, 1809, 127 died and 18 deserted.[62]

Doubtless sickness and mortality might have been sensibly diminished had there been adequate and proper supplies, particularly rations.[63] Sometimes the flour was moldy and looked like brimstone, was full of worms and bugs. Not infrequently pork was rusty, and beef not fit to be issued. Whisky was probably as good as the red-nosed might care for, but it proved no helpful panacea to men already broken by divers diseases. So bad did the rations become that Wilkinson went out and purchased one hundred barrels of flour and a small amount of fresh beef.[64]

Besides the inherent difficulties in buying good rations in the open market, there was another reason why Wilkinson did not care to do so; he was in evident collusion with the contractor, James Morrison, who had sent him eleven horses as an apparent reimbursement for official helpfulness. In a letter of July 28, 1809, Morrison revealed their unbecoming connection:

"You know whether the contract is profitable depends on the commander-in-chief.

. . . .

"Should I visit New Orleans in winding up my contract will make such arrangements on this head as will no doubt be satisfactory to

[61] "Police Officer's Report," July 12, 1809, in *Memoirs*, II, App. CVII.
[62] *Ibid.*, 373, and *Amer. State Papers, Mil. Aff.*, I, 278–290.
[63] *Amer. State Papers, loc. cit.*
[64] *Memoirs*, II, 501, 507.

you. On this head don't have a moment's uneasiness. Be as serviceable to me as you can, where you are, keeping the public in view, and
it may be in my power to be in some way serviceable to you.

.   .   .   .

"Should a part [of the flour] become unfit for use, I have directed
them [his agents] to purchase and mix with sweet flour so as to make
it palatable. Don't I pray you order an examination unless in the last
resort." [65]

Morrison believed that Wilkinson was dependable, and that his
contract would be profitable; hence he wanted to be awarded another
at a letting on October 25. In this way he worded his request for aid:

"Will you oblige me, by giving your opinion on the price which
you conceive the Ration will be furnished at each post, calculating
on a moderate profit—write briefly and without reserve marking the
letter *Private*." [66]

Until a better system was devised, corruption would continue
and soldiers would be poorly fed. Supplying by contract was a fertile
field of graft. New components of the ration were needed, such as
coffee, sugar, and vegetables. Poorly sheltered and hard-worked men
in a semitropical climate could not exist on food which was often
worse than that given slaves on some plantations. Even dull-witted
masters knew that good slaves were costly and had to be cared for;
Congressmen still believed that efficient soldiers were cheap and could
be easily obtained.

Supplies other than rations were subject to a similar uncertainty.
Most of them were forwarded to or purchased by a military agent,
who was something of a department quartermaster enjoying a civilian
status but appointed by the War Department and subject to its control.[67] In theory, he was presumed to secure what the commanding
general requisitioned; in reality, he was hamstrung by regulations
and a recurrent lack of funds. Consequently, even strategic movements might depend on whether he and the contractor could properly
function. When supplies were bad, they might be condemned and
others bought in a local market. If such purchases could be made,
the price was usually exorbitant.

This defective supply system grew worse when the administra-

[65] Morrison to Wilkinson, July 28, 1809, Wilkinson Papers, Vol. III, Chicago Hist.
Soc., and Wilkinson to Eustis, W.D., A.G.O., O.R.
[66] Morrison to Wilkinson, July 28, 1809, Wilkinson Papers, Vol. III, Chicago Hist.
Soc.
[67] Act of Mar. 16, 1802, Sec. 17, in Callan, *Military Laws of the United States*, 146.

tion lost confidence in Wilkinson and made unreasonable efforts to economize. On April 26, 1808, Henry Dearborn, Secretary of War, had written to Abraham D. Abrahams, military agent at New Orleans, that "Fifty dollars, is the highest sum to be allowed, in any case not previously authorized, except in extraordinary circumstances." [68] And the Secretary, of course, sat in final judgment on just what constituted "extraordinary circumstances." He tried also to determine what should be bought of a routine kind. In a letter of August 20 he graciously allowed the purchase of a reasonable supply of mosquito nets.[69] On December 12, $10,000 was sent to the military agent for contingencies of the Army, such as quarters, transportation, and camp equipage. Not a dollar of this amount was to be spent "except for articles actually received, or for services performed." [70] Wilkinson remonstrated, declaring that he could not always state specifically for what he drew money before a purchase was made.[71]

In March, 1809, a Dr. William Eustis stepped into Dearborn's shoes. They were somewhat oversize, but he kept their toes pointed in the same direction as his economical predecessor had done. With Abrahams' resignation before him, Eustis finally gave the office of military agent to Andrew McCulloch on the 4th of May. The letter appointing him hazarded another scheme for saving. The organization quartermasters were to be under his control, that of a civilian, and they were to make no expenditures except what were "absolutely necessary without his particular direction." [72] These orders lasted longer than the Scotchman, for on the 6th of August he was gathered to his fathers. Nevertheless, he had lived long enough to commit a grievous sin; he had purchased high-priced chickens, eggs, wine, etc. for the sick in hospital. For his action a reprimand was written, but it arrived too late; only the surgeon, his accomplice, was alive and could recall having done inadmissible things.[73] Major Pike was finally induced to take over the office as a sort of "pinch hitter." With the military chest empty and drafts in high disfavor, he had to make preparations for moving the army one hundred leagues up the river to the neighborhood of Fort Adams and Natchez.[74]

[68] Dearborn to Abrahams, Apr. 26, 1808, in Wilkinson, *Memoirs*, II, 433–434.
[69] Smith to Abrahams, Aug. 20, 1808, *Ibid.*, 435.
[70] Dearborn to Abrahams, Dec. 12, 1808, *Ibid.*, 436–437.
[71] To Eustis, May 29, 1809, Wilkinson Papers, Vol. III, Chicago Hist. Soc.
[72] Eustis to McCulloch, May 4, 1809, *Amer. State Papers, Mil. Aff.*, 1, 276.
[73] Eustis to McCulloch, Eustis to Spencer, Aug. 10, 1809, in Wilkinson, *Memoirs*, II, 451–452; list of expenditures, *Amer. State Papers, Mil. Aff.*, I, 277.
[74] Wilkinson, *Memoirs*, II, 468.

Wilkinson had at last determined to move the army thither as he had been ordered to do on April 30 and June 22. He could no longer evade or procrastinate; Eustis was obdurate; officers and men were eager for the change. On July 12 they had been on the point of mutiny, rebellious because of their misery and egged on, as Wilkinson said, by Clark and his adherents.[75] Once tranquillity had returned, the General was still bedeviled by an increasing number of resignations and requests for furloughs.[76] His own nephew, Captain Clement C. Biddle, of the Dragoons, went on leave and sent in his resignation afterwards.[77] In spite of these conditions Wilkinson wanted the troops to remain where they were; by doing so, they would enable him to avoid public admission of error in selecting Terre aux Bœufs. After ignoring War Department orders he had nothing to show for his disobedience except a demoralized and bedridden army that was a constant drain upon the public purse. He hated to see the Secretary's judgment vindicated when his own had so miserably failed. In consequence, he consistently tried to make Terre aux Bœufs appear better than it actually was and endeavored to show that the movement up the river was wholly undesirable, giving it only a perfunctory support.

On September 20 the movement to Natchez actually began— nearly three months after the order of June 22. Instead of going in small units at regular intervals, all the fifteen hundred were crowded on a few wretched boats at one time. Only the very worst cases were left behind in a New Orleans hospital. Wilkinson complained that it could handle no more and made little effort to enlarge facilities. Convalescents were put on board with others in worse condition; those who were in fair health marched overland as best they could. Wilkinson himself felt too unwell to make the journey and remained in New Orleans.

Much of the clothing had become filthy and threadbare. To save expenses a new issue was forbidden until the army reached Fort Washington.[78]

The pay of the enlisted personnel was from two to six months in arrears. A private then earned only five dollars a month.[79] The

---

[75] To Eustis, July 17, 1809, Wilkinson Papers, Vol. III, Chicago Hist. Soc.
[76] To Eustis, Aug. 27, 1809, W.D., A.G.O., O.R.
[77] Biddle to Wilkinson, July 19, 1809, *Ibid.*
[78] Depositions of Backus, Darrington, Ninian Pinkney, Chrystie, in *Amer. State Papers, Mil. Aff.*, I, 280–290, and *Memoirs*, II, 418–421.
[79] Act of Mar. 16, 1802, Sec. 4, in Callan, *op. cit.*, 143.

paymaster, hidebound and dyspeptic, did not consider it part of regulations to go to Terre aux Bœufs and pay them there, although Wilkinson and requested him to do so and had provided facilities for him to do so. When the troops stayed over three days at New Orleans, Major Backus said the General was against payment for fear that many would desert.[80] Several organizations managed to circumvent fatuity and red tape and got their dues.

A few hospital stores were distributed haphazardly to the boats. No money was available to defray contingent expenses.[81] Purchases had to be made, and money drawn for them afterwards. If they could, sick and well alike subsisted on poor flour, salt pork, and indifferent whisky.

It was a dismal pageant of incompetence that moved slowly northward over the great waste of dingy water. About fifteen hundred wards of a newly founded republic were playing the leading rôle—hired automatons about whom nobody very much cared. When rain came down in torrents over the helpless on the crowded decks, there was only a blanket to protect them from the deluge. This, too, was their only protection in the evenings when their vitality was low and the autumn winds blew cool. When the sun hung low over the cypresses and pines along the western bank, the boats drew in to shore, and camp was pitched for the night. Here was prepared the last and only hot meal of the day. Here, too, was made ready the burial of those who had died since morning. The company commander collected a few trinkets for the nearest of kin and then had the body wrapped in a blanket and covered with a few feet of soil and turf. Nothing much marked their passing, only a change in the morning report and high lush grass soon growing from where the hospital orderlies had laid them. When the sun rose and the men gathered themselves out of the mud of their bivouac, the burial squad again made the rounds to gather up what was left of the boyish recruits and worn-out veterans who had gone that night on their last great adventure; and once again scenes of the day before would be enacted.[82]

Stops were made as the boats progressed up the river. On October 3, Point Coupee was reached, and here a hospital was established and upwards of one hundred of the worst cases were left. No public

[80] Deposition of Backus, *Amer. State Papers, Mil. Aff.*, I, 280; *Memoirs*, II, 422–424.
[81] To Eustis, July 31, 1809, Wilkinson Papers, Vol. III, Chicago Hist. Soc., and Deposition of Backus, *Amer. State Papers, Mil. Aff.*, I, 281.
[82] Deposition of Darrington, *Amer. State Papers, Mil. Aff.*, I, 283.

funds being available for the purchase of necessities for these unfortunates, the officers raised one hundred dollars among themselves. The money was left with the surgeon that he might buy vegetables and fowls to supplement their revolting diet.[83] A few of those left behind lived, but most of them died. At Fort Adams, on the 17th, one hundred and twenty officers and privates were landed and put under the care of a single officer, one Dr. Thurston. Of these and fourteen others who were subsequently left there, one-half soon died.[84]

Finally, during the last days of October, the rest of the woebegone army reached Natchez—the hoped-for El Dorado of health. They still had six miles to go before they came to Fort Washington. Here Colonel Cushing, as a commanding officer, had made little or no preparation to shelter them. When once settled, the troops were better off than before. Now they could get a few vegetables, new clothing, and a little money. The coolness of autumn, too, was bracing. But nearly all still carried within them germs of pestilence; and so it was that many were merely to glimpse the better country they were destined never to enjoy. From February, 1809, to January, 1810, inclusive, losses aggregated over 1,000 out of about 2,036 men.[85] The army had passed through worse days than those of dreadful battle.

Wilkinson was not with the first contingents that reached Natchez. He was sick and lingered for a time in New Orleans, where Army business offered a plausible reason for him to remain behind. Perhaps he was also delayed by the charms of Celestine Trudeau, daughter of the Surveyor-General of Louisiana and cousin of the wife of Governor Claiborne. To leave her and lead a bedridden army to a distant station might demonstrate strength of character; but by that very act he would give tacit approval to War Department orders after he had continuously maintained that the troops should remain at Terre aux Bœufs, where they had lately improved slightly in health and might find conditions more tolerable during the approaching winter.

By November, Wilkinson had regained much of his customary

---

[83] Deposition of Darrington, *loc. cit.;* Interrogations to Williams, *Ibid.,* 288; Deposition of Backus, *Ibid.,* 281.

[84] Deposition of Preble, *Amer. State Papers, Mil. Aff.,* I, 275.

[85] Wilkinson gives losses, including desertions, from Feb., 1809, to Jan. 10, 1810, inclusive as 931 (*Memoirs,* II, 373). To these are to be added 68 deaths at Fort Adams (deposition of Preble, *Amer. State Papers, Mil. Aff.,* I, 283) and certainly some at Point Coupée where more than 100 sick were left (deposition of Darrington, *Ibid.,* 283).

strength and was able to ascend the Mississippi to rejoin his command. About the time that he arrived in Natchez, Captain Winfield Scott returned from an extended leave that he had been enjoying since June.[86] Though immature and voluble, Scott possessed marked confidence and ability. Without the experience but with the rank of much older officers, he was an object of envy to ambitious subalterns, while to some of his seniors he appeared little short of an upstart, who needed to be disciplined. For several years he had held a low opinion of Wilkinson, and since joining the Army he had not refrained from openly expressing it in scandalous language. Wilkinson, on his part, always resented criticism and was nettled because of Scott's secret correspondence with Eustis.[87] On reaching Natchez in November, Scott found that certain soldiers of his company had complained, during his absence, that they had never been paid for September and October of the year before. A court of inquiry was quickly instituted in December to investigate the complaint, and before long regular charges were preferred. A general court-martial, beginning Scott's trial on January 10, 1810, found him guilty of two specifications: withholding pay from his men, and publicly proclaiming Wilkinson a traitor, liar, and scoundrel.[88]

Rightfully enough the court could not exonerate Scott for what he had done. He had been intrusted with the pay of his men for September and October, 1808, and yet he had made no settlement with some of them until thirteen or fourteen months later. Perhaps he did have to pay scattered debts for his soldiers, but there was a balance due them, and this they very much needed during their wretched stay at Terre aux Bœufs. Distributing a few dollars might have relieved the misery of some, possibly saved the lives of a few. Taking advantage of sick and ignorant recruits cannot be excused on the ground that he was an inexperienced officer without a knowledge of Army routine. The Army has no intricate ritual for being honest. Giving another person his money is sheer simplicity; the difficulty consists in doing so after it has been spent.

Neither does uncontrolled railing at Wilkinson redound to Scott's credit. He tried to escape punishment for such tavern slander by

---

[86] Wilkinson, *Memoirs*, I, 802.
[87] To Eustis, Nov. 15, 1809, Wilkinson Papers, Vol. III, Chicago Hist. Soc.
[88] A copy of the record of Scott's trial is in W.D., A.G.O., O.F. For comments on it see Wilkinson, *Memoirs*, I, 796–813; Scott, *Autobiography*, I, 37–40; Elliott, *Winfield Scott*, 30.

declaring that the General was not his commanding officer when the opprobrious remarks were alleged to have been made between December 1, 1809, and January 1, 1810. His contention may have been true, for Wilkinson was relieved by Hampton on the 19th of December. Nevertheless, Scott must bear the reproach of being a maliciously blatant young officer uncontrolled by the rules of decent restraint. The extenuating circumstances that he offered in his defense were not altogether convincing; the members of the court sentenced him to the loss of "all rank, pay, and emoluments" for a year. Later they recommended, although unsuccessfully, that nine months of the sentence be remitted.[89]

During the trial Wilkinson was an interested observer. He was also busy with Brigadier-General Hampton, who had arrived there on the 14th of December. On the 16th he wrote a letter of about thirty-three hundred words to his successor, fully describing the disposition, condition, and mission of the scattered detachments of the Army on the lower Mississippi.[90] It was more than a routine paper; it showed a definite desire to help. Hampton, never slow in returning a courtesy or an insult, kept friendly with Wilkinson, who continued at Natchez until he had recovered his health and collected data that might be useful on his prospective visit to the Capital.

By the end of February, Wilkinson was as healthy as ever and was ready to start down the Mississippi. After a five-day trip in a twenty-oared barge, he and his staff reached New Orleans on the 2nd of March and were duly received with a "federal salute."[91] He came in full dignity and glory and was bent upon a matter of very personal concern. His fiancée was awaiting him. On Monday the 5th, he and Celestine Laveau Trudeau were married in St. Mary's Chapel of the Ursulines.[92] Protestants and Catholics, looking on, wondered at the wedding; she was in her twenties and he was fifty-two. On the other hand, she was noted for her charm and moved easily in the circles where Wilkinson, still vigorous and interesting, had many friends. A short ecstatic honeymoon of a few days, and he was once more upon his way. Bidding his wife farewell, he took ship, and soon afterwards

[89] Mansfield, *Life of General Scott*, 27–28.
[90] To Hampton, Dec. 16, 1809, W.D., A.G.O., O.R.
[91] *Louisiana Gazette*, Mar. 6, 1810, and *Memoirs*, I, 479–480.
[92] Hay, "Some Reflections on the Career of General James Wilkinson," in *Miss. Valley Historical Review*, XXI, 487.

was traveling through the deep blue waters of the Gulf on his way to Washington.

On April 16, 1810, Wilkinson, reaching Baltimore, hastened on to Washington, where two investigations concerning him were pending in the House of Representatives. Always opposing expenditures for the Army and continually criticizing its personnel, John Randolph of Roanoke seldom failed to single out Wilkinson as a target for unbridled invective. Daniel Clark was his principal fetch-and-carry helper in this business of muckraking and abuse. These two, with their allies, were not at all affected by the fact that a military court of inquiry, meeting in 1808, had cleared Wilkinson of any misconduct as an officer. Possessing a fairly intimate knowledge of the General's dubious transactions in the neighborhood of New Orleans, Clark had not failed to tell about them in various anti-administration papers. During the summer of 1809, he had gone so far as to have a book published called "Proofs of the Corruption of General James Wilkinson and His Connexion with Aaron Burr." According to current gossip, Clark had spent freely to collect the information that its three hundred and forty-nine pages contained; he had given lands and negroes liberally to those who had supplied the evidence that he wanted.[93] Although in a spirit of vindictive hate, the book has letters and documents of a kind that made Wilkinson wince and made many doubt his integrity.

Before long the House of Representatives took action. On April 4, 1810, a resolution was passed for an inquiry into Wilkinson's conduct. It was to ascertain if he had received money corruptly from Spanish agents and had been an accomplice of Burr or others for the purpose of injuring Spain or dismembering the Union. William Butler, from South Carolina, was appointed chairman of a committee with four others to carry out the inquiry. Congress was to adjourn on the 1st of May, and they could accomplish very little in this short time. However, they did collect a good deal of information, which they turned over to the House without expressing an opinion respecting the guilt or innocence of Wilkinson.[94]

Simultaneously the enemies of Wilkinson and the administration had launched another attack from a different quarter. On March 13, 1810, they secured the appointment of a committee to find out the

[93] *Ibid.*, 484.
[94] *Amer. State Papers, Miscel.*, II, 79–129.

causes of the Army's great mortality near New Orleans. On April 27, its chairman, Thomas Newton, a Representative from Virginia, submitted a report with numerous letters and depositions. According to its conclusions, deaths had come from the fact that the troops were green, fatigue details excessive, provisions unwholesome, and hospital stores, tentage, and mosquito nets inadequate; besides, the climate was unhealthy, the camp-site undesirable, and proper sanitation almost impracticable.[95] As one reads the gloomy pages of the report, the unsuitability of Terre aux Bœufs and administrative incompetence bulk largest in the somber background.

With the adjournment of the second session of the Eleventh Congress on the 1st of May, Wilkinson felt relieved; he now had a breathing spell to perfect his plans for bringing confusion on those whom he believed to be plotting his ruin. Politicians who thought Wilkinson would surrender his "injured honor" without a fight made a false reckoning. On June 24, he asked the President for a court of inquiry. Denied this request, he then asked that fourteen officers of the Army be ordered to Washington to testify in his behalf at the office of the Inspector-General. Again he was denied. Not to be outdone, and that all might know how "scurvilly" he had been treated, he began writing a sketch of his life in order to correct the views of his "deluded countrymen."[96]

To many Democratic-Republicans he was an embarrassing incubus of which they heartily wished to be rid. Open to attack from many angles, he always defended himself with extraordinary skill, caring little how others were affected as long as his own cause was well served. To a party that stood for frugality in government expenditures, Wilkinson exemplified the opposite extreme. During the summer of 1809 he had drawn $1,454.40 for rations, a sum not authorized by any provision of law. Although entitled to official transportation for himself, he used it for a great superfluity of flour, apples, horses, and household effects that he might use or sell at his journey's end. When Jefferson had wanted some "off the record" work done in diplomacy, he called in Wilkinson and furnished him with secret service money for which no expense vouchers were required. In 1807, $2,500 was given him for this purpose. Thus Wilkinson seemed forever enjoying more

[95] *Amer. State Papers, Mil. Aff.*, I, 268–295.
[96] To Eustis, July 14, 1810, Madison Papers, Vol. XXXIX; Eustis to Madison, July 16, 1810, *Ibid.*; Wilkinson to Gansevoort, Aug. 24, 1810, Gansevoort Papers.

than his legal pay and perquisites, much to the discomfiture of William Simmons, accountant of the War Department. The General would have disturbed any bookkeeper; to Simmons, mediocre and hostile, he was a perennial nuisance. Simmons retaliated by telling glibly of Wilkinson's shortcomings and holding up his pay whenever opportunity offered.[97]

Wilkinson needed all the money that he could lay his hands on in 1810; he had to win friends and collect evidence to frustrate the efforts of his persistent enemies. When the Eleventh Congress reassembled on the 3rd of December, his career was brought again under fire from the same quarters as before. Ezekiel Bacon, a Representative from Massachusetts, supplanted William Butler as chairman of the committee investigating Wilkinson's relations with Burr and the Spaniards; Thomas Newton continued as head of the other one concerned with troop mortality at New Orleans. The General was allowed to attend the hearings of both committees and offer what evidence he chose. He made good use of the privilege; for, once his relations with the Spaniards were clearly disclosed, his career as an Army officer would cease. He therefore spent most of his time and energy in trying to convince Bacon and his colleagues of his innocence; with the other group of muckrakers he was not so anxiously concerned.[98]

On February 26, both committees reported. They had been investigating since the 19th of December. Bacon's fellow workers had reached no conclusions; all of their voluminous data were ordered transmitted to the President. Newton's report, except for one member, was the same that he and the others had made during the previous April. William Crawford, of Pennsylvania, dissented; he stated that Terre aux Bœufs was not one of the causes of great mortality and Wilkinson had not disobeyed orders by moving troops thither. This lack of unanimity provoked discussion and prevented the report from being sent on to Madison; it remained to yellow in the archives of the House.[99]

After the adjournment of Congress on the 3rd of March, Eustis suggested that Wilkinson return to New Orleans and await the pleas-

[97] Depositions of William Simmons, Apr. 13, 1810, in *Amer. State Papers, Miscel.*, II, 113–144.

[98] *Journal of the House*, 11th Congress, 450, 455, 578–582; *Memoirs*, II, 15–24.

[99] Report of William Crawford, Wilkinson Papers, Vol. III, Chicago Hist. Soc.; Wilkinson to Madison, Apr. 20, 1811, Madison Papers, Vol XLII.

ure of its members when they convened in December. This suggestion was hateful to the General; rather "bare my bosom to the fire of a platoon," he angrily replied. He did not expect to remain in equivocal degradation; he would clear himself once and for all. Madison, too, wanted political enemies to cease using Wilkinson as a stalking horse for partisan purposes; they were embarrassing an already harassed administration. A court-martial would forestall further investigation. On the 1st of June, Wilkinson was ordered to appear before one. On July 7, 1811, he was furnished with a copy of the charges and told that his trial would occur in September at Frederick-Town, Maryland. His chief regret was that it would not begin earlier.[100]

He had been working hard and had collected a mass of evidence that he confidently believed would deliver him from the snares of his enemies. A good deal of it was contained in a book of some two hundred and thirty-five pages that he had finished about the first of May. It was called "Memoirs of General Wilkinson," but its subtitle is more suggestive: "Burr's Conspiracy Exposed and General Wilkinson Vindicated Against the Slanders of his enemies on that Important Occasion." Though not a finished brief completely proving the General's innocence, it contains enough to generate more than a reasonable doubt that he was in collusion with Burr. It is marred by his turgid eloquence and tiresome bombast; it is disjointed, unorganized, and pedantic, unredeemed by humor and sometimes damned by willful deception. Few men of equal ability would have written worse; few could have used the same material to better personal advantage. As his own lawyer, he was peerless. Always convinced of his innocence and confident of victory, he asked and gave no quarter. In fact, none of his contemporaries surpassed him as a vivid and deluded crusader for a questionable cause. This peculiar talent of his was soon to undergo an acid test.

In the late summer of 1811 the people in Frederick-Town, Maryland, were all agog over the court-martial soon to be held there. Eight years before, they had gossiped with interest about Colonel Thomas Butler, who was being tried because he had refused to cut his hair in the manner that Army orders prescribed. Some of his partisans had overlooked how belligerent and cantankerous he was; they had considered him only as an aged Revolutionary hero whom the command-

[100] *Memoirs*, II, 30–40.

ing general of the Army wanted to persecute. They now saw the tables turned, a sort of avenging justice at work. Wilkinson was coming to town to defend himself against charges more numerous than those Butler might have formulated in the days of his deepest bitterness.

Frederick-Town was a suitable place for such trials. It lay on one of the main highways to the West and was only fifty miles from Washington. Distinguished travelers might find hearty welcome at the red brick, stone-trimmed houses of the more affluent planters. The passing stranger could obtain comfortable accommodations at the "Golden Lamb," [101] a well known tavern over which a certain Mrs. Kimball ably presided. She furnished good fare and attracted bright company, and many a couple crossed her threshold to make merry at routs and balls. Once in a while a gay troupe of dancers came for a day or two to demonstrate their grace and skill to those who were worldly-minded. The delights of earthly things were highly valued by the near-by planters. On the rich and rolling acres of the neighborhood, they spent an easy and attractive life cultivating the soil with the help of many slaves.

Hence, not a few of the emigrants from eastern Maryland had halted on their trek to the West, establishing themselves permanently in Frederick-Town. One of these was Roger Brooke Taney, coming from Calvert County, where he and James Wilkinson had grown up as boys. Unlike many others, Taney's main interests were professional, and within a few years he had established an enviable reputation as a lawyer throughout the state. When the Burr trial occurred, he had expressed disapproval of the part Wilkinson had played in it. Later, he had changed his mind and, believing the General a persecuted victim deserving assistance, he had agreed to become the chief lawyer for the defense in the court-martial at Frederick-Town. John Hanson Thomas, of marked legal ability, joined him as colleague. These two could be depended upon to break up the well directed attack of the prosecution under the leadership of the judge-advocate, Walter Jones, who had pleaded many a case before the federal Supreme Court.[102]

On the 4th of September the court opened. In addition to the president, Brigadier-General Peter Gansevoort, it was composed of

---

[101] Scharf, *History of Western Maryland*, I, 490–491.
[102] Steiner, *Life of Roger Brooke Taney*, 66–67.

eleven officers ranging from major to colonel. When Wilkinson appeared he was in all the fine feather of Army regalia. Always a splendid showman, he surrendered his sword with melodramatic gesture, dubbing it, as he did so, "the untarnished companion of my thigh for forty years." With laconic reply Gansevoort accepted the sword and straightway proceeded to try the defendant upon a staggering list of eight charges and twenty-five specifications.[103]

In casting these into form, the prosecution had overlooked few of Wilkinson's shortcomings since 1787, when he had first drifted down the Mississippi to begin his backstairs intrigues with the agents of Spain. The first fifteen specifications declared that he had received pension money at different times in varying amounts from the Spaniards and that he had been engaged with them in treasonable projects; the next three asserted that he had been an accomplice of Burr in western conspiracy; the last seven charged him with offenses committed during the two years of 1805 and 1809: disobedience, neglect of duty, and the misuse and waste of public money and supplies.[104]

In endeavoring to make a good case against Wilkinson the prosecution had overreached itself. Since Burr had been acquitted in 1807 no reason existed for trying Wilkinson as an accomplice four years later; it was even less pertinent to arraign him for having received a pension from Spain in 1789, before he had been commissioned in the Army. In spite of the fact that sixteen or more years had elapsed since any one had seriously worked to seduce Kentucky from the Union, Wilkinson now found himself charged with complicity in this very plot. Thus ten of the twenty-five specifications might well have been outlawed. Wilkinson did not remonstrate; he longed to end being annually investigated; he wanted to silence his accusers forever on whatever complaints they had. A few meaningless ones made no difference to him; the important part of his case rested on the remaining fifteen specifications.

If once Wilkinson were proved guilty of disobedience of orders and neglect of his troops at New Orleans, he might expect to be cashiered. Therefore, he tried to excuse his flouting of orders to move northward to higher ground by declaring that they allowed liberal interpretation.[105] As commanding general he should have been al-

---

[103] *Federal Gazette* (Frederick-Town, Md.), Sept. 7, and 17, 1811; Swift, *Memoirs*, 96.

[104] Wilkinson, *Memoirs*, II, 35–40.

[105] *Ibid.*, 347–368.

lowed a reasonable latitude; but the War Department scarcely expected him to use it to bring disgrace on himself and ruin to an army. When he was finally compelled to move his troops to the neighborhood of Natchez, many of them suffered and died because he observed the letter rather than the spirit of his orders. He seemed to want the movement made to fail because it was Eustis' plan, not his own. He employed a contemptible device; he pleaded that he could have done no better with the orders that he had received. By the use of this subterfuge, he showed conclusively that he was not of the stuff from which great generals are made. That the court did not find him guilty of some of the specifications relating to this phase of his conduct may be ascribed to a deep-seated antipathy against the administration, to a lack of evidence now available, and to extenuating circumstances created by a dull-witted and parsimonious Secretary of War.

Very different reasons explain why Wilkinson was not convicted of being a pensioner of Spain while an officer of the Army. He knew that one authenticated receipt of such tainted money would have ended his career in the service and made him useless as a secret agent of Spain. Thus his two great sources of revenue would have simultaneously ceased. Wilkinson could least afford to lose this part of his case. Sparing neither himself nor his purse, he endeavored to disprove the eight specifications relating to his receipt of money from the Spanish governors at New Orleans. Fortunately for him, Miró, Gayoso, Carondelet, and Casa Calvo either were dead or had no desire to furnish incriminating evidence. That which was supplied came, according to Wilkinson, from a choice lot of stalwart knaves: Power was "utterly lost to probity and principle," Daniel Clark was a colorless wretch of cunning, treachery, and falsehood, and Andrew Ellicott was a profligate lover of washerwomen. Others of the prosecution were assailed with similar bitterness. Although they were not nearly so bad as he painted them, there was enough truth in his statements to throw doubt on the evidence they offered and to bring into question the motives that induced them to give it.

For his own part Wilkinson denied receiving any money as a pension; he said it represented balances remaining from tobacco sales in which he and Miró had been secretly engaged at New Orleans. This was an old explanation. Wilkinson now strengthened it by introducing a professed balance sheet that was the work of Philip

Nolan, who had been killed in Texas in 1801. Since no convincing evidence was produced to prove its entries erroneous, it proved a strong point in the General's system of defense. As introduced into court, it is given below:

General Wilkinson in Account with Don E. M.

Dr.

1790 June	2,	To Cash paid Philip Nolan—	$ 1800
1792 Aug.	4,	To do. remitted by Lacassan—	4000
1794 July	29,	To do. remitted by Owen—	6000
		To do. paid insurance 12½ percent	750
		To do. remitted by J. E. Collins	6350
1796 Jan.	4,	To do. paid Philip Nolan per receipt	9000
		To balance due J. W.	2095
			29,995

Cr.

By net proceeds of 235 hogshead of Tobacco condemned in the year 1790 by Arietta, and passed in the year 1791 by Brion—	17874
By so much recovered for loss sustained on the cargo of the boat Speedwell—	6121
By so much sent by H. Owen, insured—	6000
	29,995
Balance due James Wilkinson	$ 2095

New Orleans, January 4, 1796.
>   (Errors excepted) for Don E. M.
>   Gilbert Leonard.[106]

This fictitious transcript of New Orleans transactions was not fabricated in January, 1796, as dated but in the latter part of the same year when Nolan was visiting Wilkinson in Kentucky. The General was then greatly disturbed lest the truth of his Spanish connection be made public. While in this state of mind he was preparing to go to Philadelphia, the temporary Capital, with the avowed object of keeping down the military establishment, disgracing his commander, and getting for himself the command of the Army. Ruled by motives so unbecoming, he realized keenly that he himself must appear with clean hands before the seats of the mighty; consequently he wrote the following to Carondelet, the Spanish Governor at New Orleans:

"If I am questioned by Washington on my arrival at Philadelphia,

[106] *Ibid.*, 119.

I will avow a mercantile connection with New Orleans since 88 and in which I still remain interested and on this ground I will account for the money received by La C. [La Cassagne], O. [Owens], Col. [Collins] & Ca [Carondelet] but I will deny receiving a dollar by Power and I will add that a balance is still due me. To circumstantiate this assertion I will cause the faithful Philip Nolan now with me to make an account in form with a letter of advice dated at New Orleans last autumn a copy of which he will deposite with Gilberto when he returns." [107]

Thus were old transactions to hide the pension money relayed to Wilkinson by the hand of La Cassagne, Owens, Collins, and Nolan. Although Power had played a rôle like the other four, no corresponding entry was to be made for him in this conspiracy of bookkeeping. He knew too much and was known too well. As a subject of Spain and messenger of the Spanish Governor of Louisiana, he had three times been employed on trips to Wilkinson before 1798; and these, according to current belief, had objects of sinister import to the Union. Wanting to keep him "out of view," Wilkinson might well deny receiving a dollar from him. Even in this period of mud-spattered diplomacy, an aspiring brigadier could ill afford to have mysterious doings with Power and his master Carondelet. Nevertheless, Wilkinson, in his avid reach for gain, was willing to continue working in the shadow of suspicion; for his account contemplated an outstanding balance of approximately $2,000, which was obviously designed to clothe a subsequent remittance in honest raiment.

In a word, Wilkinson, by resurrecting an old business, devised a financial statement that, once filed with Gilbert Leonard, the Spanish treasurer, could be readily referred to as a prime means of vindication. Well did it serve its purpose; it is identical with the one that the General flaunted before the court as a convincing badge of innocence.

Happily for Wilkinson the papers that held the truth of his double-dealings were kept safely in the custody of the Spanish officials, who had ample reasons for silence in 1811. Long before his trial Miró, Carondelet, and Gayoso had been gathered to their fathers, and even the magnificent field of their efforts had been transferred from the service of empire. Only since the opening of the archives in Spain have the ghosts of the past come forth to tell the real story of what

[107] To Carondelet, Sept. 22, 1796, A.G.I., Seville, *Papeles de Cuba,* leg. 2375.

happened. In Seville is found a yellowed sheet, apparently Wilkinson's true bill for services. The officers, sitting as judges at Frederick-Town, knew it not; therefore no opprobrium can rest upon them for their verdict of innocence; only on the defendant must rest an added burden of guilt. The account, showing Wilkinson's receipts and services, is as follows:

Statement of Wilkinson's Account to
Pension from 1st January 89 to 1st January 96   14000.
to so much advanced by advice of Carondelet &
Gayoso to retard, disjoint and defeat the
mediated irruption of General Clark in La.   8640
                                                  22640

Credit

Received from Miró   7000 ⎱
Received from Carondelet by La Cassagne   4000 ⎰
Received from Carondelet by Collins   6000 ⎰
                                                      17000

Of the taken credited
L C has paid   2600
Collins has paid   2500
the balance is disipated [*sic*] or fraudently applyd [*sic*]
A true account upon honour   W.[108]

The account is in Spanish and English, and the two are alike except for a few unimportant variations. Naturally Wilkinson did not write out this incriminating document or sign it in full, especially since he was then under a heavy cloud of suspicion and had implored his Spanish friends neither to write nor even to mention his name.[109] Clearly his account was handled in the same way as some of his letters when they required great secrecy and the use of a code. In such cases, decoded copies are found in the handwriting of the Spanish secretary; and are usually filed, though not always, with the originals. On this hypothesis, the account might easily appear as it does.

The various items that compose the account dissipate the suspicion that it is the work of Spanish officials who were attempting to hide unwarranted disbursements. Wilkinson admitted, at one time or another, receiving the three amounts that total the $17,000 with which the Spanish government is credited. He obtained the sum

[108] Document 163, *Ibid.*
[109] To Carondelet, Sept. 22, 1796, *Ibid.*

of $7,000 only after writing various letters to Miró begging for a loan of $10,000 to strengthen his credit and fortune.[110] The variation in the Collins entries of some $350 may have had its origin in the cost of transporting the money. The difference would mean nothing to the General in the fictitious statement that he prepared for the gullible, but it might arouse the inquiries of the critical who believed that Collins had set out with $6,350. On the contrary, in a *bona fide* account prepared for his own paymasters, Wilkinson was not the type of man to lean backward with generosity and assume what appears to be the cost of delivering the money of his own pension. The La Cassagne sum of $4,000 is identical in both the Nolan and Wilkinson statements and requires no special comment.

By striking a balance between the debits and credits of the Wilkinson account the interesting figure of $5,640 is found. It is significant that Carondelet informed Wilkinson in 1797, "You ought to depend upon an annual bounty of four thousand dollars, which shall be delivered at your order and to the person you may indicate." [111] This increase of $2,000 in Wilkinson's pension may have been effective from January 1, 1796. If so, and his account was accepted as correct, the amount due to him would have been $9,640 by the end of the year 1796. According to Power, this is the amount which he turned over to Nolan at Louisville, and from which $640 was deducted at Frankfort for bringing the money from New Orleans.[112] Wilkinson publicly denied ever receiving money from Power, although he did admit that Nolan obtained $9,000 for him at New Orleans on January 4, 1796. If the General's pension was not increased, the $9,640 may have represented the sum of the annual amounts of it for 1796 and 1797 plus the balance of $5,640.

Thus did Wilkinson very cleverly try to circumvent the indictment that he was an agent of Spain. He showed uncommon vigor and persistence in presenting different phases of his defense. He had spent a good deal of money and effort in the gathering of evidence, and he was determined that the court should miss none of it. For five or six days he was engaged in merely summing up his side of the story. And of course the judge-advocate had one of a different strain that he wanted to tell. Witnesses, too, had sometimes been

---

[110] To Miró, Apr. 29, May 2, June 20, 1790, and to Gayoso, May 4, 1790, *Ibid.*
[111] Carondelet to Wilkinson, Apr. 20, 1797, *Ibid.*
[112] Deposition of Thomas Power, Mar. 18, 1809, *Amer. State Papers, Miscel.,* II, 87.

delayed, and when they appeared their testimony was long. In consequence, the trial dragged on for months; not until Christmas Day did it adjourn. Although no verdict was disclosed, many surmised that it was favorable to Wilkinson because all the members "very politely waited upon" him in a body shortly after adjournment.[113] The proceedings went immediately to Madison, and for six weeks the conscientious President occupied himself with a laborious consideration of their six hundred pages. A "most colossal paper," he termed it wearily; the minutes and printed testimony seemed endless.[114] On February 14, 1812, he somewhat ruefully approved the findings of "Not guilty" on all charges and specifications, observing that there were instances of misconduct both by the accused and by members of the court during the trial. But neither he nor any one else could change what twelve men in all honesty had decided. The explanation of the verdict lies largely in the fact that some of the evidence now available was then lacking, and that Wilkinson, Taney, and Thomas had shown themselves more than a match for Walter Jones and his federal assistants.

At last a favorable turn in Wilkinson's career had come. For over four years he had been living under a cloud of suspicion. His activities against Burr during 1806 and 1807 had cost him dear; in them he had laid bare the weaknesses of his own character. From then on he was periodically badgered with official investigations. His persistent enemies were not even deterred by the verdict of the court of inquiry that met in 1808 and completely exonerated him from any dishonorable dealings with the Spaniards. Next year they had seized upon his wretched failure as commander of the army at New Orleans, reviving old charges and drawing up a long list of new ones. Using two committees of the House of Representatives as their vehicles of attack, they still fell short of their objective. In spite of their mass of evidence damaging to the General, they could not bring him to trial. Doing so was a prerogative of the President alone. Finally yielding to pressure, Madison had directed Eustis to issue orders for a court-martial. Wilkinson had duly appeared before it. By the end of February, 1812, he could complacently read its findings acquitting him in every particular.

[113] *Niles' Weekly Register,* Jan. 4, 1812.
[114] Madison to Jefferson, Feb. 7, 1812, in *Letters and Other Writings of James Madison* (Worthington ed.), II, 525–526.

Wilkinson was now in a position of advantage. Personal and political enemies had done their worst and failed. They could not revive their efforts and make their old standardized attacks; such methods would be hailed as persecution and recoil on their own heads. War was imminent, and those like Wilkinson who had a knowledge of military science would be sought by their country. For him a great opportunity was already in the making. If he could only use it with distinction and success, his fellow citizens would quickly forget his dubious acts and compete with one another in maudlin adulation.

CHAPTER XI

PROMOTION AND FAILURE

AFTER acquittal Wilkinson returned to Washington to ascertain his future and settle a few problems that had grown out of his trial. In his defense he had often made caustic remarks, and to some of these Madison, as his commander-in-chief, had taken exception. Wilkinson, therefore, tried to make clear that they were aimed exclusively at such persons as Clark, Power, and members of the Eleventh Congress who had been persecuting him. Toward the Secretary of War he confessed having "buried every sentiment of resentment"; he expressed willingness "to vary or expunge any harsh epithet or acrimonious expression, which in agony of mind may have escaped" his pen. Before long he was looking over the court-martial record, changing "the manner but not the substance" of his remarks. At the same time he evinced no desire to have the proceedings published immediately, an attitude very acceptable to the administration.[1]

Wilkinson was trying to restore himself to the good graces of those who controlled his immediate destiny; he knew that he would be working at loose ends until the War Department gave him a definite assignment of duty. It was not until the 10th of April, 1812, that he received orders to report at New Orleans and take command of the troops there and in the adjacent territory. Fearing a war with England, Congress had lately increased the federal forces and provided them with the framework of a better organization. To make sure of his own ground Wilkinson plied Eustis with innumerable questions.[2] Some of them now seem superfluous, but the Army was then small and the Secretary liked to exert a large share of very personal control. Wishing to avoid any future charges of disobedience, Wilkinson wanted to know precisely how much latitude

[1] To Madison, Feb. 27, 29, 1812, Madison Papers, Vol. XLIV.
[2] To Eustis, April 11, 1812, W.D., A.G.O., O.R.

he might expect in the task of preparing the country of the lower Mississippi against invasion.

In order to perform his mission more readily, he insisted that his personal staff be appointed and his accounts adjusted before leaving Washington. He wanted to feel sure that he would receive his salary regularly and would be repaid for the disbursements that he had made as a former commanding general at New Orleans. He figured that the government owed him $6,941.89 [3]—a sum that he now very much needed. In trying to meet his expenses during the recent court-martial, he had been compelled to dispose of 65,000 acres in Kentucky and other property.[4] In his need for cash, he now wanted the help of Eustis, who could curb any arbitrary action on the part of William Simmons, War Department accountant. With the Secretary apparently sympathetic and important members of the Senate supporting his claims, Wilkinson began to hope that his finances were on a firmer basis than they had been for some time. After the appointment of most of those whom he had recommended for his personal staff, he was now ready to leave for his Louisiana home.

Some time in June, 1812, Wilkinson embarked on the brig *Enterprise,* and he arrived at New Orleans on the 9th of the following month. Here news greeted him that war had been declared with England on the 18th of June. As a result, he was directed to employ such means and measures as he thought best under the circumstances. The General immediately set to work, planning the defenses of an area easily vulnerable to attack. To Eustis he wrote almost continuously, asking consideration and help in solving the problem of making Louisiana safe against invasion. There were only three regular regiments with an aggregate strength of 1,680 men on the lower Mississippi. Many of the rank and file were absent on leave; those who remained with their companies were often badly scattered and poorly armed. Some of his best officers had been transferred to the North for service along the Canadian border. Arrangements had been made to call out volunteers, although they would be of little value until organized and trained. Permanent fortifications had to be erected and manned at important points, coöperation with the Navy systematized, stores laid by, and a system of rapid communi-

---

[3] To Eustis, Apr. 11, 21, May 12, 18, 21, 1812, W.D., A.G.O., O.R.
[4] Hay, "Some Reflections on the Career of General James Wilkinson," in *Miss. Valley Hist. Rev.,* XXI, 485.

cation devised and perfected.[5] The smugglers and pirates at Barataria had become openly offensive and needed exemplary punishment. To restore the confidence of the people of New Orleans, after rumors of a prospective attack by the British white and black troops, he dispatched a respectable force to English Turn and paraded his men through the streets of the city, drums beating and colors flying.[6]

Spectators grew boastful; they need fear the British no longer. News had already come that reinforcements were on the way. The backwoodsmen of Tennessee had heard the call to arms and had quickly responded. Soon two thousand of them were accepted as volunteers by the federal government. Their commander was Andrew Jackson, then a major-general, gaunt, masterful, and patriotic. Under his leadership they left Nashville on the 10th of January, 1813, marching to the Tennessee River, where boats awaited them. For days they were delayed by ice jams near the mouth of the Ohio. The wind blew strong and cold. The men huddled close together in the heavily loaded boats; sometimes they went on shore, stretched their legs, cooked their rations, and listened to Chaplain Blackman's exhortations to piety. By the 16th of February they had traveled eight hundred miles, and before them loomed the cliffs of Natchez. Here they climbed out of their thirty-odd boats and went into camp near Washington, about four miles distant; for Wilkinson had warned that the country farther south was less healthy and could furnish little feed for their horses.[7]

Jackson occupied an anomalous position: he was in Wilkinson's department, dependent upon him for many things that the Regular Army detachments could supply but at the same time enjoying the prerogatives of an independent commander. Before long he found his way cluttered with difficulties. His cavalry, six hundred strong, had not been specifically authorized, and hence the deputy quartermaster of the department, Robert Andrews, a relative of Wilkinson, refused to furnish any forage. Nor could medicines and hospital stores for the sick be obtained.[8] On the very day that Jackson reached Natchez, John Armstrong, the new Secretary of War, sent him the copy of an order dismissing his troops from the service.[9] On its receipt Jackson was incensed; to discharge his men so far

[5] To Eustis, May 18, 1812, W.D., A.G.O., O.R.
[6] To Armstrong, Mar. 23, 1813, Rawle Collection; *Bartigs' Republican Gazette*, Feb. 27, 1813.
[7] Bassett, *Correspondence of Andrew Jackson*, I, 256–268.
[8] Jackson to Armstrong, Mar. 1, Apr. 8, 1813, *Ibid.*, 285–287, 303.
[9] Armstrong to Jackson, Feb. 5, 16, 1813, *Ibid.*, 275–277.

from home, he felt, was outrageous. He foresaw the trouble that they would have in getting back to Tennessee as individuals when provided only with a stand of arms and perhaps ten dollars and forty rations. The disabled could not move without help. Jackson determined to march his men as a unit to Nashville and there discharge them. Those who were too weak for hiking were carried on horses or loaded in wagons. For their immediate wants, he turned over his own mount and spent a thousand dollars of his personal funds.[10] Two months later his men were all in Tennessee. Jackson had shown ability as a soldier. The people of the West trusted him more than ever; neither Madison nor any other political enemy could now retard his advancement.

Although frequently expressing friendliness for Jackson, Wilkinson was probably glad to be rid of him; any officer would dislike having another acting independently in a department that had been set aside as peculiarly his own. Such a situation not only was provocative of friction but had made Wilkinson understand that he did not enjoy the full confidence of the administration. Jackson was especially objectionable; Wilkinson's memory was still seared by his flamboyant abuse during the Burr trial. But each hid his ill will behind a façade of courtesy. Wilkinson kept in his own orbit, narrowly interpreting orders and Army regulations and leaving Jackson to cope alone with the supply problems of the volunteers. This procedure was probably agreeable to John Armstrong, who had no liking for the hardy Tennesseean. On the other hand, it might have offended him greatly had Wilkinson tried to modify the War Department order concerning the discharge of the volunteers. Wilkinson had just been through a court-martial and did not care to alienate the good will of his superior merely to help an old enemy return to Tennessee in the full glory of a popular hero. He may also have thought that the thinning ranks of his own regulars might be filled with stranded volunteers. In a letter to Armstrong, he gives his own official reasons; he says that he could not "exceed the provisions of the General Order of the 16th [of Armstrong] or direct the vast expense attending the march of two thousand men in military array, across a wilderness of four hundred miles; and the more especially as the commanding officer held himself independent of and insubordinate to me." [11]

For two such independent and unyielding characters as Wilkinson

---

[10] *Ibid.*, 303n.
[11] To Armstrong, Mar. 23, 1813, Rawle Collection.

and Jackson, nothing requiring mutual coöperation on a large scale could be safely planned. Fortunately their efforts were never directed toward a joint enterprise like the capture of Mobile and Pensacola. Wilkinson was restless to do this very thing on his own account, but Eustis consistently opposed the idea and would spare no troops for the purpose. The Secretary wanted to use all the recruits he could get, in regaining the territory that Hull had disgracefully lost around Detroit; he felt also that there were "reasons of a peculiar and important nature against exciting hostilities" in the Floridas. Wilkinson resolutely argued that Mobile and Pensacola should be quickly occupied in order to prevent their use as hostile bases for operations against Louisiana; in fact, New Orleans was constantly menaced so long as they remained in the hands of the Spaniards, who were then allied with the English in a war with Napoleon.[12] Personal reasons possibly abetted Wilkinson's strategic conclusions. In 1806 Forbes & Co., a great English trading house in the Floridas, had turned over to him, for an unknown consideration, Dauphin Island at the mouth of Mobile Bay.[13] The company may have been merely a blind to hide a payment that the Spanish Crown wished to make to its old-time pensioner. No matter what induced the transfer, Wilkinson knew the island would increase greatly in value once it became a part of the federal domain. He could not foresee that his title would be disallowed ultimately by United States commissioners, strangely enough on the ground that he was not a Spanish subject at the time that the tract was acquired. He did not dare to turn over to them a paper that he had drawn up and signed in 1787, a paper Miró had accepted as equivalent to an oath of allegiance to the King of Spain.

As not infrequently happened, Wilkinson's estimate of the situation was finally approved. During March, 1813, Congress, stricken with fear, authorized the seizure of West Florida, the territory lying south of the thirty-first parallel and east of New Orleans to the Perdido River.[14] For such action some lamely offered the belated excuse that it really belonged to the United States as a part of the Louisiana Purchase of 1803. Wilkinson was not concerned with these puerile afterthoughts to justify the high-handed seizure of territory belonging to a friendly country; he was elated that he could now

[12] Wilkinson to Eustis, Aug. 4, 10, etc., 1812, and Eustis to Wilkinson, Aug. 26, Sept. 12, 1812, Rawle Collection.
[13] *Amer. State Papers, Public Lands*, V, 498–499.
[14] *Memoirs*, III, 339–340.

carry through a program of defense that met with his official and personal approbation. He began to gather and organize forces for a descent on Mobile.

At the time Mobile was a town of about one hundred houses, twenty miles north of the Gulf of Mexico and a three days' journey by water from New Orleans. It lay in the midst of an attractive country and looked out upon a beautiful and tranquil bay. Nature had blessed the neighborhood. Game was abundant; the waters teemed with fish, and in the rich meadows of the adjacent islands cattle and swine waxed fat and multiplied. Cotton and rice were easily planted and yielded uncommon returns. Peach, orange, and fig trees flourished with indifferent care. In fact, many of the good things of earth were to be had for the taking.[15] Few of the inhabitants could perceive a valid reason for personal exertion; least of all, the somnolent Spanish garrison in Fort Charlotte at the entrance to Mobile Bay. The ease of living and their entire neglect by a mother country racked by civil discord, had made them listless guardians of their empire's frontier. Sunk in laziness and vice, they had lost all spirit of service and had allowed their defenses to crumble away.

Wilkinson was not sure that Mobile could be easily taken. Although he knew the Spaniards in Florida to be indifferent soldiers, he was never sure to what tricks they might resort. The British and Indians might be inveigled to come to their rescue. He planned to strike swiftly and in such numbers that resistance would be useless. Troops from New Orleans and Fort Stoddard were ordered to move on Mobile. The Navy coöperated. Before long a few gunboats blocked all exits from the town by sea and seven companies of the 2nd and 3rd regiments with a handful of volunteers were investing it by land. In spite of the loss of his baggage and a narrow escape from drowning en route, Wilkinson was on hand to direct operations.[16] On the 12th of April he sent the following note to Cayetano Pérez, the Spanish commandant:

"The troops of the United States under my command do not approach you as the enemies of Spain, but by order of the President they come to relieve the garrison which you command from the occupancy of a post within the legitimate limits of those States. I therefore hope, sir, that you may peacefully retire from Fort Char-

---

[15] Hamilton, *Colonial Mobile*, 404–407.
[16] Hamilton, *Colonial Mobile*, 409–410; Wilkinson, *Memoirs*, III, 339–340.

lotte, and from the bounds of the Mississippi Territory [and proceed] east of the Perdido River with the garrison you command, and the public and private property which may appertain thereto." [17]

Pérez thought it best for himself and his sixty soldiers to comply, and during the late afternoon of the 15th they evacuated Fort Charlotte and prepared to board the United States vessels that waited to carry them to Pensacola. For a fortnight or more Wilkinson remained at Mobile, strengthening its fortifications, organizing a garrison, and celebrating his bloodless victory. He liked this land of plenty and the flattering addresses that the people made him. But there was more work to do—he had yet to seize the right bank of the Perdido; so he marched east, possessed it, and opened up an avenue of communication with Mobile. Thus in less than two months and with little expense West Florida had become securely ours.[18] The British could no longer hope that their Spanish friends would help them by permitting the use of Mobile as a base for operating against New Orleans. To the land expansion of the Republic, Wilkinson had contributed for his last time, quickly and with distinct success.

So far in the War, Wilkinson's problems had been much simpler than those of the generals commanding along the northern frontier of the United States. In a minor rôle he had done well, while they had given one exhibition after another of sorry incompetence and failure. William Hull had proved himself a coward, Alexander Smyth a braying ass, and Henry Dearborn a colorless what not. The War Department was severely taxed to find leaders who could lead Americans to victory. Those laying claim to military fitness were confined to the Regular Army, militia, and veterans of the Revolution; and few of these possessed the elements of immediate success. Washington's one-time youthful subordinates had now turned gray and bore heavily the thirty-two years elapsing since the days of Yorktown. Their age and experience suited them for sage counsel but not for active leadership in grueling field operations. Many of the militia officers were younger. Nevertheless, they usually proved better fitted for parades, hard drinking, and political rumination than for the shock of long-continued battle far from their own homes. Once in a while they had handled the Indian in a way that had brought joy to the backwoods and embarrassment to the Capital, but for the

---

[17] Hamilton, *op. cit.*, 411.
[18] Hamilton, *op. cit.*, 414–415; Wilkinson, *Memoirs*, III, 340.

present more serious enterprises they had to undergo a change of training and viewpoint. Such a military remaking rested in the hands of the regulars who had been living isolated and inarticulate along the expanding frontier. Perhaps their friendly acts were sometimes recalled by settlers from New England who swept down the Ohio into the Northwest or by southern planters who trekked toward the setting sun with slaves and household treasures. While protecting this westward tide of immigration the regulars fought bravely in a world whose horizon shut down closely about them. When faced with new problems in a lengthened landscape they used the same tools and methods of approach that had won peace from the savages. This procedure did not always meet with favor; nor was it uniformly successful.

From sources like these, the War Department had to draw an assistant or successor for the aged Dearborn. The field of choice was barren of distinguished men; prior to March, 1813, only thirteen officers had reached the rank of general in the regular service.[19] With the exception of William Henry Harrison none of these had shown marked ability in the War, while those destined to become great leaders still lacked opportunity to demonstrate their merit and win promotion.

For a bewildered administration the choice of Wilkinson was the easiest, if not the best, way out. Only Dearborn and Thomas Pinckney outranked him; none surpassed him in length and variety of service, and with the theater of operations on the northern frontier he had become well acquainted during the Revolution. Despite his success in the facile task of acquiring West Florida, there were those who resented his presence in the 7th District.[20] His equivocal connection with the Spaniards, his high-handed measures during the Burr conspiracy, the great mortality in his command of Terre aux Bœufs, and his recent court-martial—all tended to diminish a reputation regarded by many in the Southwest with scant respect. Nevertheless, it was not possible to lay Wilkinson on the shelf and ignore him; he was too potent and expressive a personality for that. He had, also, a wealth of experience and occasionally exhibited a certain vigor of action. At one time or another, John Adams, Hamilton, Jefferson, and other distinguished men had shown respect for his

[19] *Amer. State Papers, Mil. Aff.*, I, 409.
[20] *Niles' Register*, IX, 425.

professional ability. At his worst, he was never marked down as a fool.

Hence, the administration decided to transfer Wilkinson, in spite of his desire to remain in Louisiana. For some time he had gloomily realized that a change was imminent.[21] On the 10th of March, 1813, John Armstrong, the successor of Eustis, sent him orders to proceed with the least possible delay to the headquarters of Major-General Dearborn.[22] These, Wilkinson declared, were not received until the 19th of May, when he returned to New Orleans from West Florida.[23] After sending the orders, Armstrong had written a very friendly letter urging him to come quickly "where grows the laurel," and where "we may renew the scene of Saratoga."[24] Words like these stirred pleasant recollections. And his ambition was quickened with the receipt of a commission as major-general after twenty long years of service as a brigadier. He felt aggrieved that his promotion had come so tardily, but he accepted it as a matter of duty and declared that he would start north in twelve or fifteen days.[25]

There was much to do, and apparently Wilkinson wanted something to turn up and keep him where he was. For over two years he had been happily married to Celestine Trudeau; to leave her was hard; to take her with him was difficult, for she was now heavy with child.[26] His own physique was not the kind to bear up against the severity of a climate that he had weathered with difficulty in the days of his youth. Only too well did he know the inefficiency with which the administration had so far conducted the war; he foresaw the danger to his own personal reputation in undertaking a major operation under its ægis. Success, at best, was doubtful, and defeat might mean the ruin of his military career. Whereas, in the South there were few portents of storm, here were many of his friends and fair prospects of fortune.

On the 10th of June, 1813, he regretfully left New Orleans and started for Washington.[27] Mrs. Wilkinson accompanied him.[28] Over near Mobile was a wayward son, James Biddle, who needed a bit

---

[21] *Memoirs*, III, 338–339.

[22] Armstrong to Wilkinson, Mar. 10, 1813, *Ibid.*, 341.

[23] To Armstrong, May 22, 1813, W.D., A.G.O., O.F.

[24] Armstrong to Wilkinson, Mar. 12, 1813, *Memoirs*, III, 342.

[25] To Armstrong, May 23, 1813 (two letters), W.D., A.G.O., O.F.

[26] To H. Lee, Aug. 12, 1814, Wilkinson Papers, Huntington Library and Art Gallery.

[27] *Memoirs*, III, 342.

[28] Claiborne, *Mississippi as a Province, Territory and State*, 322.

of parting advice.[29] Apparently these two slowed up his traveling; he also enjoyed open-handed hospitality along the way, and he had to take precautions against Indian attack. Whatever the reasons, he did not reach Milledgeville, Georgia, something like six hundred miles distant, until the 6th of July; on Saturday,[30] twenty-five days later, he arrived in Washington. It was nearly five months after the original orders for his transfer had been issued, and less than half of the summer remained.

During the next few days Wilkinson found a comfortable place for his family, attended one of Dolly Madison's parties, and asked for the assignment [31] of Cushing, Izard, Bomford, and Walbach to his staff. On the 5th of August the Secretary sent the General a proposed plan of campaign. In it he discussed but left open the choice of objectives—Kingston or Montreal. In the event that Montreal was chosen, the operation should be carried through in conjunction with the forces' at Plattsburg under the command of Major-General Wade Hampton, that wealthy, petulant, and none too competent officer who had relieved Wilkinson in 1810 near Natchez. Sacketts Harbor was to be the point of concentration in either contingency.[32]

The next day, the 6th, the General replied. He asked a number of questions in order to find out where his powers began and ended. In one of these he wanted to know just what instructions had been given Hampton as his subordinate. He also advised attacking Kingston as promptly as possible, provided his forces were "competent" and the command of Lake Ontario was obtained. If his forces were "incompetent," operations should begin around Fort George while Hampton menaced Montreal. Once victorious on the west end of the Lake, a "lightning" movement should be made against Kingston. After reducing this place, he and Hampton should form a juncture for an attack on Montreal, provided the weather did not prevent.[33]

Armstrong answered, promising Wilkinson considerable latitude and support in the administration of his command and giving him definite assurance that Hampton would be subject to his orders. The Secretary thought operations should not begin around Fort George,

[29] J. B. Wilkinson to Wilkinson, Apr. 5, 1805, May 11, 1808, Files of T. R. Hay.
[30] To Armstrong, July 31, 1813; W.D., A.G.O., O.F.
[31] To Armstrong, Aug. 2, 1813, Rawle Collection.
[32] Armstrong to Wilkinson, Aug. 5, 1813, *Amer. State Papers, Mil. Aff.*, I, 463.
[33] To Armstrong, Aug. 6, 1813, *Ibid.*, 463–464.

for even if successful they would leave the strength of the enemy unbroken, merely wounding the "tail of the lion." He believed, if William Henry Harrison succeeded against Malden, Fort George would be of diminished importance. In his mind, Kingston was the "first and great objective of the campaign"; and if the means were "incompetent" for a direct attack, an indirect one should be made by marching on Montreal.[34]

The Secretary and the General alike considered the reduction of Kingston imperative, but they differed greatly on how to accomplish it. Wilkinson's plan appeared the simpler, and less likely to fail. Without coming to any definite agreement, the two left Washington; time and circumstance were to determine the Army's immediate objective.

It was obvious that Kingston, being nearer Sacketts Harbor, might be more easily seized; and its loss by the British would cut their line of communications between eastern and western Canada. On the other hand, if Montreal, at the head of navigation, were left intact, England could readily dispatch reinforcements and regain Kingston. Obviously the best course of all would be to attack Quebec, provided the means were available.[35]

Appreciating that the season for active operations was daily growing shorter, Wilkinson hastened on his way. By the 14th he was in New York City, and the next day he stepped off the gangplank of the *Paragon* at Albany.[36] Here he left his traveling companions, the Secretary of War and Governor Tompkins of New York, and pushed on to Sacketts Harbor, arriving there on Friday afternoon, August 20, 1813.[37]

The post was not an inviting one, though it then boomed with a welcome of fifteen guns. Ten months earlier, Colonel Alexander Macomb, its commanding officer, had described it as a "miserable cold place." The garrison had then consisted of about 1,285 sailors, marines, militia, volunteers, and regulars; some of whom every so often got ten to forty "cobbs" on their "bare posteriors" for drunkenness. Less frequently organizations were paraded to witness the execution of one of their number for desertion.[38] Macomb was an

[34] Armstrong to Wilkinson, Aug. 5, 8, 9, 1813, *Ibid.*, 463–465.
[35] Sellar, *The U.S. Campaign of 1813 to Capture Montreal*, 7–8.
[36] *N.Y. Gazette and General Advertiser*, Aug. 16, 1813; Swift, *Memoirs*, 112–113; *Pa. Mag. of Hist. and Biog.*, XXXIX, 428–438.
[37] *N.Y. Gazette and General Advertiser*, Aug. 26, 1813.
[38] Reg. Orders, 3rd Reg. Artillery (no page numbering), N.Y. State Library.

excellent officer and endeavored to train his men in the use of their weapons and make them appreciate the value of discipline.[39]

On July 5, 1813, he had been superseded by Major-General Morgan Lewis, a brother-in-law of Armstrong and a quartermaster colonel of the Revolution.[40] Though fifty-nine years old and feeble, great responsibility rested on him as Wilkinson's second in command. Another ineffective was John Boyd, a blustering soldier of fortune who had served nearly twenty years under potentates of India. Armstrong did not trust him, and Scott declared him "vacillating and imbecile, beyond all endurance, as a chief under high responsibilities."[41] Little better was Robert Swartwout, who, without important experience, was such a military illiterate that he tried to act simultaneously as an infantry brigadier-general and as the quartermaster-general of the Army,[42] a double task that would have tried the ability of a genius. Moses Porter, chief of artillery, was fairly efficient, but was too old for the work that lay just ahead. From subordinates of this type, Wilkinson could expect very little. For all practical purposes, he was as unable to relieve them from command as he was to rid the expeditionary forces of the meddling supervision of Armstrong or the drowsy efforts of Isaac Chauncey, commodore of the protecting flotilla.

Only from some of his younger officers might he expect stalwart action. Jacob Brown was one of these, a distinguished brigadier at thirty-eight. Others, like Scott, Macomb, Swift, and Walbach, were able and enterprising; unfortunately they lacked experience and were without the rank and position to make their influence felt. Only a few of the lieutenants and captains, like Totten, Wool, and Towson, were enterprising and able; the rest were recent appointees and had little inclination or opportunity to redeem their ignorance.

Of Wilkinson's command only one organization, the 5th Infantry, had been established since 1808; the others were little more than a year old.[43] Though they were all known as regulars, they little deserved the name; for their enlisted personnel was untrained and their ill selected officers were almost wholly lacking in a knowledge of their profession. In 1808 Winfield Scott declared they were "im-

[39] Jenkins, *The Generals of the Late War with Great Britain*, 302–304.
[40] *The National Encyclopedia of American Biography*, III, 43.
[41] Armstrong, *Notices of the War of 1812*, I, 1; Scott, *Memoirs*, I, 93–94.
[42] Wilkinson, *Memoirs*, III, 50–51, 71–72.
[43] Returns of December 1, 1813, *Amer. State Papers, Mil. Aff.*, I, 474; Acts of Jan. 11 and June 26, 1812, in Callan, *Mil. Laws of U.S.*, 212, 213, 230.

beciles and ignoramuses." [44] Since then conditions had little improved; officers were still appointed chiefly for political reasons.

their subordinates. Armstrong, who was a veteran of the Revolution

Men like Wilkinson and Lewis could neither train nor inspire and a superficial student of military science, tried hard to be useful in supervising the organization of the army at Sacketts Harbor. But he and Wilkinson could seldom agree on any plan of concerted action. To the general in command the presence of the Secretary of War at the front was naturally irksome; to the impulsive Armstrong the dilatory tactics of the new major-general were exasperating and discouraging. Objectives often changed, and the work of preparation lagged. On August 25 the Quartermaster reported only fifteen vessels available for transporting men and supplies; something like three hundred were needed, along with a large number of pilots.[45] Most of the provisions and stores of the contractor were at Oswego and had to be brought to Sacketts Harbor and put aboard ship.[46] The ration then consisted chiefly of bread, meat, and whisky. Some thought that the flour was bad; almost every one knew that the bakers were lazy and mixed their dough with the inshore water near the latrines. Many had fallen sick with bowel complaints. Of the 3,483 men comprising the garrison, only 2,042 were fit for duty on the 24th of August.[47]

A lack of proper clothing also contributed to so large a sick report. No waterproof garments were issued, and only infrequently were overshoes, which were made of leather, supplied. A soldier was lucky if he had a greatcoat to protect himself from rain or snow; more often it was an issue blanket, sometimes a piece of oilcloth torn from one of the biscuit kegs. As a whole, the uniform was of comic opera design, acceptable for parades and good weather but totally unsuited for winter wear along the forty-fifth parallel. Unfortunately Wilkinson could not change the articles of clothing to be issued any more than the components of the ration; he could insist only that the quality of both should measure up to specifications.

In other things he was able to do more; he could, at least, make the preparations essential for a forward movement. On August 26, six days after his arrival, he called a council of war, which Chauncey,

[44] Scott, *Memoirs*, I, 36.
[45] Return of Transport, etc., Wilkinson, *Memoirs*, III, App. LXVII.
[46] Instructions to Brown, *Ibid.*, Appendix XXX.
[47] Statement of Lewis's Division, *Ibid.*, App. XXVIII.

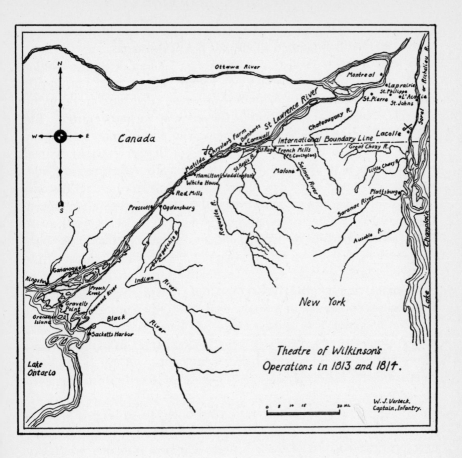

Theatre of Wilkinson's
Operations in 1813 and 1814.

W. J. Verbeck,
Captain, Infantry.

Brown, Swartwout, and Lewis attended. They decided to concentrate all available troops near Sacketts Harbor, slip by Kingston, and make for Montreal in conjunction with Hampton's forces.[48] Thus for a time the Army's objective was fixed.

To hasten the troops that were to come from Fort George, Wilkinson decided to go there himself. The decision was unwise, for he left his own natural post of command at a critical juncture and went on a mission another could have performed. Lewis, whose experience in army supply might have proved helpful, was absent on leave for nearly a month, beginning on the 28th of August. Brown, vigorous but inexperienced, took command as the next senior officer and tried to do the interminable list of things that Wilkinson had left him.[49] Working hard, he was relieved by Lewis, who returned during the last week of September. In spite of many defective arrangements, Lewis declared that troops were ready to embark on the 4th of October.[50]

During this unfortunate changing of commanding officers at Sacketts Harbor, Wilkinson was making his way to Niagara, where he arrived on the 4th of September, feeble and rather dilapidated, suffering from ague and fever brought on by six days' exposure to rain and cold.[51] From this time until his relief from duty along the northern frontier he was troubled with intermittent sickness. For ailments like his, as well as those common to camp, opium was commonly prescribed in one form or another.[52] Wilkinson apparently used it. His friend, Swift, declares that the General was exhilarated with laudanum at least once when journeying down the St. Lawrence.[53] If he used the drug frequently, this would help explain his unstable judgment, his easy belief in enemy apparitions, and his frequent suggestions of palpably impossible schemes of campaign.

At Fort George he found Boyd in command of the 3,000 men with whom the sick and "fluttery" Dearborn had taken the place in May. After the "strange fatalities" at Stony Creek and Beaver Dams, this Niagara force had contented itself with sporadic skirmishing. Wilkinson wanted more vigorous action; on September 18, he requested authority to destroy the hostile forces around the

[48] "Minutes of a Council of War," *Ibid.*, App. I.
[49] "Instructions to Brown," *Ibid.*, App. XXX.
[50] *Ibid.*, 116–117.
[51] To Armstrong, Sept. 11, 16, 1813, in *Amer. State Papers, Mil. Aff.*, I, 466–467.
[52] Mann, *Medical Sketches, etc.*, 119.
[53] Swift, *Memoirs*, 116.

west end of Lake Ontario. Armstrong had never favored any such scheme under the General's auspices; and now of course much less, for it would only delay progress to more important objectives.[54]

On September 20 Wilkinson came to conclusions entirely different. The Secretary appears to have wished that Fort George be put into a condition for defense and Moses Porter be left in command when the army moved from there to Sacketts Harbor. Wilkinson, nevertheless, discussed with a council of war the advisability of abandoning the post. The members were unanimously (with one exception) in favor of razing it.[55] The General heard them out and then obeyed Armstrong's orders in part. He left Scott—instead of Porter—in command, with eight hundred regulars, and directed him to complete the dilapidated ramparts of the fort; the rest of the garrison and near-by troops were to join him at Grenadier Island as quickly as they could.

This island was the rendezvous that Wilkinson had selected for the men coming from the neighborhood of Fort George and those that were now concentrating at Sacketts Harbor. For over a week the Fort George contingents were hindered from embarking by boisterous weather and fears of British attack. Finally on October 1 they began to ply their oars and shift their landlubber sails. Caught in a hurricane that swept the Lake clean of boats and ripped up trees along the shore, they straggled slowly along, not reaching their rendezvous until after the middle of the month, and then with their strength sapped and their morale worn down by days of continuous exposure.[56] Eluding the British was easier than escaping the elements.

Wilkinson did not accompany these troops, but made directly for Sacketts Harbor in Chauncey's trim and swift little schooner, the Lady of the Lake. He reached there on October 4; his health was so poor that he had to be helped ashore when he landed. His arrival coincided with the departure of Armstrong, who, starting for Gravelly Point, was planning to accompany the army down the St. Lawrence.[57] Changing his mind, the Secretary now had his baggage unloaded and remained at the harbor.

Armstrong liked being in the midst of things and experiencing the

[54] Wilkinson to Armstrong, Sept. 18, 1813, Amer. State Papers, Mil. Aff., I, 467.
[55] Memoirs, III, App. XII; to Armstrong, Sept. 20, 1813, in Amer. State Papers, Mil. Aff., I, 469.
[56] Testimony of Bissel, Wilkinson, Memoirs, III, 240; testimony of Boyd, Ibid., 81–82.
[57] Testimony of Swartwout and Lewis, Ibid., 56, 179; Memorandum . . . of Oct. 4, 1813, Wilkinson Papers, Vol. III, Chicago Hist. Soc.

thrill that small men enjoy in the exercise of power. He was essentially a bustler, usually a meddler, and frequently a pedant. His egotism led him to think himself infallible, but he lacked the character to assume responsibility for his own mistakes or those of his subordinates. He was gregarious, convivial, and ambitious; a rather skillful politician but a very mediocre general—one who thought less of military objectives than of safe political exits. Often a quibbler himself, he inspired fault-finding among others, much to his own injury and that of his generals.

The Secretary had been about Sacketts Harbor since the 5th of September,[58] and now that his general was back he decided to remain a little longer. His presence was more of a nuisance than a help and soon contributed to a considerable lessening of Wilkinson's prestige. Inevitably the two began to disagree while the army stood by for two weeks, waiting for equipment and stores to be packed, storms to subside, and Chauncey to return and prepare his flotilla to act as convoy. They spent the time thrusting and parrying at each other over the first point of attack for the assembling forces. For a time Wilkinson had wanted it to be Montreal; now he had changed and urged Kingston. Simultaneously Armstrong recommended just the reverse. Finally Wilkinson asked for orders based on authority of the President in case he had to make Montreal his first objective.[59] Armstrong gave none, confining himself to advice that could not be readily ignored.

Both seemed to sense that the campaign was destined to fail and each was trying to shift upon the other the burden of prospective disgrace. Armstrong, instead of accompanying the army and making sure of Hampton's coöperation, prepared to leave it and all its problems to Wilkinson. Before going, he felt that the expeditionary forces would never wrest their housing from the British, and so he ordered huts for 10,000 men to be built within the boundaries of Canada.[60] He thus proved himself without the character to cancel the campaign, change its commander, or lead it himself; while Wilkinson, unable to find any satisfactory means of escape, ruefully continued as general. Kingston was to be attacked first if conditions warranted.[61]

On October 16 the embarkation began for Grenadier Island, the

[58] Adams, *History of the United States,* VII, 179.
[59] *Amer. State Papers, Mil. Aff.,* I, 470–472.
[60] Armstrong to Swartwout, Oct. 16, 1813, in Wilkinson, *Memoirs,* III, 70–71.
[61] Lewis to Mrs. Livingston, Oct. 16, 1813, in Delafield, *Biographies of Francis Lewis and Morgan Lewis,* II, 91–92.

first stopping place, eighteen miles distant. Already snow had begun to fly; rough weather had set in on the Lake, and squalls were frequent.[62] The boats, manned by untrained crews and directed by ignorant pilots, were buffeted by wind and water. Many of them were soon piled up along the shore. About 340,000 rations had been loaded without system, and seemingly fell into the care of nobody except the agent of the contractor, whose profits mounted as losses occurred. In this short leg of the voyage 138,000 of them were ruined or lost.[63] Hospital stores, carelessly stowed, were hunted in vain by the medical officers while the contents of the casks containing port for invalids warmed the stomachs of a few successful searchers among the drenched enlisted men in the boats.[64] Many guns and much ammunition were rendered worthless. For the cold and bedraggled, Wilkinson returned to Sacketts Harbor to get more clothing. To the same place also went one hundred and ninety-six invalids who could no longer endure the hardships of campaign.[65] This initial confusion and number of casualties caused discouragement and delay.

Not until the 1st of November did the flotilla begin leaving the island and head for French Creek, about thirty miles distant. It had to reorganize and await good weather and the coming of other contingents. Wilkinson did not follow until the 3rd. He was ill again and wanted to see Colonel Randolph whose regiment had been delayed.[66] Meanwhile he wrote to Armstrong requesting that Hampton and his army near Lake Champlain threaten Chambly or join him near the confluence of the Grand and the St. Lawrence.[67] Thus was the Secretary held to a responsibility that he had assumed, that of insuring Hampton's coöperation.

The futility of the request was soon to be proved. Nor was any immediate or future help to come from the slowly moving Chauncey. The Commodore allowed two brigs and other hostile craft to elude him and fire into the camp along French Creek; and only because some enterprising artillerymen made good use of eighteen-pounders were the British compelled to retire. When they reappeared next day, they were greeted with shot, red-hot from the furnace, and soon made off to Kingston. Chauncey hove in sight almost two hours after their

[62] *Memoirs*, III, 405–406.
[63] *Ibid.*, 101–104, 423.
[64] Testimony of Major Eustis, *Ibid.*, 203–204.
[65] To Armstrong, Oct. 24, No. 2, 1813, *Amer. State Papers, Mil. Aff.*, I, 473–477.
[66] To Armstrong, Nov. 3, 1813, *Ibid.*, 474.
[67] To Armstrong, Nov. 1, 1813, *Ibid.*, 474.

departure.[68] Obviously Wilkinson could not depend upon this lethargic and constipated sailor for adequate protection against the swiftly moving fleet of a resourceful enemy.

With the arrival of the flotilla at French Creek, the British, now convinced that Montreal, not Kingston, was to be the first object of attack, were able to give better direction to obstructive tactics. The Americans' best antidote was haste. But snow and foul weather and unnecessary precautions delayed them; it was not until the 5th that their boats resumed floating down the St. Lawrence. About midnight they came straggling into Hoag's, forty miles from their starting point of the morning. The movement had been long and hard, the men were cold, and organizations were in confusion.[69]

In this neighborhood the army remained for the 6th. During the day Colonel William King arrived, bringing news of Hampton and his defeat near Spears, fifteen miles from the St. Lawrence and fifty from Montreal.[70] Wilkinson could not resist damning the Carolinian's division and swearing that his own would do better. In a return letter by Colonel King, he expressed hope of taking Montreal and a desire that Hampton and his forces join him near St. Regis.[71]

Wilkinson's spirits were high. Perhaps a glass or two of wine had helped. Toward Colonel Winfield Scott, an enemy of long standing who had just arrived from Fort George, he was openly friendly. He knew the value of this energetic young man even if he did not like him. His services might prove valuable in passing Prescott, a fortified town a few miles down the river.[72] The General planned to sneak by it during the night of the 6th and 7th. Skeleton crews were to be put on the boats, while the rest of the troops, with the powder, were to go by land on the American side under the command of Lewis. Wilkinson himself was to circulate in a gig and see that all went well. The net results were altogether satisfactory—only one man was killed and not a single boat was lost.[73]

Once past Prescott, the boats were brought to along the American shore a few miles below Ogdensburg. In this neighborhood, about sunrise of the 7th, Colonel John B. Walbach, the adjutant-general,

[68] Testimony of Eustis, *Ibid.*, 200.
[69] Testimony of Lewis and Ripley, *Ibid.*, 121, 137.
[70] Adams, *History of the United States*, VII, 193–198.
[71] Testimony of Lewis, in Wilkinson, *Memoirs*, III, 128–129; *Amer. State Papers, Mil. Aff.*, 462.
[72] Testimony of Bull, in Wilkinson, *Memoirs*, III, 211.
[73] Testimony of Pinkney, *Ibid.*, 310.

found Wilkinson sick, worn, and cold, standing by a fire in an open space in the woods. On learning that the enemy might hinder farther progress at a place called Fort Matilda, the General sent Colonel Alexander Macomb and Joseph G. Swift thither with twelve hundred men. The detachment left about four o'clock in the afternoon of the 7th, encountered a British force of three hundred militia and regulars at dusk, forced them to retreat, then burnt the hostile works that had been constructed near by.[74] With these obstacles removed, the army, still intact, reached the White House around noon of the 8th. It had now traveled about half the distance to Montreal; only a little over a hundred miles remained to be covered.

But Wilkinson, sick man that he was, had begun to worry, particularly when he realized that the British were in both his front and his rear. His spirit was without that daring quality which gives faith to the wavering; and his mind, never keenly analytical, easily gave credence to erroneous reports. The increased activity of the British had led him to magnify their forces, while he undervalued the ability of his own. Disturbed by such thoughts and grasping for the support of his subordinates, he called a council of war on the 8th at the White House, about eighteen miles below Ogdensburg and a hundred yards or more from where the river runs narrowest. Lewis, Boyd, Brown, and Swartwout were for pushing on to Montreal in spite of exaggerated reports that the enemy were nearly 25,000 strong; only Covington and Porter wavered, grudgingly accepting the others' opinion because they had no alternatives to offer.[75] The exigency called for a clear vision and an iron will; but Wilkinson saw dimly, and his natural force was abated.

In keeping with the council's decision, movement was resumed on the 9th, Brown and his brigade acting as an advance guard for clearing the Canadian shore along the day's route. So swiftly did the boats move in the rapid current that they soon passed the covering troops on land. About sunset Brown's advance guard went into camp at Chrysler's Farm, while the flotilla lay over about two miles in the rear.[76]

On the 10th Brown resumed the advance. His troops, now numbering from 2,300 to 2,500, were expected to prevent attacks on the boats while passing through the rapids. Around two o'clock in the

[74] Testimony of Macomb, *Ibid.*, 168–170.
[75] Minutes of a Council of War, Nov. 8, 1813, *Ibid.*, App. XXIV.
[76] *Ibid.*, 123, 149, 285.

afternoon, he struck the British near Hoop-pole Creek, eight or nine miles from Barnhart's; and, after defeating them, crossed the stream and went into camp a little farther along.[77]

Meanwhile the flotilla was harassed by a hostile galley and a few gunboats that the hesitant Chauncey had allowed to escape him. Men and artillery had to be landed to drive them off. The command was turned over to the sixty-year-old Lewis, who was sick and weary of living in a hole three feet high on one of the boats and stuffing himself with blackberry jelly to cure his dysentery. Even so, he was better off than bedridden Wilkinson. Partly because of this shifting of generals, the day was one of vacillation and confusion. The army made only about two miles, finally halting about a mile east of Chrysler's Farm.[78]

On the morning of November 11, the American troops on land, roused by an early reveille, ate what rations they had in the midst of drizzling, autumn rain. For hours they milled about, waiting for orders; two days without shelter, they were now cold, hungry, and drenched to the skin. At last they were told to start the march forward; before they could do so their orders were changed. Sick and volatile, Wilkinson had resumed command and thought best to countermand the arrangements Lewis had made. He did not want the boats to begin dropping down the river until he heard from Brown, in charge of the advance guard, that the route was entirely safe for a dozen or more miles to the front. Before the morning had ended, the British gunboats attacked the American rear. They had eluded the pot-bellied Chauncey and were under the able leadership of Captain Mulcaster, who was vigorously supported on land by Lieutenant-Colonel Morrison commanding about 800 troops made up of the 49th and 89th British regiments and some Canadian militia and Indians. The enemy advanced eastward from near the house on Chrysler's Farm. The farm was bounded on the north by swamp and forest, on the south by the deep and swiftly running St. Lawrence; it was composed of cleared and undulating land, broadening out toward the American position and cut by two deep gullies fringed with trees and bushes and draining into the river. In this area, little more than a mile in length and half that in width, the issue of battle ebbed and flowed.

[77] *Ibid.*, 178–179, 301–302, 325.
[78] *Ibid.*, 123–125; Lewis to Mrs. Lewis, Nov. 13, 1813, in Delafield, *Biographies of Francis Lewis and Morgan Lewis*, II, 96–100; *Amer. State Papers, Mil. Aff.*, I, 475.

About noon Boyd was ordered to beat the enemy back with his own brigade and what he could get of Swartwout's and Covington's. With a foggy notion of his mission and the whereabouts of the enemy, he hastily committed his men to the attack. Floundering around in the mud of open fields and struggling up the slippery sides of rain-washed gullies, they moved forward, often made fearful by Indian war whoops on their left flank, and frequently confused by changing and conflicting orders. Thirty yards from the enemy they began firing with slight concentration and direction; they were mostly recruits and were not easily controlled; three times they charged, only to find themselves unsupported and their twenty-six rounds of ammunition exhausted. A lieutenant came up with two six-pounders; but soon he was killed, and his pieces were captured. A squadron of cavalry forming up in one of the gullies tried to reanimate the offensive. Riding bravely forward over the rough and muddy ground it met with a well directed fire from the British infantry and supporting boats. Many a horse and rider went down. Though it had failed to break "the thin red line," it had temporarily halted a counter offensive. Boyd was able to withdraw his beaten and demoralized forces. By four o'clock they were retreating to the boats with the British in no mood to pursue.

Never have so many Americans been beaten by such inferior numbers on foreign soil. One hundred and two of them had been killed. These and the hopelessly wounded were abandoned to the enemy. Two hundred and thirty-seven other casualties managed to reach the boats and on the morrow drifted down the river to meet their more fortunate companions at Barnhart's. Those unaccounted for Wilkinson did not mention in his report. Claiming one hundred prisoners, the British gave their own losses as twenty-two killed, one hundred and forty-eight wounded, and nine missing.[79]

Upon Wilkinson must largely rest the burden of this American disaster. Jockeying the command back and forth between himself

[79] For descriptions of the battle by Americans engaged in it: Gardner's, in Gardner to Armstrong, Nov. 15, 1813, Rawle Collection; Trowbridge's, in Hough, *History of St. Lawrence County*, 647; Wilkinson's, in *Amer. State Papers, Mil. Aff.*, I, 475–476; Lewis', in Lewis to Mrs. Lewis, Nov. 13, 1813, in Delafield, *Biographies of Francis Lewis and Morgan Lewis*, II, 96–100; Boyd's, in Boyd, *Documents and Facts, etc., passim;* Swift's, in Swift, *Memoirs*, 117. For description from the British point of view, see Morrison to Rottenburg, Nov. 12, 1813, Canadian Archives, C. 681, pp. 62–64, and "Casualty Report," *Ibid.*, p. 60. For secondary source accounts: Wood, *Select British Documents of the Canadian War of 1812*, I, 89–91; Sellar, *The U.S. Campaign of 1813 to Capture Montreal*, 27–34.

and Lewis is less indicative of sickness than of a desire to escape responsibility. It shows a weakness of moral fiber, and to some extent explains how on that cheerless winter day the Americans lacked the will to conquer. He could not create in others what he himself did not feel. Without this stimulus and good tactical judgment on the part of Lewis, Boyd, and Swartwout, troops floundered about to no purpose. Boyd's plea that he was ordered merely to drive the British back is no excuse when he had the means and opportunity of annihilating them. Even if he was confused by conflicting orders, he had almost 2,500 men, and this number was ample for decisive victory. Unquestionably the rank and file were brave, but their efforts were directed by thoroughly incapable leaders. To a certain degree, Madison and Armstrong were to blame; they were the ones who were responsible for keeping Wilkinson in command when sick and antagonistic, and foisting upon him for assistants a choice coterie of high-ranking incompetents.

Perhaps if Brown and Scott had been present at the battle of Chrysler's Farm, the Americans might have won decisive victory. At the time both of them were fifteen miles away; and they did not rejoin the main body until it arrived at Barnhart's, on the following day. There foul weather and a full knowledge of recent defeat weakened still more the army's confidence that Montreal could be taken; none at all remained after news came from Hampton that no reinforcements might be expected from him.

Ever since the British victory near Spears and the receipt of Armstrong's letter directing the building of huts in Canada, Hampton seemed to think that the campaign was ended. Cherishing this idea, he had sent Colonel William King, about the 1st of November, to Armstrong with his resignation and dispatches for Wilkinson.[80] Just what the Colonel told each of them is not clear. Nothing was done immediately about the resignation, and Wilkinson sent back a request for Hampton to join him near St. Regis.[81] By this time, however, forces of Hampton had been defeated, possessed only scant supplies, and were greatly reduced by sickness. These and strong personal reasons led him to decline a juncture; and so it came about

[80] Adams, *History of the United States*, VII, 197–198, and Wilkinson, *Memoirs*, III, 461–462.
[81] To Hampton, Nov. 6, 1813, in *Amer. State Papers, Mil. Aff.*, I, 462.

that Colonel Henry Atkinson of his staff brought a letter to this effect to Wilkinson on the 12th.[82]

Thereupon the General called a council of war—his third since his arrival in the north country. Although Americans outnumbered the British forces opposed to them, the senior officers were agreed that the campaign must be abandoned.[83] Montreal, the objective, lay only three days' easy sailing to the northeast. But the fighting spirit had gone, and none of the generals had the power to inspire it again. The decision to retreat was wise. Even if joined by Hampton's division, their chance of victory was remote; without it, and the supplies that he was expected to provide, success was impossible. Wilkinson was prepared to face the fact at last. He charged Hampton with the responsibility for the failure and seized for himself a convenient exit from a field of increasing difficulty.

With the offensive abandoned, the boats drifted fourteen miles down the St. Lawrence and then worked their way for nearly half that distance up the Salmon River to French Mills. On the cold, moonlight night of November 13, a demoralized vanguard reached this melancholy settlement of a half-dozen or more houses set down in the midst of an almost impenetrable forest of hemlock and pine.[84] The blockhouse there could not hold all the sick and wounded, and so many of them were placed in tents or shanties. The body of General Covington was carried to Ware's tavern, and committed the next day to the frozen earth. As soon as possible the construction of huts began. The work progressed slowly; only a few were completed by the 14th of December; even a majority[85] of the sick remained in tents until the first of the year. Carpenter tools were scarce, and suitable lumber could not be readily obtained. The weather turned bitterly cold, reaching thirty degrees below zero. Being poorly sheltered and clothed, only the hardiest and best troops maintained their health and character. Venal officers, political appointees, appropriated the pay of the dead, swindled privates out of their eight dollars a month, and sold government rations and equipment for personal gain.[86]

Two weeks after reaching French Mills the men were put on

[82] Hampton to Wilkinson, Nov. 8, 1813, and Wilkinson to Hampton, Nov. 12, 1813, *Ibid.*, 462–463.
[83] To Armstrong, Nov. 16, 1813, in *Ibid.*, 475–476.
[84] Totten to Wilkinson, Dec. 14, 1813. Official Letter Book, 1803–1825, W.D., Engr. Dept.
[85] Mann, *Medical Sketches of the Campaigns of 1812, 1813, and* 1814, 119.
[86] Sellar, *The U.S. Campaign of 1813 to Capture Montreal*, 36–37.

short rations. Some regiments were without bread for four days. Once flour was received, they found it to be made of sprouted wheat or mixed with plaster of Paris. Food from outside sources was almost impossible to get; soldiers had little money, and Hampton's army had already eaten up the meat and vegetables of the neighborhood. Meal designed for poultices had to be cooked for the sick in order to provide them with any food at all. Hospital stores had been largely stolen or lost; the black-clad surgeons had only a very little with which to do. What they did have was of poor quality: "first grade" chocolate could not be eaten, and the wine had been watered until it had only one-tenth of its original strength. Most of the necessities for the sick had to be brought all the way from Albany, two hundred and fifty miles distant.[87] Ordinary rations should have been forwarded from Plattsburg, but there the Quartermaster's department under the good-for-nothing Colonel James Thomas had completely collapsed.[88] Supplies were piled high in the streets, rapidly deteriorating from wind and snow, while at French Mills men were on the point of starvation. It was not until along in January that so deplorable a situation was remedied through the joint action of Wilkinson and Major-General Izard, who had relieved Hampton.

As a result of these conditions many were stricken with pneumonia, diarrhoea, dysentery, typhus fever, or atrophy of the limbs. Eighteen miles away, at Malone, a general hospital was established in a few rented buildings; and here, at least, were separate beds and a little warmth for a maximum of four hundred and fifty patients. About one-third of the approximately six thousand men in camp were usually unfit for duty and needed medical treatment. During December, two hundred and sixteen died at French Mills, Sacketts Harbor, and Louisville. "The mortality spread so deep a gloom over our camps, that funeral dirges were countermanded." [89]

Few cared to remain and do their duty in misery like this. Officers advanced every conceivable reason to secure a leave, and some left without one. Soldiers deserted in the face of punishment and went home; others followed a blazed trail into Canada, whence news had come that they would be welcomed into the British service and would receive the pay that their own government owed them. Those

[87] Mann, *op. cit.*, 119–127; Wilkinson, *Memoirs*, III, App. IX.
[88] Wilkinson, to Swartwout, Dec. 2, 1813; Izard to Wilkinson, Dec. 3, 1813; Wilkinson to Izard, Dec. 7, 1813, Rawle Collection.
[89] *Memoirs*, III, App. IX.

of better stuff, who remained with the colors, half-heartedly performed their tasks. Men on guard allowed hostile patrols to penetrate the outguards and reconnoiter the camp; they had become indifferent even to their own preservation. Captain Mulcaster of the British naval service, believed that he could rout the Americans with a force only eight hundred strong.[90] Had he been permitted to make the attempt he might have succeeded.

While the army at French Mills was disintegrating from discharges, death, and desertion, Wilkinson, an ill and disappointed man, maintained his headquarters at Malone in a large frame house. He would have preferred to retire from active operations and go to Albany, where he hoped to be useful in supervising the training and equipment of troops, but, since such a transfer could not be arranged, he remained where he was, suffering many of the hardships that others were enduring. In carrying on as he did, he showed more character than his associate Wade Hampton, who had deserted his command. Wilkinson would have had him arrested and court-martialed; but he did not succeed in accomplishing either. The only thing that he could do was to write a letter to the Secretary of War, branding the Carolinian's action in a way that must have cut and seared. Thus it read:

"I will not charge this man with traitorous Designs, but I apprehend in any other Government, a military Officer who just defeated the object of a campaign by *Disobedience* of orders & then, without authority, furloughed all the *efficient Officers* of the Division he commanded on a national Frontier, in the vicinity of an Enemy, would incur heavy penalties." [91]

There was much truth in what Wilkinson wrote. William Duane, later Andrew Jackson's Secretary of the Treasury, was even more caustic in his strictures when he heard Hampton was being groomed for general-in-chief. To a friend, he pungently and feelingly wrote:

"God is my judge, I would not trust a corporal's guard nor the defense of a hen-roost to him [Hampton] against any equal number of men. His obliquity of mind and judgment would sacrifice anything military placed under his command. But he is said to be Virginian and I presume that will make him as great a General as Alexander (the Copper) Smyth." [92]

[90] Mulcaster to Provost, Dec. 2, 1813. Canadian Archives, C. 681, p. 184.
[91] To Armstrong, Dec. 8, 1813, Rawle Collection.
[92] Duane to Parker, Jan. 24, 1814, Rawle Collection.

With his wealth and political following, Hampton was able to escape being brought before a court-martial as might have happened in the case of a less fortunate man for similar conduct. During April, 1814, he was allowed to resign. Already Brigadier-General George Izard had succeeded to his command. Wilkinson welcomed him as a subordinate and coöperated with him in trying to make something out of the demoralized force at Plattsburg. To learn more about conditions, the General visited there, riding in a sled on which a box was placed for a bed. He needed a sort of ambulance handy when his legs would not carry him farther. Traveling in a fashion like this, he urged the governor of New York to provide more help for protecting the frontier, because he was worried lest the British start an offensive.[93]

To thwart any such movement, Wilkinson toyed with various plans. He thought Ile aux Noix might be taken by troops based on Plattsburg.[94] A month later, on January 7, he was intrigued with a more magnificent enterprise. If he could collect enough good rations and winter equipment, if the weather would favor and his troops turn healthy, if Governor Tompkins would coöperate with the militia and the enemy would remain immovable—then he would strike the British a blow that would "reach to the bone." And this was the way that it was to be done. Two columns of 2,000 men each from Plattsburg and Chateaugay would converge on St. Pierre, from which, after uniting, they would capture St. Philippe, L'Acadie, and St. Johns, settling down there perhaps or returning to their original cantonments. The force at French Mills would meanwhile coöperate by crossing the St. Lawrence and seizing Cornwall. If all of the plan were believed too risky, he could at least seize Cornwall or break up the hostile outposts in his immediate front. He did not like the idea of his troops eating the "bread of idleness." [95]

Several days later, January 16, 1815, after talking with the contractors, he could not even mesmerize himself into subscribing to such a harebrained operation. Barely enough bread could be got to subsist the troops, much less for a complicated offensive. He conjured up another plan: he would stay near his bases; he would merely reach out and take Prescott and Kingston with 7,500 men from French

---

[93] To Armstrong, Jan. 9, 18, 1814. W.D., A.G.O., O.R.; *Niles' Register,* Jan. 29, 1814.
[94] To Armstrong, Dec. 7, 1813, *Memoirs,* III, App. XLIII.
[95] To Armstrong, Jan. 7, 1813, *Ibid.,* App. XLVIII.

Mills and Sacketts Harbor.[96] Just how he was to raise so large a corps of "hardihood and resolution" from his sick and disabled, he did not explain. An official report declared that there were only 4,477 effectives at French Mills on the 27th of January.[97] Nor did he hint from where the necessary transportation was to be forthcoming for backtracking and mopping up what he had failed to do in a previous campaign that had presented fewer natural hazards.

Often Wilkinson seemed bewildered, groping blindly for the best thing to do; on other occasions he came to conclusions swiftly, only to repudiate them completely within a short while. He wanted ever so hard to be Napoleonic, and sometimes he originated a complicated plan of campaign and sketched its outline in an exhilarated moment. When more thoughtful and serene, he realized that it had no earthly foundations. He was wise enough to discern that it was just one of his hopeful mirages, or perhaps the product of an opium dream. Not unlikely he was still using a good deal of laudanum, a stock remedy, to allay the pains that racked his frame.

Fortunately John Armstrong, the Secretary of War, did not harken to Wilkinson's visionary schemes of immediate conquest. On the contrary, he gave orders that French Mills be abandoned. General Brown and 2,000 men were ordered to Sacketts Harbor, the rest to Plattsburg, excepting the sick and wounded, who were to be carried to Burlington. On the 3rd of February preparations for the abandonment of the camp began. The boats, three hundred and twenty-eight of them, obtained earlier at great cost, were sunk or burned, the huts, recently completed, were destroyed, and the stores that could not be carried along were either set on fire or dumped into the river. Brown, setting out with seven regiments of infantry, reached his destination quickly without the loss of either men or equipment. The distance to Plattsburg was shorter, and Wilkinson's men arrived there without incident.[98]

About four hundred and fifty casualties of the campaign were sent in relays by sleigh to Burlington. Here the hospitals provided them with single beds that were warm and free from vermin; here they were washed with vinegar and water when feverish, shaved every other day, and shirted twice a week. About them the floors were covered with fresh, clean sand, and the walls glistened with

[96] To Armstrong, Jan. 16, 1813, *Ibid.*, App. XLVIII.
[97] Report of Col. A. Y. Nicoll, Jan. 27, 1814, Rawle Collection.
[98] Sellar, *op. cit.*, 37–38.

whitewash. The food, too, was better and more abundant. For them a "new heaven and a new earth" were being tardily provided.[99]

The evacuation of French Mills marked a definite and disgraceful end to a campaign inauspiciously begun. From the very beginning its future had been mortgaged with hazards. Cold weather had already set in when the troops left Sacketts Harbor, and when once on their way they were ill protected by the clumsy flotilla of the ponderous Chauncey. The laws governing rations favored the contractor in the collection of his bills, but they hampered the army in its movements and failed to give the soldier a satisfactory diet. Issue clothing, tolerable for wear in a warmer climate, lacked necessary articles, and was fundamentally unsuited for winter wear along the Canadian frontier. The miserable roads in the north country made land transportation almost impossible, while the boats and pilots necessary for a large movement by water were hard to obtain. In the first place, because of Jefferson's and Dearborn's shortsighted policy, the Regular Army was so demoralized and insignificant at the outbreak of the war that it could not assimilate the great body of ignorant officers appointed by Madison. These neophytes could scarcely function at simple tasks; when faced with the trying demands of a rigorous campaign, they frequently failed. The staff and high command had little confidence in them, a feeling they reciprocated for vastly better reason. With Armstrong constantly invading the province of subordinates, there was even less likelihood of efficient and loyal performance.

Wilkinson, old in politics and the Army, visualized such problems; but, unlike Sir Jeffery Amherst of an earlier day, he did not have the capacity to solve them. Where close thinking and good judgment were required, he jumped to hasty conclusions; where straightforward action and quick assumption of responsibility were imperative, he procrastinated and evaded. Where dynamic enthusiasm and physical stamina were demanded, he followed without strength or genius either to lead or to inspire. Thus did he fail, and in no magnificent way that might have dulled the edge of criticism.

The people, in turn, rightly thought that they had been cheated, that victory would have been won had the campaign been ably directed.[100] Many wounded, sick, and time-expired men bore testimony

---

[99] Mann, *op. cit.*, 243.
[100] *Albany Gazette,* Jan. 13, 1814; *Gazette and General Advertiser,* Jan. 31, 1814.

that they had served to no purpose. Hobbling back to their homes in the north country they deterred recruits from filling the places they had just vacated. Enemies of the administration, ignoring the fact that they were partly responsible for some of the fundamental causes of the fiasco, scornfully pointed to Madison and his colleagues as the pusillanimous leaders of an unpopular war waged with ineptness and disgrace. Armstrong, oblivious to his own contributions to disaster, tried to thrust most of the blame on Wilkinson; he did not assail Hampton until death made retaliation impossible. Lewis and Boyd, subjects of considerable criticism, were quietly shelved in unimportant positions where they might wither away in innocuous dignity.

Wilkinson could not be handled that way; he could not be set aside so readily. He always started a scandalous racket when his importance was questioned. For the present he might just as well be left at Plattsburg; time and circumstances might take care of his case. Perhaps he thought so himself, for he never doubted his ability to cope with any situation. As his health improved and the winter began to wear away, his ideas began to revolve around a plan for reviving his moribund reputation. Just across the border at Lacolle Mill, thirty miles north of Plattsburg, was a small detachment of the British blocking any advance the Americans might make in the Champlain valley. To take this outpost looked easy and might help General Brown, who was fighting farther to the west. Even a demi-tasse victory would gratify the administration and perhaps thwart an investigation of his own shortcomings. Such an inquiry appeared to be imminent. The operation would furnish excellent training for troops and would pave the way for a more important offensive during the summer—provided, of course, it was successful.

During the last days of March an oversized raiding party marched out of Plattsburg; it was made up of 3,999 troops and eleven pieces of artillery. By the 29th it had covered twenty-two miles and had decided to attack Lacolle Mill, provided reconnaissance warranted. With the auspices apparently favoring, the men moved forward next day. All were urged to do their duty, and tried sergeants were ordered to kill those who turned and fled. With only eight miles for the column to go, ignorant guides led it astray, and Lacolle was not reached until between one and two in the afternoon. Here some six hundred British lay in wait, most of whom were safely protected behind the two-foot walls of a three-story stone mill. The Americans closed in until about one hundred and fifty yards from the enemy, opening up with ineffective musketry fire. The British replied in kind to better advantage. Artillery was then invoked to relieve the stalemate; but only twelve-pounders got into action, for heavier guns had broken down along the trail and no one seemed able to bring them up. The walls could not be breached with the light pieces employed, and so the battle went on as indecisively as before. The British made a sally or two, but the Americans failed to use these opportunities for driving home the attack; they contented themselves by shooting from the edges of the clearing at the various openings of the mill and other buildings along the Lacolle River. As evening approached, the attack petered out. The raiders had suffered a few casualties and were ready to quit. Disturbed by the signs of bad weather and the menace of the British, Wilkinson ordered a retreat. About sunset the column started on the four-mile march to Odeltown.[101] Next day it wearily set out from there for Plattsburg, demoralized with its own contempt.

As at Chrysler's, the Americans had been defeated. On both occasions Wilkinson had a chance to demonstrate able leadership; each time he had failed. In moving down the St. Lawrence he proved his inability to command successfully 8,000 men in a difficult offensive; now he showed that he could not handle even half the number in one of much greater simplicity. At Lacolle Mill fundamental details of preparations were neglected; reconnaissance was spasmodic and indifferent, and, once troops were committed to battle, they fought without plan or cohesion. Wilkinson had hoped to enhance his military reputation; instead, he had irretrievably ruined it. The public would not allow the War Department to bear with him longer. On April 12,[102] he received orders relieving him from command of the 9th District. His days as an Army officer on the northern frontier were over.

[101] Testimony of Clark, 155–159; Totten, 224–238; Bissel, 238–250; M'Pherson, 317–331: all in Wilkinson, *Memoirs*, Vol. III.
[102] To Armstrong, Apr. 12, 1814, W.D., A.G.O., O.R.

CHAPTER XII

THE EX–GENERAL TURNS TO BOOKS AND FOREIGN TRAVEL

BEFORE the opening of the year 1814, England, exulting in victory on the Continent, had released some of her best regiments and ablest generals to fight her war in America. Madison and his cabinet soon saw that the strengthened forces of the enemy could not be defeated by political hucksters and military ignoramuses who were capable only of yapping on patriotism; they realized that they must replace Revolutionary heirlooms with young and vigorous officers who had lately performed with brilliance the tasks that their country had set them. Hence Henry Dearborn, Morgan Lewis, John Boyd, and others were relegated to unimportant positions. Into their places stepped men of stout hearts and clear vision. Jacob Brown and Andrew Jackson were promoted to the grade of major-general, Alexander Macomb, Edmund P. Gaines, Winfield Scott, and Eleazer W. Ripley to brigadier. Within a year, engagements at Chippewa, Lundy's Lane, Fort Erie, Plattsburg, and New Orleans had furnished glorious examples of their marked ability and stubborn courage. In this rebirth of our arms, Wilkinson played no part; he was only an angry, interested spectator. On April 11, he had received an order relieving him from command of the 9th District.[1] Major-General George Izard, as the next ranking officer, became his successor.

Knowing that he must sooner or later face an investigation for his failures on the northern frontier, Wilkinson had previously asked for and had been granted a court of inquiry. Its personnel did not please him; compared with himself, the officers selected as his judges were much younger and of an inferior grade. The War Department then ordered a court-martial, which would meet some time when the large number of senior officers necessary for trying him could be assembled without injury to the service.[2] Such an arrange-

[1] To Armstrong, Apr. 12, 1814, W.D., A.G.O., O.R.
[2] Wilkinson, *Memoirs*, III, 492–493; *Niles' Register*, Apr. 23, 30, 1814; *Albany Gazette*, May 5, 1814; Madison to Sec. of War, May 17, 1814, in *Letters and Other Writings of James Madison* (Worthington ed.), III, 397–398

ment would mean months of delay; but in the interval a better solution of the General's case might arise, and the administration might be spared the embarrassment of having one of its stock skeletons paraded before the public eye. Wilkinson detested any delay; he felt that it was just a clever ruse to lay him disgracefully on the shelf while the war was being waged by those of less ability and experience.

While waiting for his trial, Wilkinson had been directed to choose Philadelphia, Baltimore, or Annapolis as his place of residence and there await orders.[3] But he lingered at Fort George until about the middle of May. He then started for Albany, writing to Solomon Van Rensselaer to join him en route that together they might ride over the field of Saratoga, a place that kindled bright memories of brilliant exploits during the General's younger and happier days. Van Rensselaer was sympathetic, for he, too, had failed so far to win distinguished laurels in the last two years. After visiting him and other friends along the way, Wilkinson reached New York in "an elegant barge" during the first days of June.[4] Here he found Morgan Lewis, then in charge of the city's defenses, a task assigned him after the failure of the offensive against Montreal. Their friendship, begun during the Revolution, had continued unbroken, and both found pleasure in being together. Mrs. Lewis, too, was comforting. Perhaps he would have enjoyed such hospitality longer, had he not received a letter serving him with "an arrest" and an outline of the charges that he would ultimately have to face.[5] Under the circumstances, he decided to leave for Baltimore, from which he might easily go on to Washington, rejoin his family, and find out more about his ever darkening future.

Arriving at the Capital on June 26, 1814, Wilkinson continued there and in the neighborhood for the next few months. Restrictions governing his place of residence had been removed, for the War Department did not care to separate the General from the members of his family, who had been living comfortably in the city for some time.[6]

[3] Sec. of War to Wilkinson, Apr. 28, 1814, in *Memoirs*, III, 493.
[4] To Van Rensselaer, May 12, 1814, Wilkinson Papers, N.Y. State Library; Nicoll to Kingsbury, June 14, 1814, Kingsbury Papers, Vol. III.
[5] To S. Van Rensselaer, June 8, 1814, Wilkinson Papers, N.Y. State Library.
[6] To S. Van Rensselaer, July 17, 1814, Huntington Library and Art Gallery; Madison to Sec. of War, June 20, 1814, in *Letters and Other Writings of James Madison* (Worthington ed.), III, 407; Wilkinson to Armstrong, June 16, 1814, Rawle Collection.

Restless, angry, and ignored except by a few of his friends, he turned with bitterness on those who, he believed, had brought misfortune to him and his country. The *Aurora* and other anti-administration papers were vehicles for his tirades. John Armstrong, a favorite target, was denounced in private as a "vile, unprincipled villain" whose place no one would take on account of the critical state of affairs that had been created by the "folly and duplicity of his arrangements, and the disasters which await the headlong operations of Jacob [Brown] and others." [7]

Although the General's prejudice sometimes clouded his judgment, he still could estimate some situations correctly. As early as the 17th of July he foresaw that an attack on Washington was imminent and railed at the inadequate measures taken for defense. He himself could do nothing; he was sick and without command, his sword resting in the scabbard "to uphold the imposition of Armstrong and to gratify his malignant spirit." [8] Never had he been so useless in a time of peril to the nation. He raged but to no purpose. When the battle of Bladensburg occurred, he offered to drive back the British or perish in the attempt. [9] This offer may have been just a vainglorious gesture of a discarded old man. But had he been permitted to do as he wished, he would hardly have exhibited more ramifications of failure than did Brigadier-General William H. Winder with the Maryland militia.

The raid on Washington over, the curtain rang down on Armstrong. No later opportunity was given him to retrieve his ruined reputation as a military executive. In fact, he was repudiated sooner than Wilkinson. Scarcely were the ashes of the government buildings cold before the public, already incensed at failures elsewhere, demanded a sacrifice for this crowning act of incompetence. On September 27 Armstrong resigned as Secretary of War. Another earthworm that had come to the surface during the rain of opportunity, now sought obscurity.

With his archenemy Armstrong out of office, Wilkinson still faced a cheerless and uncertain future. To the frustration of his military hopes had been added a very personal loss during the middle of the summer. An infant of seven months, the firstborn child of his second

[7] To S. Van Rensselaer, July 17, 1814, Huntington Library and Art Gallery.
[8] To S. Van Rensselaer, July 17, 1814, Huntington Library and Art Gallery.
[9] *Memoirs*, I, 760–761.

marriage, had died, leaving "beloved Celestine" ill with grief and the General sorely distressed.[10] He had regained only a little of his usual strength, and his small narrow world seemed to be breaking into bits. Tired of enforced idleness, he wanted to move about and visit his friends, gather evidence for his defense, and try the curative waters of Bedford Springs. But his household was economically and comfortably situated in the city, and it was expensive to travel with his wife and her sister, a negro maid, and a black boy or two, and support them in becoming style. For years his accounts with the government had been in a tangle, and now he had little money to spare. Hence, his family stayed at home while he wandered to and fro in Virginia and Maryland, feeling inconsolable because he was playing no part in the war. Going to Montpelier, Virginia, he importuned Madison to arraign him quickly or restore his sword.[11] Weeks passed and his plea went unheeded. Then he went hunting in the mountains, thinking a jaunt of this kind and a diet of venison would tone up his health and quicken his spirit. Meanwhile he asked about winter accommodations for his dependents at Frederick, where, among his friends, his "devoted Celestine" might be spared many of the remarks that some of his caustic critics might make. What he wanted was two bedrooms, a dining room, parlor, and places for servants, horses, and coach; a "snug Box," if you please, where, if meals were not furnished, Celestine and her sister might prepare "neat, sweet, little French dinners" of their own.[12] But a haven like this was not easily found, so they seem to have stayed in Washington or the neighborhood awaiting the time of the General's trial.

Wilkinson's court-martial first met at Utica, New York, on January 3, 1815. It was composed of thirteen generals and colonels. Major-General Henry Dearborn acted as its President; Morgan Lewis, next in rank, was senior member.[13] These two and a majority of the others knew Wilkinson intimately because of years of service either with or under him.

At this time Utica was a village of about two thousand inhabitants and afforded poor accommodations for the officers and men concerned with the trial. Lewis was reduced to a single room, small enough for

[10] To H. Lee, Aug. 12, 1814, Huntington Library and Art Gallery.
[11] To Madison, Sept. 15, 1814, W.D., A.G.O., O.R.; to Williams, Oct. 3, 1814, Williams Papers, Vol. VI.
[12] To Williams, Oct. 3, 1814, Williams Papers, Vol. VI.
[13] Wilkinson, *Memoirs*, III, 4–5.

one; but when his body servant Stephen, an ex-slave, broke out with the measles, he, too, was moved in. The ex-governor and major-general was a kindly man, and he carefully waited on the old negro until convalescent. Then the two, master and servant, journeyed on to Troy, whither the court had moved in the hope of avoiding the "incessant storms" and obtaining better and less expensive quarters.[14]

On January 16 the court-martial resumed its sessions in the courthouse at Troy. There Martin Van Buren, a civilian, appeared as "special judge-advocate." Everet A. Bancker, who was the Army judge-advocate regularly assigned by the order convening the court, found himself merely an assistant. Van Buren's penchant for the party in power was self-evident. After he had deserted De Witt Clinton, the unsuccessful candidate for President, he had become an able supporter of Madison. With an eye to his own advancement, he was keenly sensitive to the administration's wishes. Wilkinson knew that all the craft of the "Little Magician" would be turned against him. Therefore, with justice on his side, he manfully objected to the appointment of Van Buren. The court sustained his contention; and, as a result, Bancker had to shoulder entire responsibility for winning a conviction of the prisoner on four charges and seventeen specifications.[15]

The indictments were entirely concerned with Wilkinson's career on the northern frontier since 1813. The majority of them were of a purely military character: they alleged that Wilkinson had delayed unnecessarily in leaving Fort George and Sacketts Harbor, that he had afterwards given proof of procrastination, poor tactical judgment, and neglect in the care of provisions and stores, that he had disparaged the Army and encouraged others to cowardice and disobedience of War Department orders, and that he was chiefly responsible for the fiasco at Lacolle Mill. To this list of shortcomings were added two very personal accusations: scandalous drunkenness and willful lying. To the entire lot, Wilkinson pleaded not guilty.

Poorly phrased and lacking in specific character, the indictments were extremely difficult to prove. Delays certainly had existed, but they were the results, not the cause, of widespread incompetence, and very probably would have been overlooked if the campaign had

---

[14] Lewis to Mrs. Lewis, Jan. 5, 1815, in Delafield, *Life of Francis Lewis and Morgan Lewis,* II, 108–109.
[15] Wilkinson, *Memoirs,* III, 6–22.

cott. Colonel Joseph G. Swift, later chief of engineers, whose veracity and knowledge of the facts cannot be questioned, declares the General's condition arose from taking too much laudanum, a stock remedy for alleviating bowel complaints from which most of the Army suffered. Such an explanation is more convincing than the contrary evidence produced by the enemies of the General and by those who knew little about him.[17]

When it came to the accusation that Wilkinson had lied in declaring that Armstrong had categorically ordered Montreal to be the first object of attack, the members of the court again rendered a verdict of not guilty. They were acquainted with Armstrong's methods. They knew he was not always truthful, that his orders were sometimes changed, frequently enigmatic, and once in a while verbally delivered. No one ever will know exactly what he said to the General; all can readily perceive that their common aim was to escape responsibility for the campaign's failure. In their welter of words one thing alone is clear: the offensive against Montreal would have been better off without the presence of either.

In respect to Wilkinson's advising cowardice, the prosecution had to base its case on a letter that he had written to Morgan Lewis on June 10, 1813, advising his old friend not to neglect personal safety in battle since his task was more to direct than to lead.[18] Although this advice might well have been omitted, the War Department evinced a lack of good sense in spreading it broadcast. Whatever unfortunate implications the letter contained, Wilkinson had previously proved his bravery on many occasions. For this lapse in judgment he deserved being cautioned and having his letter censored, but he should never have been court-martialed.

A somewhat similar procedure might have been employed in reference to the second specification of the third charge; namely, that of "damning the Army, the expedition, and himself" near Ogdensburg on the very same night that his tongue got to wagging with salacious yarns. At the time, the flotilla was attempting to sneak by Prescott; and, as he went here and there, he tried to correct the errors he saw, with compelling profanity. He was usually very casual about whom he damned, and on this occasion he showed no variation from habitual form except that he reserved for himself a proportionate share of his

[17] Testimony of King, Thorne, Walbach, Macomb, Bull, in Wilkinson, *Memoirs*, III, 73, 104, 144–145, 163, 211; testimony of Swift, in Swift, *Memoirs*, 116.
[18] To Lewis, July 6, 1813, in *Memoirs*, III, 115–116.

own abuse. His inhibitions were loosened, and he rejoiced to proclaim what a finished fool he was to head an expedition under the direction of Armstrong. This public outburst was unbecoming, especially from one who held the position that he did. On the other hand, Armstrong, as an old soldier, knew that, in war, moments arise when only by scathing abuse and personal violence are the lethargic stirred into action and the cowardly held in restraint. He knew that those who live in a small world of make-believe cannot fashion the patterns of conduct for men who run the gantlet of battle. The action of the Secretary in drawing up this indictment against Wilkinson savored of persecution; it looked as if he were trying to magnify a common molehill into an unusual mountain for partisan purposes.

All of the above charges and specifications and others less important were carefully and impartially considered by the court. Wilkinson was given full opportunity for cross-examining the prosecution's witnesses and delivering his own extensive plea of innocence. He somewhat regretted that certain officers did not appear to give testimony for him, but the War Department insisted that they could not be spared from the work in which they were then engaged. Some, it seemed, were not especially eager to come, for the General had done them favors in the past and they did not care to show themselves apparently ungrateful by testifying in a way that might hurt his cause. The trial was long and tedious and did not end until the ice began to break and steamboats were seen again upon the Hudson. Not until the 21st of March did Henry Dearborn have ready the verdict—an honorable acquittal of Wilkinson on all charges and specifications. Shortly afterwards President Madison received the voluminous proceedings and began to read them carefully through. By this time he was well acquainted with Wilkinson's verbosity and could hasten through the distasteful task. On April 18, 1815, he took up his pen and signed them. Above his signature was this laconic comment: "The sentence of the court is approved." [19]

While Wilkinson's trial was going on, the War ended, and as a sequel laws were enacted for the reorganization of the Army on a peace-time basis. The act of March 3, 1815, reduced it to 10,000 men, who were to be commanded by two major-generals and four brigadier-generals.[20] Consequently there could be retained in the serv-

[19] Wilkinson, *Memoirs*, III, 496.
[20] Callan, *The Military Laws of the U.S.*, 234–235.

ice only 39 of the approximately 216 field officers, and 450 of the 2,055 regimental officers. On Generals Brown, Jackson, Scott, Gaines, Macomb, and Ripley fell the unwelcome task of weeding out those considered less desirable.[21] Those designated for discharge were to be given only three months' pay, no matter how long and honorable their service had been. On the older officers the law operated with cruel severity. They no longer possessed the physical stamina "competent to engage an enemy on the field of battle"—the standard that those sitting in judgment were directed to employ. A letter of Colonel Kingsbury is pitifully revealing:

"At the commencement of the Revolutionary War I entered the service of my country in which I have continued except [for] a few months at the close of the War and I am now at the advanced age of sixty turned out upon the world destitute of support with a large and helpless family and can expect no relief but from the Government whom I have served faithfully for more than forty years which is longer than any other officer or soldier in the United States." [22]

After his discharge, the colonel tried to earn something as a justice of the peace; almost nothing came from his efforts. A little homemade account book clearly discloses his record of failure. Two of its well worn pages are partly filled with entries of fees since May 15, 1815; there are eleven all told and they amount to ninety-nine cents.[23]

Many other officers succeeded no better than Kingsbury in fitting themselves into the grooves of civilian life. As a partial consequence, they felt that the government had treated them shabbily, and bitterly voiced their complaints in the *Aurora* and other anti-administration papers. Wilkinson, of course, was in the number. Perhaps he had never entertained much hope of being retained after reading the provisions of the March law and finding out who were to compose the selection board. His discharge was none the less affecting when it came. Nearly thirty years of service, often spotted with failure but sometimes brilliant, honorable acquittals by court-martials, vindications by investigating committees, humiliating efforts to please the parties in power—all had availed him nothing; he was now let out by the back door and had to begin life over. His pride was hurt; he bitterly complained. Joining the "Association of Disbanded Of-

---

[21] Dallas, *Life and Writings of Alexander James Dallas*, 370–375.
[22] Kingsbury to Crawford, Apr. 16, 1816, Kingsbury Papers, Vol. III.
[23] Account Book, *Ibid.*

ficers," [24] he became an ardent crusader for their relief. Little good came from Wilkinson's efforts; adjustments were individual and had to be slowly and painfully made without any help from the government.

But the Democratic-Republicans, already preening themselves for the Era of Good Feeling, were disconcerted. They were plagued with his virulent comments and the embarrassing information that he scattered broadcast in letters and papers. Here was a man they would silence. Since he could not be intimidated, he might be bought off with kindness. "Have you been able to find any provision for General Wilkinson?" Madison inquired of Monroe.[25] Between them, they admitted that his case was distressing. At a later date Madison continued: "I am willing to do the best we can for Wilkinson, and hope he may not frustrate our dispositions by insinuations or threats that must be defied. Whether he would suit at what you hint, I am at a loss to say." [26] They soon found out; he tartly refused to be one of three on an Indian Commission.[27] They thought he might be "touchy" about a return to the Canadian border where its duties would take him. They might have known that he was bitter from humiliation and his heart was full of hate. Dallas, the acting Secretary of War, was anxious. "General Wilkinson," he wrote, "has broken through all decorum, and indulges in the most malignant rage in every conversation. He will leave Washington next week to engage in active mischief elsewhere, his vehicle to be the *Aurora*. I wish you would provide for him abroad." [28] Again they counseled together; they wanted to placate him with a dignified and remunerative position. What they had and would offer, he threw back in their faces. He did not want any "hush" money office; he was through with the Virginia dynasty; he detested their almsgiving proffers of peace.

The General had plans of his own; he wanted to complete his memoirs. He burned to express himself without the restraint that he might be expected to observe as a federal officeholder, although he never quite gave up the idea of getting once more on the government pay roll. Settling down near Philadelphia, he began the task of trying

---

[24] Hay, "General James Wilkinson—the Last Phase," in *Louisiana Hist. Quarterly,* XIX (Apr., 1936), 410.

[25] Madison to Monroe, Apr. 18, 1815, Monroe Papers (Library of Congress), Vol. XV.

[26] Madison to Monroe, May 2, 1815, *Ibid.*

[27] Madison to Dallas, May 24, 1815; Dallas to Madison, May 27, 1815; Madison to Dallas, June 1, 1815; all in Dallas, *op. cit.*, 427, 430–432.

[28] Dallas to Monroe, May 28, 1815, Monroe Papers (Library of Congress), Vol. XV.

to correct the viewpoint of his "deluded country-men" in reference to the leading characters and events of his time.

The General was a news-hawk for sources, especially since his own ideas of truth and justice were to be established. He went over the battleground of Queenstown with Solomon Van Rensselaer, that of Germantown with another friend; he minutely studied these and other places of military importance and obtained proof of what actually occurred by interviewing not one but many an officer of the day.[29] To assist him, friends and helpers searched reading rooms, pored over contemporary news files, haunted places where Congressmen were found, gathered information from old soldiers and faithful politicians, and checked and rechecked statements. In spite of his antipathy for the War Department, he called on it again and again for copies of its records.[30]

Sometimes visitors came and interrupted his work. They carried away with them a vivid picture of a round-faced, stocky man, knee-deep in papers that littered the floor, writing like one possessed.[31] Celestine had left him, and gone to New Orleans as a passenger on the good ship *Marmion*. He missed her, wanted her; but she was more comfortable where she was, waiting the day of her confinement. He was then living modestly on five dollars a week, vigorously pushing a quill pen that never seemed to waver.[32] For a while he lodged at Beggars Town (Bebberstown, Pennsylvania), and from here and elsewhere he wrote and rewrote to War Department officials for copies of papers that he needed to complete his narrative. Clerks were slow and appeared to have much to do. Burning with desire to quicken their efforts, Wilkinson explained to them his reasons for haste. "I have not a day to spare," said he, "from the labors necessary to protect my old age from penury—my humble means nor my time will permit longer delay." And "the press," he added, "has been stopped, at a considerable daily expense," for the lack of papers that have been requested.[33]

At the same time he was worrying because the War Department had not yet settled his accounts. He needed the three months' pay to which he was entitled when he had been discharged. And during

---

[29] Wilkinson to Van Rensselaer, Dec. 29, 1815, Wilkinson Papers, N.Y. State Library.
[30] To Graham, Sept. 13, Dec. 16, 28, 1815. W.D., A.G.O., O.R.
[31] Hay, *op. cit.*, 412.
[32] To Dearborn, Mar. 17, 1817, Wilkinson Papers, Library of Congress.
[33] To Graham, Dec. 16, 28, 1815, W.D., A.G.O., O.R.

his late campaign he had spent $3,317 as secret service money and paid out $4,006.14 for soldiers' damage to civilian property at French Mills and Chateaugay; besides there was $3,656.03 that had gone for the purchase of goods and services in the Southwest. Some items in the above amounts lacked Presidential approval, proper vouchers, and legal authority; and Wilkinson was called on for an explanation. He gave a plenty. He knew that, once these stoppages were removed, the old charges against him for fuel and transportation would be taken care of by the relieving act passed in his favor on July 1, 1812. He therefore went to Washington and skillfully pressed his case. About the beginning of the year 1816 he seems to have won a satisfactory settlement. Had he not been successful, he planned to petition Congress for relief.[34]

Thus, in spite of disappointing delays and financial tribulations, his work went on, page following page in rapid succession. Such progress had been made that on October 28, 1815, the following announcement appeared in *Niles' Weekly Register:*

"Literary—Mr. Small of Philadelphia, has issued proposals for publishing, in 3 vols. 8vo. a work entitled—Memoirs of my own times, by James Wilkinson, late major-general in the service of the United States; and the work will commence with the period of partial investment of the town of Boston, by the American Militia, in 1775, and terminate with the disorganization of the Army in 1815. Each volume to contain 500 pages, at $3 per vol. payable on delivery."

But not until April, 1817, were the volumes of his *Memoirs* ready for delivery. The narrative intended for posterity had been finished, "written with freedom and only regardful of the truth," [35] designed "to set forth every act of my life that may denote zeal or demonstrate patriotism." [36] "Though with numerous blemishes," Wilkinson modestly admits, "it is approved by all persons except official sycophants —a testimonial for which I shall be remembered after the grave has received me, and my enemies are forgotten." [37]

The book is a rich personal document. Wilkinson struts across something less than two thousand pages in magnificent conceit. Maladjusted and irreconcilable, he would shine unblemished in a world

[34] A copy of Wilkinson's account by Tobias Lear, Nov. 22, 1815; Worthington to Lear, Sept. 20, 1815; Wilkinson to Crawford, Nov. 22, 1815; Act of July 1, 1812—all in W.D., A.G.O., O.R.
[35] Wilkinson to Van Rensselaer, Feb. 14, 1817, Wilkinson Papers, N.Y. State Library.
[36] To Madison, Apr. 5, 1816, Madison Papers, Vol. LVIII.
[37] To (?) Apr. 15, 1817, Miscellaneous Papers, N.Y. Public Library.

of sin. Seizing upon his enemies' shortcomings, he describes them with almost iniquitous delight. To strengthen his own defense and his accusations against others, document after document swells the end of each volume. Usually these have been accurately printed, yet the inferences drawn from them are often no compliment to any one's logic. In all his croaking rhetoric, he is a virile, picturesque old general, a gossiping chronicler of unpolished and unexpurgated narratives in which most of the heroes of two wars are not effigies in cocked hats; they are men who are still alive as Wilkinson knew them, strong, violent, clashing forces that had wrecked his dreams of greatness.

In spite of the defects of haste, stalwart prejudice, personal animus, and an almost total lack of organization, his *Memoirs* met with heartening sales. By April 15, 1817, "the subscriptions had so far exceeded the impression" that Wilkinson was having some difficulty in making distributions. With this encouragement, he toyed with the idea of writing more volumes and revising the ones already printed. His friends and admirers inspired him to do more. Dearborn wrote him a highly complimentary letter asking him "to go on and tell the truth of which they have been kept in the dark." [38] The *Aurora* declared that the General had shown himself able to *"unmask imposture* in a spirit worthy of Sallust and with an energy worthy of Tacitus." [39] Alexander Graydon, a friend and contemporary critic, thought the style was often lame and the narrative sometimes flat without "seducing embellishment." In spite of these defects, he still had kind words for the General:

"I must say that the General's work has improved my estimate both of his heart and intellect and that with all his vanities, his ambition and love of splendor, his heretofore faulty politics and management to stand well with the ruling power, his old age discovers a good deal of honorable and manly feeling, and shows a disposition to correct former errors." [40]

Others, however, were not so generous in praise. In 1820 the *Literary and Scientific Repository and Critical Review* published, as a leading article of the July issue, an essay on the General's *Memoirs*. Instead of being a literary criticism, it proved to be only a vehicle for a lengthy, heavy, and scandalous personal attack. Without any

[38] Wilkinson to (?), Apr. 15, 1817, Miscellaneous Papers, N.Y. Public Library.
[39] Hay, *op. cit.*, 414.
[40] Graydon to Lardner, May 5, 1817, Gratz Collection.

signature, it continued in the same abusive manner for three subsequent numbers. Then, without warning, its solid paragraphs suddenly stopped while the author, with grotesque efforts, attempted to conceal the fact that his publishers refused to have more of what he had written.[41] Undismayed he returned to the attack twenty years later in a book of his own.

Wilkinson knew that John Armstrong was the hostile critic. He would have been disappointed without his attention. In 1816, the General had remarked, "I shall give Jack more than one topic to employ his Pen on, when my Books get out. . . . His abuse of me will not wipe out the infamy I shall attach to him." [42] According to Wilkinson, Armstrong's later attack was made with "such acrimony and virulence" that its object was defeated. He was flattered that his "clumsy book" of *Memoirs* had attracted "the attention of a fiend." In retaliation he planned to publish a brief in his own defense, perhaps review the entire career of Armstrong.[43]

As it was, Wilkinson found himself too busy for incendiary polemics. His family needs were by no means covered by the generous pension that the Maryland legislature had almost unanimously voted him for Revolutionary services. It amounted to the half-pay of a colonel of dragoons.[44] The expenses incident to his last court-martial and the publication of his books had been a heavy drain on his finances. And he had always chosen to be a prominent personage, a notable with a grand manner. As Poinsett observed, "he moved in the highest ranks of society." [45] He had traveled far, and had always been careful to appear in a style befitting his position. He had loved laughter and good company, and had delighted to arrange an ostentatious background for his hospitality. Of course he had lived beyond his means, never hesitating in his demands on the future. Thus he needed all the profit that he could get from his *Memoirs*. With the assistance of others he tried to dispose of them privately in order to outwit "scoundrel booksellers." His scheme partly succeeded. Thanks to friendly and gratuitous aid he was able to collect ten dollars and a half for sets previously engaged and twelve to fifteen dollars for most

[41] *Literary and Scientific Respository*, June, 1820, pp. 1–24, Oct., pp. 441–471; Jan. 1821, p. 86, July, pp. 106–137.
[42] To Van Rensselaer, June 30, 1816, Wilkinson Papers, N.Y. State Library.
[43] To Van Rensselaer, Jan. 16, 1821, *Ibid.*
[44] Brumbaugh, Maryland Records, II, 408.
[45] Fragment from the Poinsett Papers, Vol. II, Hist. Soc. of Pa. Library.

of the rest.[46] Three years later, when sales of his second edition began to slacken, he lowered the price to nine dollars on a hundred copies for which subscribers had failed to pay.[47]

In business and politics his energies were absorbed. True to form, he expressed himself without restraint upon the leading men and events of the day. Monroe was a "liar"; Jacob Brown, a "dirty dog"; Dallas, a "scoundrel"; Armstrong, a "rascal"—thus the roll-call of his enemies went on.[48] For De Witt Clinton he had only flattering words, offering to support his candidacy for Governor of New York by writing articles in his behalf. In spite of Andrew Jackson's being an old enemy, he declared him possessed of more honor, independence, and patriotism than any of the others who were trying to be President. At Irish societies and political organizations, Wilkinson was often a guest, freely voicing his views. Wined and dined wherever he appeared, he was always ready with a hearty reply when flattering toasts to him were proposed. Happy at such gatherings in Baltimore, Philadelphia, and elsewhere,[49] he made the most of them, knowing that he would soon be far away from his friends in the East.

He was expecting to join his family soon in the Southwest. On June 7, 1817, the packet ship *Orleans* held out to sea with Wilkinson aboard as a passenger, and in about four weeks it reached the Mississippi.[50] After disembarking, he departed in high spirits for the mouth of Wolf River, on the Bay of St. Louis, "to grow sugar cane and cotton," happily oblivious of the "miasmas" of the river bottom, that had so nearly spelled disaster for him eight years before. He must be at it, he said, clearing rich delta lands to keep good people warm, and to line his empty pockets.[51] Cotton was then thirty-five cents a pound, sugar nine cents. Counting only ten or fifteen thousand dollars a year for net gain, surely in five years, or at the most seven, he would be able to return with his fortune restored and make fitting acknowledgments to his friends. He had hoped that his stanch supporter, Solomon Van Rensselaer, would join him, lured by the prospect of a profit of $5,000 the very first season. He did not come;

[46] To (?), Apr. 15, 1817, Miscellaneous Papers, N.Y. Public Library.
[47] To Thompson, June 7, 1820, Libr. of the City of Boston.
[48] To Van Rensselaer, Dec. 29, 1815, June 30, Sept. 24, 1816, Wilkinson Papers, N.Y. State Library; to Van Rensselaer, Mar. 25, 1816, Darlington Papers.
[49] Hay, *op. cit.*, 412–413.
[50] *The Aurora*, June 9, 1817.
[51] To Thompson, Jan. 14, 1818, Darlington Papers.

he preferred to remain among the rolling hills of New York, where his ancestors had long lived in honor and comfort.[52]

Wilkinson's own plantation could scarcely be expected to yield these gratifying returns. He had paid $1,400 for it, giving only $400 in cash. It was a portion of the rich delta land of the Live Oak Grove estate, but not large enough to produce a handsome revenue, under the most favorable conditions.[53] Nevertheless, Wilkinson liked to live there. In spite of illness and financial anxieties, he was enjoying a pastoral interlude of content such as he had not experienced in years. Celestine Trudeau was his "divine little creole." Truly French, she was obedient, courageous, self-forgetful, and charming —a wife whose virtues Wilkinson delighted to praise. He hated to be separated from her; while in the East he had kept her with him as long as he could. Then, attended only by her sister and servants, she had prepared to return to the home of her father in New Orleans. Wilkinson had arranged for their traveling with solicitous care, doing all he could for their comfort. They went by sea, and he engaged cabins and accommodations such as are necessary for "the sweetest female delicacy." [54] Yet the voyage proved distressing. It was late summer and storms were frequent in the Atlantic and the Gulf. Celestine was also pregnant. Yellow fever prevailed, and slightly lesser plagues, those "epidemical visitations with which it pleased God to scourge" particularly the ports of the Southern coast. Five or six months after reaching New Orleans, she gave birth to a pair of charming daughters. They were born on January 23, 1816,[55] and were given the names Stephanie and Theofannie,[56] and were Wilkinson's superlative delight. When they were two years old and he had joined the family at New Orleans, he was still vastly proud: "Select two of your handsome boys for my angelic twins and we will mix the best Blood of America, England and France." Along with this injunction to his old friend Thompson went news of his own domestic peace: "Adhering to my determination to make myself independent by exertion and industry, before I again go into the world, I decline all Company, refuse all public appointment, and in my Books, my Pen, my divine little Creole & our charming little Girls, I enjoy more tran-

[52] To Van Rensselaer, Mar. 10, 1817, Wilkinson Papers, N.Y. State Library.
[53] Wilkinson, *General James Wilkinson, Soldier and Pioneer*, 32.
[54] To Thompson, May 23, 1815, Gratz Collection.
[55] To Van Rensselaer, Feb. 25, 1816, Wilkinson Papers, N.Y. State Library.
[56] To Williams, Dec., 1822, courtesy of T. W. Streeter and T. R. Hay.

quility [*sic*] & Happiness, than I have experienced in my variegated Life." [57]

In another letter of a somewhat later date, Wilkinson told of his literary aims. "I have not abandoned the idea of continuing my *Memoirs*," he says, "and am therefore desirous to collect every original scrap relative to Revolutionary transactions." [58] He was elated because he had Washington's first Army order in manuscript. He was forever pestering his friends to obtain important data. He planned to write General Starrett and ask him about "a diagram of the Theatre and the merits of the military operations before Baltimore in 1814." [59] He was bent on a task that would have daunted a much younger man. He hated to halt his pen after writing a mere two thousand pages; he wanted to round out what he had already written. He planned to enlarge his story of the Revolution, to describe the War of 1812 in greater detail, and sketch his own career from the time that he had resigned as secretary of the Board of War until the opening days of the Burr conspiracy. The volumes that he had published in 1816 covered "only a fifth" of his life; three more of about the same size would enable him "to render justice to the living and the dead, to record information for posterity." [60] For the purpose, he had material on hand unknown to any one else. Unfortunately he never made use of it, for by 1820 his literary ardor had cooled. It was then that the agreeable gentleman and scholar, Darth Caldwell, visited Magnolia Grove Plantation. Shortly afterwards Wilkinson wrote to an old friend in Baltimore about the visit and the sale of a few remaining copies of his *Memoirs*.[61] If he had been at work on another book, he would not have resisted the opportunity to say so.

His mind and energy were focused on another object. By 1820, ideas of democratic government had spread through France and the United States, and even to the Spanish possessions in America, each national group making its own interpretation of Republicanism. The force was contagious; Wilkinson felt a missionary urge. He hoped for American expansion, he wanted greater opportunities for commercial gain; but he looked for the two only after the South American countries had freed themselves from Old World tyranny. His spirit,

[57] To Thompson, Jan. 14, 1818, Darlington Papers.
[58] To Van Rensselaer, Dec. 14, 1819, Abstract in *Henkel's Cat.* No. 842 (1900).
[59] To Thompson, Jan. 4, 1818, Darlington Papers.
[60] To Dearborn, Mar. 17, 1817, Wilkinson Papers, Library of Congress.
[61] To Thompson, June 7, 1820, A.L.S., Public Library of the City of Boston.

ever volatile, burned to assist Mexico in her struggle for independence.

For a rôle like this Wilkinson was exceptionally fitted. Most of his career had been spent in dealing with the Spaniards. Although not speaking their language fluently, he knew how to control and circumvent them. Their minds were an open book to him. He resembled them greatly in the way that he sometimes contended for the appearance rather than for the essence of things. Americans generally offended the dons with their crudeness, but he charmed with the graceful ease of his manners and a meticulous consideration for their Castilian pride. Procrastination seldom caused him to worry, and often he chose the longest and most intricate path to an important objective. Careless with money, he generously spent his own or government funds —whichever came handy. Out of his long association with the Army he had learned the trick of producing impressions through colorful and ostentatious display. These characteristics were usually esteemed as virtues by the oversea children of Spain. In Mexico lay Wilkinson's opportunity; there strong men had risen to the pinnacle of success in the twinkling of an eye.

For years he had been in contact with filibusters who would overthrow the existing regime in the land of the Montezumas. In New Orleans was the Mexican Association, a group of business men who were trying to free Mexico. In Baltimore and Philadelphia he had become acquainted with many young patriots who were eager to overthrow tyranny in Latin America. Simon Bolívar, who justly won the title, "El Libertador," was probably one of them. He was a Venezuelan of excellent family, educated, an interested student of government, and one who had actually observed the French Revolution. In 1809 he had come to North America and traveled through the United States to see how a republic functioned. On his arrival in Venezuela, he had immediately identified himself with the revolutionists. Wilkinson's interest in Spain and her American dependencies, his own movements that year, as well as his familiar reference to Bolívar, bespeak their early acquaintance.

Much the same can be said of Xavier Mina. After splendid resistance to French armies in Spain, he had suffered imprisonment in Vincennes at the hands of Napoleon. Then, disappointed with Ferdinand VII and his promises, he had fled to London after a revolutionary fiasco in his native land. In 1816, accompanied by English and Italian followers, he had come to Baltimore, where he hoped to assist those already rebelling in Mexico. Here he purchased a brig that was to be converted into a vessel of war, and procured equipment, clothing, and food for his troops. When the expedition left Baltimore, in September, 1816, it consisted of two sailing vessels carrying two hundred infantry and a company of artillery, most of whom were from the United States. It was easy to find volunteers. The War of 1812 had left many out of the new economic system. Some were disappointed in the government they had fought to establish in 1775. Others had their idealism strangely mixed with a spirit of adventure. Whoever they were, they stood ready to proclaim liberty to the oppressed.

The Mexican Company of Baltimore sold arms and supplies to Xavier Mina, expecting him to pay for them as soon as circumstances would permit. José Manuel Herrera had also obtained munitions for the insurgents from Americans. Wilkinson had an interest in both these claims, although it may have been only his 15 per cent commission for collection.[62] If he actually assisted in the acquisition of these supplies the proof is only circumstantial. Nevertheless, the members of the Mexican Company were his friends; and if any one in America could lay hands on old war matériel, Wilkinson could. Furthermore, the attention paid him on his subsequent visit to Mexico was more than his pleasing personality and his military title would justify. Apparently the Mexicans regarded him as a real godfather to the Revolution.

In helping them to freedom, Wilkinson discovered an agreeable outlet for his energies. He could not find it in his neighbors' worldly concerns—negroes and cotton. Though experienced in the handling of tobacco, he knew little about the cultivation of cotton. No matter how hard he tried, he never made his plantation yield a comfortable livelihood. Shortly after reaching Louisiana in 1816, he and his brother Joseph and others became interested in buying slaves in Maryland and adjacent states and selling them in Louisiana.[63] Apparently Wilkinson shared only once in this sordid business. He hated the revolting aspects of slavery and inveighed against it. In 1821, he warned the people of Missouri against legalizing it. According to his opinion they were inviting a curse, they were reasoning with bias, they were actuated from habit, indolence, and a desire for ease. At the same time he called on his countrymen to hold fast to the Union—"the Rock

[62] Goodwin to Wilkinson, July 15, 1822, Records Md. Court of Appeals, Hall of Records, Annapolis, Md.

[63] Wilkinson to Van Rensselaer, Nov. 7, 1816, Wilkinson Papers, N.Y. State Library.

of our Political Salvation." Its preservation meant more to those in the South and the West, though they were the very ones, as he thought, who were hastening its ruin through their "insatiate desire for limitless domain." [64] A philosophy like this made only enemies in Louisiana; he found greater advantage in helping to spread ideas of a different brand.

In most of the important places where he had visited and had made strong friends, were influential groups who were interested in seeing Latin America win its independence. In New Orleans was the Association of Three Hundred, a group of Americans and Creoles interested in fostering commerce with Mexico, and purposefully effecting the spread of American ideas along with the sale of their merchandise. The business of outfitting Mexican rebel armies had grown to such proportions in New Orleans that both the Louisiana legislature and the United States Congress had passed laws to destroy it. In spite of legal handicaps it continued to flourish. In Philadelphia the press of Mr. Carey assisted in propaganda by publishing *The Rights of Man*, by Thomas Paine. It was translated into Spanish and designed for "the particular use and benefit of Spanish America." [65] A copy was sent to Stephen F. Austin, who was expected to present it to the governor of Texas for his perusal and then forward it to Mexico, "or where it may be most useful." In Baltimore existed the Mexican Company, from which filibusterers might obtain financial backing to carry out their designs. Planters along the lower Mississippi constantly heard of the rich land in the valleys of the Trinity, Brazos, and Colorado; they burned with desire to march out and possess it; Spanish ownership was no bar to their overweening cupidity. Thus Wilkinson could easily maintain contact with trouble-makers for Old World despotism in Latin America, either by writing to his friends in the East or by talking to his neighbors on adjacent plantations.

While many were centering their efforts on moving the United States border another step nearer the Pacific, Wilkinson, full of trouble, tried to find a part for himself in a world that seemed turning against him. "Hard labor with his own hands" had failed to line his empty pockets. His "divine Celestine" had been ill and suffered a miscarriage. When she had recovered and was "round and firm as a billiard ball," Wilkinson had a twenty-day siege of yellow fever, which

[64] To Van Rensselaer, Jan. 16, 1821, Wilkinson Papers, N.Y. State Library.
[65] Sibley to J. E. B. Austin, June 6, 1822, "Austin Papers," in *Annual Report Amer. Hist. Assn., 1919*, Vol. II, Part 1, p. 525.

left him "a mere skeleton." Neighbors were growing rich on cotton selling at thirty-five cents per pound, but he made little from his crops and trading ventures.[66] During January, 1819, General Adair brought suit against him for false imprisonment during the Burr conspiracy. The Natchez court decided in favor of the plaintiff, and Wilkinson, without money to meet the judgment, was faced with a debtors' prison. In this predicament friends came to the rescue. They introduced a bill in Congress by the terms of which Wilkinson was given three thousand dollars, five hundred more than was actually necessary.[67] The additional sum helped the frail old man, now sixty-three years old and working for his bread. In spite of troubles, his spirit was unbroken; and his mind was active as ever in plans for the future. One of them involved trying to get the pension of St. Clair, who had died, transferred to himself.[68] Only Wilkinson would have entertained so unusual a notion.

While the court at Natchez was hearing General Adair's suit against General Wilkinson, there was a great stir along the southwestern frontier over the fact that President Monroe had signed away all claims to Texas. In Natchez a meeting of indignation was held and an expedition organized. Almost anything that would bring trouble to the "leather-headed ass Monroe" found favor with Wilkinson. When Dr. Long was chosen general of the invading force, Wilkinson's interest became deep and personal. Without strength or inclination to lead a campaign into Mexico or material resources to carry it on, Wilkinson made available his pen, influence, and all the lore of an old and far-traveled soldier to "the young Lion" of the battle of New Orleans. To this intrepid soldier, Wilkinson's niece, Jane H. Wilkinson, was already married. She and Wilkinson were both on hand while plans were ripening for the expedition to "jump off" from Natchez.

A republic, Texas by name, was to be established in the eastern part of the adjacent Spanish province. Once connections were made with the insurgents of Mexico, the republic would be a center from which to carry on a campaign to free the whole country. Long, a man of means in Natchez, staked his entire fortune on the result. After he had captured Nacogdoches, he found it necessary to leave for New

[66] To Thompson, Jan. 14, 1818, *Darlington Papers.*
[67] *Niles' Weekly Register*, Jan. 23, 1819, and *Annals of Congress*, 16th Cong., 1st Session, 613, 619, 675, 678, 1298.
[68] To Van Rensselaer, Dec. 14, 1819, *Henkel's Cat.* No. 842 (1900), p. 76.

Orleans to seek more capital. When he returned, his followers had scattered to the four winds. He had proved a better fighter than executive; he had trusted too much to the forms of government that he had set up; the men who had joined him were inherently filibusterers and adventurers, not colonists.

Long, however, was not to be stopped by the loss of his fortune or the failure of his first attempt. General Ripley, who had resigned from the Army, had recently turned to politics and the practice of law in New Orleans, and the new movement was guided by the united wisdom of himself and Wilkinson. To insure coöperation or, at least, recognition from the Republican Junta in Mexico, Ripley arranged for General Trespalacios, a recent exile in Cuba because of activities against the Spaniards in Mexico, to take nominal command. And Long, who appreciated the importance of connection with this most important group of revolutionists, submitted.

A constitution was adopted, probably of the joint composition of Ripley and Wilkinson. Ripley was invited by the Supreme Council of the Republic of Texas to become President and "ex-officio Commander-in-Chief of the armies and navies thereof." As head of the republic, so neatly laid out on paper, Ripley outlined and sent to Long the policy that he expected to pursue. He would cultivate peace, foreign trade, and religion. Education, manufacture, and agriculture, were to be encouraged. Roads would be built, canals dug, and the forests and waste places turned into plowed fields. Slavery would not be permitted. Ripley was a northern man and an idealist. Wilkinson was southern with practical ideas, thoroughly convinced of the evil effects of slavery.

Texas proved not so easy to reclaim as members of the expedition had hoped. Long's new establishment at Bolivar Point was again deserted by every one except his wife, her child Ann, and one small negro maid. He and his soldiers had advanced only to be captured by Spanish government troops. After the Treaty of Cordova, when Mexican independence had been made certain, they were escorted to Mexico City, where they were on the point of being rewarded as patriots when Long was shot by a Mexican sentry, a few days before the arrival of Wilkinson. Long's friends believed that death was due to assassination directed by Trespalacios, whom Americans had grudgingly made their leader in the recent expedition. In that capacity he had proved to be untruthful, and a dangerously ambitious trouble-maker. It was easy to see that the presence of Long interfered with his influence and advancement in Mexico. After he had been killed, Trespalacios was appointed Governor of Texas, thus receiving honors that rumor had already given to his rival.

General Ripley never came to Texas; his efforts for her independence now ended. An only son, however, was destined to take up his work, and be among the valiant few who died at Fannin's massacre in 1836.

Wilkinson's years of activity seemed definitely finished. It was not so; he was cherishing a great plan; he was determined to go to Mexico. He could not see Long play the rôle that he wanted himself. Yet neither separately nor together were his former business associates willing to finance for him a trip to Mexico. If they refused to consider him dishonest, they probably suspected him of being incapable, senile, and visionary. His uncertain health was definitely broken. His favorite of the angelic twins had died. His beloved Theofannie, as her father said, "was too good and too perfect for this world so God took her." [69] Wilkinson had neither the means nor the desire to carry on further with the plantation.

In March, 1822, he sailed for Vera Cruz; he was going to Mexico, as he said, to improve his health. For his triumphant entry, sword, gold braid, and buttons were refurbished. There were newly tailored uniforms. His portrait of Washington by Stuart was packed to go with him.[70] The old portmanteau was stuffed with notes on Mexican commercial relations, tariff reduction, tunnage, etc., and facts concerning Texas colonization—all to be brought forward at a convenient season. He wanted to be ready to discharge any kind of mission. The United States would be needing a representative in Mexico. That "ass" of a President might come to his senses and do something for him yet. Wilkinson would like being Minister to Mexico. He thought best to keep this hope of his to himself; he explained that he was going to Mexico for the sake of his health. He would probably be there a long while; bills were difficult to collect. He had a mass of them for the supplies that the Mexican Company of Baltimore had furnished to General Xavier Mina and his followers. If he succeeded in getting the Mexican Congress to pay them, he would be given a commission of 15 per cent.[71]

Wilkinson left his family and his plantation in the care of his son,

[69] To Williams, Dec., 1822, courtesy of T. W. Streeter and T. R. Hay.
[70] To Monroe, May 11, 1822, Monroe Papers, Vol. XX, Library of Congress.
[71] Goodwin and others to Wilkinson and Smith, July 15, 1822, *Account Book,* Md. Court of Appeals, Hall of Records, Annapolis, Md.

who with filial devotion later corresponded with the General about matters of business at home; as times became difficult for them both, the General quoted Scriptures for mutual consolation.[72] Joseph Biddle Wilkinson believed in his father's plans, fully expecting success. Through his assistance and apparently that of the Mexican Company, the General went on his last, long journey in relative comfort.

He was going to a country rent with civil strife. On September 27, 1821, Agustín de Iturbide had been proclaimed "El Libertador," organizing the Regency of five members of which he was the *de facto* head. One of its members was O'Donojú, who had come over as Viceroy from Spain and, from necessity and convenience, had joined the patriots. After a constitution had been drawn up, Iturbide was proclaimed Emperor. On July 25, 1822, he was crowned with regal ceremony as Agustín I. During October he tried to create an "Instituting Junta" to take the place of Congress, which he dissolved. As a result he was forced to abdicate, and Congress appointed an Executive Triumvirate to assume the reins of control while a new constitution was written. In drawing it up Miguel Ramos Arizpe, leader of the Federalist group, played a dominant part. He was appointed head of the committee for an *ad interim* constitution, and produced in three days the "Acta Constitutiva." [73] Under his leadership Mexico began to function under the Constitution of October 4, 1824. Guadalupe Victoria was elected as President. On November 25, 1825, the last Spanish soldiers in Mexico, quartered at San Juan de Ulúa, surrendered.

They were in possession of the island fortress when Wilkinson appeared off Vera Cruz in April, 1822. They could readily train their guns upon the town or the approaches to it by water. Perhaps they prevented his ship from drawing up along the wharf and discharging her cargo and passengers. Perhaps customhouse officials objected. The ruling faction in the town may have been unwilling to admit a distinguished foreigner who might ally himself with the opposition. Whatever the reason, Wilkinson did not land for several days.[74] He chafed at delay. His ship was no pleasant place to stay if it lay beyond the reefs, subjected to the rough water of the open sea. He was a poor sailor and usually fell sick in stormy weather. If it cast anchor

[72] Wilkinson to J. B. Wilkinson, Mar. 24, 1825, courtesy of Mrs. W. H. Palmer, Jr., and T. R. Hay.
[73] Priestley, *The Mexican Nation, a History*, 261–262.
[74] Sibley to J. E. B. Austin, June 6, 1822, *Annual Report Amer. Hist. Assn., 1919*, Vol. II, Part 1, p. 525.

Panorama of Vera Cruz in 1846 from an old print in the Public Library of Vera Cruz, Mexico. Vera Cruz appeared almost the same in 1846 as when Wilkinson saw it in 1822.

in the lee of the island of San Juan de Ulúa, he was exasperated that he could not cross the eight hundred yards or more of water and enter the old Spanish town with its thick gray walls of coral stone. He was eager to pass through its gates, follow the road westward through the shifting sand hills, ride past the mountain Orizaba, forever snow-clad and brilliant in a tropic sun. He was restless to be traveling to the highlands, where the climate was bracing and his business might be accomplished.

While he paced the deck or lay in his cabin waiting to land, Wilkinson made notes for the "Observations" that he was to present Iturbide in November. In final form they concerned the existing evils of the Mexican tariff. Some of them were "those vexatious delays which merchants experience in the imperial custom's office, or through defect in organization of the service." To give point to his remarks, he told of the time when he "was a prisoner in the port of Vera Cruz"; he declared ships were detained for weeks before they were permitted to depart. To him the tariff was more than a political problem: it concerned the moral and social life of the swarming sans-culottes. The United States, he believed, could do much for her neighbors if only the Mexican trade laws were revised. Thus with an array of facts gathered far and wide over a long period of years, he argued for closer relations with the United States.[75]

Finally, after landing at Vera Cruz, he hastened on to Mexico City. Along the way he scattered advice freely, made friends, and stored his mind with facts that might help him later. About the 23rd of April he reached Puebla,[76] a stronghold of Iturbide's supporters and the second largest city of all Mexico. Wilkinson decided to rest at this place three days before starting on the remaining seventy miles of his journey; he wanted "to recover from an indisposition produced by fatigue." During his convalescence, he met Dr. Ramos Arizpe, an important official of the Cathedral. He had represented Mexico in the Cortes of León, when the Spanish constitution had been written, and had led a successful struggle for its application to Mexico. Through his influence "the meritorious O'Donojú" had come to Mexico as the last of the viceroys, turning patriot at Vera Cruz. Now O'Donojú had died, leaving a vacancy in the Regency, to which Ramos

---

[75] "Reflections on the Province of Texas," in *Hispanic American Historical Review*, I, 163–175.

[76] Reilly to Hawkins, Apr. 26, 1822, in *Annual Report Amer. Hist. Assn., 1919*, Vol. II, Part 1, p. 500.

Arizpe's superior, the Bishop of Puebla, had been appointed. Ramos Arizpe was a statesman after Wilkinson's own heart, and a politician fit to give him a sensitive appreciation of the Mexican public. Their first meeting may have turned on constitutional comparisons. Significantly, the next year Ramos Arizpe was campaigning for a government by federation after the manner of the United States. Certainly the friendship between him and Wilkinson flourished with a constitutional bent. The General probably had a more powerful influence upon him than Austin is reputed to have exerted.

Austin took great credit for having sent Ramos Arizpe a copy of the United States Constitution. Ramos Arizpe's draft of the "Acta Constitutiva" does show points of resemblance with it. As a learned man and a student of government he was fully competent to make use of any American ideas that might be suitable for incorporation into Mexican law. Doubtless he adopted some of the suggestions of Wilkinson, who had a much wider and deeper knowledge of Spanish-American affairs than Austin. For this reason the General's indirect contribution to Mexico's constitution was probably greater. In apportioning credit to either of the two, it must be remembered that Ramos Arizpe was intelligent and did not need to lean upon others for intellectual guidance.

Wilkinson's connection with Ramos Arizpe apparently continued during the whole of his Mexican sojourn. As late as May, 1825, Baron de Bastrop was complaining to Austin of his influence. The "Plan of Colonization" sent by Ramos Arizpe to the first "constituent legislature" of the province of Texas, he said, was a piece of Wilkinson's work. The part of the "cursed plan" prohibiting slavery gave Bastrop "no end of trouble." "Wilkinson," he commented, "is like the dog in the garden, not being able to eat grass, he will not permit the ox to enjoy it either." [77]

When these remarks were made, Wilkinson was in Mexico City trying to get the government to pay in land the debts of the Mexican Company and others. He had reached there on April 28, 1822. Three days later Stephen F. Austin wrote that the General had the confidence of the Mexican government "to a high degree," received "distinguished attention," lived with the Captain-General of the province, and was visited by General Iturbide and members of the Regency. [78]

[77] Bastrop to S. F. Austin, May 6, 1825, *Ibid.*, 1088.
[78] Austin to Hawkins, May 1, 1822, *Ibid.*, 504–505.

José Manuel Herrera was minister of state, the very same person who had purchased arms in New Orleans about the time of Long's first expedition. Perhaps he helped Wilkinson become favorably known to the existing powers in the capital. Being so well received induced Wilkinson to believe that he was especially qualified to discharge any mission that the United States Government might entrust to him. He therefore wrote and offered his services. The President had nothing to suggest; a year later the same was true. Though disappointed, Wilkinson still could boast of the independence which he declared that he never would barter away for all the "gifts and graces" at the disposition of the "little Jesuit Madison or his Bifaced successor Monroe." [79]

Unquestionably Wilkinson stood well with the Mexican government, if not his own. One news item in the United States declared that he had "an office under Iturbide worth $15,000 per year." [80] If, indeed, Wilkinson was one of his paid foreign advisors, the position permitted him to make no comment. At the banquet following the coronation of the Emperor, he was present.[81] Three days before, Austin had forwarded to Iturbide a "Petition" and a copy of a "Memorial" to Congress. With these two important documents he thought best to include the letter of introduction that the General had given him.[82] After A. C. Rodney, a member of Congress especially interested in South American affairs, had heard of Wilkinson's letter to Monroe, he forwarded to the President this interesting bit of gossip: "Wilkinson has prevented sending minister to U.S. after Minister has been selected." [83] Rodney happened to be wrong. Wilkinson was on good terms with the minister-elect, and was anxious for him to be on his way; only the state of the Mexican treasury detained him.[84]

Wilkinson was learning and planning much; he thought of writing a history of Mexico that would correct some of the errors in Humboldt's work.[85] His unused notes on the American Revolution were still available; the startling comparisons that he had observed in regard to the two American revolutions would furnish excellent copy. He

---

[79] To Aspinwall, Apr. 17, 1823, printed in *Bulletin N.Y. State Library*, III, 362.
[80] Draper MSS. 5 J 16, State Hist. Soc. Wis.
[81] *National Intelligencer*, Oct. 12, 1822.
[82] Austin to Iturbide, May 25, 1822, "Austin Papers," in *Annual Report of Amer. Hist. Assn., 1919*, Vol. II, Part 1, pp. 518–519.
[83] Rodney to Monroe, July 13, 1822, Monroe Papers, Library of Congress.
[84] To De Witt Clinton, Aug. 1, 1822, Clinton Papers, Columbia Univ. Library.
[85] Clinton to Wilkinson, July 29, 1823, *Ibid.*

knew intimately the men who had fought with Washington, and those who were driving Spain out of the New World were his frequent guests. Whether they were Mexicans or Americans, he judged them with unusual acumen.

From his first acquaintance Wilkinson was disappointed with Iturbide, who was to become Emperor as Agustín I. When the Emperor and his wife paid the General a call, he said nothing "worth recording." About a fortnight later, on May 11, 1822, Wilkinson avoided any characterization of the distinguished guest in a letter to Monroe.[86] On the 1st of August he correctly described the political situation to De Witt Clinton. He told of his own efforts to play the rôle of a "minister of Peace," to conciliate the warring factions; he hoped that the Emperor would act "fairly, uprightly and justly," although his enemies charged him with the determination "to dissolve the Cortez, restore the Jesuits, and reëstablish the Inquisition." Any one of these errors, Wilkinson believed, would be the forerunner of the Emperor's downfall.[87] Within a year his worst forebodings were verified. He declared Iturbide to be a man who had cheated his followers, more of "the Lamb than the Lion," "the Spinster than the Soldier," an unhappy combination of ambition and vanity, "a stranger to Integrity." [88] To save himself Iturbide abdicated on February 19, 1824. Although enjoying a comfortable pension as an exile in Italy and faced with a decree against his return, he had the temerity to attempt a c. 'p after the manner of Napoleon and entered Soto la Marina, Mexico, in disguise. He was captured and almost immediately executed, July 14, 1824, by order of the Congress of Tamaulipas.

Neither Wilkinson nor Stephen F. Austin had faith in the ability of the Mexicans to form a stable government. Austin's opinion of them was none too flattering. Of them he wrote:

"The population, however, is very much mixed and a great proportion of them are miserably poor and wretched, beggars are more numerous than I ever saw in any place in my life—robberies and assasins [sic] are frequent in the streets, the people are biggoted [sic] and superstitious in the extreme, and indolence seems to be the general order of the day—in fact the City Magnificant [sic] as it is in appearance is at least a century behind many other places in point of

---

[86] To Monroe, May 11, 1822, Monroe Papers, Library of Congress.
[87] To Clinton, Aug. 1, 1822, Clinton Papers, Columbia Univ. Library.
[88] To Aspinwall, Apr. 23, 1823, printed in *Bulletin N.Y. State Library*, III, 362.

intelligence and improvement in the Arts. The majority of the people of the whole nation, as far as I have seen them, want nothing but tails to be more brutes than Apes . . . thank God there are no Fryars [*sic*] near the Colorado, and if they come to distress me, I shall hang them for a certainty unless an army protects them." [89]

Wilkinson held similar views about the character and ability of the Mexicans. He declared, they "are resolutely determined to resist a despotism and yet are utterly! utterly! unqualified to organize, administer or enjoy a free republic—an idolatrous, ignorant, unmoral people, without disposition or capacity for rational Government founded on Liberty." [90]

From the spring of 1822 to the winter of 1825, a period of more than three years, Wilkinson saw first one, then another, Mexican faction rise and fall. He always managed to be on friendly terms with the one in power. He was at home in a government of military men. After years of experience he had finally added wisdom and persuasive graces to his unique personality. He had become a mellowed and discerning diplomat.

To escape the violence and pandemonium in the heart of the city Wilkinson retired to lodgings in a quiet and remote section of the city. Even there he was sought out by those who would recover claims against the government or who were asking favors or grants of land. The Capital was swarming with American and other foreign adventurers. Travelers and representative citizens sat round his hospitable board. Many others might have written, like Joel R. Poinsett, United States Minister to Mexico: "We stopped at the lodgings of our countryman, General W——, who received us in the kindest manner; he has been sometime here, and we sat up to a late hour, listening to his interesting account of the country." [91]

Wilkinson carefully avoided giving offense by associating with the enemies of the government. When Long and his followers were under the ban, he denied having sympathy with them, although he had been of great aid to them in the past. In his "Reflections on the Province of Texas," prepared for Iturbide, he declared they were demoralized wanderers, "slothful, ready to vice, insensible to social affection and really permanent social life"; no one with any goodness

[89] S. F. Austin to J. E. B. Austin, "Austin Papers," in *Annual Report Amer. Hist. Assn., 1919,* Vol. II, Part 1, p. 531.
[90] To Clinton, Aug. 1, 1822, Clinton Papers, Columbia Univ. Library.
[91] Poinsett, *Notes on Mexico, etc.,* 63.

or religion would associate with them, and Long, he added, was nothing but an "imposter." At the time of these strictures Long had been killed. Trespalacios, the probable instigator of his assassination, had been appointed Governor of the Province of Texas, and Wilkinson was trying to get a grant of land for himself in this very territory.

Toward the latter part of December, 1822, Wilkinson was hopeful of success: "I am making an effort to acquire a precious tract of land in the province of Texas divinely situated on the Coast of the Gulph with a good harbour & salubrious climate, with Fish and oysters at the Door and droves of Buffalo & wild horses in thousands on our rear. If I succeed I am desirous to make a settlement of the well born & break out the second year in extensive production of Sugar and Cotton—you will be permitted to introduce negroes—the voyage is only three days west of the Mississippi—say at Galvez Town . . . not a breath of this project because it may not succeed." [92]

If by "negroes" Wilkinson meant slaves, he showed that even in his old age he was willing to be inconsistent if himself or his friends benefited thereby. Perhaps his very inconsistency helped him to keep in favor with the Regency, the Constitutional Empire, the Instituting Junta, the Triumvirate, the Constituent Congress, the administration of Victoria Guadalupe, and various *ad interim* powers. Throughout the period covered by them all, he labored with patience and long-suffering to collect "Revolutionary debts" and to secure his "precious tract of land."

Though often duped by the Imperial and Republican governments and exhausted with anxiety, he continued his determination to serve the Mexican people. He sought to strengthen their connection with the United States. He tried to convert Iturbide to this idea, reminding him that the two countries should be bound together in "one body politic," neither trespassing upon the rights of the other. [93] He wrote to De Witt Clinton expressing the hope that the "Guardian Angel of Columbia may extend Her beneficient [sic] protection to an Idolatrous, Ignorant, unmoral People, without disposition or capacity for rational government." [94]   To Thomas Aspinwall, United States Consul at London, he hinted that there might be reasons to fear British and French efforts at joint control of Mexico; he thought

[92] To Williams, Dec., 1822, courtesy of T. W. Streeter and T. R. Hay.
[93] "Reflections on the Province of Texas," printed in *Hispanic American Historical Review*, I, 163–175.
[94] To Clinton, Aug. 1, 1822, Clinton Papers, Columbia Univ. Library.

15,000 of their troops could march unimpeded to the Capital after a single combat.[95] Perhaps Wilkinson wanted Aspinwall to transmit this information back to the State Department at Washington. The Monroe Doctrine had not yet been proclaimed. After it had been, Wilkinson warned Jefferson on March 21, 1824, that a United States minister to Mexico was needed; he thought the British were exercising undue influence through their loans. In the same letter he expressed "the desire to behold the People of the Western Hemisphere a close knit League of National Republicans, Independent of European Alliances and Conexions [sic]"; he believed that the United States in concert with the "enlightened and virtuous few of Mexico could control the rest of the benighted inhabitants and keep them "within the pale of Republicanism." Bolívar, he declared, would be an efficient agent in promoting such friendly concert.[96]

During July, 1823, Wilkinson presented his large Stuart portrait of Washington to the Congress of Mexico. The time was opportune; the great Mexican Constitution was before the people for adoption. To them, only less than to Americans, Washington typified the great soldier and statesman who, after freeing his country, had preserved it from confusion and anarchy. His portrait would be a constant inspiration for others to emulate his distinguished example. The Mexicans were deeply appreciative of the gift, and Wilkinson was heartily thanked. Thus he deftly made friends for himself and the United States.[97]

He needed to be favorably and widely known. Congress was not moved entirely by the intrinsic merits of a case: the popularity of the petitioner was important. The character of claims for which Wilkinson sought adjustment varied. He wanted an appropriation for the "widowed children of two citizens of the United States," reimbursement of the Mexican Company for supplies it had furnished, disposition made of the flimsy bill of Cox and Elkins of New Orleans, a cash settlement of $15,000 for services rendered by some one else, possibly himself.[98] These and other claims, some honest, others fictitious, Wilkinson handled with consummate skill. Working for others did not retard his efforts to obtain a princely grant for himself. Doing

[95] To Aspinwall, Apr. 17, 1823, printed in *Bulletin N.Y. State Library*, III, 361–363.
[96] To Jefferson, Mar. 21, 1824, Jefferson Papers, Vol. CCXXVI.
[97] Mateos, *Historia Parlamentaria de los Congresos Mexicanos*, II, 451, 457.
[98] Hay, "General James Wilkinson—the Last Phase," *La. Hist. Quarterly*, XIX (Apr., 1936), pp. 429–430.

business like this in a foreign land was not easy. Changing administrations considered his claims and filed them away. Procrastination followed procrastination. Toyed with by some, duped by others, he still persisted. To his friends Samuel Smith and Thomas Jefferson he wrote in the early days of 1824, inveighing against the people and the government that had deceived him.[99] He knew that he had only a short span of life remaining, and he yearned to spend it with his faithful Celestine, his charming Stephanie, and that interesting son Theodore, who was now only four or five. He did not care to remain longer in the barren Mexican uplands; he wanted to be back in the Valley of the Mississippi, where his friends were old and understanding.

Not until March 17, 1824, were there prospects that his business would soon be ended. Then a law was enacted establishing the principles on which his claims were to be adjusted. By its provisions the different states in the Republic could make their own dispositions covering their unoccupied land. On March 24, 1825, the *empresario* system was authorized. An *empresario* was none other than a promoter to whom the government gave a large tract of land contingent on bringing into Mexico a number of colonists in accordance with certain conditions. Wilkinson wished to obtain a grant in Texas, and here Trespalacios, for whom he had probably done favors, was Governor. The tide was beginning to turn in the General's favor. On September 1, 1824, he was able to write to his son Joseph that he had made a contract that would enable him to leave Mexico in two or three weeks.[100] He may have thought best to abandon all the remaining unsettled claims except one for $15,000 in cash. This one, as well as the final details covering others, detained him much longer than he expected.

While he waited, his never idle mind turned to a variety of interests. He investigated the possibility of silver mining in Mexico. The difficulties proved insurmountable; mines were inaccessible, machinery unobtainable, and potential competitors were established already in the industry. At one time he thought of buying mules and driving them overland to Louisiana, where they might be sold at a handsome profit. But such a business involved long, hard riding—and he was growing old. As a life member of the American Bible Society he

[99] To Smith, Jan. 27, 1824, *Amer. Art Assn. Cat. No. 376,* Apr. 13, 1921; to Jefferson, Mar. 21, 1824, Jefferson Papers, Vol. CCXXVI.
[100] Wilkinson to J. B. Wilkinson, Sept. 1, 1824, Files of T. R. Hay.

Major-General James Wilkinson
from a portrait by Charles W. Peale.

Courtesy of the Curator, Horace T. Carpenter,
Independence Hall, Philadelphia.

requested a large number of Testaments for distribution among the ignorant and ungodly. Before they could be shipped, his work in Mexico had ended.[101] When Stephen F. Austin started north in 1823, he and Wilkinson conceived the idea of selling thirteen-dollar watches to people along the way. Austin did the peddling. On reaching Saltillo he wrote back that the speculation *on one side* was profitable; he did not mention the buyer, whose thoughts may have been profanely different.[102] From time to time Wilkinson wrote and told his friends of the plans that he was perfecting to colonize in Texas; their success, of course, depended on the grant of land for which he adroitly and continuously labored. When swindlers cheated him—and there were several—he tried to have them apprehended when they landed in New Orleans; they were a heavy tax upon his purse and patience. Although he lived modestly, he needed a small and dependable revenue, and sometimes he was hard put to get it.

During March, 1825, Wilkinson wrote in deep distress to his son Joseph, asking for a loan. For previous advances and what he hoped to obtain the General sent him a "grant for 100,000 acres" on either of two tracts that he expected to colonize. Both contained something more than 5,000,000 acres; one was in the northeast corner of Texas, the other in the vicinity of Galveston Bay.[103] Not to be thwarted by other *empresarios* or defeated by the well known trickery of Tres-palacios, Governor of Texas and Coahuila, he planned to make his grants doubly sure through the influence of Joel R. Poinsett, who had arrived at the Capital in June as United States Minister to Mexico. He asked Poinsett for a letter of introduction to the Governor, and apparently it was given in the form desired.[104] Still not confident that the government's promise to him would be fulfilled, Wilkinson continued in Mexico. As affairs turned out, he was unable to perform his own part of the bargain, and neither he nor his family profited from the magnificent estate that might have been theirs. His failure was not unusual. Stephen F. Austin was about the only one of the *empresarios* who really succeeded. Wilkinson's wife, Celestine, had to be content with a parcel of one hundred and sixty acres that the United States gave her because of her husband's service in the Army.[105]

[101] Hay, *op. cit.*, 433–434.
[102] S. F. Austin to Wilkinson, May 11, 1823, Wilkinson Papers, Vol. III, Chicago Hist. Soc.
[103] To J. B. Wilkinson, Feb. 25, Mar. 24, 1825, Files of T. R. Hay.
[104] To Poinsett, July 9, 1825, Poinsett Papers, I, 179.
[105] Hay, *op. cit.*, 435.

If Wilkinson had kept strong and active, his last great enterprise might have ended happily. It was far otherwise. From the summer of 1825, the refreshing breeze of the highlands no longer lent vigor to his declining health. The chronic diarrhoea from which he had suffered for many years became more aggravated. Opium, the common remedy of the time, gave little relief. In December those near his "little villa on La Vega" failed to see him mount his horse and ride out for his morning exercise. He had taken to his bed and was daily growing weaker. Only large doses of opium eased his protracted pain. Celestine had come, but her efforts were unavailing. Three days after Christmas his friends stood by and closed his unseeing eyes. The General had finished his travels and had made his first and last surrender.[106]

He was removed to the home of Poinsett, and there gathered the distinguished of the city to pay their final tribute before his interment in consecrated ground. Friends would have buried him with military honors, but these were not permitted even to citizens of Mexico. The General's obsequies were therefore simple. Dr. Don Ciro Villaurutia read the service of the Catholic faith, and in the cemetery of the Archangel San Miguel the sexton placed a marker on a newly made grave. In time his remains, with those of others, were gathered up and indiscriminately buried in a common vault. Afterwards his countrymen were too late when they would have returned them to his native land; they could do nothing, only leave them beneath the floor of the Church of the Archangel San Miguel until the course of Earth is finished.[107]

[106] *Daily National Intelligencer*, Feb. 11, 20, 1826.
[107] *Gulf Coast Historical Magazine*, I, 288; Senate Executive Documents, No. 6, 42nd Cong., 3rd Session.

BIBLIOGRAPHY

I. PRIMARY SOURCE MATERIAL

A. Unpublished

Because of Wilkinson's extensive travels and correspondence, his letters are widely scattered. The locations of manuscript material relating to his career are arranged below in alphabetical order. Sources marked at the beginning with a [1] probably contain not more than five papers concerning Wilkinson. Besides the manuscripts enumerated below, there are a few Wilkinson letters in the hands of his descendants and of manuscript dealers.

Albany, New York
> In New York State Library are eleven letters written by Wilkinson from 1814 to 1821 to Solomon Van Rensselaer; some of the papers of Isaiah and John Townsend, contractors for Wilkinson's army during 1813 and 1814, and a book without page numbering containing orders of the 3rd Regiment of Artillery while it was stationed at Sacketts Harbor.

Annapolis, Maryland
> Hall of Records: [1] Account Book of the Maryland Court of Appeals contains letters relating to Wilkinson in 1822 and 1824.

Baltimore, Maryland
> [1] The Library of Maryland Historical Society: Otho Holland Williams Papers, Vols. I and VI; Isaac Briggs Papers.

Boston, Massachusetts
> The Massachusetts Historical Society has about thirty-five letters that Wilkinson wrote to Winthrop Sargent between 1797 and 1800. In the Henry Knox Papers are a few more.
> The Public Library of the City of Boston has at least five Wilkinson letters. They are in different collections and date from 1797 to 1820.

Buffalo, New York
> [1] The Buffalo Historical Society Library has at least two Wilkinson letters of 1813.

Chicago, Illinois
> Chicago Historical Society owns three volumes of Wilkinson's letters covering the period from 1779 to 1809. Those from 1796 through 1809 are especially valuable. A few others written at later dates are scattered in several collections.
> The Newberry Library has approximately twenty letters written to or by Wilkinson, all but two of which are before 1800. In the Ayer Collection are twenty

341

bound volumes of "typescripts" entitled Despatches of the Spanish Governors of Louisiana; it also contains copies of many important papers found in the Library of Congress.

In the Library of the University of Chicago are located the Durrett Collection and the Gardoqui Papers. In the former are thirty or forty papers covering Wilkinson's Kentucky career and the Journal of the Kentucky Conventions for Statehood; in the latter are several letters relating to Wilkinson's applications for land and trade dispensations.

Cincinnati, Ohio

The Historical and Philosophical Society of Ohio, at the University of Cincinnati Library Building, has several letters of Wilkinson written while he was prominent in the Northwest.

Frankfort, Kentucky

The Library of the Kentucky State Historical Society has a number of letters that Wilkinson wrote between 1784 and 1791. Seven of them were addressed to Dr. Shiell and have been published in the *Register* (Kentucky State Historical Society) of September, 1926.

Hanover, New Hampshire

[1] The Library of Dartmouth College: Papers of Josiah Bartlett.

Hartford, Connecticut

The Connecticut State Library has several letters that Wilkinson wrote to John Pratt and Jeremiah Wadsworth between 1790 and 1795. It has also other manuscripts in which Wilkinson is mentioned. See the Library's Supplementary Index to Revolutionary Manuscripts.

Havana, Cuba

In the National Archives are at least five letters that Wilkinson wrote to Miró, Jorda, Harmar, and Martinez between 1789 and 1790. They are in the Second bundle of Florida papers.

Jackson, Mississippi

In the Mississippi Department of Archives and History are found many letters of Winthrop Sargent and William C. C. Claiborne, some of which were written by Wilkinson or relate to him, particularly from 1798 to 1804.

Lexington, Kentucky

In the Fayette County Clerk's office are the records of Wilkinson's land purchases and sales. They are found in Burnt Records, Vols. 3–5, Deed Book Q, and District Court Books, C. and A. The Burnt Records (eight volumes) are composed of copies of burnt records that were salvaged from a fire that destroyed the County Clerk's office in 1803; the contents of each volume are arranged without unity of time, person, or place.

Madison, Wisconsin

In the Library of the Historical Society of Wisconsin are the Harmar Papers (two volumes), Draper Notes (thirty-three volumes), Kentucky MSS. (thirty-two volumes), and Newspaper Extracts (four volumes). The first of these has information covering Wilkinson's career along the Ohio up to 1799; the others, found in the Draper Collection, are only incidentally concerned with the General.

Mexico, D.F., Mexico
See Bolton, *Guide to Materials for the History of the United States in the Principal Archives of Mexico*, published by the Carnegie Institution of Washington, Washington, D.C.

New Haven, Connecticut
The Yale University Library has a collection of Philip Nolan manuscripts acquired from Henry I. Wagner. In them are eight Wilkinson and Cordero letters of 1806.

New Orleans, Louisiana
The Library of the Cabildo contains a few Wilkinson items; among them is H. C. Castellano, Scrap Book, interesting for its data on local conditions shortly after the Louisiana Purchase.

In the Louisiana State Historical Society are the Pontalba Papers, a collection of hand-written copies of manuscripts owned by the Pontalba family at Senlis, France. They are helpful in supplementing information gained from the Spanish Archives concerning the relations of Wilkinson and Miró.

New York City
[1] The Library of Columbia University has a few Wilkinson letters. With one exception they are in the De Witt Clinton Papers and were written while Wilkinson was in Mexico.

The Library of the New York Historical Society owns the Gates Papers, in which are a number of letters that Wilkinson wrote to Gates and others during the Revolution.

The New York Public Library has at least four Wilkinson letters in the Emmet Collection. In the Military Papers of General Peter Gansevoort, Jr., are about a dozen written from 1808 to 1811. Miscellaneous Papers have about twenty, ranging in date from 1776 to 1823. A few others are found in the James Monroe Papers, Richard Varick Papers, etc.

Ottawa, Canada
The Public Archives of Canada contain considerable information relating to Wilkinson's campaign of 1813–1814. Most of it is found in Series C.

Philadelphia, Pennsylvania
The Historical Society of Pennsylvania Library has approximately two hundred Wilkinson letters. The Gratz Collection, McKean Papers, etc. contain a few of them. In the Joel R. Poinsett Papers (twenty-two volumes) are several manuscripts concerned with Wilkinson's activities in Mexico from 1822 to 1825. The Rawle Collection has many data relating to Wilkinson's operations on the Canadian border in 1813 and 1814. The Anthony Wayne Papers (seventy-three volumes) furnish essential information about Wilkinson, Wayne, and the Army, especially between 1792 and 1796.

The Library of the American Philosophical Society has Early Minutes of the American Philosophical Society, which Wilkinson joined January 19, 1798, and two Meteorological Journals and two Meteorological Tables kept by Wilkinson in 1797.

Pittsburgh, Pennsylvania

The Library of the University of Pittsburgh has the Darlington Collection, containing thirty-eight letters of Wilkinson. They are dated from 1790 to 1816 and were written in most cases to General Samuel Smith of Baltimore.

St. Louis, Missouri

The Missouri Historical Society Library has the Thomas Jefferson Papers, Amos Stoddard Papers, and the General James Wilkinson Papers. They respectively contain seven, six, and sixteen manuscripts relating to Wilkinson, all of which were written after 1801. In other collections additional Wilkinson data may be found.

San Marino, California

¹ The Henry E. Huntington Library and Art Gallery.

Ticonderoga, New York

The Ticonderoga Museum has a number of manuscripts in which Wilkinson is referred to, and one long letter that Dearborn wrote to him in 1815.

Washington, D.C.

Here are the largest depositaries of Wilkinson material. In the Library of Congress are the following relevant manuscripts.

Archivo General de Indias, Papeles Procedentes de Cuba: Under this title are found a great number of photostats that the Library of Congress has made of important papers in the archives of Spain at Seville. They are grouped in bundles (*legajos*), each of about three hundred pages. For Wilkinson's relations with the Spaniards, *legajos* 2373, 2374, and 2375 are most important. The Library has also photostats of manuscripts from the Archivo Histórico Nacional, Madrid; they contain frequent references to Wilkinson. For pertinent papers in the Spanish Archives, see Hill, *Descriptive Catalogue of the Documents Relating to the History of the United States, etc.*

The James Brown Papers (five volumes): several letters relating to Wilkinson during 1803, 1804, and 1805.

Public Archives of Canada: Series C: Military Papers, vol. 681. This volume is composed of photostats of letters, orders, reports, etc. of British officers operating against Wilkinson during 1813 and 1814.

The Papers of the Continental Congress furnish information about Wilkinson's promotion in 1777 and his work as a clothier-general, 1779–1781.

Andrew Ellicott Papers (three volumes): correspondence between Wilkinson and Ellicott between 1797 and 1800.

Thomas Flournoy Papers (one box): a number of Wilkinson's letters and orders while at New Orleans during 1812 and 1813.

Alexander Hamilton Papers (1st Series, eighty-four volumes; 2nd Series, twenty-four volumes; Reports to Congress, two): The volumes covering from 1795 through 1801 supply considerable information concerning the administration of the Army and the relations of Hamilton and Wilkinson. There are about fifty letters written by Wilkinson.

Harry Innes Papers (thirty-two volumes) are essential for any study of Wilkinson's career from 1784 to 1796. For this purpose Vols. XIX, XXII, and XXIII are the most important.

Thomas Jefferson Papers (two hundred and thirty-six volumes) contain a number of letters from and relating to Wilkinson, especially for the period from 1804 to 1809.

Jacob Kingsbury Papers (three volumes): several letters to and from Wilkinson and Kingsbury, especially between 1800 and 1804.

Letters in Relation (one volume): they concern the Burr Conspiracy.

The James Madison Papers (one hundred and five volumes): about twenty letters that Wilkinson wrote to Madison. In others' correspondence Wilkinson is frequently mentioned.

The James Monroe Papers (twenty-two volumes): approximately fifteen letters relating to Wilkinson of no particular period.

Northwest Territory Papers (eight packets). This collection contains little of direct bearing on Wilkinson but a good deal concerning early conditions in the Ohio country.

David Porter Papers, 1805–1812; data concerning Wilkinson at New Orleans during the Burr Conspiracy and while his troops were at Terre aux Bœufs.

John Stark Collection: "Minutes of the Battle of Bunker Hill. Answers to Questions of General Wilkinson, 1815–1816."

Joseph Meredith Tonei Papers (Ohio Collection): the Official Letter Book of Fort Washington, 1794–1795.

United States Revolution (Miscellaneous Papers): several letters relating to Wilkinson.

The George Washington Papers (approximately three hundred volumes in customary, one hundred in original, bindings). They contain a number of Wilkinson letters. See calendar of the Correspondence with the Officers.

Wilkinson Papers (one volume and one folder): They are composed mostly of letters Wilkinson wrote between 1793 and 1812.

In the Interior Department, Indian Office, are some of Wilkinson's letters and reports while he was acting as a commissioner to the Indians; the Land Office contains his correspondence with the Secretary of the Treasury concerning surveyors, boundaries, roads, public lands, etc.

In the State Department, Bureau of Indexes and Archives, are a few Wilkinson letters; the Bureau of Rolls and Library has the correspondence of Wilkinson with the Secretary of State during 1805 and 1806.

The War Department Archives have a very great number of Wilkinson's official letters. They are mostly found in the Adjutant-General's Office, Old Files and Old Records Divisions. In the Engineer Office are several maps and other important information concerning the War of 1812. In the Judge-Advocate's Office is the record of Wilkinson's court-martial in 1815.

West Point, New York

The Library, United States Military Academy: Wayne Order Books, 1792–1794, invaluable for information of the early Army.

B. Published

1. Books and Pamphlets

Adams, John Quincy, Memoirs, ed. C. F. Adams, 12 vols. Philadelphia: Lippincott, 1877.

American Archives, ed. Peter Force *et al.* 9 vols. Washington, 1837–1853.
Valuable for Revolutionary data.

American State Papers, selected and ed. Walter Lowrie *et al.* Washington: Gales & Seaton, 1832–1861.
The following volumes are relevant: Claims; Foreign Relations, Vol. II; Military Affairs, Vol. I; Miscellaneous, Vols. I and II; Public Lands, Vol. V.

AMES, FISHER, Works, ed. Seth Ames. 2 vols. Boston: Little, Brown, 1854.

Annals of Congress of the United States. 42 vols. Washington: Gales & Seaton, 1834–1856.
See Annals of the Eighth, Ninth, Tenth, and Eleventh Congresses.

BIDDLE, CHARLES, Autobiography. Philadelphia: E. Claxton & Co., 1883.
Charles Biddle was a friend of Wilkinson and a cousin of his wife.

BOYD, JOHN PARKER, Documents and Facts, Relative to Military Events, During the Late War. (1816?)
A rather rare pamphlet of about forty pages. Both the date of publication and the publisher are lacking. Copies are in the Library of the U.S. Military Academy, West Point, and the N.Y. Public Library. In spite of his own explanations Boyd's burden of incompetence appears as heavy as before.

BOYER, LIEUT., A Journal of Wayne's Campaign, printed with A Biographical Sketch of the Life of the Late Michael Cresap. Cincinnati, 1866.

BRANNON, JOHN, Official Letters of the Military & Naval Officers of the U.S. . . . in the Years 1812, 1813, 1814, 1815. Washington, 1823.

Broadsides
The Library of Congress has about one hundred and fifty packets and fifty-seven bound volumes of broadsides. Several written in 1806 and 1807 give the viewpoints of Wilkinson's friends and foes.

BURGOYNE, JOHN, A State of the Expedition from Canada as Laid Before the House of Commons. London: J. Almon, 1780.
The testimony of Burgoyne and others to free him from blame for the failure of his campaign.

BURNETT, E. C., ED., Letters of Members of the Continental Congress. 8 vols. Washington: Carnegie Institution of Washington, 1921–1936.

BURR, AARON, The Private Journal of Aaron Burr During His Residence of Four Years in Europe. 2 vols. New York: Harper, 1838.

CALLAN, J. F., The Military Laws of the United States. Philadelphia, 1863.
A convenient book of reference. Unfortunately, some of the laws are not given as a whole, they are merely briefed.

CIST, CHARLES, The Cincinnati Miscellany. 2 vols. Cincinnati, 1845.
The two volumes contain numerous letters between Wilkinson and John Armstrong during 1792.

CLAIBORNE, W. C. C., Official Letter Books, 1801–1816, ed. Dunbar Rowland. 6 vols. Jackson, Miss.: State Dept. of Archives and History, 1917.

CLARK, DANIEL, Proofs of the Corruption of General James Wilkinson and of His Connexion with Aaron Burr. Philadelphia, 1809.
A bitter denunciation of Wilkinson by one of his worst enemies. If for no other reason, the book deserves reading for the documents that it contains.

DALLAS, GEORGE M., Life and Writings of Alexander James Dallas. Philadelphia: Lippincott, 1871.
A book without interest except for the letters that it frequently quotes.

ELLICOTT, ANDREW, Journal. Philadelphia: Thomas Dobson, 1803.
It covers the period while Ellicott and Wilkinson were in the neighborhood of Natchez and New Orleans and were friendly. Wilkinson is frequently mentioned.

Expenditures in the Naval and Military Establishments by the Quarter Master General and Navy Agents, 1797–1801.
Both date of publication and publisher are lacking. The book is relatively rare. A copy is in the War College Library, Washington. It gives the purchase price of many commonplace things used by early frontier posts.

"A Faithful picture of the political situation in New Orleans at the close of the last and beginning of the present year, 1807."
Probably written by Edward Livingston or James Workman. It is reprinted in the *Louisiana Historical Quarterly*, Vol. II.

FORD, WORTHINGTON C., AND HUNT, GAILLARD, EDS., Journals of the Continental Congress. 34 vols. Washington, 1904–1937.
The volumes contain the proceedings of Congress from Sept. 5, 1774, to Mar. 2, 1789.

GRAYDON, ALEXANDER, Memoirs of His Own Time. Philadelphia, 1846.
Although Graydon was a constant friend of Wilkinson, he mentions the General only a few times in his Memoirs. The book was written when Graydon was old.

HAMILTON, ALEXANDER, Works, ed. J. C. Hamilton. 7 vols. New York: J. F. Trow, 1850–1851.

HECKEWELDER, JOHN, "Narrative of [His] Journey to the Wabash in 1792." *Pennsylvania Magazine of History and Biography*, XII (1888), 34–54, 165–184.

HEITMAN, F. B., Historical Register and Dictionary of the United States Army. 2 vols. Washington: Government Printing Office, 1903.

HENING, W. W., ED., The Statutes at Large; Being a Collection of All the Laws of Virginia. Vols. XII and XIII, Richmond and Philadelphia, 1823.

JACKSON, ANDREW, Correspondence, ed. J. S. Bassett. 7 vols. Washington: Carnegie Institution of Washington, 1926–1935.

JAY, JOHN, Correspondence and Public Papers, ed. H. P. Johnston. 4 vols. New York: Putnam, 1890.
It contains several significant letters relating to Burgoyne's campaign and its aftermath.

JILLSON, W. R., Old Kentucky Entries and Deeds (Filson Club Publications, No. 34). Louisville: Standard Printing Co., 1926.

—— The Kentucky Land Grants . . . 1782–1924 (Filson Club Publications, No. 33). Louisville: Standard Printing Co., 1925.

KING, RUFUS, Life and Correspondence, ed. Charles R. King. 6 vols. New York: Putnam, 1894–1900.

MACLAY, WILLIAM, Journal, ed. Charles A. Beard. New York: A. & C. Boni, 1927.
Maclay was U.S. Senator from Pennsylvania, 1789–1791.

MELISH, JOHN, Military Atlas and Register. Philadelphia, 1813.

PIKE, ZEBULON M., The Expeditions of Zebulon Montgomery Pike to Headwaters of the Mississippi River, etc., ed. Elliott Coues. 3 vols. New York: Francis P. Harper, 1895.
    This work contains the journals of Pike's expeditions to Santa Fe and the headwaters of the Mississippi.

Reports of the Trials of Colonel Aaron Burr . . . 2 vols. Philadelphia: Hopkins & Earle, 1808.

ROWLAND, DUNBAR, ED., The Mississippi Territorial Archives. Nashville, Tenn.: Brandon Printing Co., 1905.
    The volume contains a few letters and numerous references to Wilkinson, *ca.* 1800.

ST. CLAIR, ARTHUR, The St. Clair Papers, ed. William H. Smith. Cincinnati: Robert Clarke & Co., 1882.

SULLIVAN, MAJOR–GENERAL JOHN, Letters and Papers, ed. O. G. Hammond (Collections of New Hampshire Historical Soc., Vols. XIII–XIV). Concord, N.H.: New Hampshire Historical Society, 1931.
    They contain several letters concerning Wilkinson, a number relating to the invasion of Canada during 1775 and 1776.

SWIFT, GEN. JOSEPH GARDNER, Memoirs, ed. Harrison Ellery. Worcester, Mass.: Privately printed, 1890.

TOMPKINS, DANIEL D., Public Papers, ed. Hugh Hastings. 3 vols. Albany, N.Y.: State of New York, 1898–1902.
    Tompkins was Governor of New York from 1807 to 1817. He urged vigorous prosecution of the War of 1812; he frequently wrote to Wilkinson asking him to help equip the state militia properly.

WILKINSON, JAMES, Memoirs of General Wilkinson, Volume II.
    There are two editions, 1810 and 1811; they were published at Washington, D.C., and are entirely alike. The edition of 1816, given below, includes little of the material found in the earlier ones.

—— Memoirs of My Own Times. 3 vols. and an atlas. Philadelphia: A. Small, 1816.

WINTERFIELD, CHARLES (?), A Plain Tale, etc. 24 pp. New York, 1807.

WOOD, WILLIAM, Select British Documents of the Canadian War of 1812 (Champlain Society Publications, Vols. XIII–XV, XVII). Toronto: Champlain Society, 1920–1928.

WORKMAN, JAMES, A Letter to the Respectable Citizens, Inhabitants of the County of Orleans; Together with Several Letters to His Excellency Governor Claiborne, and Other Documents Relative to the Extraordinary Measures Lately Pursued in This Territory. New Orleans, 1807.

2. Newspapers and Magazines

Those enumerated below were published during Wilkinson's time and contain items about him. The places of publication follow titles.

Albany Argus (Albany, N.Y.)
Albany Register (Albany, N.Y.)

Augusta Chronicle and Gazette of the State (Augusta, Ga.)
Aurora (Philadelphia, Pa.)
Baltimore Whig (Baltimore, Md.)
Cincinnati Miscellany (Cincinnati, Ohio)
Continental Journal and Weekly Advertiser, The (Boston)
Enquirer (Richmond, Va.)
Federal Gazette (Frederick-Town, Md.)
Federal Republican and Commercial Gazette (Baltimore, Md.)
Frederick-Town Herald (Frederick-Town, Md.)
Gazette of the United States (Philadelphia, Pa.)
Kentucky Gazette (Lexington, Ky.)
Literary and Scientific Repository, and Critical Review (New York)
Louisiana Gazette (New Orleans, La.)
National Intelligencer (Washington, D.C.)
New York Evening Post (New York, N.Y.)
New York Gazette and General Advertiser (New York, N.Y.)
New York Packet, The (Fish-Kill, N.Y.)
Niles' National Register (Philadelphia, Pa.)
Ohio Gazette (Marietta, Ohio)
Palladium (Frankfort, Ky.)
Patriot, The (Utica, N.Y.)
Pittsburgh Gazette (Pittsburgh, Pa.)
Pittsburgh Mercury (Pittsburgh, Pa.)
Virginia Gazette & Richmond Chronicle (Richmond, Va.)
Western World (Cincinnati, Ohio)

II. SECONDARY SOURCE MATERIAL

A. GENERAL WORKS

ADAMS, HENRY, History of the United States of America. 9 vols. New York: Scribner, 1921.

AVERY, E. M., A History of the United States and Its People. 7 vols. Cleveland: The Burrows Bros. Co., 1904–1910.

CHANNING, EDWARD, A History of the United States. 7 vols. New York: Macmillan, 1921–1932.

GANOE, W. A., The History of the United States Army. New York: Appleton, 1932.

HART, A. B., ED., The American Nation: A History from Original Sources by Associated Scholars. 28 vols. New York: Harper, 1904–1918.
    Especially useful in this series are: The Confederation and the Constitution, by A. C. McLaughlin (Vol. X, 1905), and The Federalist System, by J. S. Bassett (Vol. II, 1906).

HEITMAN, F. B., Historical Register and Dictionary of the United States Army. 2 vols. Washington: Government Printing Office, 1903.

JENKINS, J. S., The Generals of the Last War with Great Britain. Auburn, N.Y., 1849.

JOHNSON, ALLEN, AND MALONE, DUMAS, EDS., Dictionary of American Biography. 20 vols. New York: Scribner, 1928–1936.

McMASTER, J. B., A History of the People of the United States, from the Revolution to the Civil War. 8 vols. New York: Appleton, 1924.

ROOSEVELT, THEODORE, The Winning of the West. 3 vols. New York: Putnam, 1894–1896.

STEELE, M. F., American Campaigns. 2 vols. Washington: Byron S. Adams, 1909.

TURNER, F. J., The Frontier in American History. New York: Holt, 1921.

UPTON, EMORY, The Military Policy of the United States. Washington: Government Printing Office, 1912.

B. WORKS DEALING WITH A PARTICULAR PERSON, PLACE, OR PERIOD

ALEXANDER, HOLMES, Aaron Burr, the Proud Pretender. New York: Harper, 1937.

ARMSTRONG, JOHN, Notices of the War of 1812. 2 vols. New York: Wiley & Putnam, 1840.
    Biased and superficial; written in his old age, about a quarter of a century after the events he recounts.

ARNOLD, I. N., The Life of Benedict Arnold: His Patriotism and His Treason. Chicago: Jansen, McClurg & Co., 1880.

BEMIS, S. F., Pinckney's Treaty. Baltimore: The Johns Hopkins Press, 1926.
    A very scholarly piece of work covering a limited field in detail.

BEVERIDGE, A. J., The Life of John Marshall. 4 vols. Boston: Houghton Mifflin, 1916–1919.
    The standard biography of John Marshall.

BOLTON, C. K., The Private Soldier Under Washington. New York: Scribner, 1902.
    A small, interesting volume.

BOND, B. W., The Civilization of the Old Northwest. New York: Macmillan, 1934.
    A well written and informing book.

BOYD, THOMAS A., Mad Anthony Wayne. New York: Scribner, 1929.
    A dispassionate biography pleasingly written.

BROWN, JOHN M., The Political Beginnings of Kentucky (Filson Club Publications, No. 6). Louisville: J. P. Morton & Co., 1889.

BRUCE, W. C., John Randolph of Roanoke. 2 vols. New York: Putnam, 1922.
    The standard biography of John Randolph.

CHRISTIAN, P. W., General James Wilkinson and Kentucky Separatism, 1784–1798 (Ph.D. thesis, unpublished). Evanston, Ill.: Northwestern University, 1935.
    An accurate and detailed account of Wilkinson's rôle in Kentucky politics.

COX, I. J., "Opening the Santa Fe Trail," *Mo. Hist. Review*, XXV, 30–66 (Oct., 1930).

—— "The New Invasion of the Goths and Vandals," *Miss. Valley Hist. Assn. Proceedings*, VIII (1914–1915), 176–200.

—— "The Pan-American Policy of Jefferson and Wilkinson," *Miss. Valley Hist. Rev.*, I, 212–239 (Sept., 1914).

—— The West Florida Controversy, 1798–1813. Baltimore: Johns Hopkins Press, 1918.

—— "Wilkinson's First Break with the Spaniards," *Biennial Report, Dept. of Archives and History of the State of West Virginia, 1911–1912, 1913–1914*, Appendix, pp. 49–56. Charleston, W. Va.: State of West Virginia, 1914.

—— "General Wilkinson and His Later Intrigues with the Spaniards," *Amer. Hist. Rev.*, XIX, 749–812 (July, 1914).

Through the above scholarly articles, Professor Cox has made valuable contributions to a better understanding of Wilkinson.

DREWRY, E. B., Episodes in Western Expansion as Reported in the Writings of James Wilkinson (Ph.D. thesis, unpublished). Ithaca, N.Y.: Cornell University, 1933.

ELLIOTT, C. W., Winfield Scott. New York: Macmillan, 1937.

The standard biography of Winfield Scott.

Filson Club Publications, No. 31: Reprints of Littell's Political Transactions in and Concerning Kentucky, and Letters of George Nicholas to His Friend in Virginia, also Gen. Wilkinson's Memorial. Louisville: J. P. Morton & Co., 1926.

Temple Bodley's Introduction (pp. i–cxviii) relates Wilkinson's part in Kentucky politics.

FISKE, JOHN, The Critical Period of American History, 1783–1789. Boston: Houghton Mifflin, 1897.

FORTIER, ALCÉE, A History of Louisiana, 4 vols. New York: Goupil & Co. of Paris—Manzi, Joyant & Co., Successors, 1904.

The best history of Louisiana yet published.

GREEN, T. M., The Spanish Conspiracy, etc. Cincinnati: R. Clarke & Co., 1891.

HAMILTON, P. J., Colonial Mobile. Boston: Houghton Mifflin, 1910.

HATCHER, M. A., The Opening of Texas to Foreign Settlement (University of Texas Bulletin, No. 2714).

Very helpful in any study of Wilkinson's relations with Texas.

HAY, T. W., "General James Wilkinson—the Last Phase," *La. Hist. Quarterly*, XIX, 407–435 (Apr., 1936).

—— "Some Reflections on the Career of General James Wilkinson," *Miss. Valley Historical Review*, XXI, 471–494 (Mar., 1935).

—— "Letters of Mrs. Ann Biddle Wilkinson from Kentucky, 1788–1789," *Pa. Mag. of Hist. and Biog.*, LVI, 33–55 (Jan., 1932).

The Hay articles are of distinct importance; they evince painstaking research and an honest effort to learn the truth about Wilkinson.

HENSHAW, LESLIE, "The Aaron Burr Conspiracy in the Ohio Valley," *Ohio Archaeological and Hist. Quarterly*, XXIV, 121–137 (Apr., 1915).

HOUCK, LOUIS, A History of Missouri. 3 vols. Chicago: R. R. Donnelley & Sons Co., 1908.

"An Interview of Governor Folch with General Wilkinson" (document), *Amer. Hist. Rev.*, X, 832–840 (July, 1905).

JAMES, J. A., The Life of George Rogers Clark. Chicago: University of Chicago Press, 1928.

KING, GRACE, Creole Families of New Orleans. New York: Macmillan, 1921.

Charming sketches of people whose faults the author has mostly forgotten.

LUCAS, C. P., The Canadian War of 1812. Oxford: Clarendon Press, 1906.
One of the best secondary accounts of the War from the English viewpoint.

McCALEB, W. F., The Aaron Burr Conspiracy. New York: Dodd, Mead, 1903.
The best work of its kind yet published.

McELROY, R. M., Kentucky in the Nation's History. New York: Moffat, Yard, 1909.

McKEE, MARGUERITE M., "Service of Supply in the War of 1812," Quartermaster Review, Vol. VI (Jan.–Feb., 1927, pp. 6–19; Mar.–Apr., 1927, pp. 45–54).

McMAHON, J. V. L., An Historical View of the Government of Maryland. Baltimore: Lucas & Deaver, 1831.

MAHAN, A. T., Sea Power in Its Relations to the War of 1812. 2 vols. Boston: Little, Brown, 1905.

MANN, JAMES, Medical Sketches of the Campaign of 1812, 13, 14. Dedham, Mass.: H. Mann & Co., 1816.
Discerning observations of an able doctor.

MARSHALL, HUMPHREY, The History of Kentucky. 2 vols. Frankfort, Ky.: G. S. Robinson, Printer, 1824.
The earliest, perhaps the most biased, history of Kentucky.

MATHEWS, C. V. C., Andrew Ellicott: His Life and Letters. New York: Grafton Press, 1908.

NICKERSON, HOFFMAN, The Turning Point of the Revolution. Boston: Houghton Mifflin, 1928.
An excellent account of Burgoyne's campaign.

PRIESTLEY, H. I., The Mexican Nation, a History. New York: Macmillan, 1923.

REED, W. B., Life and Correspondence of Joseph Reed. 2 vols. Philadelphia: Lindsay & Blakiston, 1847.

ROBERTSON, J. A., Louisiana Under the Rule of Spain, France, and the United States, 1785–1807. 2 vols. Cleveland: The A. H. Clark Co., 1911.
It contains several important documents not easily available.

SCHACHNER, NATHAN, Aaron Burr. New York: Stokes, 1937.

SCHARF, J. F., History of St. Louis City and County. 2 vols. Philadelphia: L. H. Everts & Co., 1883.
Filled with odds and ends of information difficult to find elsewhere.

SCOTT, WINFIELD, Memoirs of Lieutenant-General Scott. 2 vols. New York: Sheldon & Co., 1864.
Written when Scott was seventy-eight and his natural forces were abated.

SEAVER, F. J., Historical Sketches of Franklin County and Its Several Towns. Albany, N.Y.: J. B. Lyon Co., 1918.

SELLAR, ROBERT, The U. S. Campaign of 1813 to Capture Montreal. Huntingdon, Quebec, 1913.
One of the best accounts of this campaign; not documented.

SHEPHERD, W. R., "Wilkinson and the Beginnings of the Spanish Conspiracy," Amer. Hist. Rev., IX, 490–506 (Apr., 1904).

SHREVE, R. O., The Finished Scoundrel: General James Wilkinson. Indianapolis: Bobbs-Merrill, 1933.
Written without fairness and adequate study.

STEINER, B. C., The Life and Correspondence of James McHenry. Cleveland: The Burrows Bros. Co., 1907.
More desirable for the documents that it quotes than for the interpretations that it offers.
—— Life of Roger Brooke Taney. Baltimore: Williams & Wilkins Co., 1922.
Of the same character as Steiner's Life of McHenry.

STRYKER, W. S., The Battles of Trenton and Princeton. Boston: Houghton Mifflin, 1898.
Written by a person of military understanding in an interesting way.

SWISHER, E. B., Roger B. Taney. New York: Macmillan, 1935.

TRUMAN, B. C., The Field of Honor. New York: Fords, Howard & Hulbert, 1886.

VERHOEFF, MARY, The Kentucky Mountains: Transportation and Commerce, 1750 to 1911 (Filson Club Publications, No. 26). Louisville: J. P. Morton & Co., 1911.
—— The Kentucky River Navigation (Filson Club Publications, No. 28). Louisville: J. P. Morton & Co., 1917.

VOLSTORFF, V. V., William Charles Cole Claiborne, A Study in Frontier Administration (Ph.D. thesis, unpublished). Evanston, Ill.: Northwestern University, 1933.
It contains a thoughtful study of the relations between Claiborne and Wilkinson about 1803.

WANDELL, S. H., AND MINNIGERODE, MEADE, Aaron Burr. 2 vols. New York; Putnam, 1925.

WHITAKER, A. P., The Mississippi Question, 1795–1803. New York: Appleton-Century Co., 1934.
—— The Spanish-American Frontier. Boston: Houghton Mifflin, 1927.
These two books are the happy result of a long study of a great mass of material from the Spanish archives.

WILKINSON, JAMES, "General James Wilkinson," *La. Hist. Quarterly,* Vol. I, No. 2 (Sept. 14, 1917), 79–166.

WRONG, G. M., Canada and the American Revolution. New York: Macmillan, 1935.
An impartial narrative written with almost biblical beauty.

INDEX

Abercrombie, 71
Abraham, Plains of, 23
Abrahams, Abraham D., 257
Ackland, Major John Dyke, 39
Act of 1802, 211–212
Acta Constitutiva, 330, 332
Adair, John, attacked near Fort St. Clair, 127; writes to Wilkinson, 214; arrest of, 234; suit of, against Wilkinson, 327
Adams, John, and Matthew Lyon, 42; and Wilkinson, 156; President-elect, 159; his judgment of Wilkinson, 161–162; and Spaniards, 163; calls special session of Congress, 173; and Wilkinson, 182; and Wilkinson's promotion, 190; the "flatterer" of, 201; administration of, 207; and opinion of Wilkinson, 283–284
Adams, Samuel, 6
Agustin I, of Mexico, 334
Agustín, Matías, 183
Albany, N.Y., Wilkinson reaches, 8; W. leaves for, 14; concentration at, 17; Wilkinson's trip to, 18; Wilkinson's letter from, 27; line of communications with, 28; Schuyler moves toward, 33; securing the road to, 36; advance of Clinton to, 42; Wilkinson leaves, 43; Wilkinson back at, 46; Gates at, 48; Wilkinson returns to, 49; Wilkinson leaves, 50; Paragon reaches, 286; necessities of sick from, 299; Wilkinson's preference for, 300; Wilkinson starts for, 307
Alien and Sedition Acts, 187
All Saints Church, 2
Alleghenies, 77; Wilkinson crosses, 83
America, Wilkinson's knowledge about land in, 72; Spanish colonies in, 135; war in, 306; Wilkinson twins and "best Blood" of, 322; democratic ideas in, 323. See also Latin America
American Bible Society, 338, 339
American Philosophical Society, 163
Americans, and Arnold, 9; and new spirit, 17; at Princeton, 25; and Brit-

ish, 31; advance of, 36; casualties of, 37; reinforcements of, 38; capture of material by, 39; waiting of, 41; and aid from French, 56; and closing of Mississippi, 76; bordering Louisiana, 79–80, 81; at St. Clair's defeat, 117–118, 121; of the backwoods, 135; and invasion of Louisiana, 163, 164, 178; Gayoso coöperates with, 183; and deposit at New Orleans, 201; interrupt French quadrille, 204; and banquet, 205; and attacks on Spanish territory, 206; north of Ohio, 207; limits of advance of, 231; to supply funds, 216; eager for hostilities, 230; as neutrals, 247; need of haste for, 293; and defeat, 296; and will to conquer, 297; and British forces, 298; and Captain Mulcaster, 300; advance of, 304; at Lacolle Mill, 305; and the Spaniards, 324; and Herrera, 325; and Association of Three Hundred, 326; and Washington, 337
Ames, Fisher, on reduction of Army, 146
Amherst, Sir Jeffery, 303
Andrews, Robert, 278
Angelus, 2
Annapolis, Md., Wolf leaves, 248; Wilkinson's orders in reference to, 307
Apalachicola River, 198
Appalachian Mountains, 70
Arietta, and condemnation of tobacco, 270
Arkansas River, 220, 224, 225
Armesto, Don Andrés, 205
Armstrong, John (captain, general, Secretary of War), at Battle of Saratoga, 39; at Fort Hamilton, 123–124; the new Secretary of War, 278; and Jackson's troops, 279; and orders to Wilkinson, 284; promises to Wilkinson of, 285; brother-in-law of Lewis, 287; efforts at Sacketts Harbor, 288–291; and request of Wilkinson, 292; and Wilkinson's command, 297; orders evacuation of French Mills, 302; and subordinates, 303; and blame of Wilkinson, 304;